C. P. SNOW

a reference guide

Reference
Guides
to
Literature

Ronald Gottesman
Editor

C. P. SNOW

a reference guide

PAUL BOYTINCK

G.K. HALL & CO.

70 LINCOLN STREET, BOSTON, MASS.

Library of Congress Cataloging in Publication Data
Boytinck, Paul W
    C.P. Snow : a reference guide.

    Bibliography: p.
    Includes index.
    1. Snow, Charles Percy, Baron Snow, 1905-
—Bibliography. I. Title.
Z8823.37.B69 [PR6037.N58] 016.823'9'12 79-27529
ISBN 0-8161-8357-0

This publication is printed on permanent/durable acid-free paper
MANUFACTURED IN THE UNITED STATES OF AMERICA

Contents

Introduction

C.P. Snow (1905–) English novelist, biographer, critic, and moralist, was born in the Midlands city of Leicester. The son of a clerk in a shoe factory, he was educated at Alderman Newton's Grammar School, University College (Leicester) and Christ's College, Cambridge. He made his way largely by means of scholarships, obtained a Ph.D. in physics (1928) and in 1930 was elected a Fellow of Christ's College.

His scientific research resulted in contributions to Nature and the Proceedings of the Royal Society of London between the years 1929 and 1935. J.D. Bernal has written that Snow was a "brilliant physical chemist whose work on photo-chemistry in the solid state could easily have opened up for him a new field of research."[1] A later, more temperate estimate of Snow's scientific work observes that he performed "some significant though not earth-shaking research, particularly in infrared spectroscopy and the physical chemistry of vitamins."[2]

During World War II, he left the university, entered the government, and eventually became the technical director of the Ministry of Labour. In this capacity he interviewed and placed scientists in positions to serve British military objectives during World War II, including radar and the atomic bomb project. He became a Commander of the British Empire (C.B.E.) in 1943, and was awarded a knighthood in 1957 in recognition of his con-tributions during the war and his post-war work as a civil service commissioner (1945-1960).

Snow's interest in the problems of technology and industry caught the attention of Harold Wilson in 1964, and he became a parliamentary secretary, or junior minister, in the Ministry of Technology under Frank Cousins. At this time, in 1964, he was raised to the peerage and officially styled Baron Snow of the City of Leicester. He remained a member of the Labour government from 1964 to 1966, when he resigned to resume his writing career.

This sketch illustrates that much of Snow's life has been spent among scientists and non-scientists in University circles and in the upper ranks of the civil service. The members of this intellectual "squirearchy" are dissected and celebrated in his eleven-volume-novel sequence entitled <u>Strangers and Brothers</u>. He has, to use an expressive neologism, a large acquaintance with the men and women who make up the intelligentry.

Snow has often been praised in terms which intimate that he is a polymath, if not a Renaissance man, equally at home in the world of the arts and sciences; but it is probably better to think of him as a civil servant who, ever since his student days, wanted to be a writer. There have been very few writers, certainly in the twentieth century, with Snow's scientific background, and his varied experience of officialdom. He is, it may be said, the Ulysses of Whitehall.

The relation between Snow's fiction and his career as a civil servant has not been explored to date, and yet the link between the two is clear. The English civil service, it may be presumed, is not the first or last haven of anarchists, romantics, or other extremists; and the qualities the civil servant brings to administration are the qualities Snow brings to his fiction. One gets an intimation of this fact from what might be called the civil servant's credo, written by H.E. Dale, himself a member of that corps for many years.

> First, pure reason is not at present the most important factor in human affairs. Second, even in the realm of pure reason there is much to be said for both sides on any complicated question which is fiercely disputed, and in the modern world nearly all serious questions are complicated. Third, in a vast and highly organized society great social, economic, and political changes (call them reforms if you like) cannot be made quickly without arousing widespread opposition, much of it natural and reasonable, and without causing some un-merited suffering. Fourth, a minority which feels strongly and shouts loudly will often prevail both against the majority and the merits, unless the major-ity itself feels strongly. Fifth, in this complex and rapidly changing world any great measure, whether legislative or executive, is sure to have results, of often very grave results, which no-one foresaw; in other words, the strongest intellect and the keenest insight cannot predict anything like the full conse-quences of important decisions.[3]

The striking feature of this passage is that the contents, with only a few changes in wording ("call them reforms if you like" is a little cool for Snow), could well have been written by Snow himself. The second observation is that the style reflects precisely those qualities of moderation and restraint--grayness, flatness,

utilitarian newspeak are the complaints of his more grim critics--
which are typical of Snow's fiction. Third, the quotation reflects
a resolute awareness of the complexity, or potential complexity, of
any serious issue. It strongly suggests that a suspension of judgment should precede the final verdict on that issue. It is
precisely this quality which marks the deliberations of Lewis Eliot,
the narrator of Snow's fictional novel sequence. The trait is,
incidentally, entirely apt for a barrister and it is not foreign to
Snow himself. The character Swan in William Cooper's novel Young
People is a fictional depiction of the younger Snow. At one point
in the narrative, Swan remarks that "Passing moral judgments seems
to me to be the chief intellectual recreation of the human race
. . . . The first moral compulsion ought to be to understand . . . .
passing moral judgments should be open to you only when you understand what you're judging, not before."[4] The pervasive presence
of this sentiment in his fiction accounts for the prevailing sense
of moral complexity in that fiction. It gives his descriptions of
the conflicts between the moral romantics or berserkers and the
quiet elderly puffins, who long for a painless solution preferably
without the inordinate fuss of publicity and preferably by means
of a long, slow tango with that siren, Compromise, its own curious
nagging power.

Snow's Literary Credo

Realist in fiction, Labourite in politics, and pious agnostic
in religion, he has made a shibboleth only of the first of these
propositions, and a compressed version of Snow's literary credo
reads as follows. Science has invaded fields previously occupied
by literature; it has also enshrined a complex technological
culture. Faced with the difficulties inherent in describing modern
society, twentieth century novelists have divorced external life
from art and have concentrated on the expression of private moods.
Aided and abetted by certain critical trends, the expression of
these private moods has become dominant in the type of novel best
typified by Finnegans Wake. The cult of the anti-novel leads to
cultural suicide. A code of realism will reverse this process
and close the dangerous gap between fastidious and supercilious
critics and the average intelligent reader. Modern psychology is
excluded from the credo of realism, partly on the ground that it
is not sufficiently scientific and partly in the belief that it
erodes notions of individual responsibility. Symbolism leads to
clumsiness, naturalism to literary porridge, and both are excluded
from the credo. These guiding principles, compressed, abstract, and
necessarily oversimplified, pervaded and prompted Snow's critical
judgments as reviewer for the London Sunday Times (1949-1952) and,
to a lesser extent, when he reviewed books for the London Financial
Times (1970-).

Introduction

The Reception of His Fiction

The critical reception of Snow's fiction can perhaps be divided into three phases: obscurity, acclaim, and decline. In the first phase, from 1932 to 1934, he published <u>Death Under Sail</u>, <u>New Lives for Old</u>, and <u>The Search</u>. He undoubtedly received some encouragement, but no unanimous endorsement. In the second, from <u>George Passant</u> (1940) to <u>The Affair</u> (1960), his writing was at first conscientiously condemned and later, toward 1960, widely and uniformly praised. After 1964, from <u>Corridors of Power</u> to <u>The Sleep of Reason</u> (1968) the reviewers in the major reviewing organs, and certainly the academic critics, denounced Snow's fiction with a relentless energy.

The American commercial reception of Snow's novels roughly parallels, with some delay, the critical reception. <u>The Search</u> appeared in the United States in 1934, but it was barely noticed at the time. <u>The Masters</u>, often considered one of the best of Snow's books, and arguably his one enduring masterpiece, sold only 1,100 copies in its first year of American publication. After 1951, the situation showed a dramatic improvement, and <u>The New Men</u>, <u>Homecomings</u>, and <u>The Conscience of the Rich</u> each sold about 10,000 copies in the American market.[5] <u>The Affair</u> (1960), <u>Science and Government</u> (1961) all became selections of the Book-of-the-Month Club.[6] However, sales of the Scribner Omnibus Edition of <u>Strangers and Brothers</u>, an edition intended mainly for libraries, resulted in the disappointing sale of only 475 sets.[7]

Snow's commercial success in the United States has been equaled or surpassed, in the Soviet Union. Walter Allen writes:

There are times when it seems you are almost as likely to glimpse his burly figure, with its great bespectacled dome of a head, and hear his grunts and barks of delighted laughter, in Moscow as in New York.[8]

Soviet-sized editions of <u>The Affair</u> (100,000 copies) and <u>Time of Hope</u> (75,000 copies) appeared in 1962.[9] <u>The Search</u> and <u>Homecomings</u> were published in 1964. An extract from <u>Corridors of Power</u> appeared in <u>Pravda</u>,[10] and translations of <u>The Masters</u> and <u>Corridors of Power</u> have made a recent appearance.

The main problem which confronts the readers and critics of Snow's fiction is to decide whether Snow's version of reality is, to use one of Mencken's formulations, "manifestly true, and free of popular sentimentality and illusion." Is Snow's masculine world, full of strenuous ambition strenuously observed, in fact at one with the world we know? Snow himself is under no illusions on that score, and in an interview conducted by Frank Kermode, he observed that it is possible to describe the world with objective truth; and he denied that he permits a myth of his own invention, the imposition of a formal pattern by the novelist, to obscure or change that objective reality.[11]

He has received a good deal of support for this belief. Here is J.D. Scott on George Passant:

> Its form was tragic, its method traditional, and it dealt
> with English people who were living, and had jobs in
> England, and were not professional derelicts, on holiday
> in Italy, or living in the future, the Edwardian past,
> or Hollywood. Mr. Snow displayed an unfashionable grasp
> of the mundane, of jobs and salaries and committees and
> legal processes.[12]

A.S. Byatt writes in a similar vein almost three decades later. She is clearly writing, not about one novel alone, but about the whole sequence: "There is room for a study of bureaucracy, or jobs, or heritage that is not presented only as a grotesque phantasmagoria."[13] J.I.M. Stewart, in a review of Homecomings, makes a similar observation somewhat more wildly and therefore more effectively:

> Mr. Snow's writing won't let us down. . . . No; contem-
> porary men, women and institutions are like this. The
> tycoons and the permanent secretaries, the womanists
> and the virgins, the stuffed shirts and the prima donnas
> do tick just as Mr. Snow says they do; it is thus that
> careers are made and broken. . . . So we read and learn.
> Our instructor is extremely knowledgeable, and not a
> crackpot as so many writers are. . . . His world remains
> very liveable in and readable about.[14]

This perception of Snow as a Balzac of the Office and Proust of the Committee has two effects. On the one hand, it gives Snow's critics an opportunity to describe his realistic posture, to assess his human cunning, and to suggest the accomplishments and limits of his art. In the best of these critical essays--in Lionel Trilling's review of The New Men (B435), in Alfred Kazin's slightly horrified appreciation of Snow's cut-throat intellectuals scrupulously and not so scrupulously on the make (B164), in Patrick Swinden's punctilious enumeration of the merits and faults of Snow's novels (B309)--we find criticism that threatens to depart from its object and seditiously aims to set itself up as a work of art.

The same perception with which Snow has endowed the workaday world, with its quota of calculation and its share of sorrows and delight, tends, on the other hand, to soften adverse criticism. Edmund Wilson is a case in point.

INTERVIEWER: How do you feel about Sir Charles Snow?
WILSON: My only objection to his novels is that I find them
almost completely unreadable. But I always stand up for him
in opposition to the virtually united front against him of
the London literary world. He does have "something to say"
--put that in quotes. He's been bold enough to disregard
the literary rules and to open up a whole new geography of
the intellectual world, so everybody is furious with him.[15]

The reasoning of the last passage is open to question. After
all, most critics do not object to a writer who opens up a whole
new geography of the intellectual world. On the other hand, the
word "fury" adequately describes part of the later critical response.
Here, for example, is Frederick Crews on Corridors of Power:

Emotional shallowness is elevated to a kind of moral ideal
in the narrative method of C.P. Snow. Plausibly believing
that men of action tend to be out of touch with their inner
experience, Snow chooses to chronicle important deeds at
the expense of nuances of feeling. . . . The narrator,
colorless and familiar Lewis Eliot, speaks of his own
emotional life merely as something that might be "dangerous
for me," and he tells of adultery in high places with a
chilly and distant broadmindedness.[16]

Daniel Curley, in a review of the same novel, remarks that the
characters are "professionally inscrutable and [their] very existence depends on a surface that defies dramatization."[17] Frank
McGuiness in London Magazine finds that Snow moves with assurance
through Whitehall, but:

More relevantly perhaps to its merit as a novel, I find it
hard to believe that even the most vehement left-winger
would expect the Tory mandarins to be quite so massively
dull and emotionally constipated as Snow depicts them.
Indeed, by the side of this lot, those footling academics
suddenly seem vital and amusing.[18]

Another:

Why do we put up with Snow's long-distance treatment of
the human heart--his stubborn refusal to come to intimate
terms with either good or evil? The answer is that while
he may be remote, he is never cold. There is a generosity
and, within limits, a curiosity to Snow. Keeping his
balance once again, he wins--or loses, depending on how
you look at it.[19]

Still another:

Sometimes, by preaching a doctrine of such desperate inhibition, Snow leaves us wondering whether he is actually
contributing to the collision he so anxiously seeks to
avoid.[20]

A fourth:

It may be that [Snow] is not really very interested in
people except as vehicles. Take the case of Quaife and
his mistress, Ellen. We are told that they are genuinely
in love, but they seldom contrive to meet without old
Uncle Lew bustling along too. And when Roger does exhibit
the wish to embrace her it is with the meditative pre-
cipitation of the slug upon a cool garden lettuce.[21]

Anthony Burgess, in his own civilized way, clearly perceives the
same trend, and shows an awareness of the dangers:

Lord Snow's progress isn't towards a more accurately realised world of the senses and the emotions, to greater
flexibility of language or a more subtle probing of character: it is towards a dissatisfaction with the novel
as a mirror of life. . . . Lord Snow. . . . sustains manly
reticence and never gives anything away: he fulfills the
British ideal by being both artist and man of affairs.
The question is one of gain and loss. More novels like
Corridors of Power, and the novelist must be admired
more and loved less. A novel that shuts more doors than
it opens can, when it has the weight and majesty of a
Snow behind it, do more harm to the progress of the form
than one dares think of.[22]

What these observations have in common is the suggestion that the
supremacy of public relations in Snow's later fiction leads to the
loss of private relations. This loss is clearly evident in the
later fiction, but it has been noted that Lewis Eliot's slide into
reportorial techniques in The New Men is another example of this
resolute, apparently planned, avoidance of the emotional and the
merely personal and private.

The Question of Style

Critical attempts to define Snow's position as a novelist show
unusually startling differences of opinion. The debate revolves
around Snow's ability or inability to create character, the moral
implications lurking in his novels, and the virtues and defects of
his prose style. On the subject of style alone it is possible to
compile a small catalog of praise and abuse.

William Cooper tells us that Snow's style is designed to "give
absolute conviction on the plane of immediate fact" and at its best

--he selects a passage from <u>Homecomings</u>--he finds it both clear and compact.[24] Pamela Hansford Johnson, in an early assessment, praises the style with oxymoronic elegance:

> Snow is a flawless writer of unadorned prose; stylistically,
> he might even be considered icily regular and splendidly
> null. What matters, however, is whether this scientific
> prose is the best medium for setting down the process of an
> exploratory operation; and I think it is. He is the only
> novelist of under forty years of age of whose future I am
> not in the slightest doubt.[25]

Both Geoffrey Wagner and Bernard Bergonzi, two of Snow's early critics, represent the opposing point of view. Wagner observes that Snow, who has argued, in his literary criticism, against the aesthetic novels,

> . . . writes (as a consequence?) in a style so lame, lab-
> oured, and insensitive to words and sentence rhythms that
> his <u>roman-fleuve</u> really comes to read like a parody of
> John Marquand parodying a stodgy and inarticulate Bostonian
> writing his class record. [If the trend continues] the
> prose writing of a purely utilitarian society is simply
> going to be C.P. Snow's brand of Soviet realism, Sartre's
> committed communication, and eventually the arid Newspeak
> of <u>1984</u>.[26]

A bilious Bernard Bergonzi considers Snow's style functionally disabling, which means--if it means anything at all--that it is not designed to give an impression of absolute conviction on the plane of immediate fact.[27] An adroit Charles A. Brady makes a virtue of a defect, and presents us with the considered judgment that

> . . . the artfully controlled flatness of Snow's style is
> admirably suited to the exact sort of reality he so subtly
> reduces to its symbolic essentials, and then reproduces
> for us.[28]

Similar judgments of the same cheerful perversity are now common form. Helen Gardner chose to recant her former coldness toward the series when she wrote a review of <u>The Conscience of the Rich</u>. Her defense of Snow's style is a slightly extended version of Pamela Hansford Johnson's remarks:

> The grayness is deliberate. . . . To complain of the nar-
> rator's priggishness or of the lack of humor with which
> he views the world is to complain of the things which are
> necessary concomitants of the kind of prolonged and serious
> self-inquisition which is at the centre of the whole long
> work.[29]

Introduction

There is a good deal of cunning circularity in this passage.
Serious self-inquisition possibly requires a lack of humor; we do
not expect to find buffoonery in the judgments of the Supreme Court.
Why it should require priggishness is more difficult to see. In
any case, serious self-inquisition probably is not an adequate
description of Snow's themes which remain, as he himself puts it
in the preface to the Omnibus Edition, possessive love, man in
society, and man alone.[30]

This necessarily brief discussion of Snow's fiction demonstrates
some of the areas of critical concern. There are, of course, others,
and the bibliography which follows should be a preliminary guide to
these questions. Is the first-person narrator a useful device or
should it be abandoned for the traditional device of the omniscient
narrator? What can be said of the moral implications embedded in
the novels? In the last few years, a minor critical movement (if
it deserves the name) has freely admitted that Snow is a "competent
craftsman" not quite up to Balzac's standards, or even of the first
rank; but, the same critics who believe that Snow's style is not
imaginatively compelling, violently defend the Greek ideal of
political participation which they detect in the series. What can
usefully be said of Snow's treatment of morality, conscience and
the passions? Maxwell Geismar believes that Snow's continuing
moral concern is not enough for great fiction (B361). Robert K.
Morris (B302) finds Lewis Eliot drained of all passion by the
murderous barrage of reason to which he has been subjected. Is
this process possibly the sum and substance of Snow's myth, the
imposition of a formal pattern by the novelist, a process from
which Snow believes himself immune? John LeCarré finds himself
speculating whether Snow does not preach a doctrine of such desperate inhibition that he may be contributing to the very anarchy
and murderousness he seeks to prevent; cap the emotions and you can
elicit chaos. Then what of Snow's famous distinction between the
tragic individual condition and the "untragic" social condition?
Is it a tenable distinction, and are the characters who are most
aware of this tragic self (Roy Calvert, Paul Jago, George Passant,
Dr. Rubin) singularly uninteresting as Patrick Swinden (B309) con-
tends? These, it seems to me, are all serious, interesting and
pertinent questions that are worth asking about the work of this
considerable novelist, and generous and amiable man.

COVERAGE. This bibliography includes Snow's novels, pamphlets,
essays, book reviews, and open letters. It excludes his papers,
manuscripts, letters, and press clippings on file at the Humanities
Research Center of the University of Texas in Austin. The Center
reportedly owns 50 linear feet of such material. Some of the
letters in the collection are restricted. A smaller part of Snow's
manuscripts remains in private hands, and this material is also
excluded.

Introduction

This bibliography also attempts to list all books, pamphlets, essays,
open letters, and various _jeux d'esprit_ which have been written
about him in his two roles as novelist and social critic. The "Two
Cultures" debate is covered in depth. A word about the annotations
is in order. The diction is almost invariably that of the critic
or reviewer, and I have made extensive use of paraphrase without
resorting to the annoying and distracting practice of giving a
series of short quotations. Direct quotations are used when the
critic, or reviewer, made a memorable statement about Snow's achievement pro or con; when the sentiment in the review was difficult to
paraphrase without a loss of meaning; when the reviewer aired an
apparently meaningful statement which I found unable to penetrate
without the help of block and tackle, cryptoanalyst, or prayer.

ARRANGEMENT. The arrangement is predominately chronological in all
sections. The one exception is the list of Snow's book reviews.
These reviews are arranged in alphabetical order. They are not
otherwise indexed.

FICTION. This chapter includes Snow's fictional works up to the year
1975. Novels originally published as part of the "Strangers and
Brothers" sequence are so described in a note. However, it must be
emphasized that the "Omnibus Edition" of Strangers and Brothers
(London: Macmillan; New York: Scribner, 1972) supersedes all previous editions. The revised order of the novels in this edition is the
final one, and the text is the definitive text.

ARTICLES, ESSAYS, ETC. The works listed in this chapter convey some
idea of Snow's range of interests. The first articles were published
in Discovery when Snow was editor of that journal from 1938 to 1940.
In these early publications, we see the first evidence of Snow's
concern with issues of broad political and military significance
and not just with scientific subjects alone.

The genesis and growth of Snow's "Two Cultures" lecture is also
traced in this chapter--from its first, relatively quiet publication
in the New Statesman and Nation (1956) to its later elaboration
and defence in the Times Literary Supplement (1963). Some curios-
ities are in evidence. "Confidences on a Summer Evening," chapters
one and two of The Conscience of the Rich, was published in 1945;
the complete novel was issued in 1958. Snow writes that the publication of the work was delayed for entirely private and non-literary
reasons, and it is reasonable to speculate that publication was
delayed to protect the interests of a character or characters still
alive between 1945 and 1958. "An Object of Love" is apparently part
of that literary ghost of a novel The Devoted, a work pulped by the
stoical author himself. Its place in the series was later taken
by The Sleep of Reason.

Many of the articles, and some of the reviews listed in this chapter,
were collected and published in C.P. Snow, A Spectrum: Science,
Criticism, Fiction (New York: Scribner, 1963). The compendium was
edited by Stanley Weintraub.

INTERVIEWS. Interviews often appear in publications not indexed by conventional bibliographical tools. All the available examples of the genre which left a bibliographical trace have been put in a separate chapter on the ground of their rampant biographical and autobiographical appeal. More formal, brief biographical sketches may be found in the index under the heading "C.P. Snow."

BOOK REVIEWS. This chapter includes Snow's book reviews published in Discovery, Encounter, the London Financial Times, New Statesman, New Statesman and Nation, New York Herald Tribune Book Review, New York Times Book Review, Spectator, Time and Tide and the London Sunday Times. The London Sunday Times, by the way, should not be confused with the London Times.

Most of the reviews were contributed to the London Sunday Times and the London Financial Times. Snow became a regular reviewer of fiction for the first newspaper on January 9, 1949, and held the position until December 18, 1952. In the public statement of his resignation Snow observed he found it impossible to maintain indefinitely his "interest in any kind of new fiction." The remark is surely pardonable and somewhat prophetic. In 1970, when Snow became a reviewer for the London Financial Times, he primarily reviewed works of non-fiction.

The arrangement of the book reviews is alphabetical by author, and the title of the review is given as an aid to location only. It should not be accepted as a clue to Snow's treatment of the author in question. Snow wrote omnibus reviews in the harried way of the modern reviewer of fiction. Five or even six works were reviewed every two weeks. The title of his column, apt for one of the books reviewed, is often bizarre when extended to any or all of the others. So we get, for example, G.B. Stern's Ten Days of Christmas listed under the column headed "In the Jungle," a title chosen to fit Jon Godden's The Peacock.

Those readers or students who want to read all of Snow's reviews from one journal (say the New Statesman) are advised to consult the bibliography by Rubin Rabinovitz (B251). It includes a chronological arrangement of Snow's articles and reviews under the newspaper or periodical title.

WORKS ABOUT SNOW: BOOKS. The "Two Cultures" dispute gave rise to a furious and impassioned hubbub in the early part of the 1960s, and the proof of that contention is found in this chapter. Almost an equal number of books has been written about Snow the novelist and Snow the advocate and partisan of science and industrialization. The "Two Cultures" debate, a discussion of politics, science, and literature gorgeously studded with much ad hominem abuse, is a pervasive theme in works written about Snow, and it is probably desirable to give a brief historical introduction to the whole affair.

The Rede lecture is an ancient British tradition. The first
lecture was delivered in the year 1525, and the first lecturer
received the sum of nine guineas (about $27) for his pains. Snow
delivered the lecture in May 1959, and he was paid the same princely
sum. It is fitting, in this context, to observe that the main
thrust of the argument was for equality. "Liberty without equality
is a name of noble sound and squalid meaning." This sentiment,
attributed to L.T. Hobhouse, is probably shared by C.P. Snow, and
the Rede lecture argued for a greater equality, not between individuals of the Western world, but between the rich nations of the
Western world and the poor, undeveloped nations.

The lecture, however, had an uncertain emphasis. It appeared to
some to be an attack on literature. It was read by others as a
long hymn in praise of all science and all scientists. It annoyed
some by reason of its undoubted vulgarities. It pleased others by
the sheer seductiveness of a new moral demand. It displeased or
repelled others for the same reason. It struck still others as a
renewed call for a form of education which reconciles the sciences
and the humanities. It led still others on a search, often painstaking and fruitless, to identify the men and women equally at home
in both the arts and sciences. This diffuse response later prompted
Snow to say:

> I feel something like Upton Sinclair. He wrote about pov-
> erty among the stockyard workers in Chicago and the result
> was to get people remarkably concerned about the hygenic
> properties of canned meats--missed the main target by a
> mile.[31]

The Rede lecture was duly published under the title The Two
Cultures and the Scientific Revolution. It had a favorable reception, went through several reprintings, and promised to make Snow
a sage as well as a novelist. In March of 1962, ferocity, not
fraternity, came in the form of F.R. Leavis. Dr. Leavis, who com-
bines, it is commonly observed, a religious depth of feeling about
literature with a style that relies heavily on self-assertion,
serpentine periphrasis, and the repetition of talismanic value terms,
attacked Snow's reputation, his fiction, and his grasp of history.
He observed that Snow was ignorant. He denounced the novels as
intellectual nullities. He claimed that Snow's interpretation of
the literary response to the Industrial Revolution was a locus
classicus of bland ignorance. Snow was as intellectually undistinguished as it was possible to be. In short the lecture (see B123)
attacked Snow in terms so atrabilious as to be near libelous, and
Snow first had to give his assurance to the editors of the Spectator,
the magazine in which Leavis aired his grievances, that he would not
sue for libel on its appearance. Snow laughingly did so, and ex-
horted Mr. Ray, the Spectator's emissary, to publish the lecture
without cuts.[32]

WORKS ABOUT SNOW: ARTICLES, ESSAYS, ETC. The literature about Snow is voluminous and contentious; it often suggests that literary criticism is a continuation of war by other means. English language publications predominate in this chapter. Some German and East European articles are given when indexed in English language sources.

If the literature about Snow the writer of fiction forms a considerable total, then the material about Snow's "Two Cultures" lecture has become galactic. To record all the material everywhere is a plain impossibility: dicta on this subject, I am convinced, adorn Urdu. However, given that qualification, all the major English and American glosses, explications, diatribes, and exorcisms occasioned by the famous debate are recorded. Those other numerous works on this theme found in technical journals, or intended for a scientific or specialist audience, may be found in B218, B280, B286, and B316.

SNOW IN THE LONDON TIMES: A CHRONOLOGICAL ACCOUNT. This section, a cumulation of references to Snow in the index to the London Times, gives an outline of Snow's career, speeches, and activities as reported in the London Times.

The chronology must be used with care. The index to the London Times includes, not merely the London Times itself, but also the London Sunday Times, the Higher Education Supplement, and the Times Literary Supplement. The reference may be to any of these papers and journals, and the exact citation is important.

This chapter gives a brief report of Snow's speeches in the House of Lords. In fact, it serves as a rough index to Hansard's Parliamentary debates (Great Britain. Parliament. Hansard's Parliamentary debates is the common entry in library catalogs). To find the full debate in Hansard, simply refer to the issue immediately preceding the date of publication in the London Times. Occasionally, the text includes a cryptic notation in parentheses (6*, 7*, and the like) which means that the newspaper report is found in the edition with 6 or 7 stars.

WORKS ABOUT SNOW: BOOK REVIEWS. This chapter represents a cumulation of the reviews indexed in the Book Review Digest, Book Review Index, and the Index to Book Reviews in the Humanities. These three indexes concentrate on North American coverage, and so they are by no means exhaustive. A brief account of the reception of just one of Snow's books shows the nature of the problem. When he published Strangers and Brothers (London: Faber, 1940) the novel received, by his own ready reckoning, "three good notices out of approximately forty-seven." Almost all the reviews of that novel included in this chapter are prompted by the publication of the American edition of Strangers and Brothers in 1960. Those who want to read all the reviews from all sources must consult the press clippings at the Humanities Research Center, University of Texas at Austin. Furthermore, although these reviews are selective and not exhaustive, they include approximately 600 citations, and they should be numerous enough to satisfy all but the most unabashed Snovians.

1. J.D. Bernal. "Letter to the Editor." Spectator, 208 (23 March 1962) 365.

2. "Can Science Save Britain's Industry?" Business Week, no. 1862 (8 May 1965) 118-21.

3. H.E. Dale. The Higher Civil Service of Great Britain. Oxford: Oxford University Press, 1941, p. 92.

4. Quoted by Francis Wyndham. Review of The Conscience of the Rich. London Magazine, 5 (June 1958) 70.

5. "An Interview with C.P. Snow and Pamela Hansford Johnson." Publishers Weekly, 176, no. 22 (30 November 1959) 28.

6. "Like The Sleep of Reason, which is the tenth and latest in the series, The Affair and Corridors of Power were Book-of-the-Month Club selections. Thus Snow's audience has continued to grow, until the series today is almost certainly the most widely read fictional cycle in the English language; indeed, it has been called "the most remarkable creative effort of its kind since Balzac's Comedie Humaine." Book-of-the-Month Club News, December 1968, p. 13.

7. Letter from Charles Scribner III to the author. Lord Snow writes that this three volume, eleven novel work will probably be made available to its readers by the Book-of-the-Month Club beginning December 1978.

8. Walter Allen. "C.P. Snow." Book-of-the Month Club News, August 1964, p. 5.

9. V. Ivasheva. "Meeting Sir Charles Snow." Soviet Literature, no. 8 (1963) 180-82.

10. The London Times, 7 December 1964, p. 8d.

11. Frank Kermode. "The House of Fiction: Interviews with Seven English Novelists." Partisan Review, 30, no. 1 (Spring 1963) 74-76.

12. J.D. Scott. "New Novels." New Statesman and Nation, 38, no. 970 (8 October 1949) 402.

13. A.S. Byatt. "Worldly Wise." New Statesman, 96, no. 2485 (3 November 1978)586.

14. J.I.M. Stewart. Review of Homecomings. London Magazine, 4 (January 1957) 71-73.

15. Edmund Wilson. "An Interview with Edmund Wilson." New Yorker, 38 (2 June 1962) 118.

16. Frederick Crews. "Private Lives, Public Lives." New York Review of Books, 3, no. 6 (5 November 1964) 14.

17. Daniel Curley. "Satan is Missing." New Leader, 47, no. 25 (7 December 1964) 24.

18. Frank McGuiness. Review of Corridors of Power. London Magazine, 4, no. 10 (January 1965) 102.

19. Melvin Maddocks. "'Take It Off' Cry the C.P. Snow Fans." Life, 66, no. 2 (17 January 1969) 8.

20. John LeCarré. "Vocation in a World of Pain." London Sunday Times, 25 October 1970, p. 27.

21. Alan Pryce-Jones. "A Structure Built for Business, Not for Living." Washington Post (San Francisco Examiner, etc.) Book Week, 13 September 1964, p. 5.

22. Anthony Burgess. "Power That Be." Encounter, 24, no. 1 (January 1965) 74-76.

23. Jay R. Halio. "C.P. Snow's Literary Limitations." Northwest Review, 5, no. 1 (Winter 1962) 97-102.

24. William Cooper. C.P. Snow. London: Published for the British Council by Longmans Green, 1959, p. 35.

25. Pamela Hansford Johnson. "With Prejudice." Windmill, 1, no. 1 (1944) 10.

26. Geoffrey Wagner. "Sociology and Fiction." Twentieth Century, 167, no. 996 (February 1960) 114.

27. Bernard Bergonzi. "The World of Lewis Eliot." Twentieth Century, 167 (March 1960) 215.

28. Charles A. Brady. "The British Novel Today." Thought, 24, no. 135 (Winter 1959-60) 539.

29. Helen Gardner. "The World of C.P. Snow." New Statesman, 55, no. 1411 (29 March 1958) 409-410.

30. C.P. Snow. "Preface." Strangers and Brothers. Omnibus Ed. New York: Scribner, 1972, p. xii.

31. New York Times, 2 November 1968, p. 37c.

32. Cyril Ray. "Letter to the Editor." Times Literary Supplement, 30 April 1970, p. 478. Mr. Ray remarks: "I sat with the Snows in the drawing room of their Cromwell Road flat, admired their Sidney Nolans, and listened to Charles reading the Leavis lecture to Pamela. Some of it nettled them--Pamela I seem to recall was the more indignant of the two--and some of it amused them. But there was no hesitation at the end: 'Of course you must go ahead and publish--and no cuts.'"

Acknowledgments

Every stage of this opuscule has entailed the sacrifice of more sustained voluptuousness, dolce far niente, and a greater consumption of tobacco in a growing atmosphere of rank despair, than I ever thought possible. Here are some of the people and institutions who were helpful, and more than helpful, kind in the course of its compilation: Carl Bode of the Department of English, University of Maryland; Frank Carroll of the Newspaper Division of the Library of Congress; my friend, Mr. Prudencio de Pereda, for his unrelenting scrutiny of style and content; Ruth Drozin and Gene Spencer of the Freas Rooke Computer Center, Bucknell University; Ellen Dunlap, Humanities Research Center, University of Texas at Austin; Mr. Ronald Hingley, formerly of the Sunday Times; Laurene Lozoski, Catalog Department, Ellen Clarke Bertrand Library, for dilating on the benefits of dumping; Ann Lusk and Nancy Weyant, Interlibrary Loan Department, Bucknell University, who learned that a harassed individual inflicts a modicum of harassment; Pamela Maloney, for her rapid learning of TEXT; Marion Peters, the Norman F. Sprague Memorial Library, Harvey Mudd College; Charles Scribner, III; Lord Snow, for his unfailing generosity and kindness; John Wain; Stanley Weintraub, Department of English, Pennsylvania State University, State College, Pennsylvania; Audrey Zuch, for her invariable helpfulness in all things. For permission to reprint material, I am indebted to the New York Times and Abstracts of English Studies. I am grateful, for many services, to the librarians of the New York Public Library, the Library of Congress, and Pennsylvania State University. I am also grateful to Bucknell University, Lewisburg, Pennsylvania, for an administrative leave in the year 1976–1977, which enabled me to make a beginning on this project.

Chronology

1905   Born October 15, 1905, son of William Edward and Ada Sophia (Robinson) Snow, in Leicester, England.

1925   Entered University College, Leicester (now University of Leicester) to study chemistry. Awarded B.Sc. in chemistry, 1927; M.Sc. in physics, 1928.

1928   Entered Christ's College, Cambridge, to do research in molecular structure. Awarded Ph.D., 1930.

1930   Elected fellow of Christ's College, Cambridge. Remained a Fellow from 1930-50 (in residence 1930-40). Honorary Fellow, 1966-.

1932   Death Under Sail.

1933   New Lives for Old.

1934   The Search.

1935   Elected tutor, Christ's College (1935-45). In Marseilles, on January 1, first thought of writing the Strangers and Brothers sequence.

1938   Richard Aldington: An Appreciation. Editor, Discovery (1938-1940).

1940   Strangers and Brothers, first novel in the Strangers and Brothers sequence published in this year. Later issued under the title George Passant to avoid confusion with the series as a whole. Technical director, Ministry of Labour, 1940-44.

1943   Made C.B.E. (Commander of the British Empire) for his work as technical director, Ministry of Labour, in recruiting and placing Britain's scientific manpower in World War II.

Chronology

1944   Director of scientific personnel, English Electric Company (1944-64).

1945   Civil service commissioner (1945-60).

1947   The Light and the Dark. Member, board of directors, English Electric Company (1947-64).

1949   Time of Hope. Regular fiction reviewer for the London Sunday Times (1949-52).

1950   Married Pamela Hansford Johnson. "View Over the Park," a play. First performed at the Lyric Opera House, Hammersmith, August 29.

1951   The Masters.

1952   Birth of Philip Hansford Snow.

1954   The New Men. In conjunction with The Masters, this novel gained Snow the James Tait Black Memorial Prize for fiction.

1956   Homecomings.

1957   Awarded knighthood for his service during the war and his postwar work as a civil service commissioner.

1958   The Conscience of the Rich.

1959   The Two Cultures and the Scientific Revolution (The Rede lecture, 1959).

1960   The Affair.

1961   Science and Government (The Godkin lectures at Harvard University, 1960). The Affair dramatized by Ronald Millar and performed at the Strand Theatre, Aldwich (September 21, 1961-62). President, Library Association. Rector, University of St. Andrews, Scotland (1961-64).

1962   The New Men dramatized by R. Millar and performed at the Strand Theatre.
Two Cultures? The Significance of C.P. Snow, attack by F.R. Leavis.

1963   The Masters dramatized by R. Millar and performed at the Savoy and Piccadilly Theatres (1963-64).

1964   Corridors of Power. The Two Cultures: and a Second Look. Created life peer and styled Baron Snow of Leicester. Parliamentary secretary, Ministry of Technology (1964-66).

Chronology

1967   <u>Variety of Men</u>.

1968   <u>The Sleep of Reason</u>.

1969   <u>The State of Siege</u> (The John Findley Green Foundation
        lectures, 1968).

1970   <u>Last Things</u>.
        Regular reviewer for the London <u>Financial Times</u>.

1971   <u>Public Affairs</u>. Member, Arts Council.

1972   <u>The Malcontents</u>. All eleven novels of the "Strangers and
        Brothers" sequence published in a three volume "Omnibus
        edition." This set includes the definitive reading to date,
        and the revised order of the novels is also final and
        definitive.

1973   <u>George Passant</u>. New title of the one novel first issued under
        the title <u>Strangers and Brothers</u>.

1974   <u>In Their Wisdom</u>.

1975   <u>Trollope; His Life and Art</u>. <u>The Case in Question</u>, a play by
        Ronald Millar, based on <u>In Their Wisdom</u>. First performed at
        the Theatre Royal, Haymarket, March 11.

1978   <u>The Realists</u>.

1979   <u>A Coat of Varnish</u>.

Writings by Snow

Death Under Sail. 1932.

A1 London: Heinemann, 1932.

A2 Garden City, N.Y.: Published for the Crime Club by
        Doubleday, Doran, 1932.

A3 London: Heinemann, 1959. Rev. ed.

A4 Harmondsworth, Middlesex: Penguin Books, 1963.

A5 Harmondsworth, Middlesex: Penguin Books, 1973. Pbk.

A6 Arabic: Jarimat al-yakht. al-Qahirah: al-Dar al-Qawmiyah,
        1966. Translated by 'Abd al-Mun'im Sadiq.

A7 German: Mord unterm Segel. Stuttgart: Deutsche Verlags-
        Anstalt, 1971. Translated by Liselotte Michel.

A8 Italian: Morte a vele spiegate. Milano: Rozzoli, 1967.
        Translated by Marina Valente.

A9 Japanese: Yacht senjo no satsujin; shinriteki suiri
        shosetsu. Tokyo: Kobundo, 1964. Translated by
        Sakurai Masuo.

A10 Polish: Smierc pod zaglami. Warsaw: Iskry, 1961.
        Translated by Jadwiga Milnikiel.

A11 Ukrainian: Smert'pid vitrylami; roman. Kyiv: Dnipro,
        1965. Translated by I. Halyns'ka and M. Pinchevs'kyi.

New Lives for Old. 1933.

    A12   London: Gollancz, 1933.

The Search. 1934.

    A13   London: Gollancz, 1934.

    A14   Indianapolis: Bobbs-Merrill, 1935.

    A15   London: Macmillan, 1958. Rev. ed.

    A16   London: Macmillan, 1959. 2d ed.

    A17   New York: Scribner, 1959.

    A18   New York: New American Library, 1960.

    A19   New York: Scribner, 1967. Pbk.

    A20   Russian: Poiski. Moskva: Progress, 1964. Translated by
           B. Gribanov.

Strangers and Brothers. 1940.

    A21   London: Faber and Faber, 1940.

    A22   London: Faber, 1944.

    A23   London: Macmillan, 1951. 2d ed.

    A24   London: Macmillan, 1958. "Uniform ed."

    A25   New York: Macmillan, 1958.

    A26   New York: Scribner, 1960.

    A27   New York: Scribner, 1963. Pbk. (Strangers and Brothers,
           1)

    A28   German: Fremde und Bruder. Stuttgart: Deutsche Verlags-
           Anstalt, 1964. Translated by Grete Felten.

    A29   Spanish: Extranos y hermanos. Barcelona: Plaza & Janes,
           1962. Translated by Rosa S. de Naveira.

The Light and the Dark. 1947.

    A30   London: Faber, 1947.

    A31   London: Macmillan, 1948.

A32   London: Macmillan, 1951. 2d impression.

A33   London: Macmillan, 1957.

A34   New York: Scribner, 1961.

A35   Harmondsworth, Middlesex: Penguin Books, 1962. Pbk.

A36   New York: Scribner, 1964. Pbk.

A37   Harmondsworth, Middlesex: Penguin Books, 1972. Pbk.
        (Strangers and Brothers, 4)

A38   French: La lumiere et les tenebres. Paris: Laffont,
        1951. Translated by Renee Villoteau.

A39   German: Die lichten und dunklen Gewalten. Vienna:
        Zsolnay, 1948. Translated by Walter Puchwein.

A40   Polish: Jasnosc i mrok. Warsaw: Panstowe Instytut
        Wydawn, 1961. Translated by Henryk Krzeczko.

Time of Hope. 1949.

A41   London: Faber and Faber, 1949.

A42   London: Macmillan, 1950.

A43   New York: Macmillan, 1950.

A44   London: Macmillan, 1951. 2d impression.

A45   London: Macmillan, 1958. "Uniform ed."

A46   New York: Harper, 1961. Pbk.

A47   New York: Scribner, 1966. Pbk.

A48   French: Le temps de l'espoir. Paris: Laffont, 1952.
        Translated by Renee Villoteau.

A49   German: Jahre der Hoffnung. Vienna: Zsolnay, 1948.
        Translated by Th. Kauer.

A50   German: Zeit der Hoffnung. Stuttgart: Europaischer
        Buchklub, 1963. Translated by Grete Felten.

A51   German: Zeit der Hoffnung. Zurich: Buchclub Ex Libris,
        1963. Translated by Grete Felten.

A52   Hungarian: <u>A remenyseg kora</u>. Budapest: Europa, 1962.
        Translated by Peter Nagy.

A53   Polish: <u>Czas nadziel</u>. Warsaw: Panstowe Instytut Wydawn,
        1963. Translated by Jadwiga Milnikiel.

A54   Russian: <u>Pora nadezhd; roman</u>. Moskva: Izd-vo Inostrannoi
        lit-ry, 1962. Translated by N. Vasil'eva and T.
        Kudriavtsevoi.

<u>The Masters</u>. 1951.

A55   London: Macmillan, 1951.

A56   New York: Macmillan, 1951.

A57   London: Macmillan, 1954. "Uniform ed."

A58   London: Macmillan, 1959.

A59   Garden City, N.Y.: Doubleday, 1959. Pbk.

A60   New York: Scribner, 1960.

A61   New York: Scribner, 1965. Pbk.

A62   London: Macmillan, 1966. Abridged, with introduction
        and notes, by K.M. Lobb.

A63   London: Macmillan, 1972. (<u>Strangers and Brothers</u>, 5)

A64   Czechoslovakian: <u>Professori</u>. Praha: Statni nakl krasne
        lit-ry a umeni, 1963. Translated by Eliska
        Hornatova.

A65   German: <u>Die Lehrer; Roman</u>. Munchen: Desch, 1952.
        Translated by Georg Goyert.

A66   Rumanian: <u>Universitarii</u>. Bucuresti: Editura pentru
        literatura universala, 1967. Translated by Veronica
        Suteu.

A67   Swedish: <u>Rektorsvalet</u>. Stockholm: Norstedt, 1954.
        Translated by Jane Lundblad.

<u>The New Men</u>. 1954.

A68   London: Macmillan, 1954.

A69   New York: Scribner, 1955.

A70   Toronto: Macmillan, 1954.

A71   London: Macmillan, 1958. "Uniform ed."

A72   London: Macmillan, 1960.

A73   New York: Scribner, 1961. Pbk.

A74   New York: Scribner, 1965. (<u>Strangers and Brothers</u>, 6)

A75   German: <u>Entscheidung in Barford</u>. Stuttgart: Deutsche
         Verlags-Anstalt, 1970. Translated by Grete Felten.

A76   Italian: <u>Gli uomini nuovi</u>. Milano: Club Degli Editori,
         1965. Translated by Maria R. Schisano.

A77   Spanish: <u>Nueve hombre del siglo xx</u>. Madrid: Alianza
         Editorial, 1969. Translated by Mercedes Garcia
         Arenal.

A78   Swedish: <u>De nya Mannen</u>. Stockholm: Norstedt, 1956.
         Translated by Jane Lundblad.

<u>Homecomings</u>. 1956.

A79   London: Macmillan, 1956.

A80   New York: Scribner, 1956.

A81   New York: Scribner, 1965. Pbk.

A82   Bulgarian: <u>Zavrastaija u doma</u>. Sofija: Nar. Kultura,
         1966. Translated by Todor Valcev.

A83   German: <u>Wege nach Haus</u>. Stuttgart: Deutsche Verlags-
         Anstalt, 1962. Translated by Grete Felten.

A84   Russian: <u>Vozrasceni ja momoj</u>. Moskva: Hudoz, 1964.
         Translated by N. Emel-Jannikoua.

<u>The Conscience of the Rich</u>. 1958.

A85   London: Macmillan, 1958.

A86   New York: Scribner, 1958.

A87   New York: Scribner, 1960. Pbk. (<u>Strangers and Brothers</u>,
         2)

A88   German: <u>Das Gewissen der Reichen</u>. Stuttgart: Deutsche
       Verlags-Anstalt, 1961. Translated by Dorothea
       and Rolf Michaelis.

The Affair. 1960.

A89   London: Macmillan, 1960.

A90   New York: Scribner, 1960.

A91   Harmondsworth, Middlesex: Penguin Books, 1962. Pbk.

A92   New York: Scribner, 1962. Pbk. (<u>Strangers and Brothers</u>,
       8)

A93   Danish: <u>Affaeren</u>. Kobenhaven: Gyldendal, 1963.
       Translated by Anton Kjaedegaard.

A94   Dutch: <u>De zaak-Howard</u>. Amsterdam: Contact, 1963.
       Translated by G. Messelaar.

A95   French: <u>L'affaire Howard</u>. Paris: Laffont, 1963.
       Translated by Suzanne Desternes.

A96   German: <u>Die Affäre; Roman</u>. Stuttgart: Deutsche Verlags-
       Anstalt, 1963. Translated by Grete Felten.

A97   German: <u>Die Affäre</u>. Berlin, Darmstadt: Deutsche
       Buchgemeinschaft, 1965. Translated by Grete Felten.

A98   Italian. <u>Il caso Howard</u>. Torino: Einaudi, 1962.
       Translated by Vincanzo Mantovani.

A100   Polish: <u>Spawa Howarda</u>. Warsaw: Panstowe Instytut Wydawn,
       1964. Translated by Zofia Kierszys.

A101   Russian: <u>Delo</u>. Moskva: Goslitizdat, 1962. Translated
       by V. Efanova.

A102   Swedish: <u>Affaren</u>. Stockholm: Norstedt, 1963. Translated
       by Erik Frykman.

A103   Yugoslavian: <u>Afera</u>. Zagreb: Zora, 1970. Translated
       by Gordana Buncic.

Corridors of Power. 1964.

A104   London: Macmillan, 1964.

A105   New York: Scribner, 1964.

A106   Toronto: Macmillan, 1964.

A107   New York: Bantam Books, 1965.

A108   Harmondsworth, Middlesex: Penguin Books, 1967. Pbk.
        (Strangers and Brothers, 9)

A109   Bulgarian: Koridori na vlastta. Sofijia: NSOF, 1967.
        Translated by Zeni Bozilova.

A110   Estonian: Voimu telgitagused. Tallin: Eesti raamat,
        1968. Translated by U. Lehtsalu.

A111   German (East): Korridore der Macht. Berlin: Verlag Volk
        und Welt, 1967. Translated by Grete Felten.

A112   German: Korridore der Macht. Stuttgart: Deutsche
        Verlags-Anstalt, 1967. Translated by Grete Felten.

A113   Latvian: Varas gaiteni. Riga: Liesman, 1968. Translated
        by Vanda Vikane.

A114   Swedish: Maktens Korridorer. Stockholm: Norstedt, 1967.
        Translated by Gunnar Barklund.

The Sleep of Reason. 1968.

A115   London: Macmillan, 1968.

A116   New York: Scribner, 1969.

A117   Harmondsworth, Middlesex: Penguin Books, 1970. Pbk.
        (Strangers and Brothers, 10)

Last Things. 1970.

A118   London: Macmillan, 1970.

A119   New York: Scribner, 1970. (Strangers and Brothers, 11)

The Malcontents. 1972.

A120   London: Macmillan, 1972.

A121   New York: Scribner, 1972.

Strangers and Brothers. Omnibus Ed. 1972.

A122   London: Macmillan, 1972. 11 v. in 3.

A123   New York: Scribner, 1972. 11 v. in 3.
        CONTENTS: Volume 1. <u>Time of Hope</u> (1914–33).
        <u>George Passant</u> (1925–33). <u>The Conscience of the</u>
        <u>Rich</u> (1927–37). <u>The Light and the Dark</u> (1935–43).
        Volume 2. <u>The Masters</u> (1937). <u>The New Men</u> (1939–47)
        <u>Homecomings</u> (1938–51). <u>The Affair</u> (1953–54).
        Volume 3. <u>Corridors of Power</u> (1955–59). <u>The Sleep</u>
        <u>of Reason</u> (1963–64). <u>Last Things</u> (1964–68).
        This edition includes a preface and a five page
        index of characters. Snow writes that this edition
        "contains the text which I should like to be read.
        The arrangement of the volumes is different from
        that in which they have been separately published,
        and there is a fair amount of amendment both in
        structural detail and in words."--Pref.

<u>George Passant</u>. 1973.

A124   Harmondsworth, Middlesex: Penguin Books, 1973. First
        published under the title <u>Strangers and Brothers</u>
        in 1940. Later given this title to avoid confusion
        with the "Omnibus Edition" published under the
        title <u>Strangers and Brothers</u>.

<u>In Their Wisdom</u>. 1974.

A125   London: Macmillan, 1974.

A126   New York: Scribner, 1974.

<u>Non-Fiction: Books, Pamphlets and Translations</u>

<u>Richard Aldington: An Appreciation</u>. 1938.

A127   London: Heinemann, 1938. 26 p.

<u>Writers and Readers in the Soviet Union</u>. 1943.

A128   Watford, Hertfordshire: Farleigh Press, 1943.
        (Attributed to Snow by the Library of Congress and
        Stanton (B328) but not one of his works.)

<u>The Two Cultures and the Scientific Revolution</u>. 1959.

A129   Cambridge: Cambridge University Press, 1959. 51 p.

A130   New York: Cambridge University Press, 1959. 58 p.

A131   Cambridge: Cambridge University Press, 1959. 51 p.

A132   Cambridge: Cambridge University Press, 1961.   58 p.

A133   Cambridge: Cambridge University Press, 1964.   2d. ed.

A134   London: Cambridge University Press, 1964.   2d ed.
       Originally delivered as the Rede Lecture for 1959.

A135   Catalan: Les dues cultures i la revolucio cientifica.
       Barcelona: Edicions, 1965.   Translated by Jordi
       Sole-Tura.

A136   French: Les deux cultures.   Paris: Pauvert, 1968.

A137   German: Die zwei Kulturen.   Literarische und Naturwiss-
       enschaftliche Intelligenz.   Stuttgart: Klett, 1967.
       Translated by Grete and Karl-Eberhardt Felten.

A138   Norwegian: De to Kulturer.   Oslo: Cappelen, 1963.
       Translated by Ragnar Kvam.

A139   Russian: Dve kul'tury.   Moscow: Progress, 1973.

A140   Spanish: Las dos culturas y la revolucion cientifica.
       Buenos Aires: Sur, 1963.   Translated by Maria
       Raquel Bengolca.

A141   Swedish: De tva kulturerna.   Malmo: Cavefors, 1961.
       Translated by Claes-A. and Lillemor Wachtmeister.

The Moral Un-Neutrality of Science.   1961.

A142   Philadelphia: Peace Education Program, American Friends
       Service Committee, 1961.
       Reprint of A273.   See also: A278.

Recent Thoughts on the Two Cultures.   1961.

A143   London: Birkbeck College, 1961.   11 p.   An oration
       delivered at Birkbeck College, London, 12 December
       1961, in celebration of the 138th anniversary of
       the foundation of the college.

Science and Government.   1961.

A144   Cambridge: Harvard University Press, 1961.   Appendix
       published separately as supplement, 1962.

A145   London: Oxford University Press, 1961.

A146   Toronto: S.J. Reginald Saunders, 1961.

A147   New York: New American Library, 1962.

A148   London: New English Library, 1963. (Four Square Books,
        no. 3002). Originally delivered as the Godkin
        lecture, Harvard University, 1960.

A149   Danish: <u>Videnskap og stat</u>. Kobenhavn: Gyldenal, 1962.
        Translated by Bjarne Norretranders.

A150   German: <u>Politik hinter verschlossenen Türen</u>.
        (<u>Wissenschaft und Staatsfuhrung</u>.) Stuttgart:
        Deutsche Verlags-Anstalt, 1961. Translated by
        Grete and Karl-Eberhardt Felten.

A151   Icelandic: <u>Valdstjor og visindi</u>. Reykjavik: Hith Isenzka
        Bokmenntafelag, 1970. Translated by Baldur
        Simonarson.

A152   Italian: <u>Scienza e governo</u>. Torino: Einaudi, 1966.
        Translated by Luciano de Maria.

A153   Japanese: <u>Kagaku to seiji</u>. Tokyo: Otawa Shobo.
        Translated by Natsuo Shumata.

A154   Norwegian: <u>Vitenskap og statsstyre</u>. Oslo: Cappelen,
        1962. Translated by Ragnar Kvam.

A155   Spanish: <u>Ciencia y govierno</u>. Barcelona: Seix barral,
        1963. Translated by Manuel Escalera.

<u>Appendix to Science and Government</u>. 1962.

A156   Cambridge: Harvard University Press, 1962.

<u>Magnanimity</u>. 1962.

A157   London: University of St. Andrews, Students Representative
        Council, 1962. Rectorial address delivered at the
        University of St. Andrews, 13 April 1962. 23 p.

<u>A Postscript to Science and Government</u>. 1962.

A158   Cambridge: Harvard University Press, 1962. 37 p.

A159   London: Oxford University Press, 1962. 37 p.

<u>C.P. Snow, a Spectrum: Science, Criticism, Fiction</u>. 1963.

A160   New York: Scribner, 1963. Edited by Stanley Weintraub.
        (A Scribner research anthology)

The Two Cultures: and A Second Look.   1963.

    A161   New York; Toronto: New American Library, 1963.   (Mento
            Book, MP 557)

    A162   Cambridge: Cambridge University Press, 1964.   107 p.

    A163   Toronto: Macmillan, 1964.

    A164   New York: New American Library, 1964.   92 p.

    A165   Cambridge: Cambridge University Press, 1965.

    A166   London: Cambridge University Press, 1969.   107 p.

    A167   New York: New American Library, 1970.   92 p.   Expanded
            versions of The Two Cultures and the Scientific
            Revolution first published in 1959.

Variety of Men.   1967.

    A168   London: Macmillan, 1967.

    A169   New York: Scribner, 1967.

The State of Siege.   1969.

    A170   New York: Scribner, 1969.   Originally delivered as the
            John Findley Green Foundation lecture for 1968.

Public Affairs.   1971.

    A171   London: Macmillan, 1971.

    A172   New York: Scribner, 1971.

Medical Possibilities and Human Conscience.   1974.

    A173   Chapel Hill, North Carolina: The School of Medicine,
            The University of North Carolina, 1974.   13 p.

Trollope; His Life and Art.   1975.

    A174   London: Macmillan, 1975.

    A175   New York: Scribner, 1975.

The Realists.   1978.

    A176   London: Macmillan, 1978.

A177   New York: Scribner, 1978

Contributions to Books

A178   JOHNSON, PAMELA HANSFORD. Family Party. London:
        Evans Brothers, 1951. A one-act play of 24 pages.
        Co-author: C.P. Snow.

A179   _____. Her Best Foot Forward. London: Evans Brothers,
        1951. A one-act play of 31 pages. Co-author:
        C.P. Snow.

A180   _____. The Pigeon with the Silver Foot. London: Evans
        Brothers, 1951. A one-act play of 24 pages.
        Co-author: C.P. Snow.

A181   _____. Spare the Rod. London: Evans Brothers, 1951.
        A one-act play of 23 pages. Co-author: C.P. Snow.

A182   _____. The Supper Dance. London: Evans Brothers, 1951.
        A one-act play of 23 pages. Co-author: C.P. Snow.

A183   _____. To Murder Mrs. Mortimer. London: Evans
        Brothers, 1951. A one-act play of 30 pages.
        Co-author: C.P. Snow.

A184   Congress for Cultural Freedom. Two Cultures: A
        Discussion. By C.P. Snow and others. New
        Delhi [1960?].

A185   ROGOW, ARNOLD A. The Jew in a Gentile World. New
        York: Macmillan, 1961. Introduction by C.P.
        Snow.

A186   Winter's Tales: Stories from Modern Russia. Edited
        by C.P. Snow and Pamela Hansford Johnson.
        London: Macmillan; New York: St. Martin's
        Press, 1961

A187   MILLAR, RONALD. The Affair; A Play in Three Acts.
        From the novel by C.P. Snow. London: S. French,
        1962. (French's acting edition)

A188   _____. The Affair; A Play. From the novel by C.P.
        Snow. New York: Scribner, 1962. Performed at
        the Strand Theatre, Aldwich, 21 September 1961-
        62.

12

A189 REZNIKOFF, CHARLES. <u>By the Waters of Manhattan; Selected</u>
<u>Verse</u>. New York: New Directions, 1962. Introduction
by Snow.

A190 <u>Stories from Modern Russia</u>. Edited by C.P. Snow and
Pamela Hansford Johnson. New York: St. Martin's
Press, 1962. (Winter's Tales, 7)

A191 YOUNG, JESSICA (HANKINSON) BRETT. <u>Francis Brett Young;</u>
<u>A Biography</u>. London: Heinemann, 1962. Includes
a preface by C.P. Snow.

A192 MILLAR, RONALD. <u>The Affair, The New Men and The Masters</u>.
Three plays based on the novels and with a preface
by C.P. Snow. London: Macmillan, 1964. <u>The New</u>
<u>Men</u> performed at the Strand Theatre, 1962. <u>The</u>
<u>Masters</u> at the Savoy Theatre and Piccadilly Theatre
in 1963-64.

   BODE, CARL. <u>The Half-World of American Culture: A</u>
<u>Miscellany</u>.

A193 Carbondale: Southern Illinois University Press, 1965.

A194 Carbondale: Southern Illinois University Press, 1965.
Pbk.

A195 London: Feffer & Simons, 1967. Introduction by Snow,
pp. vii-ix.

A196 WILSON, MITCHELL. <u>Energy</u>. Amsterdam, 1965. C.P. Snow
is one of the consulting editors.

   HOLLOWAY, JOHN. <u>A London Childhood</u>.

A197 London: Routledge and K. Paul, 1966.

A198 New York: Scribner, 1967. Introduction by Snow, p. xi-
xiii.

A199 HARDY, GODFREY HAROLD. <u>A Mathematician's Apology</u>.
London: Cambridge University Press, 1967. Includes
a foreword written expressly for this work by
C.P. Snow, p. 9-58. Reprinted under title "G.H.
Hardy" in Snow's <u>Variety of Men</u>. See A168-A169.

A200 DZHAGAROV, GEORGI. <u>The Public Prosecutor; A Play</u>.
Translated from the Bulgarian by Marguerite
Alexieva, adapted by C.P. Snow and Pamela Hansford
Johnson, with an introduction by C.P. Snow.
London: Owen, 1969. (International play series, 2)

A201   DOYLE, ARTHUR CONAN. The Casebook of Sherlock Holmes.
        London: J. Murray and J. Cape, 1974. C.P. Snow
        argues convincingly that these stories are Doyle's
        masterpieces, because in them his remarkable
        romantic imagination was tied down (as it was not
        in the historical novels) by a commitment to the
        concrete facts of the London he saw about him.
        The Year's Work in English Studies, v. 55 (1974)
        447.

A202   MILLAR, RONALD. The Case in Question; A Play. London;
        New York: S. French, 1975. Based on Snow's novel
        In Their Wisdom.

                        Articles, Essays, Etc.

A203   "Science of the Year." Bookman, 85 (December 1933)
        159-61.

A204   "Chemistry." In University Studies, Cambridge, 1933.
        Edited by Harold Wright. London: Nicholson &
        Watson, 1933, pp. 97-127.

A205   "Rejuvenation Promises an End of Old Age." Pictorial
        Review, 35 (May 1934) 4+. New Lives for Old
        marked the beginning of Snow's interest in the
        subject of rejuvenation; this article marks its
        end.

A206   "The Enjoyment of Science." Spectator, 156 (12 June
        1936) 1074+. Reprinted: A160, A209.

A207   "False Alarm in Physics." Spectator, 157 (16 October
        1936) 628-29.

A208   "What We Need from Applied Science." Spectator, 157
        (20 November 1936) 904.

A209   "The Enjoyment of Science." Living Age, 351 (November
        1936) 205-208. Reprint of A206.

A210   "Superfluity of Particles." Spectator, 157 (4 December
        1936) 984-5.

A211   "The Original of the Mona Lisa," in Imaginary Biographies.
        Edited by Arthur Bryant, et al. London: Allen &
        Unwin, 1936. A short story.

A212   "Humanity of Science." Spectator, 158 (16 April 1937) 702-03.

A213   "Controlling Reproduction." Spectator, 159 (22 October 1937) 678-79.

A214   "Brightest Things in the Universe." Spectator, 160 (28 January 1938) 124-25.

A215   "Discovery Comes to Cambridge." Discovery, N.S., 1 (April 1938) 1.

A216   "The Progress of Discovery." N.S., 1 (June 1938) 103.

A217   "Science in a Modern World." Discovery, N.S., 1, no. 7 (October 1938) 318.

A218   "Science and Conscience; A Letter from Mr. Aldington." Discovery, N.S., 1, no. 9 (December 1938) 421-24. Includes Snow's editorial reply to the letter.

A219   "Scientific Prophecies." Discovery, N.S., 2 (January 1939) 1-2.

A220   "Blueprint of Future Science." Discovery, N.S., 2 (March 1939) 107.

A221   "The First Excitement That Knowledge Gives." Discovery, N.S., 2, no. 13 (April 1939) 161-62.

A222   "Science and Air Warfare." Discovery, N.S., 2 no. 14 (May 1939) 215-217. Snow dismisses speculations that German air power will reduce London to rubble in a week.

A223   "Race, Nations, Class: Lessons of Genetics." Discovery, N.S., 2, no. 15 (June 1939) 271.

A224   "A New Attempt to Explain Modern Physics." Discovery, N.S., 2, no. 16 (July 1939) 329.

A225   "A New Means of Destruction?" Discovery, N.S., 2, no. 18 (September 1939) 443. Snow discusses the possible construction of an atomic bomb. He suspects it will first be made in the United States.

A226   "The Fate of Homo Sapiens." Discovery, N.S., 2, no. 19 (October 1939) 449.

A227   "Against Destructiveness." Discovery, N.S., 2, no. 20 (November 1939) 557.

A228　"Stretches of Time." <u>Discovery</u>, N.S., 3, no. 22
　　　　(January 1940) 1-2.

A229　"Scientists and War Discoveries." <u>Discovery</u>, N.S., 3,
　　　　no. 23 (February 1940) 59-60.

A230　"The End of <u>Discovery</u>." <u>Discovery</u>, N.S., 3, no. 24
　　　　(March 1940) 117.

A231　"Careers." <u>Political Quarterly</u>, 15 (October 1944) 310+.

A232　"Confidences on a Summer Evening." <u>Windmill</u>, no. [2]
　　　　(June 1945) 95-101.
　　　　Chapters I and II of <u>The Conscience of the Rich</u>.
　　　　(London: Macmillan, 1958)

A233　"The Mathematician on Cricket." <u>Saturday Book</u>, no. 8
　　　　(1948) 65-73.

A234　"The Wisdom of Niels Bohr." <u>The Saturday Book</u>, no. 9
　　　　(1949) 180+.

A235　"Books and Writers." <u>Spectator</u>, 185, no. 6378 (22
　　　　September 1950) 320. A hearty attack on the
　　　　aesthetic credo of Henry Green.

A236　"View Over the Park." A play written by C.P. Snow.
　　　　First performed at the Lyric Opera House,
　　　　Hammersmith, 29 August 1950.

A237　"Books and Writers." <u>Spectator</u>, 186 (19 January 1951)
　　　　82.

A238　"Valedictory." <u>Sunday Times</u>, 28 December 1952, p. 7.
　　　　Snow's goodbye to the readers of his book review
　　　　column in the London <u>Sunday Times</u>.

A239　"Illiteracy." <u>Author</u>, 64 (Winter 1953) 64.

A240　"New Trends in First Novels." <u>Sunday Times</u>, 27 December
　　　　1953, p. 3. Reflects on the decline of the stream
　　　　of consciousness novel and praises Brigid Brophy's
　　　　<u>Hackenfeller's Ape</u> and six other books, including
　　　　John Wyllie's <u>The Goodly Seed</u>.

A241　"Reflections on Mr. Dean's Report." <u>Spectator</u>, 192
　　　　(12 March 1954) 283-84.

A242   "The Well Endowed." <u>New Statesman and Nation</u>, 48, no.
        1212 (25 December 1954) 850. An essay on Canada.
        He writes about Canadian universities, income per
        capita, Labrador and Roger Lemelin.

A243   "Storytellers for the Atomic Age." <u>New York Times Book
        Review</u>, 30 January 1955, p. 1.

A244   "Irregular Right." <u>Nation</u>, 182 (24 March 1956) 238-29.

A245   "Irregular Right," in <u>The Nation: One Hundred Years of
        the Nation</u>. Edited by Henry M. Christman. New
        York: Macmillan, 1956, pp. 305-08. Reprint of A244.

A246   "New Minds for the New World." <u>New Statesman and
        Nation</u>, 52, no. 1330 (8 September 1956) 279-82.
        On scientific and technical education in Russia,
        the United States and Great Britain. Originally
        "contributed by an expert who must necessarily
        remain anonymous" but subsequently identified
        by Snow as his own work.

A247   "The Two Cultures." <u>New Statesman and Nation</u>, 52, no.
        1334 (6 October 1956) 413-14. The first printed
        version of Snow's much debated "Two Cultures"
        thesis. For correspondance, see <u>New Statesman
        and Nation</u>, 52, no. 1335 (13 October 1956) 453;
        52, no. 1336 (20 October 1956) 486; 52, no. 1337
        (27 October 1956) 519. Reprinted: A294, A296,
        B190. Reprinted, enlarged and revised ed.: A129-
        A134; A171-A172.

A248   "London Diary." <u>New Statesman and Nation</u>, 53, no. 1354
        (23 February 1957) 226-27.

A249   "London Diary." <u>New Statesman and Nation</u>, 53, no. 1355
        (2 March 1957) 266-67.

A250   "Britain's Two Cultures; A Study of Education in a
        Scientific Age," London <u>Sunday Times</u>, 10 March
        1957, p. 12. [The second appearance of Snow's
        "Two Cultures" thesis in print. For conclusion,
        see A251.]

A251   "Britain's Two Cultures; A Revolution in Education."
        London <u>Sunday Times</u>, 17 March 1957, p. 5.

A252   "The Corridors of Power." <u>Listener</u>, 57 (18 April 1957)
        619-20.

A253   "The English Realistic Novel." <u>Moderna Sprak</u>, 51
       (1957) 265–70.

A254   "Changing Nature of Love." <u>Mademoiselle</u>, 46 (February
       1958) 105, 180–81.

A255   "Men of Fission." <u>Holiday</u>, 23 (April 1958) 95+.

A256   "Man in Society." <u>Observer</u>, 13 July 1958, p. 12.
       [Another statement of the "Two Cultures" theme.]

A257   "Challenge to the Intellect." <u>Times Library Supplement</u>,
       15 August 1958, p. iii.

A258   "New Men for a New Era." London <u>Sunday Times</u>, 24 August
       1958, p. 12.

A259   "Which Side of the Atlantic: The Writer's Choice."
       <u>New Statesman</u>, 56, no. 1434 (6 September 1958)
       287–288.

A260   "Future of Man." <u>Nation</u>, 187 (13 September 1958) 124–25.

A261   "The Two Cultures and the Scientific Revolution."
       <u>Encounter</u>, 12, no. 6 (June 1959) 17–24.
       [Part I. For the conclusion and pt. II see
       <u>Encounter</u>, 13, no. 1 (July 1959) 22–27. Extracts from
       the original lecture delivered in Cambridge, England,
       in May 1959.] Snow later supplied a summary of the
       lecture in the following terms. "I will now remove
       the qualifications and the pictures and rephrase the
       essence of the lecture as quietly as I can.--It is
       something like this. In our society (that is, advanced
       western society) we have lost even the pretence of a
       common culture. Persons educated with the greatest
       intensity we know can no longer communicate with each
       other on the plane of their major intellectual concern.
       This is serious for our creative, intellectual and,
       above all, our normal life. It is leading us to
       interpret the past wrongly, to misjudge the present,
       and to deny our hopes of the future. It is making it
       difficult or impossible for us to take good action.
       I gave the most pointed example of this lack of com-
       munication in the shape of two groups of people, repre-
       senting what I have christened 'the two cultures'. One
       of these contained the scientists, whose weight, achieve-
       ment and influence did not need stressing. The
       other contained the literary intellectuals. I did not
       mean that literary intellectuals act as the main
       decision-makers of the Western world. I meant that

literary intellectuals represent, vocalise, and to some
extent shape and predict the mood of the non-scientific
culture: they do not make the decisions, but their
words seep into the minds of those who do. . . . There
is, of course, no complete solution. In the conditions
of our age, or any age which we can foresee, Renaissance
man is not possible. But we can do something. The
chief means open to us is education--education mainly
in the primary and secondary schools, but also in
colleges and universities." Snow, C.P. The Two Cultures:
and A Second Look. Cambridge: Cambridge University
Press, 1964, pp. 60-61.

A262   "Two Cultures." Science, 130, no. 3373 (21 August
          1959) 419.
          Reprint of the prefatory note from The Search.
    It serves as editorial comment for this issue.

A263   "Conflict of Cultures." Saturday Evening Post, 232
          (12 September 1959) 28-29.

A264   "Letter to the Editor." London Magazine, N.S., 6, no. 10
          (October 1959) 57-59.
          Snow's response to Herbert Read's "Mood of the
    Month--X," London Magazine, N.S., 6, no. 8 (August 1959)
    39-43. See also: B57.

A265   "Which Side of the Atlantic?" Harper's, 219, no. 1313
          (October 1959) 163-66.
          "The balance of advantage between being an English
    or American writer seems to me surprisingly even," but
    there is one argument which decisively tips the balance
    to the English side of the Atlantic: in the more
    homogenous, more compact English society, where the
    reading audience scatters itself throughout society,
    "quite wide and quite deep," the writer knows his audience;
    but "in America the writers don't really know whom they
    are writing for--apart from their fellow writer-scholars."
    AES, 3, no. 2 (February 1960) 71. For digest and
    popularization, see B52. Reprinted: A272.

A266   "The 'Two Cultures' Controversy: Afterthoughts."
          Encounter, 14, no. 2 (February 1960) 64-68.
          The "Two Cultures" lecture was intended as a call
    to action; it is becoming the cause of argument. Here
    Snow responds to some of the critics who argued for and
    against the "Two Cultures" thesis in "The Two Cultures:
    A Discussion of C.P. Snow's Views," in Encounter, 13,
    no. 2 (August 1959) 67-73. See B58. He replies to
    J.H. Plumb by observing sharply that William Shakespeare

and William Perkins, a Puritan preacher, would have
found it possible to communicate with each other on
the plane of their major intellectual concern. Approves
Soviet curricular changes which require some craft and
student apprenticeship as well as a stint of industrial
labor. He refines and restates the charge leveled
against the reactionary literary culture. It is the
major creative artists (Yeats, Eliot, Proust, Joyce,
Lawrence, Gide) who have no truck with liberalism as
Snow and Lionel Trilling understand the term (emphasis
supplied). He quotes a well known passage from Sea and
Sardinia by D.H. Lawrence ("It is a great mistake to
abolish the death penalty. . . . And because the instinctive heart recognized a man as evil, I would have that
man destroyed. Quickly. Because good warm life is now
in danger") and observes that the instinctive heart,
unless bounded by custom and fiat, will end up as
Hitlerism. Bantocks' observation that a study of
literature leads to sensuous awareness is dismissed.
Industrialization leads to a greater individuality; and
it entails less truckling to the assertive will. "Tell
us. In what place, or in what time, did men have these
benefits which we have lost? Where and when was this
Eden?"

A267   "Billiard Room Talks." London Sunday Times, 6 March
             1960, p. 18.
             An exchange of open letters between Leonard Russell
        and Snow. Both letters advert to the publication of
        The Affair. They also descirbe the events which led
        Snow to become, in January 1949, a regular fiction
        reviewer for the London Sunday Times.

A268   "Adding Up Einstein." Newsweek, 55, no. 15 (11 April
             1960) 82.
             Digests Snow's review of Albert Einstein, Philosopher-
        Scientist, edited by Arthur Paul Schilpp. For the
        complete review, see "The Moral Grandeur of Einstein."
        New Statesman, 59, no. 1515 (26 March 1960) 453-54.

A269   "The Two Cultures and the Scientific Revolution,"
             Library Journal, 85, no. 13 (July 1960) 2523-28.
             Extracts.

A270   "An Object of Love," Meanjin, 19, no. 3 (9 September
             1960) 229-35.
             A chapter from a novel once tentatively called
        The Devoted. The novel itself was never published.

A271   "News Notes." Science, 132, no. 3443 (23 December 1960)
        1878.
        A synopsis of Snow's Godkin lecture entitled
        Science and Government. Includes excerpts from the
        address.

A272   "Which Side of the Atlantic: The Writer's Choice,"
        in Writing in America. Edited by John Fischer and
        Robert B. Silvers. New Brunswick, N.J.: Rutgers
        University Press, 1960, pp. 78-87.

A273   "The Moral Un-Neutrality of Science." Science, 133,
        no. 3448 (27 January 1961) 255-62.
        An address delivered 27 December 1960, before the
        American Association for the Advancement of Science.
        Printed in Science with an introduction by Warren Weaver
        and comments by Theodore Hesburgh and William C. Baker.
        [See also A278.]

A274   "Whether We Live or Die," Life, 50, no. 5 (3 February
        1961) 90-104.
        Excepts from Snow's Godkin lectures later published
        in book form under title Science and Government.

A275   "A Secret War of Whitehall; Two Scientists Clash in a
        a Secret War of Whitehall." Sunday Times Magazine
        Section, 12 March 1961, p. 25.

A276   "A Secret War of Whitehall; The Battle for Radar."
        Sunday Times Magazine Section, 19 March 1961, p. 27.

A277   "A Secret War of Whitehall; Mass Bombing--The Great
        Fallacy." Sunday Times Magazine Section, 26 March
        1961, p. 25.
        The essence of the argument of Science and Government
        serialized for the readers of the London Sunday Times.
        [See also: A275 and A276.]

A278   "The Moral Un-Neutrality of Science." Science Digest,
        49, no. 3 (March 1961) 19-24.

A279   "Writer's Luck." American Academy of Arts and Letters
        and the National Institute of Arts and Letters.
        Proceedings. Series 2, no. 12 (1 April 1961-
        November 1961) 190-96.
        Snow reminisces about his career and the critical
        reception of his books.

A280   "Western Values and Total War." Commentary, 32, no. 4
         (October 1961) 277-304.
         A "slightly abridged transcript" of a three-hour
symposium. Snow observes that, with some qualifications,
the Soviet Union has become the model of emulation
throughout the world. England, in any thermonuclear
war, would be eliminated as a country. After such a
war, democratic institutions would probably not survive
in the West. Speaks out against nuclear proliferation,
the total reliance on a nuclear deterrant (rather than
conventional armies) after 1945, against British
neutralism, but favors a British reliance on American
nuclear weapons. He also puts up a case for the view
that the Russians have a right to be suspicious of
American intentions.

A281   "Presidential Address." Library Association Record,
         63 (November 1961) 359-63.

A282   "Quarter Century: Its Great Delusions." Look, 25, no.
         26 (19 December 1961) 116-26.

A283   "The Great Delusions; An Open Letter to an American Friend."
         Sunday Times Magazine Section, 31 December 1961, pp.
         13, 17.
         On engineering and racial supremacy, the Soviet
space flight, spread of atomic bombs, waning of British
power, the myth of United States invulnerability in the
event of war.

A284   "Italo Svevo: Forerunner of Cooper and Amis." Essays
         and Studies, N.S., 14 (1961) [7]-16.
         Italo Svevo, whose real name was Ettore Schmitz,
might never have achieved literary fame if James Joyce,
who was Svevo's language teacher in Trieste in 1907, had
not asked him to send La Coscenza di Zeno (The Confessions
of Zeno) to Valery Larbaud, T.S. Eliot, and others. Thus
Svevo could become a literary influence on Kingsley
Amis and William Cooper. The common features of these
three writers are their truthfulness and their innocent
unworldliness, from which they create a "mysterious,
inconsequential, and often hilarious universe." AES, 7,
no. 4 (April 1964) 162.

A285   "The Literati and the Scientists," in The Fate of Man.
         Edited by Clarence Crane Brinton. New York:
         Braziller, 1961, pp. 296-303.
         An excerpt from the Two Cultures and the Scientific
Revolution (New York: Cambridge University Press, 1969).

A286   "Science, Politics, and the Novelist: Or, The Fish and
            the Net." Kenyon Review, 23, no. 1 (Winter 1961)
            1-17.
            The verbal-aesthetic criticism which has dominated
        the twentieth century is best adapted to novels whose
        range is narrow; a parallel movement among writers has
        been the production of fiction of restricted range, best
        seen in the vogue of stream-of-consciousness novels.
        But the great tradition of the novel, to which Tolstoy
        and Proust belong, defies verbal-aesthetic criticism.
        Science and politics, themes which a serious novel should
        be able to treat, are not amenable to stream-of-conscious-
        ness techniques; "we have got to find new strategies,
        and review old ones, to widen the range again." AES,
        4, no. 4 (April 1961) 157-58.

A287   "C.P. Snow on Magnanimity." Sunday Times Magazine
            Section, 22 April 1962, p. 17.
            Rectorial address at the University of St. Andrews.
        "This is a slightly abbreviated version of the full
        text." [See also: A288.]

A288   "On Magnanimity." Harper's, 225 (July 1962) 37+.
            [See also: A287.]

A289   "Myth, Reality, and Fiction." Listener, 68, no. 1744
            (30 August 1962) 311-13.
            Recorded conversations with Iris Murdoch, Graham
        Greene, Angus Wilson, Ivy Compton-Burnett, John Wain,
        Muriel Spark and C.P. Snow. Introduced by Frank Kermode.
        Broadcast in the Third Programme of the B.B.C. on
        29 March 1962. For Snow's contribution to the discussion,
        see p. 312.

A290   "The Cold War and the West." Partisan Review, 29, no.
            1 (Winter 1962) 81-83.
            A symposium.

A291   "Churchill." Look, 27 (26 February 1963) 26-33.
            Reprinted under title "We Must Never Deny Our
        Gratitude." Reader's Digest, 82 (May 1963) 66-71.

A292   "Education and Sacrifice." New Statesman, 65, no. 1679
            (17 May 1963) 746-50.

A293   "The Two Cultures: A Second Look." Times Literary
            Supplement, 25 October 1963, pp. 839-44.

A294   "The Two Cultures," in The Scientist vs. the Humanist.
            Edited by George Lewis Levine and Owen Paul Thomas.
        New York: Norton, 1963. Reprint of A247.

A295   "Higher Education in America." <u>NEA Journal</u>, 53, no. 4
          (April 1964) 11.
          A guest editorial in praise of the American system
of higher education.

A296   "The Two Cultures," in <u>The Open Form</u>. Edited by Alfred
          Kazin. New York: Harcourt, 1965, pp. 36–49.

A297   "Government, Science and Public Policy." <u>Science</u>, 151
          no. 3711 (February 11, 1966) 650–53.
          [Adaptation of an address delivered (25 January)
before the Advisory Panel on Science and Technology of
the United States House of Representatives Committee
on Science and Astronautics.] Concerned with the issue
of making choices among various competing areas of
scientific research. How, for example, can a government
choose between the claims of high-energy physics,
molecular biology, radio astronomy and observational
astronomy in deciding where to put its research funds?
Reiterates that men charged with the duty of making
these decisions should have a scientific and technological
training. Explains why the British chose to establish
a Ministry of Technology as opposed to, say, a Ministry
of Science, Technology and Education. Discusses the
internal organization of the Ministry, and states that
the cybernetic revolution will call for rigorous selection
and education of gifted young mathematicians. Ends with
the observation that the cybernetic revolution will add
to the wealth of rich nations, and states that "the world
cannot survive in peace half-rich and half-poor."

A298   "J.D. Bernal; A Personal Portrait," in <u>The Science of
          Society</u>. Edited by Maurice Goldsmith.
          Harmondsworth, Middlesex: Penguin, 1966, pp. 19–31.

A299   "Lloyd George: Britain's Great Radical." <u>Atlantic</u>, 219,
          no. 2 (February 1967) 68+.
          Also published under title "Lloyd George" in
Snow's <u>Variety of Men</u>. [See also: A168, A169.]

A300   "G.H. Hardy: the Pure Mathematician." <u>Atlantic</u>, 219
          no. 3 (March 1967) 106+.
          First written by way of introduction to G.H. Hardy's
<u>A Mathematician's Apology</u> (London: Cambridge University
Press, 1967). Also published under title "G.H. Hardy"
in Snow's <u>Variety of Men</u>. [See also: A168, A169.]

A301   "On Albert Einstein." <u>Commentary</u>, 43, no. 3 (March 1967)
          45–55.
          Also published under title "Einstein" in Snow's
<u>Variety of Men</u>. [See also: A168, A169.]

A302   "Unwitting Rival." Saturday Review, 50, no. 13
            (1 April 1967) 48-49.
        A fragment in which Snow captures H.G. Wells
    brooding over love and marriage. For Snow's complete
    biographical sketch, see "H.G. Wells" in Snow's Variety
    of Men. [See: A168, A169.]

A303   "On Stalin's Triumph, On Stalin's Madness." Esquire,
            67, no. 5 (May 1967) 114+.

A304   "Georgi Dzhagarov; or, The Problems of a Liberal
            Communist," London Magazine, 8 (September 1968)
            75-95.

A305   "Liberal Communism; the Basic Dogma, the Scope for
            Freedom, the Danger in Optimism." Nation, 207
            (9 December 1968) 617-23.

A306   "Views from Earth on the Odyssey Into Space." Look,
            33, no. 3 (4 February 1969) 77.
        Snow's reaction to the voyage of Apollo 8. Other
    contributors include Arthur C. Clarke, I.I. Rabi, and
    Leslie Dewart.

A307   "The Moon Landing." Look, 33 (26 August 1969) 68-70.

A308   "Out of the Air: Sam Would Have Said It." Listener, 82,
            no. 2112 (18 September 1969) 376.
        In fifty words praises Priestley as a "very
    original writer."

A309   "How 'Equal' Are We Really?" Daily Telegraph, 5 June
            1970, pp. 14-17.
        Discusses the reluctance to accept inborn genetic
    differences of intellectual ability, responds to Dr.
    Short, the Secretary of State for Education and Science,
    and argues that innate intellectual differences should
    not affect the major strategy of education, but that
    individuals gifted in mathematics and music should
    receive special training from an early age.

A310   "The Case of Leavis and the Serious Case." Times Literary
            Supplement, 9 July 1970, pp. 737-40.

A311   "Hope for America." Look, 34, no. 24 (1 December 1970)
            30-41.
        Written with the collaboration of Philip Snow.

25

A312   "Dickens and the Public Service," in <u>Dickens 1970;</u>
        <u>Centenary Essays</u>. Edited by Michael Slater.
        New York: Stein & Day, 1970, pp. 125-49.
        A defence of the British Civil Service of 1857.
        Dickens' rhetorical attack on the Treasury (the
        "Circumlocution Office" of <u>Little Dorrit</u>) includes
        historical errors, and the appeal of the rhetoric lies
        in the fact that it is a manic "cry against all admin-
        istrative systems anywhere."

A313   <u>The Two Cultures of C.P. Snow: A Contemporary English</u>
        <u>Intellectual Discusses Science and State of Man.</u>
        [PHONOTAPE CASSETTE] Learning Plans, 1970. One
        cassette, mono, fifty-seven minutes duration.

A314   "In the Communities of the Elite." <u>Times Literary</u>
        <u>Supplement</u>, 15 October 1971, pp. 1249-50.
        A general discussion--not an autobiographical
        fragment. Observes the rise of elites--soccer players,
        scientists--in all societies. Points to the presence
        of unsung elitist cells (mathematicians, theoretical
        physicists, etc.) within the egalitarianism of the
        liberal body politic. Calls for studies on the family
        background and social class of certain elitist groups,
        and finds members of these groups "slightly freer in
        personality than the rest of us."

A315   "Testimony of Four Peers." <u>Esquire</u>, 76, no. 6 (December
        1971) 159+.
        The ethical problem faced by a man in Daniel
        Ellsberg's position is difficult, and no satisfactory
        answers exist to the problem of the individual conscience
        as against duty to the state. Trust is an important
        matter, not to be violated lightly. One would wish
        the problem in the Ellsberg case to have been "much
        graver," with "assertion of the individual conscience"
        possibly having some effect, to justify Ellsberg's
        actions. AES, 15, no. 10 (June 1972) 653.

A316   "Trollope: The Psychological Stream," in <u>On the Novel:</u>
        <u>A Present for Walter Allen on His 60th Birthday</u>
        <u>from his Friends and Colleagues,</u> edited by B.S.
        Benedikz. London: Dent, 1971, pp. 3-16.

A317   "The Faces of Maugham: A Portrait for His Centenary."
        <u>Listener</u>, 91, no. 2341 (7 February 1974) 170.
        Includes Snow's brief appraisal of Somerset Maugham.

A318   "Priestley: One Hell of a Lot of Talent. . . A Birthday
        Portrait by Paul Bailey." Listener, 92, no. 2372
        (12 September 1974) 335.
        Includes Snow's brief appraisal of Priestley.

A319   "P.L.R." [Public Lending Right] New Review, 2 (December
        1975) 12-13.
        Quotes Snow's House of Lords speech in favor of the
Public Lending Right.

A320   "The Classical Detective Story," in From Parnassus.
        Essays in Honor of Jacques Barzun. Edited by Dora
        B. Weiner and William R. Keylor. New York: Harper
        and Row, 1976, pp. 16-22.
        The classical detective story is marked by
hypothetico-deductive reasoning. In the romantic practitioners, a private investigator wanders "in an impenetrable
haze on the fringes of society, gun under the arm pit
and on the hip." Discusses some practitioners of the
classical mode (R. Austen Freeman, H.C. Bayley, Freeman
Wills Croft, Anthony Berkeley, Dorothy L. Sayers,
Agatha Christie, P.D. James) and predicts the revival
of the classical form.

A321   "The Literary Legacy." Saturday Review, 4, no. 18
        (11 June 1977) 14-15.
        Praises the English literary legacy left behind
by Chaucer, Shakespeare and Dickens.

Interviews

A322   DOLBIER, MAURICE. "Building Bridges Between Two Cultures,"
        New York Herald Tribune Book Review, 2 March 1958,
        p. 2.
        On his start as a writer, the strong inner structure
of the "Strangers and Brothers" sequence, the gap between
the literary and scientific cultures (and the tendency to
British educational specialization), the different
approaches to book reviewing taken by British and
American reviewers, and some promising young British
writers. "I'd put a lot of money on John Wain to become,
in time, a respectable man of letters."

A323   "Interview with C.P. Snow and Pamela Hansford Johnson,"
        Publishers' Weekly, 176 (30 November 1959) 28-29.
        Includes a short summary of The Two Cultures and the
Scientific Revolution, a biographical sketch of Snow,
some sales figures of Snow's books in the United States,
short sketch of Lady Snow (Pamela Hansford Johnson) and

her recent books, and describes the literary collaboration
between the two. "If one of us is really up against a
technical problem," Lady Snow says, "we always ask the
other." "She," her husband says modestly, "is much
better at providing the solutions than I am."

A324   CAMPBELL, KENNETH. "Snow in the Wings; English Writer
          Talks about The Affair," New York Times, 16 September
          1962, Section II, p. 1, c. 7.
          Interview occasioned by the opening of The Affair
at Henry Miller's theatre in New York City.

A325   "An Interview with C.P. Snow," Review of English
          Literature, 3, no. 3 (July 1962) 91-108.
          On the autobiographical element in his novels, the
reason for the anonymous publication of New Lives for
Old, his conception of the scope and role of resonance,
his writing habits ("If you can only write in a purple
dressing-gown, in a room facing north-east, temperature
67, then the prognosis for your art isn't very hopeful"),
the extent to which fictional characters are based on
real people, the absence of psychological terms in his
fiction, the world's greatest novelists (Tolstoy, Proust,
Balzac, Dickens and Dostoevsky), his aesthetic beliefs,
and the relation between his political beliefs and
fiction.

A326   MUGGERIDGE, MALCOLM. "Conversation Piece," Encounter,
          18, no. 2 (February 1962) 90-93.
          Partial transcript of an interview transmitted by
Granada Television on 18 August 1961. Snow replies
to questions about science in government, the Lindemann-
Tizard row, America, Russia and the "Two Cultures"
thesis.

A327   KERMODE, FRANK. "The House of Fiction: Interviews
          with Seven English Novelists," Partisan Review,
          30, no. 1 (Spring 1963) 61-82.
          [For Kermode's interview with Snow, see p. 74-76.]
Snow replies to questions about the degree to which
myth, defined as the imposition of a formal pattern by
the novelist, distorts or reflects reality. He replies
that it is possible, roughly speaking, to tell the truth
in fiction. He also comments on the fictional experiments of Dorothy Richardson and Virginia Woolf.

A328   HAGERTY, SHEWARD. "Walking the Corridors of Power."
          Newsweek, 64, no. 26 (28 December 1964) 25.
          Snow responds to his appointment as number two man

in the Ministry of Technology. Includes Snow's assessments of the Labour government, Prime Minister Harold
Wilson and the role of technology in British industry.

A329 NEWQUIST, ROY. "C.P. Snow," in his Counterpoint.
New York: Simon & Schuster, 1964, pp. 554-60.
Snow interviewed by Roy Newquist. After a brief
autobiographical sketch, Snow comments on the English
Establishment, the Angry Young Men, the "Two Cultures"
lecture, Sheila Knight, the obligations of the novelist,
his own literary detestations ("I dislike art trickling
away into a kind of gifted insanity, an esoteric
nonsense. . . ."), the pornography of violence, the
extraordinary resevoir of moral concern found in Great
Britain and the United States, some Soviet writers
neglected in the West (Sholokhov, Leonid Leozov,
Konstantin Fediv, Alexander Tvardovsky), and his own
literary objectives.

A330 MARSH, PAMELA. "Dialogue with C.P. Snow," Christian
Science Monitor, 4 May 1967, p. B11.
Includes Snow's brief comments on the best novelists
writing today, the working-class novel, future themes
of the young novelists, the historical periods which
favor the growth of the novel and whether his stint in
the Ministry of Technology provided new material for
fiction. Snow was interviewed in his Strand office and
he seemed animated by secret amusement. Marsh comments:
"The seriousness of his answers came as a surprise."

A331 WHITMAN, ALDEN. "C.P. Snow Reflects on Growth of
Violence Among the Affluent," New York Times, 17
November 1968, p. 123.
On the role of reason in society, the moot question
of man's basic goodness, and the root causes of violence--
issues prompted by the publication of The Sleep of Reason.

A332 COLEMAN, TERRY. "Flummery Rampant on a Field of Snow,"
Guardian, 8 September 1970, p. 15.
After a biographical sketch, which gives details
about Snow's coat of arms, his current duties as
chairman of the Post Office think-tank, Snow's early
education in Leicester, Coleman quotes Snow's opinions
on food, metrication, the think-tank, education and
sexual jealousy.

A333 _____. "A Various Man, " Guardian Weekly, 103 (19
September 1970) 15.
Reprint of interview first published under title:
"Flummery Rampant on a Field of Snow." For annotation,
see A332.

A334   MOSKIN, J.R. "Interview with C.P. Snow," Saturday
        Review/World, 1 (6 April 1974) 20-22+.
        Comments on the relation between national power
and literary greatness, some of the younger British
writers, the loss of Empire. The British, he states,
have a talent for state ceremony, acting and collecting
Nobel prizes in science, and many of the great British
scientists came from lower middle-class backgrounds
(Faraday, Rutherford, Thompson). Talks about American
fiction (Bellow, Malamud, Mailer), journalism and
realism in fiction, the prevailing prudishness about
money, the American veneration for coaches, the anarchic
and permissive sixties, the rise of a more spartan and
neo-puritannical attitude among the young, literary
life in London and New York, the work of Dr. Irving
Cooper, the problem of poverty in India, Ruth Jhabwalla
and Watergate. [The interview includes frequent
references to a novel called The Onlookers, published
that same year under the title In Their Wisdom.]

A335   POLAND, NANCY. "A Conversation with C.P. Snow: You've
        Got to Understand How the World Ticks." Harvard
        Magazine, 77, no. 10 (June 1975) 40-47.
        Snow discusses the absence of great writers in the
twentieth century compared to the nineteenth, Russian
adulation of their writers (Tvardovsky), education for
the gifted, the problem of reconciling social justice
to intellectual excellence, his wife's engagement
to Dylan Thomas, the sacrifices which must be made by
the rich nations to benefit the poor, the rise in world
population, envy as the motivating force in human
affairs, the cruelty of the human species, the characteristics of the young, the sense of purpose in Russia,
the sense of limitless expectations which afflicts
most people until old age, the stable lives of artists
(Renoir, Henry Moore, Dostoevsky, D.H. Lawrence), the
themes of his novels and Churchill, Einstein, Lloyd
George and Frost. [Includes six photographs of Snow
and his wife, and two caricatures of Snow from his days
as the Parliamentary secretary for the Ministry of
Technology.]

A336   FRASER, JOHN. "C.P. Snow Looks Ahead," Atlas, 22, no.
        9 (September 1975) 23-24.
        Snow, now aged seventy, laments the absence of
drive in British society, confides his suspicion that
"socialist influences are inimical to a dynamic society,"
gives his impression of the sixties ("an appalling decade"),
deprecates the use of drugs, and talks briefly about the
oil crisis and the business of writing novels. Reprinted
from the Toronto Globe and Mail.

A337   TURNER, JILL. "Fifteen Years On: C.P. Snow Interviewed,"
        Library Association Record, 78, no. 1 (January 1976)
        22-23.
        On librarians and Public Lending Rights (P.L.R.),
        James Joyce, permissiveness in literature, and the
        necessity of middle-class standards in life and literature.

Scientific Articles

A338   "Infra-Red Investigations of Molecular Structure. Part I:
        Apparatus and Technique." Royal Society of London.
        Proceedings, Series A, 124 (1929) 442.

A339   "Infra-Red Investigations of Molecular Structure. Part II:
        The Molecule of Nitric Acid." Royal Society of
        London. Proceedings, Series A, 124 (1929) 453.

A340   "Infra-Red Investigations of Molecular Structure.
        Part III: The Molecule of Carbon Monoxide." Royal
        Society of London. Proceedings, Series A, 125
        (1929) 462.

A341   "Infra Red Investigations of Molecular Structure.
        Part IV: The Overtone of Nitric Acid." Royal
        Society of London. Proceedings, Series A, 126 (1930)
        355.
        Co-author: E.K. Rideal.

A342   "Infra-Red Investigations of Molecular Structure. Part V:
        The Simplest Kind of Polyatomic Molecule." Royal
        Society of London. Proceedings, Series A, 126
        (1930) 294.

A343   "The Optical Rotary Power of Quartz on Either Side of
        an Infra-Red Absorption Band." Royal Society of
        London. Proceedings, Series A, 127 (1930) 271.

A344   "Colours of Inorganic Salts." Nature, 125, no. 3149
        (8 March 1930) 349-50.
        Co-author: F.I.G. Rawlins.

A345   "Absorption Spectra of Aldehydes." Nature, 133, no.
        3372 (16 June 1934) 908-09.
        Co-author: E. Eastwood.

A346   "Physico-Chemical Studies of Complex Organic Molecules.
        Part I: Monochromatic Irradiation." Royal Society
        of London. Proceedings, Series B, 115 (1934) 261.

A347   "Sources of Error in Absorption Spectroscopy." <u>Nature</u>,
       135, no. 3405 (2 February 1935) 186.
       Co-author: E Eastwood.

A348   "Electronic Spectra of Polyatomic Molecules. 1: Saturated
       Aldehydes. 2: Acrolein." Royal Society of London.
       <u>Proceedings</u>, Series A, 149 (1935) 434.

Book Reviews

ABERCROMBIE, P.B. <u>The Rescuers</u> (Derek Verschoyle). "Most
   Musical, Most Melancholy." London <u>Sunday Times</u>, June 29,
   1952, p. 5.

ABRAHAMS, PETER. <u>The Path of Thunder</u> (Faber). "Episode in
   Siberia." London <u>Sunday Times</u>, June 1, 1952, p. 8.

_____. <u>Wild Conquest</u> (Faber). "Atmospherics." London <u>Sunday
   Times</u>, May 20, 1951, p. 3.

ACTON, HAROLD. <u>More Memoirs of an Aesthete</u>. "From a Garden in
   Florence." London <u>Financial Times</u>, April 23, 1970, p. 28.

_____. <u>Nancy Mitford: A Memoir</u>. "Pursuit of Nancy." London
   <u>Financial Times</u>, September 11, 1975, p. 29.

ADAM, RUTH. <u>A Woman's Place, 1910-1975</u>. "Those Conquering
   Heroes." London <u>Financial Times</u>, November 20, 1975, p. 28.

AITMATOV, CHINGIZ. <u>The White Steamship</u>. "Death of a Boy."
   London <u>Financial Times</u>, September 14, 1972, p. 31.

ALBARET, CELESTE. <u>Monsieur Proust</u>. "Croissants for the
   Master." London <u>Financial Times</u>, May 27, 1976, p. 12.

ALDANOV, MARK. <u>The Escape</u> (Cape). "Mauriac for Beginners."
   London <u>Sunday Times</u>, April 6, 1952, p. 3.

ALDRIDGE, JAMES. <u>The Diplomat</u> (Bodley Head). "Interest
   Without Art." London <u>Sunday Times</u>, December 4, 1949, p. 3.

ALI, TARIQ. <u>The Coming British Revolution</u>. "Modern
   Revolutionaries." London <u>Financial Times</u>, February 3,
   1972, p. 22.

ALLEN, GRACE. <u>This to Be Love</u> (Cape). "Personal Flavours."
   London <u>Sunday Times</u>, June 12, 1949, p. 3.

ATLICK, RICHARD D. <u>Victorian People and Ideas</u>, "Victorian
   Values." London <u>Financial Times</u>, April 18, 1974, p. 18.

_____. Victorian Studies in Scarlet. "Crop of Crimes."
London Financial Times, April 12, 1973, p. 37.

ALVAREZ, A. The Savage God: A Study of Suicide. "To End It. .
. . " London Financial Times, November 18, 1971, p. 16.

AMBLER, ERIC. Judgment on Deltchev (Hodder & Stoughton). "No
Loving-Kindness." London Sunday Times, July 29, 1951, p. 3.

_____. Send No More Roses. "Ambling On." London Financial
Times, July 28, 1977, p. 12.

AMBROSE, STEPHEN E. The Supreme Commander: The War Years of
General Dwight D. Eisenhower. "Light on Ike." London
Financial Times, September 9, 1971, p. 24.

AMIS, KINGSLEY. Lucky Jim. "Novels of 1954: Counter-Revolution."
London Sunday Times, December 26, 1954, p. 5.

_____. Riverside Villas Murder. "Crop of Crimes." London
Financial Times, April 12, 1973, p. 37.

ANSTRUTHER, IAN. I Presume (Blas). "Explorer's World." London
Financial Times, May 17, 1973, p. 31, c. 1.

ARLOTT, JOHN. The Oxford Companion to Sports and Games.
"Playing to Win." London Financial Times, June 27, 1975,
p. 18.

ARMYTAGE, W.H.G. Sir Richard Gregory. "The Trusted Rebel."
New Statesman, 53 (February 9, 1957) 176.

ARONSON, THEO. Victoria and Disraeli. "Victoria's Loves."
London Financial Times, May 26, 1977, p. 10.

ASCH, SHOLEM. The Apostle (Macdonald). "A Playwright's
Novel." London Sunday Times, December 17, 1950, p. 3.

_____. Mary (Macdonald). "A Playwright's Novel." London
Sunday Times, December 17, 1950, p. 30.

ASHTON, HELEN. Letty Landon (Collins). "Pestilent Plants."
London Sunday Times, August 26, 1951, p. 3.

_____. Parson Austen's Daughter (Collins). "Two Entertainments."
London Sunday Times, May 29, 1949, p. 3.

ASHTON-JINKS, CICELY. The Rise of Francoise Scarron (Hammond,
Hammond). "A Playwright's Novel." London Sunday Times,
December 17, 1950, p. 3.

ASKWITH, BETTY. A Broken Engagement (Gollancz). "Quality from America." London Sunday Times, July 9, 1950, p. 3.

ATHERTON, H.M. Political Prints in the Age of Hogarth. "Savage Lines." London Financial Times, August 22, 1974, p. 22.

ATIYAH, EDWARD. The Thin Line (Peter Davies). "Mauriac Country." London Sunday Times, November 18, 1951, p. 3.

AUSTEN, JANE. Sanditon. "Satirical Spinster." London Financial Times, July 31, 1975, p. 20.

AYER, A.J. Part of My Life. "Young Don." London Financial Times, July 1, 1977, p. 14.

AYLING, STANLEY. The Elder Pitt. "Power of Pitt." London Financial Times, March 4, 1976, p. 24.

AYME, MARCEL. The Fable and the Flesh (Bodley Head). "Two Entertainments." London Sunday Times, May 29, 1949, p. 3.

_____. The Miraculous Barber (Bodley Head). "English, French, Jamaican." London Sunday Times, March 5, 1950, p. 3.

BACCHELLI, RICCARDO. The Mill on the Po (Hutchinson). "The Man Behind the Story." London Sunday Times, February 24, 1952, p. 3.

BAILEY, TREVOR. Sir Gary. "Master Players." London Financial Times, May 21, 1976, p. 37.

BAINBRIDGE, BERYL. Injury Time. "Intimate Relations." London Financial Times, October 6, 1977, p. 30.

_____. A Quiet Life. "Intimate Relations." London Financial Times, October 6, 1977, p. 30.

BAKER, DOROTHY. The Street (Wingate). "Atmospherics." London Sunday Times, May 20, 1951, p. 3.

BALCHIN, NIGEL. A Sort of Traitors (Collins). "A Varied Trio." London Sunday Times, June 19, 1949, p. 3.

_____. A Way Through the Wood (Collins). "A Matter of Pace." London Sunday Times, June 3, 1951, p. 3.

BALSDON, J.P.V.D. Oxford Now and Then. "That Sweet City." London Financial Times, December 10, 1970, p. 8.

BARCLAY, GLEN ST. J. Twentieth Century Nationalism. "Generous Social Critic." London Financial Times, December 9, 1971, p. 12.

BAREA, ARTURO. The Broken Root (Faber). "A New Talent." London Sunday Times, May 6, 1951, p. 3.

BARING, MAURICE. Maurice Baring Restored. Edited by Paul Horgan. "The Insider." London Financial Times, October 1, 1970, p. 24.

BARKER, A.L. Novelette, and Other Stories (Hogarth). "Susannah's Husband." London Sunday Times, November 4, 1951, p. 3.

BARKER, GEORGE. The Dead Seagull (Lehmann). "Character Drawing." London Sunday Times, September 17, 1950, p. 3.

BARON, ALEXANDER. Rosie Hogarth (Cape). "A Memorable Story." London Sunday Times, September 9, 1951, p. 3.

_____. There's No Home (Cape). "A Novelist to Watch." London Sunday Times, February 19, 1950, p. 3.

_____. With Hope Farewell (Cape). "Millionaire Among the Miners." London Sunday Times, May 4, 1952, p. 6.

BARRINGTON, PAMELA. The Triangle Has Four Sides (Evans). "Eye on the Ball." London Sunday Times, December 25, 1949, p. 3.

BARTLEY, WILLIAM W. Wittgenstein. "Bounds of Possibility." London Financial Times, April 11, 1974, p. 32.

BARTON, DEREK. An Englishman's Breakfast. "Second Sex." London Financial Times, September 23, 1976, p. 13.

BARZUN, JACQUES. The House of Intellect. "Coriolanus of the Intellectuals." Encounter, 13, no. 5 (November 1959) 66-68.

BATES, H.E. Colonel Julian, and Other Stories (Michael Joseph). "The Seeing Eye." London Sunday Times, July 1, 1951, p. 3.

_____. The Jacaranda Tree (Michael Joseph). "The Visual Gift." London Sunday Times, January 16, 1949, p. 3.

_____. Love for Lydia (Michael Joseph). "The Love Story of Lydia." London Sunday Times, October 5, 1952, p. 5.

BATES, RALPH. The Dolphin in the Wood (Hart-Davis). "Wild
Men." London Sunday Times, November 5, 1950, p. 3.

BAXTER, WALTER. Look Down in Mercy (Heinemann). "Collapse
in Burma." London Sunday Times, December 2, 1951, p. 3.

BAZIN, HERVE. Head Against the Wall (Secker & Warburg).
"First Novel Success." London Sunday Times, January 27, 1952,
p. 3.

BEAUCLERK, HELEN. There Were Three Men (Gollancz). "The Visual
Gift." London Sunday Times, January 16, 1949, p. 3.

BEDFORD, SYBILLE. Aldous Huxley. V. 1: 1894-1939 (Collins).
"Attitudes of Aldous." London Financial Times, November 1,
1973, p. 34, c. 1.

_____. Aldous Huxley. V. 2: 1939-1963. "Aldous Concluded."
London Financial Times, September 19, 1974, p. 29.

BEERBOHM, MAX. The Bodley Head Max Berbohm. "Almost Too
Exquisite." London Financial Times, September 10, 1970,
p. 10.

BEHAINE, RENE. Day of Glory (Allen & Unwin). "A Novelist
to Watch." London Sunday Times, February 19, 1950, p. 3.

BELL, NEIL. I Am Legion (Eyre & Spottiswoode). "A Remarkable
Novel." London Sunday Times, July 23, 1950, p. 3.

BELLOW, SAUL. Mr. Sammler's Planet. "A Man for Our Time."
London Financial Times, July 9, 1970, p. 26.

BENNETT, ARNOLD. Arnold Bennett: The 'Evening Standard' Years.
Edited by Andrew Mylett. "Foreman on the Job." London
Financial Times, July 11, 1974, p. 26.

_____. Arnold Bennett in Love: Arnold Bennett and his Wife
Marguerite Soulie; A Correspondance. Edited by George and
Jean Beardmore. "Bennett's Hidden Self." London Financial
Times, December 21, 1972, p. 29.

_____. Letters of Arnold Bennett. V. 3: 1916-1931. Edited by
James Hepburn. "The Old Creature." London Financial Times,
June 18, 1970, p. 14.

BENTLEY, PHYLLIS. Quorum (Gollancz). "Bees in the Bonnet."
London Sunday Times, July 16, 1950, p. 3.

BERGENGRUEN, WERNER. A Matter of Conscience (Thames & Hudson). "The Pilgrimage of Grace." London Sunday Times, March 23, 1952, p. 3.

BERLIN, ISAIAH. Russian Thinkers. "Constructing Our World." London Financial Times, January 12, 1978, p. 28.

BERMANT, CHAIN. The Cousin-Hood. "Relations and Friends." London Financial Times, December 2, 1971, p. 28.

BERNAL, J.D. The Extension of Man. "Elder Scientists." London Financial Times, March 16, 1972, p. 24.

_____. The Social Function of Science. "Blueprint of the Future of Science." Discovery, N.S., 2 (March, 1939) 107-11.

_____. Science and Industry in the Nineteenth Century. "Using Science." New Statesman & Nation, 48, no. 1202 (March 20, 1954) 374.

_____. World Without War. "Act in Hope." New Statesman, 56 (15, November 1958) 698-700.

BERNARD, J.F. Talleyrand. "Wily Statesman." London Financial Times, August 3, 1973, p. 12.

BERNARD, MARC. As Little Children (Dobson). "Personal Flavours." London Sunday Times, June 12, 1949, p. 3.

BIDDIES, MICHAEL D. Gobineau: Selected Political Writings. "How It All Began." London Financial Times, March 5, 1970, p. 10.

BINGHAM, JOHN. The Hunting Down of Peter Manuel (Macmillan). "Crimes of a Killer." London Financial Times, September 20, 1973, p. 33, c. 1.

BINGHAM, MADELINE. Henry Irving and the Victorian Theatre. "Performers." London Financial Times, April 20, 1978, p. 36.

_____. The Making of Kew. "All in Miniature." London Financial Times, April 17, 1975, p. 16.

_____. Masks and Facades: Sir John Vanbrugh, the Man in His Setting. "Great Van a Wit." London Financial Times, September 12, 1974, p. 23.

_____. Sheridan. "Triumph and Fall." London Financial Times, March 9, 1972, p. 32.

BIRKENHEAD, FREDERICK WINSTON FURNEAUX SMITH. The Prof in Two
Worlds: The Official Life of Professor F.A. Lindemann,
Viscount Cherwell. "Politicians and Scientists." Encounter,
18, no. 1 (January 1962) 103-6.

BLACK, MICHAEL. The Literature of Fidelity. "What You Will."
London Financial Times, June 19, 1975, p. 28.

BLAKE, GEORGE. The Piper's Tune (Collins). "Fashion." London
Sunday Times, September 3, 1950, p. 3.

BLAKE, ROBERT. The Office of Prime Minister. "No. 10 People."
London Financial Times, December 18, 1975, p. 16.

BLAKE, WILLIAM. The Copperheads (Cassell). "The Pursuit of
Money." London Sunday Times, January 23, 1949, p. 3.

BLOCH, MARC. The Royal Touch. Translated by J.E. Anderson
(Rutledge). "Sages and Plagues." London Financial Times,
March 22, 1973, p. 34, c. 1.

BOLL, HEINRICH. Group Portrait with Lady (Secker & Warburg).
"Pert Maidens." London Financial Times, May 3, 1973, p. 16,
c. 1.

BOLTON, ISABEL. The Christmas Tree (Chapman & Hall). "Dramatic
Values." London Sunday Times, January 1, 1950, p. 3.

BONINGTON, CHRISTIAN. Annapurna South Face. "The Airy
Mountain." London Financial Times, March 25, 1971, p. 14.

BORN, EDITH de. The Bidou Inheritance (Chapman & Hall).
"Mauriac Country." London Sunday Times, November 18, 1951,
p. 3.

BORN, MAX. The Born-Einstein Letters. With commentaries by
Max Born. "Meeting of Minds." London Financial Times,
June 24, 1971, p. 14.

BOSTON, RICHARD. An Anatomy of Laughter. "Causes of Mirth."
London Financial Times, June 6, 1974, p. 30.

BOTTOME, PHYLLIS. Under the Skin (Faber). "Conflicts."
London Sunday Times, June 25, 1950, p. 3.

BOYD, MARTIN. Such Pleasure (Cresset Press). "Real People."
London Sunday Times, September 11, 1949, p. 3.

BOYER, FRANCOIS. The Secret Game (Bodley Head). "A Brave
Talent." London Sunday Times, March 19, 1950, p. 3.

BOYLE, ANDREW. <u>Only the Winde Will Listen: Reith of the BBC</u>. "Soldier at Savoy Hill." London <u>Financial Times</u>, November 16, 1972, p. 14.

_____. <u>Poor, Dear Brendan</u>. "B.B." London <u>Financial Times</u>, October 31, 1974, p. 34.

BOYLE, KAY. <u>The Smoking Mountain</u> (Faber). "Summer in Paris." London <u>Sunday Times</u>, May 18, 1952, p. 9.

BRADBURY, RAY. <u>The Silver Locusts</u> (Hart-Davis). "From Far and Near." <u>London Sunday Times</u>, September 23, 1951, p. 3.

BRADFORD, ERNEST. <u>Nelson: The Essential Hero</u>. "Admiral's Attitude." London <u>Financial Times</u>, July 7, 1977, p. 37.

BRANDEL, MARC. <u>The Choice</u> (Eyre & Spottiswoode). "Mauriac for Beginners." London <u>Sunday Times</u>, April 6, 1952, p. 3.

BRANNER, H.C. <u>The Riding Master</u> (Secker & Warburg). "Susannah's Husband." London <u>Sunday Times</u>, November 4, 1951, p. 3.

BRAY, JEREMY. <u>Decision in Government</u>. "Less Fun than Machiavelli." <u>New Statesman</u>, 79, (January 9, 1970) 50.

BRENDON, PIERS. <u>Hawker of Morwenstow</u>. "Parson Who Loved Cream." London <u>Financial Times</u>, July 1975, p. 14.

BRIDGE, ANN. <u>The Dark Moment</u> (Chatto & Windus). "A Visit to Turkey." London <u>Sunday Times</u>, January 13, 1952, p. 3.

BRIDGES, YSEULT. <u>Poison and Adelaide Bartlett. Two Studies in Crime. How Charles Bravo Died. Saint with Red Hands</u>. "Seasonal Sleuths." London <u>Financial Times</u>, November 26, 1970, p. 14.

BRIGGS, ASA. <u>Essays in the History of Publishing in Celebration of the 250th Anniversary of the House of Longman, 1724-1974</u>. "Long Arm." London <u>Financial Times</u>, August 15, 1974, p. 22.

BRITTAIN, VERA. <u>Born 1925</u> (Macmillan). "The Visual Gift." London <u>Sunday Times</u>, January 16, 1949, p. 3.

BRODIE, FAWN M. <u>Thomas Jefferson: An Intimate History</u>. "Mr. President's Mistress." London <u>Financial Times</u>, March 27, 1975, p. 40.

BRODRIBB, GERALD. <u>The Croucher</u>. "Old-Time Cricket." London <u>Financial Times</u>, January 2, 1975, p. 8.

———. Maurice Tate. "Master Players." London Financial
Times, May 21, 1976, p. 37.

BROMFIELD, LOUIS. Mr. Smith (Cassell). "Crusaders--and
Mr. Smith." London Sunday Times, September 7, 1952, p. 5.

BRONOWSKI, J. Science and Human Values. "Habit of Truth."
New Republic, 139, no. 17-18 (August 18, 1958) 26.

———. Science and Human Values. "Both Cultures." New
Statesman, 61 (April 21, 1961) 630.

BROOK-SHEPHERD, GORDON. Uncle of Europe. "Tum-Tum." London
Financial Times, May 1, 1975, p. 32.

BROOKE, JOCELYN. The Image of a Drawn Sword (Bodley Head).
"Puritan Ireland." London Sunday Times, April 16, 1950,
p. 3.

BROOKS, RICHARD. The Producer (Heinemann). "Inside Hollywood."
London Sunday Times, December 14, 1952, p. 5.

BROPHY, JOHN. Turn the Key Softly (Collins). "Collapse in
Burma." London Sunday Times, December 2, 1951, p. 3.

BROWN, GEORGE. In My Way. "Brown Study." London Financial
Times, April 1, 1971, p. 24.

BUCHANAN, GEORGE. Rose Forbes (Faber). "Productivity."
London Sunday Times, February 5, 1950, p. 3.

BUCKMASTER, CELIA. Village Story (Hogarth). "Florentine
Summer." London Sunday Times, June 17, 1951, p. 3.

BUECHNER, FREDERICK. A Long Day's Dying (Chatto & Windus).
"Mauriac's Way." London Sunday Times, February 11, 1951,
p. 3.

BULGAKOV, MIKHAIL. The White Guard. "The White and the Red."
London Financial Times, February 12, 1971, p. 27.

BULLETT, GERALD. The Trouble at Number Seven (Michael Joseph).
"Unusual Quintet." London Sunday Times, March 9, 1952,
p. 3.

BULLITT, ORVILLE H., ed. For the President (Deutsch).
"Bullitt on Target." London Financial Times, June 1, 1973,
p. 16, c. 1.

BURN, MICHAEL. The Midnight Diary (Hart-Davis). "The Love Story of Lydia." London Sunday Times, October 5, 1952, p. 5.

BURNEY, FANNY. Fanny Burney, Journals and Letters. "Innocent but Determined." London Financial Times, May 4, 1972, p. 24.

BURNS, JOHN HORNE. Lucifer with a Book (Secker & Warburg). "Lively Quartet." London Sunday Times, October 30, 1949, p. 3.

BUSH, DOUGLAS. Jane Austen. "Satirical Spinster." London Financial Times, July 31, 1975, p. 20.

BUTRON, MICHEL. Hans (Derek Verschoyle). "A Rising Reputation." London Sunday Times, September 21, 1952, p. 5.

BUTT, JOHN AND TILLOTSON, KATHLEEN. Dickens at Work. "Dickens at Work." New Statesman, 54, no. 1376 (July 27, 1957) 119-20.

C.K. OGDEN: A COLLECTIVE MEMOIR. Edited by P. Sargant Florence. "Odd Fish." London Financial Times, February 16, 1978, p. 28.

CADOGAN, SIR ALEXANDER. The Diaries of Sir Alexander Cadogan, 1938-45. "Careering Along." London Financial Times, November 11, 1971, p. 24.

CAMBERTON, ROLAND. Rain on the Pavements (Lehmann). "Susannah's Husband." London Sunday Times, November 4, 1951, p. 3.

CANNING, VICTOR. Venetian Bird (Hodder & Stoughton). "Games of Hide and Seek." London Sunday Times, August 12, 1951, p. 3.

CAPON, PAUL. The Other Side of the Moon (Heinemann). "A Gifted Writer." London Sunday Times, November 19, 1950, p. 3.

CARGOE, RICHARD. The Tormentors (Gollancz). "Robust Realism." London Sunday Times, July 17, 1949, p. 3.

CARPENTIER, ALEJO. Reasons of State. "Cuban Master." London Financial Times, March 12, 1976, p. 12.

CARVER, SIR MICHAEL. The War Lords. "From Agincourt Onwards." London Financial Times, July 1, 1976, p. 12.

CARY, JOYCE. A Fearful Joy (Michael Joseph). "Lively Quartet."
London Sunday Times, October 30, 1949, p. 3.

CASSER, GEORGE H. Kitchener. "Under Fire." London Financial
Times, February 9, 1978, p. 28.

CAUSLEY, CHARLES. Hands to Dance (Carroll & Nicholson).
"Witch-Hunting Today." London Sunday Times, December 16,
1951, p. 3.

CAUTE, DAVID. The Fellow Travellers (Weidenfeld & Nicholson).
"Seeing Red." London Financial Times, February 15, 1973,
p. 34, c. 1.

CECIL, DAVID. The Cecils of Hatfield House (Constable).
"Parliament Men and Press." London Financial Times, October
4, 1973, p. 31, c. 1.

CECIL, HENRY. The Painswick Line (Chapman & Hall). "A Home
Disrupted." London Sunday Times, July 15, 1951, p. 3.

CENDRARS, BLAISE. Antarctic Fugue (Pushkin Press). "The
Pursuit of Money." London Sunday Times, January 23, 1949,
p. 3.

CHANDLER, RAYMOND. The Simple Art of Murder (Hamish Hamilton).
"In the Jungle." London Sunday Times, December 3, 1950,
p. 3.

CHANDOS, JOHN. In God's Name: Examples of Preaching in
England, 1534-1662. Edited by John Chandos. "Captive
Audiences." London Financial Times, December 30, 1971, p. 8.

CHAPLIN, SID. My Fate Cries Out (Phoenix House). "A Minor
Classic?" London Sunday Times, January 8, 1950, p. 3.

CHAPMAN, GUY. The Dreyfus Trials. "All the Military
Conspirators." London Financial Times, August 31, 1972,
p. 7.

CHAPMAN, HESTER W. Anne Bolyn. "Love in a Cruel Climate."
London Financial Times, March 8, 1974, p. 29.

_____. Ever Thine (Cape). London Sunday Times, April 8, 1951,
p. 3.

CHARLES, GERDA. The Destiny Waltz. "Books as Presents."
London Financial Times, December 2, 1971, p. 28.

_____. The Destiny Waltz. "Facing the Music." London
Financial Times, April 15, 1971, p. 26.

_____. A Slanting Light. "Books as Presents." London Financial Times, December 2, 1971, p. 28.

CHARQUES, DOROTHY. Men Like Shadows (Murray). "Crusaders-- and Mr. Smith." London Sunday Times, September 7, 1952, p. 5.

CHATTERTON, RUTH. Homeward Borne (Harrap). "Masks and Faces." London Sunday Times, April 22, 1951, p. 3.

CHEKHOV, A.P. Chekhov: Stories 1889-91. Translated and edited by Ronald Hingley. "Our Very Own Chekhov." London Financial Times, April 2, 1970, p. 28.

CHESTERTON, G.K. G.K. Chesterton: A Selection from His Non-Fictional Prose. Selected by W.H. Auden. "A G.K.C. Revival?" London Financial Times, February 26, 1970, p. 12.

CHEVALLIER, GABRIEL. Mascarade (Secker & Warburg). "Entertaining But--." London Sunday Times, April 30, 1950, p. 3.

CHILCOTT, TIM. A Publisher and His Circle. "Paying the Piper." London Financial Times, March 23, 1972, p. 32.

CHILDERS, ERSKINE. The Riddle of the Sands. "Behind the Best-Sellers." London Financial Times, July 6, 1972, p. 33.

CHITTY, SUSAN. The Beast and the Monk: A Life of Charles Kingsley. "Lion Rampant." London Financial Times, January 23, 1975, p. 30.

CHRISTIE, AGATHA. Curtain: Poirot's Last Case. "Deaths and Entrances." London Financial Times, October 17, 1975, p. 12.

CHURCH, RICHARD. The Nightingale (Hutchinson). "Most Musical, Most Melancholy." London Sunday Times, June 29, 1952, p. 5.

CLARK, ELEANOR. Eyes, Etc. "Time of Insight." London Financial Times, January 19, 1978, p. 16.

CLARK, KENNETH. Another Part of the Wood. "Dawn of Civilization." London Financial Times, October 17, 1974, p. 23.

_____. The Nude (Murray). "Books of the Year-II; Chosen by Eminent Contemporaries." London Sunday Times, December 30, 1956, p. 10.

CLARK, RONALD W. Einstein: The Life and Times. "Two Aspects of Science's Giant." Life, 71, no. 8. (August 20, 1971) 14.

_____. The Life of Bertrand Russell. "Mind and Body." London Financial Times, October 30, 1975, p. 29.

CLARKSON, TOM. The Pavement and the Sky (Wingate). "The Seeing Eye." London Sunday Times, July 1, 1951, p. 3.

CLEWES, HOWARD. An Epitaph for Love (Macmillan). "Hot War and Cold War." London Sunday Times, November 16, 1952, p. 5.

_____. Green Grow the Rushes (Bodley Head). "Simenon's Best Yet." London Sunday Times, June 26, 1949, p. 3.

CLEWES, WINSTON. Troy and the Maypole (Michael Joseph). "Interest Without Art." London Sunday Times, December 4, 1949, p. 3.

COCKBURN, CLAUD. Bestseller: The Books That Everyone Read. "Behind the Best-Sellers." London Financial Times, July 6, 1972, p. 33.

COCKSHUT, A.O.J. Truth to Life: The Art of Biography in the Nineteenth Century. "Portraits of People." London Financial Times, March 1, 1974, p. 28.

COHEN, J.M. The Life of Ludwig Mond (Methuen). "Industrial Dynamo." New Statesman and Nation, 51, no. 1318 (June 16, 1956) 702-03.

COLE, SONIA. Leakey's Luck: The Life of Louis Seymour Bazett Leakey, 1903-1972. "In Search of Man." London Financial Times, June 12, 1975, p. 35.

COLLOMS, BRENDA. Charles Kingsley: The Lion of Eversley. "Lion Rampant." London Financial Times, January 23, 1975, p. 30.

_____. Victorian Country Parsons. "Clerical Cuttings in Golden Era." London Financial Times, September 29, 1977, p. 31.

COLVILLE, J.R. Footprints in Time. "Cheerful Soul." London Financial Times, November 18, 1976, p. 41.

_____. Man of Valour: Field Marshall Lord Gort, V.C. "Leader of the BEF." London Financial Times, January 6, 1972, p. 20.

COMFORT, ALEX. <u>On This Side Nothing</u> (Routledge & K. Paul). "An Outstanding Novel." London <u>Sunday Times</u>, January 30, 1949, p. 3.

COMMAGER, HENRY STEELE. <u>Britain Through American Eyes</u>. "Ourselves Observed." London <u>Financial Times</u>, August 30, 1974, p. 22.

COMPTON-BURNETT, IVY. <u>Two Worlds and Their Ways</u> (Gollancz). "Simenon's Best Yet." London <u>Sunday Times</u>, June 26, 1949, p. 3.

CONSTABLE, JOHN WILSON. <u>C.A.: The Life of Sir Henry Campbell-Bannerman</u> (Constable). "Good-Living P.M." London <u>Financial Times</u>, February 1, 1973, p. 14, c. 1.

COOK, DAVID. <u>Walter</u>. "Real People." London <u>Financial Times</u>, March 23, 1978, p. 33.

COOK, WILFRED. <u>The Amateurs</u> (Cresset Press). "To Dream Again." London <u>Sunday Times</u>, April 20, 1952, p. 3.

COOPER, I.S. <u>The Victim Is Always the Same</u>. "Surgery That Cuts Two Ways." <u>New York Times Book Review</u>, August 12, 1973, pp. 3-4.

COOPER, WILLIAM. <u>Scenes from Provincial Life</u> (Cape). "English, French, Jamaican." London <u>Sunday Times</u>, March 5, 1950, p. 3.

_____. <u>Young People</u>. London <u>Sunday Times</u>, February 9, 1958, p. 3. Reviewed by "Atticus." [Note: "Atticus" is <u>not</u> C.P. Snow.]

CORMAN, AVORY. <u>Kramer's Kramer</u>. "Real People." London <u>Financial Times</u>, March 23, 1978, p. 33.

COTTLE, BASIL. <u>The Plight of English</u>. "English as She Is Spoke." London <u>Financial Times</u>, December 4, 1975, p. 29.

COTTRELL, ALAN. <u>Portrait of Nature</u>. "In Love with Nature." London <u>Financial Times</u>, May 22, 1975, p. 34.

COURAGE, JAMES. <u>Desire Without Content</u> (Constable). "In the Jungle." London <u>Sunday Times</u>, December 3, 1950, p. 3.

COWIE, A.P. <u>Oxford Dictionary of Current Idiomatic English</u>. "English as She Is Spoke." London <u>Financial Times</u>, December 4, 1975, p. 29.

COWLING, MAURICE. The Impact of Hitler. "So Are They All, All Honourable Men." London Financial Times, August 22, 1975, p. 8.

COXHEAD, ELIZABETH. A Play Toward (Faber). "To Dream Again." London Sunday Times, April 20, 1952, p. 3.

COZZENS, JAMES GOULD. By Love Possessed. "Mr. Cozzens Hits the Jackpot." London Sunday Times, December 8, 1957, p. 8.

_____. Guard of Honour (Lehmann). "Artists in Contrast." London Sunday Times, November 20, 1949, p. 3.

CRAIG, DENYS. Man in Ebony (Gollancz) "A Brave Talent." London Sunday Times, March 19, 1950, p. 3.

CRANKSHAW, EDWARD. Tolstoy. "The Real Tolstoy." London Financial Times, June 13, 1974, p. 26.

CROFT-COOKE, RUPERT. Brass Farthing (Werner Lowrie). "Entertaining, But--." London Sunday Times, April 30, 1950, p. 3.

_____. Three Names for Nicholas (Macmillan). "A Matter of Pace." London Sunday Times, June 3, 1951, p. 3.

_____. The White Mountain (Falcon Press). "Sentimental Stories." London Sunday Times, December 18, 1949, p. 3.

CRONE, ANNE. Bridie Steen (Heinemann). "An Outstanding Novel." London Sunday Times, January 30, 1949, p. 3.

CROSS, COLIN. Who Was Jesus. "Quest for the Truth." London Financial Times, August 21, 1970, p. 8.

CULLEN, TOM. Maundy Gregory: Purveyor of Honours. "How Maundy Made Money." London Financial Times, May 10, 1974, p. 34.

CURTIS, ANTHONY. The Pattern of Maugham. "Supreme Story-Teller." London Financial Times, January 24, 1974, p. 25.

CUSACK, DYMPHNA. Say No to Death (Heinemann). "Susannah's Husband." London Sunday Times, November 4, 1951, p. 3.

DANIELL, DAVID. The Interpreter's House: A Critical Assessment of the Work of John Buchanan. "Scottish Power House." London Financial Times, August 28, 1975, p. 17.

DAVIE, GEORGE ELDER. The Democratic Intellect. "Miasma, Darkness and Torpidity." New Statesman, 62 (August 11, 1961) 186-87.

DAVIES, JOHN PETER. Dragon by the Tail. "Old China Hand." London Financial Times, April 25, 1974, p. 19.

DAVIES, RHYS. Boy With a Trumpet (Heinemann). "Captivating Satire." London Sunday Times, November 27, 1949, p. 3.

DAVIS, MELTON S. Who Defends Rome? "Stylish Soldier." London Financial Times, April 5, 1973, p. 32.

DEAN, GORDON. Report on the Atom (Eyre & Spottiswoode). "Revolution for Our Time." London Sunday Times, January 31, 1954, p. 5.

DE HARTOG, JAN. Stella (Hamish Hamilton). "Local Knowledge." London Sunday Times, December 30, 1951, p. 3.

DELVES-BROUGHTON, JOSEPHINE. I Saw No Sun (Faber). "Unusual Quintet." London Sunday Times, March 9, 1952, p. 3.

DENNY, NORMAN. Story in a Half-Light. "Novels of 1954: Counter-Revolution." London Sunday Times, December 26, 1954, p. 5.

DERBY, MARK. Element of Risk (Collins). "Crusaders—and Mr. Smith." London Sunday Times, September 7, 1952, p. 5.

_____. Malayan Rose (Collins). "Games of Hide and Seek." London Sunday Times, August 12, 1951, p. 3.

DESANI, G.V. All About H. Hatterr (Saturn Press). "A Novelist to Watch." London Sunday Times, February 19, 1950, p. 3.

DE SHERBININ, BETTY. The Monkey Puzzle (Putnam). "Millionaire Among the Miners." London Sunday Times, May 4, 1952, p. 6.

DESMOND, ADRIAN J. The Hot-Blooded Dinosaurs: A Revolution in Palaeontology. "Primevil Powers." London Financial Times, December 11, 1975, p. 10.

DEVLIN, PATRICK. Too Proud to Fight. "Political Ego." London Financial Times, October 24, 1974, p. 39.

DE VOTO, BERNARD. Mountain Time (Hammond, Hammond). "Personal Flavours." London Sunday Times, June 12, 1949, p. 3.

DE VRIES, PETER. Madder Music. "Real People." London
Financial Times, March 23, 1978, p. 33.

DE WOHL, LOUIS. Attila (Gollancz). "The Visual Gift."
London Sunday Times, January 16, 1949, p. 3.

_____. The Quiet Light (Gollancz). "English, French,
Jamaican." London Sunday Times, March 5, 1950, p. 3.

DICEY, EDWARD. Spectator of America. "Englishman Among
Yankees." London Financial Times, August 17, 1972, p. 12.

DICKENS, CHARLES. Letters of Charles Dickens. V. 4. Edited
by K. Tillotson. "Performers." London Financial Times,
April 20, 1978, p. 36.

_____. Pictures from Italy. "The English on Tour." London
Financial Times, January 17, 1974, p. 32.

DICKSON, LOVAT. H.G. Wells. "Hint of Joy Amid the Misery."
Life, 67, no. 5 (August 1, 1969) 8.

DILLARD, ANNIE. Pilgrim at Tinker Creek. "In Love with
Nature." London Financial Times, May 22, 1975, p. 34.

DI VINE, DAVID. The King of Fassarai (Murray). "Human
Kindness." London Sunday Times, December 31, 1950, p. 3.

DJILAS, MILOVAN. The Unperfect Society. "The Djilas Enigma."
London Financial Times, January 15, 1970, p. 8.

DONOGHUE, BERNARD. Herbert Morrisson: Portrait of a Politician
(Weidenfeld & Nicolson). "London Pride." London
Financial Times, September 27, 1973, p. 14. c. 4.

DOS PASSOS, JOHN. The Grand Design (Lehmann). "Simenon's
Best Yet." London Sunday Times, June 26, 1949, p. 3.

DOUGLAS-HOME, SIR ALEC. The Way the Wind Blows. "Straight
Bat." London Financial Times, October 7, 1976, p. 25.

DOVIE, G.E. The Democratic Intellect (Edinburgh University
Press). "Miasma, Darkness and Torpidity." New Statesman,
62 (August 11, 1961) 186-87.

DRABBLE, MARGARET. Arnold Bennett. "Foreman on the Job."
London Financial Times, July 11, 1974, p. 26.

_____. The Needle's Eye. "The Drabble Touch." London
Financial Times, March 30, 1972, p. 34.

DRAKE, BURGESS. Chinese White (Falcon Press). "Intelligent Mr. Sartre." London Sunday Times, August 6, 1950, p. 3.

DUGGAN, ALFRED. Conscience of the King (Faber). "Mauriac's Way." London Sunday Times, February 11, 1951, p. 3.

_____. Knight With Armour (Faber). "English, French, Jamaican." London Sunday Times, March 5, 1950, p. 3.

DU MAURIER, DAPHNE. My Cousin Rachel (Gollancz). "No Loving-Kindness." London Sunday Times, July 29, 1951, p. 3.

DUNBAR, JANET. J.M. Barrie: The Man Behind the Image. "Captain Hook." London Financial Times, September 17, 1970, p. 10.

DUNHAM, VERA S. In Stalin's Time: Middle Class Values in Soviet Fiction. "Ordinary Russians." London Financial Times, January 21, 1977, p. 11.

DUNN, RICHARD S. Sugar and Slaves. "Planters' Punches." London Financial Times, January 25, 1973, p. 12.

DUPRE, CATHERINE. John Galsworthy. "Sour Face of Success." London Financial Times, July 15, 1976, p. 25.

DUTTON, GEOFFREY. The Literature of Australia. "Australia Comes Into Its Own." London Financial Times, March 10, 1978, p. 15.

DYOS, H.J. The Victorian City: Images and Realities. Edited by H.J. Dyos and Michael Wolff. "Victoriana." London Financial Times, August 30, 1973, p. 10.

DYSON, A.E. Between Two Worlds. "Two Critics." London Financial Times, April 20, 1972, p. 14.

_____. The Inimitable Dickens. "Salute to Dickens." London Financial Times, June 4, 1970, p. 12.

EAVES, T.C. DUNCAN, AND KIMPEL, BEN D. Samuel Richardson. "Bohemian and Bourgeois." London Financial Times, May 20, 1971, p. 12.

EDEL, LEON. Henry James: The Master, 1901-1916. "Napoleon of the Novel." London Financial Times, August 3, 1972, p. 31.

ELIOT, ELIZABETH. Alice (Cassell). "Lively Quartet." London Sunday Times, October 30, 1949, p. 3.

_____. Henry (Cassell). "Fashion." London Sunday Times, September 3, 1950, p. 3.

ELLIN, STANLEY. Stronghold. "Policeman and Psychopath." London Financial Times, July 24, 1975, p. 12.

EMERSON, DAVID. Dark Bright Rose (Hurst & Blackett). "A New Talent." London Sunday Times, May 6, 1951, p. 3.

EPSTEIN, JASON. The Great Conspiracy Trial. "Modern Revolutionaries." London Financial Times, February 3, 1972, p. 22.

ERGAZ, DOUSSIA. The Favours of Heaven (Secker & Warburg). "Away from Conflict." London Sunday Times, May 15, 1949, p. 3.

EVE, A.S. Rutherford. "Lord Rutherford." Spectator, 163 (October 13, 1939) 512, 514.

_____. Rutherford. "Rutherford." Discovery, N.S., 2 (November 1939) 611, 613.

FABER, RICHARD. Proper Stations: A Study of Class in Victorian Fiction. "The Likes of Us." London Financial Times, June 17, 1971, p. 24.

FABIAN FEMINIST: BERNARD SHAW AND WOMAN. Edited by Rodelle Weintraub. "Gradual People." London Financial Times, July 15, 1977, p. 27.

FALSTEIN, LEWIS. The Sky is a Lonely Place (Hart-Davis). "The Seeing Eye." London Sunday Times, July 1, 1951, p. 3.

FARR, DIANA. Gilbert Cannan: A Georgian Prodigy. "Poor Gilbert." London Financial Times, February 2, 1978, p. 31.

FARRAR-HOCKLEY, ANTHONY. Goughie. "Victim of the System." London Financial Times, May 9, 1975, p. 16.

FARRELL, KATHLEEN. Mistletoe Malice (Hart-Davis). "A New Talent." London Sunday Times, May 6, 1951, p. 3.

FAULKNER, WILLIAM. Intruder in the Dust (Chatto & Windus). "Cult of the Atrocious." London Sunday Times, October 16, 1949, p. 3.

FENBY, CHARLES. The Other Oxford. "That Sweet City." London Financial Times, December 10, 1970, p. 8.

FENWICK, KENNETH. Dark Was the Dawning (Heinemann). "Entertaining, But--." London Sunday Times, April 30, 1950, p. 3.

FEST, JOACHIM C. Hitler. "Fathoming the Fuhrer." London Financial Times, July 25, 1974, p. 24.

FEUCHTWANGER, LION. This Is the Hour (Hutchinson). "Most Musical, Most Melancholy." London Sunday Times, June 29, 1952, p. 5.

FINLEY, M.I. The World of Odysseus (Chatto & Windus). "Books of the Year--II; Chosen by Eminent Contemporaries." London Sunday Times, December 30, 1956, p. 10.

FIRBANK, RONALD. Caprice (Duckworth). "Books and Writers." Spectator, 186, no. 6395 (January 19, 1951,) 82.

_____. Inclinations (Duckworth). "Books and Writers." Spectator, 186, no. 6395 (January 19, 1951) 82.

_____. Vainglory (Duckworth). "Books and Writers." Spectator, 186, no. 6395 (January 19, 1951) 82.

FISHER, MARGERY. Field Day (Collins). "From Far and Near." Sunday Times, September 23, 1951, p. 3.

FITZGERALD, F. SCOTT. The Last Tycoon (Grey Walls Press). "Miss Mitford Up to Date." London Sunday Times, July 31, 1949, p. 3.

FITZGERALD, RICHARD. Art and Politics. "Savage Lines." London Financial Times, August 22, 1974, p. 22.

FITZHUGH, ROBERT T. Robert Burns: The Man and the Poet. "Literary Lover." London Financial Times, March 4, 1971, p. 24.

FITZSIMMONS, RAYMUND. Edmund Kean. "Players' King." London Financial Times, April 23, 1976, p. 20.

FLAIANO, ENNIO. Mariam (Lehmann). "Cult of the Atrocious." London Sunday Times, October 16, 1949, p. 3.

FOOT, MICHAEL. Aneurin Bevan: A Biography. 2: 1945-60. (Davis-Poynter.) "Nye's Mara." London Financial Times, October 18, 1973, p. 18.

FORBES, BRYAN. Ned's Girl. "Millamant." London Financial Times, October 13, 1977, p. 18.

FORBES, ESTHER. The Running of the Tide (Chatto & Windus). "Writing in Exile." London Sunday Times, December 11, 1949, p. 3.

FORESTER, C.S. Mr. Midshipman Hornblower (Michael Joseph). "A Matter for Pride." London Sunday Times, May 28, 1950, p. 3.

FORSTER, E.M. <u>Maurice</u>. "Open Windows." London <u>Financial Times</u>, October 7, 1971, p. 28.

FOSS, MICHAEL. <u>The Age of Patronage</u>. "Paying the Piper." London <u>Financial Times</u>, March 23, 1972, p. 32.

FOWLES, JOHN. <u>Daniel Martin</u>. "Intimate Relations." London <u>Financial Times</u>, October 6, 1977, p. 30.

FOX, ROBIN LANE. <u>Alexander the Great</u> (Allen Lowe with Longman). "The Real Alexander." London <u>Financial Times</u>, November 15, 1973, p. 33, c. 1.

FRANCIS, DICK. "Over the Sticks." London <u>Financial Times</u>, July 19, 1973, p. 33, c. 2. A general essay on Francis' crime fiction writing.

FRANKLIN, ROBERT. <u>Queen Wolf</u>. "In Love with Nature." London <u>Financial Times</u>, May 22, 1975, p. 34.

FRASER, ANTONIA. <u>Cromwell</u> (Weidenfeld & Nicolson). "The Protector." London <u>Financial Times</u>, June 7, 1973, p. 17.

FRASER, MORRIS. <u>Children in Conflict</u> (Secker & Warburg). "Cruel Climate." London <u>Financial Times</u>, May 10, 1973, p. 20. c. 1.

FRASER, RONALD. <u>Beetle's Career</u> (Cape). "Masks and Faces." London <u>Sunday Times</u>, April 22, 1951, p. 3.

FREELING, NICHOLAS. <u>What Are the Bugles Blowing For</u>? "Deaths and Entrances." London <u>Financial Times</u>, October 17, 1975, p. 12.

FREUD, SIGMUND. <u>The Freud/Jung Letters</u>. Edited by William McGuire. "Bounds of Possibility." London <u>Financial Times</u>, April 11, 1974, p. 32.

FRISON-ROCHE, ROGER. <u>The Last Crevasse</u> (Methuen). "Facts as Well as Fiction." London <u>Sunday Times</u>, June 25, 1952, p. 11.

FROST, ERNEST. <u>Dark Peninsula</u> (Lehmann). "The Novelist's Ear." London <u>Sunday Times</u>, October 2, 1949, p. 3.

_____. <u>The Lighted Cities</u> (Lehmann). "A Gifted Writer." London <u>Sunday Times</u>, November 19, 1950, p. 3.

FULLER, KAY. <u>The Silken Cord</u> (Peter Davies). "Putting Down the Thugs." London <u>Sunday Times</u>, August 24, 1952, p. 5.

FUSSELL, PAUL. The Great War and Modern Memory. "Mud Into Myth." London Financial Times, November 13, 1975, p. 23.

GABOR, DENNIS. The Mature Society. "Too Many Too Soon." London Financial Times, June 8, 1972, p. 32.

GALLO, MAX. Mussolini's Italy. "Brio and Bayonets." London Financial Times, February 7, 1974, p. 26.

GALSWORTHY, JOHN. Ten Best Plays. "Sour Face of Success." London Financial Times, July 15, 1976, p. 25.

GARY, ROMAIN. The Company of Men (Michael Joseph). "Fashion." London Sunday Times, September 3, 1950, p. 3.

GASKIN, CATHERINE. All Else is Folly (Collins). "Stout-Hearted Stories." London Sunday Times, February 25, 1951, p. 3.

GATHORNE-HARDY, JONATHAN. The Public School Phenomenon: 1597-1977. "Boys into Men." London Financial Times, November 17, 1977, p. 17.

GAUTHIER, JEAN JACQUES. The Triple Mirror. "From Far and Near." London Sunday Times, September 23, 1951, p. 3.

GAYE, PHOEBE FENWICK. On a Darkling Plain (Cape). "Puritan Ireland." London Sunday Times, April 16, 1950, p. 3.

GEER, ANDREW. The Sea Chase (Collins). "Good Short Stories." London Sunday Times, August 14, 1949, p. 3.

George Orwell: The Critical Heritage. Edited by Jeffrey Myers. "Blasting Off." London Financial Times, January 29, 1976 p. 25.

GERHARDI, WILLIAM. Collected Work of William Gerhardi (Macdonald). "William Gerhardi." London Sunday Times, June 6, 1948, p. 3.

GERIN, WINIFRED. Emily Bronte: A Biography. "Emily the 'Major'." London Financial Times, December 23, 1971, p. 17.

GIBSON, ROBERT. The Land Without a Name: Alain-Fournier and His World. "Faraway Princess." London Financial Times, March 6, 1975, p. 26.

GIJSEN, MARNIX. The Book of Joachim of Babylon (East and West Library). "Susannah's Husband." London Sunday Times, November 4, 1951, p. 3.

GILBERT, EDWIN. The Squirrel Cage (Heinemann). "The
Pursuit of Money." London Sunday Times, January 23, 1949,
p. 3.

GILBERT, MARTIN. Sir Horace Rumbold (Heinemann). "Rumbold's
Realism." London Financial Times, December 21, 1973,
p. 21, c. 1.

_____. Winston S. Churchill. Vol. 3: 1914-16. "Grandiose
Failure." London Financial Times, October 28, 1971, p. 34.

_____. Winston S. Churchill. Vol. 4. "In and Out of the
Wilderness." London Financial Times, June 5, 1975, p. 34.

GILBERT, STEPHEN. The Burnaby Experiments (Faber). "Putting
Down the Thugs." London Sunday Times, August 24, 1952, p. 5.

GILLEN, MOLLIE. The Prince and His Lady. "Royal Lady."
London Financial Times, January 14, 1971, p. 26.

GIMPEL, JEAN. The Cult of Art. "Too Big for Their Palettes?"
London Financial Times, February 5, 1970, p. 8.

GITTING, ROBERT. Young Thomas Hardy. "Hardy Quest." London
Financial Times, April 17, 1975, p. 34.

GLOAG, JOHN. All England At Home (Cassell). "Miss Mitford
Up to Date." London Sunday Times, July 31, 1949, p. 3.

GODDEN, JON. The Peacock (Michael Joseph). "In the Jungle."
London Sunday Times, December 3, 1950, p. 3.

GOES, ALBRECHT. Arrow to the Heart (Michael Joseph).
"A New Talent." London Sunday Times, May 6, 1951, p. 3.

GOLDIE, GRACE NISBET. Facing the Nation: Television and
Politics, 1936-1976. "M.P.'s as Performers." London
Financial Times, April 28, 1977, p. 33.

GOLDMAN, WILLIAM. A Saint in the Making (Constellation Books).
"A Visit to Turkey." London Sunday Times, January 13, 1952,
p. 3.

GOLDSMITH, MAURICE. Frederic Joliot-Curie. "Frenchman
in the Lab." London Financial Times, June 18, 1976, p. 19.

GOLLANCZ, EMMA LATHEN. Murder to Go. "Thriller Writer on
Wall Street." London Financial Times, May 8, 1970, p. 14.

GORDAN, JOHN D. <u>Mrs. Gamp. Facsimile of Prompt Copy</u>.
"Dickens at Work." <u>New Statesman</u>, 54, no. 1376, (July 27,
1957) 119-20.

GRAFTON, C.W. <u>Beyond a Reasonable Doubt</u> (Heinemann). "Rough
Stuff." London <u>Sunday Times</u>, January 28, 1951, p. 3.

GRANT, MICHAEL. <u>The Jews in the Roman World</u> (Weidenfeld &
Nicolson). "Unto Caesar." London <u>Financial Times</u>, July 12,
1973, p. 18, c. 1.

GRANT, NIGEL. <u>Soviet Education</u>. "High-Fliers and Others."
London <u>Financial Times</u>, November 23, 1972, p. 33.

GRANT, ROBERT M. <u>Augustus to Constantine</u>. "Creed Like
Wildfire." London <u>Financial Times</u>, June 10, 1971, p. 26.

GRAVES, AFFLECK. <u>Willa, You're Wanted</u> (Faber). "Unusual
Quintet." London <u>Sunday Times</u>, March 9, 1952, p. 3.

GRAVES, ROBERT. <u>The Isles of Unwisdom</u> (Cassell). "Four
Exceptional Novels." London <u>Sunday Times</u>, May 14, 1950,
p. 3.

_____. <u>Seven Days in Crete</u> (Cassell). "The Novelist's Ear."
London <u>Sunday Times</u>, October 2, 1949, p. 3.

GREEN, ALAN. <u>What a Body</u> (Redman). "Human Kindness." London
<u>Sunday Times</u>, December 31, 1950, p. 3.

GREEN, DAVID. <u>Queen Anne</u>. "Royal Lady." London <u>Financial
Times</u>, January 14, 1971, p. 26.

GREEN, F.L. <u>Ambush for the Hunter</u> (Michael Joseph). "Living
People." London <u>Sunday Times</u>, November 30, 1952, p. 5.

_____. <u>The Magician</u> (Michael Joseph). "A Charming Heroine."
London <u>Sunday Times</u>, March 25, 1951, p. 3.

GREEN, HENRY. <u>Nothing</u> (Hogarth). "Four Exceptional Novels."
London <u>Sunday Times</u>, May 14, 1950, p. 3.

GREEN, JULIAN. <u>If I Were You</u> (Eyre & Spottiswoode). "A
Brave Talent." London <u>Sunday Times</u>, March 19, 1950, p. 3.

_____. <u>Moira</u> (Heinemann). "Atmospherics." London <u>Sunday
Times</u>, May 20, 1951, p. 3.

GREEN, MARTIN. <u>Children of the Sun: A Narrative of Decadence
in England after 1918</u>. "Just Dandy." London <u>Financial
Times</u>, June 2, 1977, p. 31.

GREEN, PETER. Armada from Athens. "Syracuse Shambles." London Financial Times, March 20, 1971, p. 10.

_____. The Year of Salamis. "The Brave and the Free." London Financial Times, July 30, 1970, p. 8.

GREENE, GRAHAM. The Collected Edition of Graham Greene. V. 1-4. "The Novelist on Himself." London Financial Times, April 9, 1970, p. 28.

GRIGG, JOHN. The Young Lloyd George (Eyre Methuen). "Welsh Wizzard from Criccieth." London Financial Times, June 29, 1973, p. 32, c. 1.

GROSSMAN, LEONID. Dostoevsky. "Dostoevsky, Crime and Punishment." London Financial Times, February 13, 1975, p. 28.

GROSVENOR, PETER, AND MCMILLAN, JAMES. The British Genius (Dent). "Waving the Flag." London Financial Times, February 22, 1973, p. 29, c. 1.

GUARESCHI, GIOVANNI. The Little World of Don Camillo (Gollancz). "Human Kindness." London Sunday Times, December 31, 1950, p. 3.

GUNN, NEIL M. The Last Chart (Faber). "Personal Flavours." London Sunday Times, June 12, 1949, p. 3.

GUNTEKIN, RESAT NURI. Afternoon Sun (Heinemann). "Five Good Stories." London Sunday Times, March 11, 1951, p. 3.

GUTHRIE, JOHN. Journey by Twilight (Werner Laurie). "Eye on the Ball." London Sunday Times, December 25, 1949, p. 3.

HAFFNER, SEBASTIAN. Failure of a Revolution (Andre Deutsch). "Seeing Red." London Financial Times, February 15, 1973, p. 34, c. 1.

HAGGLOF, GUNNAR. Diplomat: Memoirs of a Swedish Envoy in London, Paris, Berlin, Moscow, Washington. "Clear-Sighted Swede." London Financial Times, October 26, 1972, p. 14.

HAIGHT, G.S. The George Eliot Letters. "George Eliot's Way; Conflicting Impulses in Work and Life." London Sunday Times, June 17, 1956, p. 4.

HAILSHAM OF SAINT MARYLEBONE, QUINTIN MCGAREL HOGG. The Door Wherein I Went. "Boisterous and Magnanimous Peer." London Financial Times, October 9, 1975, p. 12.

HALE, A.M. The Ordeal of Alfred M. Hale: The Memoirs of a Soldier Servant. Edited by Paul Fussell. "Mud Into Myth." London Financial Times, November 13, 1975, p. 23.

HALLIDAY, F.E. The Excellency of the English Tongue. "English as She Is Spoke." London Financial Times, December 4, 1975, p. 29.

HALPERIN, JOHN. Trollope and Politics. "Victorian Masters." London Financial Times, September 1, 1977, p. 14.

HALSBAND, ROBERT. Lord Harvey: Eighteenth Century Courtier (Oxford University Press). "Versatile Courtier." London Financial Times, November 29, 1973, p. 16, c. 1.

HAMILTON, ALASTAIR. The Appeal of Fascism. "Black-Shirt Leanings." London Financial Times, April 8, 1971, p. 26.

HAMILTON, BRUCE. So Sad, So Fresh (Cresset Press). "Hot War and Cold War." London Sunday Times, November 16, 1952, p. 5.

HAMILTON, NIGEL. The Brothers Mann. "Mann to Mann." London Financial Times, March 30, 1978, p. 27.

HAMILTON, PATRICK. Hangover Square. "Behind the Best-Sellers." London Financial Times, July 6, 1972, p. 33.

_____. The Light Went Out: A Biography. "Behind the Best-Sellers." London Financial Times, July 6, 1972, p. 33.

_____. The Slaves of Solitude. "Behind the Best-Sellers." London Financial Times, July 6, 1972, p. 33.

HAMMETT, DASHIELL. The Continental Op. "Deaths and Entrances." London Financial Times, October 17, 1975, p. 12.

HAMPSON, JOHN. A Bag of Stones (Verschoyle). "Inside Hollywood." London Sunday Times, December 14, 1952, p. 5.

HANLEY, JAMES. The Closed Harbour (Macdonald). "Salute to a Fine Novelist." London Sunday Times, July 13, 1952, p. 3.

_____. Winter Song (Phoenix House). "A Matter for Pride." London Sunday Times, May 28, 1950, p. 3.

HANNAH, W.H. Bobs, Kipling's General; The Life of Field Marshal Roberts of Kandahar. "Humane Bravery of Bobs." London Financial Times, January 4, 1973, p. 26.

HANNAM, CHARLES. <u>A Boy in Your Situation</u>. "Torn Roots."
London <u>Financial Times</u>, April 21, 1977, p. 37.

HARCOURT-SMITH, ROSAMOND. <u>Fever of Love</u> (Longmans). "Living
People." London <u>Sunday Times</u>, November 30, 1952, p. 5.

HARDY, BARBARA. <u>The Exposure of Luxury: Radical Themes in
Thackeray</u>. "Snobs and Sinners." London <u>Financial Times</u>,
August 10, 1972, p. 19.

HARRIMAN, W. AVERELL AND ABEL, ELIE. <u>Special Envoy to
Churchill and Stalin: 1941-1946</u>. "Shrewd Observer."
London <u>Financial Times</u>, June 10, 1976, p. 25.

HARRISSON, T.H. <u>Living Through the Blitz</u>. "When Bombs Fell."
London <u>Financial Times</u>, August 5, 1976, p. 12.

HARROD, R.F. <u>The Prof; A Personal Memoir of Lord Cherwell</u>.
"Lord Cherwell." <u>New Statesman</u>, 58 (September 26, 1959)
398-99.

HARTLEY, L.P. <u>The Boat</u> (Putnam). "Old Brandy." London
<u>Sunday Times</u>, January 22, 1950, p. 3.

_____. <u>The Travelling Grove, and Other Stories</u> (Barrie).
"Five Good Stories." London <u>Sunday Times</u>, March 11, 1951,
p. 3.

HARVEY, OLIVER. <u>The Diplomatic Diaries of Oliver Harvey,
1937-40</u>. Edited by John Harvey. "Inside the Nightmare."
London <u>Financial Times</u>, July 16, 1970, p. 24.

HARWOOD, RONALD. <u>Articles of Faith</u> (Secker & Warburg).
"Boer Blockbuster." London <u>Financial Times</u>, November
22, 1973, p. 30, c. 1.

HASLIP, JOAN. <u>Catherine the Great</u>. "Queenly Passion."
London <u>Financial Times</u>, April 7, 1977, p. 27.

HAWKES, JACQUETTA. <u>The First Great Civilizations</u> (Hutchinson).
"Old Times." London <u>Financial Times</u>, October 25, 1973,
p. 33, c. 1.

HAWKINS, A.H. <u>Sophy of Kravonia</u>. "In Balk of the Balkans."
London <u>Financial Times</u>, July 17, 1975, p. 10.

HAYES, ALFRED. <u>All Thy Conquests</u> (Gollancz). "A Novelist
to Watch." London <u>Sunday Times</u>, February 19, 1950, p. 3.

HAYTER, TERESA. Hayter of the Bourgeosie. "Modern Revolutionaries." London Financial Times, February 3, 1972, p. 22.

HAYTER, SIR WILLIAM. A Double Life. "Wisdom of a Warden." London Financial Times, May 24, 1974, p. 16.

_____. Spooner; A Biography. "Speed of Crooner." London Financial Times, March 10, 1977, p. 28.

HAZLEHURST, CAMERON. Politicians at War, July 1914 to May 1915: A Prologue to the Triumph of Lloyd George. "Minds of the Ministers." London Financial Times, February 25, 1971, p. 14.

HEALEY, EDNA. Lady Unknown: The Life of Angela Burdett-Coutts. "Rich Lady." London Financial Times, January 5, 1978, p. 9.

HEATTER, BASIL. The Dim View (Hammond, Hammond). "Eye on the Ball." London Sunday Times, December 25, 1949, p. 3.

HEILBRON, J.L. H.G.J. Moseley: The Life and Letters of an English Physicist, 1887-1915. Books and Bookmen, 20 (June 1975) 64-65.

HEMINGWAY, ERNEST. Islands in the Stream. "Playing a Fish." London Financial Times, October 22, 1970, p. 27.

HEMMING, JOHN. Red Gold; The Conquest of the Brazilian Indians. "Colonial Man." London Financial Times, May 1, 1978, p. 18.

HENDERSON, PHILLIP. Swinburne. "Acting Like Artists." London Financial Times, August 1, 1974, p. 14.

HEPPENSTALL, RAYNER. Reflections of the Newgate Calendar. London Financial Times, February 6, 1975, p. 24.

HERBERT, XAVIER. Capricornia. "Australia Comes Into Its Own." London Financial Times, March 10, 1978, p. 15.

HEREFORD, JOHN. The May Fair (Hodder & Stoughton). "The Pursuit of Money." London Sunday Times, January 23, 1949, p. 3.

HERVEY, HARRY. The Veiled Fountain (Allen). "Action and Analysis." London Sunday Times, January 9, 1949, p. 3.

HESSE, HERMAN. Magister Ludi (Aldus). "Away from Conflict." London Sunday Times, May 15, 1949, p. 3.

HEYERDAHL, THOR. Fatu-Hiva: Back to Nature? "In Search of Eden." London Financial Times, November 14, 1974, p. 16.

HEYM, STEFAN. The Crusaders (Cassell). "Productivity." London Sunday Times, February 5, 1950, p. 3.

HIBBERT, CHRISTOPHER. The Rise and Fall of the House of the Medici. "Ruling Clan." London Financial Times, January 9, 1975, p. 19.

HICKLING, HUGH. The Furious Evangelist (Alvin Redman). "Laws of Promise." London Sunday Times, October 1, 1950, p. 3.

HIGHAM, DAVID. Literary Gent. "Feast or Famine?" London Financial Times, April 13, 1978, p. 18.

HILL, A.V. What Science Stands For. "The Humanity of Science." Spectator, 158,(April 16, 1937) 702-03.

HILTON, JAMES. Morning Journey (Macmillan). "Witch-Hunting Today." London Sunday Times, December 16, 1951, p. 3.

HINDE, THOMAS. Mr. Nicholas (MacGibbon & Kee). "Summer in Paris." London Sunday Times, May 18, 1952, p. 9.

HINDE, WENDY. George Canning (Collins). "Parliament Men and Press." London Financial Times, October 4, 1973, p. 31, c. 1.

HINGLEY, RONALD. A New Life of Anton Chekhov. "Doctor in the House." London Financial Times, May 13, 1976, p. 32.

HITREC, JOSEPH. Son of the Moon (Michael Joseph). "Two Entertainments." London Sunday Times, May 29, 1949, p. 3.

HOBHOUSE, HERMIONE. Thomas Cubitt, Master Builder. London Financial Times, August 12, 1971, p. 10.

HODGE, JANE AIKEN. The Double Life of Jane Austen. "Shrewd Spinster." London Financial Times, June 1, 1972, p. 32.

HOEL, SIGURD. Meeting at the Milestone (Secker & Warburg). "From Far and Near." London Sunday Times, September 23, 1951, p. 3.

HOFFMAN, DANIEL. Poe, Poe, Poe, Poe, Poe, Poe, Poe. "Extravagant Poe." London Financial Times, January 10, 1974, p. 32.

HOLLOWAY, DAVID. Derby Day. "All in Miniature." London
Financial Times, April 17, 1975, p. 16.

HOLLOWAY, MARK. Norman Douglas. "Hard-Hearted Hedonist."
London Financial Times, December 1976, p. 12.

HOLT, EDGAR. The Tiger: The Life of Georges Clemenceau.
"A French Churchill." London Financial Times, February
12, 1976, p. 15.

HOPKINSON, TOM. Down the Long Slide (Hopkinson). "Another
Jumbo." London Sunday Times, November 13, 1949, p. 3.

HORNE, ALASTAIR. A Savage War of Peace: Algeria, 1954-1962.
"Algerian Agony." London Financial Times, October 22,
1977, p. 12.

HORNUNG, E.W. Raffles: The Amateur Cracksman. "Raffles Rides
Again." London Financial Times, April 3, 1975, p. 34.

_____. Raffles: The Black Mask. "Raffles Rides Again."
London Financial Times, April 3, 1975, p. 34.

HOUGH, RICHARD. Louis and Victoria: The First Mount-Battens.
"Royals Aboard." London Financial Times, October 4, 1974,
p. 14.

HOUGHTON, CLAUDE. Birthmark (Collins). "Dramatic Values."
London Sunday Times, January 1, 1950, p. 3.

HOWARD, CECIL, ed. West-African Explorers (Oxford University
Press). "Professional Exploration." Spectator, 188, no.
6461 (April 25, 1952) 554-56.

HOWARD, ELIZABETH JANE. The Beautiful Visit (Cape).
"Entertaining, But--." London Sunday Times, April 30,
1950, p. 3.

HOWARTH, DAVID. 1066: The Year of the Conquest. "King's
Luck." London Financial Times, September 8, 1977, p. 14.

HOWE, GEORGE. Call It Treason (Hart-Davis). "Plot or No
Plot?" London Sunday Times, January 14, 1951, p. 3.

HOWE, IRVING. The Immigrant Jews of New York: 1881 to the
Present. "Into the Melting Pot." London Financial Times,
December 16, 1976, p. 35.

HOYLE, FRED. A Decade of Decision (Heinemann). "A 25-Year
Plan." London Sunday Times, October 11, 1953, p. 5.

HUDSON, LIAM. <u>The Cult of the Fact</u>. "Too Many Too Soon."
London <u>Financial Times</u>, June 8, 1972, p. 32.

HUGHES, CLEDWYN. <u>The Civil Strangers</u> (Phoenix House).
"Dramatic Values." London <u>Sunday Times</u>, January 1, 1950,
p. 3.

HUGHES, DAVID. <u>J.B. Priestley</u>. London <u>Sunday Times</u>,
November 9, 1958, p. 16.

HUIZINGA, J.H. <u>The Making of a Saint</u>. "Natural Force."
London <u>Financial Times</u>, January 16, 1976, p. 29.

HUMPHREYS, EMYR. <u>A Change of Heart</u> (Eyre & Spottiswoode).
"Five Good Stories." London <u>Sunday Times</u>, March 11, 1951,
p. 3.

_____. <u>Hear and Forgive</u> (Gollancz). "A Rising Reputation."
London <u>Sunday Times</u>, September 21, 1952, p. 5.

_____. <u>Voice of a Stranger</u> (Eyre & Spottiswoode). "Love
and Hate." London <u>Sunday Times</u>, August 28, 1949, p. 3.

HUNTER, N.C. <u>The Losing Hazard</u> (Robert Hale). "Local
Knowledge." London <u>Sunday Times</u>, December 30, 1951, p. 3.

HUXLEY, JULIAN. <u>Memories</u>. "Huxley Heritage." London
<u>Financial Times</u>, May 28, 1970, p. 30.

HYAMS, EDWARD. <u>Not In Our Stars</u> (Lehmann). "Dramatic Values."
London <u>Sunday Times</u>, January 1, 1950, p. 3.

HYDE, H. MONTGOMERY. <u>Oscar Wilde</u>. "Eye-Opener About Oscar."
London <u>Financial Times</u>, June 3, 1976, p. 12.

HYNES, SAMUEL. <u>The Auden Generation</u>. "When We Were Very
Young." London <u>Financial Times</u>, July 9, 1976, p. 29.

IBUSE, MASUJI. <u>Black Rain</u>. "One Day in August." London
<u>Financial Times</u>, February 20, 1970, p. 8.

INGLIS, BRIAN. <u>Natural and Supernatural: A History of the
Paranormal</u>. "Passing Beyond Belief." London <u>Financial
Times</u>, January 26, 1978, p. 18.

INNES, HAMMOND. <u>The White South</u> (Collins). "Interest Without
Art." London <u>Sunday Times</u>, December 4, 1949, p. 3.

IRVINE, WILLIAM AND HONAN, PARK. The Book, The Ring and the Poet: A Biography of Robert Browning. "Browning Version." London Financial Times, March 16, 1975, p. 16.

IRVING, DAVID. Hitler's War. "Another Hitler." London Financial Times, June 17, 1977, p. 15.

ISHERWOOD, CHRISTOPHER. Christopher and His Kind: 1929-1939. "Ego Trip." London Financial Times, April 1, 1977, p. 14.

_____. Kathleen and Frank. "Family Figures." London Financial Times, October 21, 1971, p. 10.

JACKSON, CHARLES. The Outer Edges (Peter Nevill). "Murder Most Foul." London Sunday Times, April 2, 1950, p. 3.

JACOB, W.W. Selected Short Stories. "In Balk of the Balkans." London Financial Times, July 17, 1975, p. 10.

JAMES, P.D. An Unsuitable Job for a Woman. "Crop of Crimes." London Financial Times, April 12, 1973, p. 37.

JAMES ROBERT RHODES. Ambitions and Realities: British Politics, 1964-1970. "The Decent Society." London Financial Times, May 25, 1972, p. 36.

JAMESON, STORM. The Green Man (Macmillan). "Divided Households." London Sunday Times, July 27, 1952, p. 5.

JEAL, TIM. Livingstone (Heinemann). "Explorer's World." London Financial Times, May 17, 1973, p. 31, c. 1.

JHABVALA, RUTH PRAWER. An Experience of India. "Aimless Elite." London Financial Times, December 16, 1971, p. 12.

_____. A New Dominion. "Women and Gurus." London Financial Times, March 1, 1973, p. 29.

JOHNSON, EDGAR. Charles Dickens. "Performers." London Financial Times, April 20, 1978, p. 36.

_____. Sir Walter Scott: The Great Unknown. "Man of Honor." London Financial Times, October 29, 1970, p. 22.

JOHNSON, EYVIND. Return to Ithaca (Thames & Hudson). "Newcomers." London Sunday Times, October 19, 1952, p. 5.

JOHNSON, LYNDON BAINES. The Vantage Point. "L.B.J. at Large." London Financial Times, January 20, 1972, p. 12.

JOHNSON, PAUL. Enemies of Society. "Threatened Values." London Financial Times, May 20, 1977, p. 29.

JOHNSON, SAMUEL. Johnson as Critic. Edited by John Wain.
"Mind of the Great Cham." London Financial Times,
January 3, 1974, p. 36.

JONAS, KLAUS W. The World of Somerset Maugham. "Very Odd
Fish." Time and Tide, 40, no. 11 (March 14, 1959) 303-04.

JONES, GWYN. The Flowers Beneath the Scythe (Dent). "First
Novel Success." London Sunday Times, January 27, 1952, p. 3.

JONES, JAMES. From Here to Eternity (Collins). "The Ugliest
Trend." London Sunday Times, February 3, 1952, p. 3.

JONES, MERVYN. No Time to Be Young (Cape). "First Novel
Success." London Sunday Times, January 27, 1952, p. 3.

JONES, R.V. Most Secret War; British Scientific Intelligence
1939-1945. "Monitoring the Enemy in Wartime." London
Financial Times, March 2, 1978, p. 32.

JOSEPH, MICHAEL. Katherine Mansfield: The Memories of E.M.
"Third Party." London Financial Times, July 8, 1971, p. 26.

JOVINE, FRANCESCO. The Estate in Abruzzi (McGibbon & Kee).
"Facts as Well as Fiction." London Sunday Times, June 15,
1952, p. 11.

JUDD, DENNIS. Edward VII. "Tum-Tum." London Financial Times,
May 1, 1975, p. 32.

_____. Radical Joe: A Life of Joseph Chamberlain. "Birmingham
Boss." London Financial Times, May 1, 1977, p. 36.

JUNGK, ROBERT. Brighter Than a Thousand Suns. "The Atomic
Pioneers." New Republic, 139 (October 27, 1958) 18-19.

_____. Brighter Than A Thousand Suns (Gollancz with Hart-Davis).
"Not the Whole Truth." New Statesman, 55, no. 1422 (June
14, 1958), 771-72.

_____. Tomorrow is Already Here (Hart-Davis). "Revolution of
Our Time." London Sunday Times, January 31, 1954, p. 5.

KAPITSA, P.L. Peter Kapitsa on Life and Science. "Soviet
Scientific Impressario." Book World, 2 (September 8, 1968)
p. 4.

KAPLAN, H.J. The Plenipotentiaries (Secker & Warburg).
"Mauriac's Way." London Sunday Times, February 11, 1951,
p. 3.

KEATING, H.F.R. <u>Murder Must Appetise</u>. "Digging Up Clues."
London <u>Financial Times</u>, February 5, 1976, p. 16.

KEATING, P.J. <u>The Working Classes in Victorian Fiction</u>. "The
Likes of Us." London <u>Financial Times</u>, June 17, 1971, p. 24.

KEEGAN, JOHN. <u>The Face of Battle</u>. "From Agincourt Onwards."
London <u>Financial Times</u>, July 1, 1976, p. 12.

KEIR, URSULA. <u>The Sun Behind Me</u> (Collins). "The Man Behind
the Story." London <u>Sunday Times</u>, February 24, 1952, p. 3.

KELLY, LAWRENCE. <u>Lermentov: Tragedy in the Caucasus</u>.
"Sour Hero." London <u>Financial Times</u>, December 8, 1977, p. 31.

KENNAN, GEORGE F. <u>Memoirs, 1925-1950</u>. "George F. Kennan: Too
Extraordinary for His Own Good." <u>Book World</u>, 1 (November
5, 1967) 1.

KENNEDY, LUDOVICK. <u>A Presumption of Innocence: The Amazing
Case of Patrick Meehan</u>. "Scottish Connection." London
<u>Financial Times</u>, January 8, 1976, p. 20.

KENNELLY, ARDYTH. <u>The Peacable Kingdom</u> (Gollancz). "Reflected
Glory." London <u>Sunday Times</u>, August 20, 1950, p. 3.

_____. <u>The Spur</u> (Gollancz). "Unusual Quintet." London <u>Sunday
Times</u>, March 9, 1952, p. 3.

KEPPEL, SONIA. <u>The Sovereign Lady</u>. "Whigs and Woman."
London <u>Financial Times</u>, June 27, 1974, p. 14.

KEYNES, MILO. <u>Essays on John Maynard Keynes</u>. "Worldling of
Genius." <u>Books and Bookmen</u>, 20 (May 1975) p. 11.

KHRUSHCHEV, N.S. <u>Khrushchev Remembers</u>. With an introduction,
commentary and notes by Edward Crankshaw. London: Deutsch,
1971. "Who Is Speaking, Please?" London <u>Financial Times</u>,
January 21, 1971, p. 12.

KINCAID, DENNIS. <u>British Social Life in India</u> (Routledge).
"How We Quit India." London <u>Financial Times</u>, July 15, 1973,
p. 39, c. 1.

KING, FRANCIS. <u>The Dark Glasses</u>. "Novels of 1954: Counter-
Revolution." London <u>Sunday Times</u>, December 26, 1954, p. 5.

_____. <u>The Dividing Stream</u> (Lehmann). "Florentine Summer."
London <u>Sunday Times</u>, June 17, 1951, p. 3.

KINNEAR, MICHAEL. <u>The Fall of Lloyd George</u> (Macmillan).
"Welsh Wizzard from Criccieth." London <u>Financial Times</u>,
June 29, 1973, p. 32, c. 1.

KREUDER, ERNEST. The Attic Pretenders (Putnams). "Action and Analysis." London Sunday Times, January 9, 1949, p. 3.

KRIM, SEYMOUR. Views of a Near-Sighted Cannonneer. "The Case of Mr. Krim." London Financial Times, April 30, 1970, p. 14.

KUHNELT-LEDDIHN, ERIK VON. Black Banners (The Hand and Flower Press). "Newcomers." London Sunday Times, October 19, 1952, p. 5.

KYLE, ELISABETH. Douce (Peter Davies). "Puritan Ireland." London Sunday Times, April 16, 1950, p. 3.

LACEY, ROBERT. Majesty: Elizabeth and the House of Windsor. "Majestic Majesty." London Financial Times, February 3, 1977, p. 29.

LAMBERT, ELIZABETH. The Sleeping House Party (Michael Joseph). "Plot or No Plot?" London Sunday Times, January 14, 1951, p. 3.

LAMBERT, ERIC. The Twenty Thousand Thieves (Frederick Muller). "Hot War and Cold War." London Sunday Times, November 16, 1952, p. 5.

LANE, JANE. Fortress in the Forth (Dakers). "Bees in the Bonnet." London Sunday Times, July 16, 1950, p. 3.

LANGER, WALTER. The Mind of Adolf Hitler (Secker & Warburg). "Fuhrer's Kinks." London Financial Times, March 8, 1973, p. 30.

LARKIN, PHILIP. The Less Deceived (Marvell Press). "Books of the Year-II; Chosen by Eminent Contemporaries." London Sunday Times, December 30, 1956, p. 10.

_____. The Oxford Book of Twentieth Century Verse. Chosen by Philip Larkin (Oxford). "Poets of our Time." London Financial Times, March 29, 1973, p. 37. c. 1.

LASH, JOSEPH P. Eleanor and Franklin. "First Lady's Fears." London Financial Times, June 15, 1972, p. 14.

LASKY, MELVIN J. Utopia and Revolution. "Happier Places." London Financial Times, February 11, 1977, p. 35.

LAVIN, MARY. A Single Lady, and Other Stories (Michael Joseph). "Local Knowledge." London Sunday Times, December 30, 1951, p. 3.

LEAR, WINIFRED. Shady Cloister (Macmillan). "More Mauriac." London Sunday Times, June 11, 1950, p. 3.

LECARRÉ, JOHN. Tinker, Tailor, Soldier, Spy. "Smiley Comes Back." London Financial Times, July 19, 1974, p. 19.

LEE, CHARLES M. Meeting at Potsdam. "Super Summit." London Financial Times, August 7, 1975, p. 19.

LEE, RAYMOND E. The London Observer: The Journal of Raymond E. Lee, 1940-1941. Edited by James Lentze. "Blitzed American." London Financial Times, July 13, 1972, p. 23.

LEESON, R.A. Strike--A Live History (Allen & Unwin). "Coming Out." London Financial Times, March 15, 1973, p. 16, c. 1.

LEMELIN, ROGER. The Plouffe Family (Cape). "Facts as Well as Fiction." London Sunday Times, June 15, 1952, p. 11.

LEPPMANN, WOLFGANG. Winckelmann. "Man of Steel." London Financial Times, March 11, 1971, p. 14.

LESSING, DORIS. This Was the Old Chief's Country (Michael Joseph). London Sunday Times, April 8, 1951, p. 3.

LEVERSON, ADA. The Limit (Chapman & Hall). "Books and Writers." Spectator, 186, no. 6395 (January 19, 1951) 82.

_____. Love's Shadow (Chapman & Hall). "Books and Writers." Spectator, 186, no. 6395 (January 19, 1951) 82.

LEWIN, RONALD. Churchill as Warlord. "Re-Fighting Old Battles." London Financial Times, February 14, 1974, p. 25.

_____. Slim: the Standard Bearer. "Strategic Slim." London Financial Times, December 30, 1976, p. 8.

LEWIS, DAVID L. Prisoners of Honour. "Victim of the System." London Financial Times, May 9, 1975, p. 16.

LEWIS, R.W.B. Edith Wharton: A Biography. "In Old New York." London Financial Times, November 7, 1975, p. 14.

LEWIS, SINCLAIR. World so Wide (Heinemann). "A Memorable Story." London Sunday Times, September 9, 1951, p. 3.

LEWIS, WYNDHAM. <u>Enemy Salvoes: Selected Literary Criticism.</u>
Edited by C.J. Fox. "Blasting Off." London <u>Financial</u>
<u>Times</u>, January 29, 1976, p. 25.

_____. <u>Self-Condemned</u>. "Novels of 1954: Counter-Revolution."
London <u>Sunday Times</u>, December 25, 1954, p. 5.

LIDDELL, ROBERT. <u>Some Principles of Fiction</u>. London <u>Sunday</u>
<u>Times</u>, June 7, 1953, p. 5.

LINDSAY, JACK. <u>Fires in Smithfield</u> (Bodley Head). "Murder
Most Foul." London <u>Sunday Times</u>, April 2, 1950, p. 3.

LINKLATER, ERIC. <u>Laxdale Hall</u> (Cape). "Mauriac Country."
London <u>Sunday Times</u>, November 18, 1951, p. 3.

_____. <u>A Spell for Old Bones</u> (Cape). "Captivating Satire."
London <u>Sunday Times</u>, November 27, 1949, p. 3.

LIPPINCOTT, DAVID. <u>The Voice of Armaggedon</u>. "Case for the
Cliffhanger." London <u>Financial Times</u>, May 15, 1975, p. 18.

LIPSKY, ELEAZAR. <u>The Scientists</u>. "The Missing Scientists."
<u>Reporter</u>, 20 (February 19, 1959) 38-39.

LISTER, R.P. <u>The Way Backwards</u> (Collins). "Intelligent Mr.
Sartre." London <u>Sunday Times</u>, August 6, 1950, p. 3.

LLEWELYN, MICHAEL GARETH. <u>To Fame Unknown</u> (Murray). "A
Minor Classic?" London <u>Sunday Times</u>, January 8, 1950, p. 3.

LLOYD, SELWYN. <u>Mr. Speaker, Sir</u>. "High Office Hindsight."
London <u>Financial Times</u>, November 4, 1976, p. 27.

LOCKRIDGE, ROSS. <u>Raintree County</u> (Macdonald). "A Varied
Trio." London <u>Sunday Times</u>, June 19, 1949, p. 3.

LODWICK, JOHN. <u>Just a Song at Twilight</u> (Heinemann). "Personal
Flavours." London <u>Sunday Times</u>, June 12, 1949, p. 3.

_____. <u>First Steps Inside the Zoo</u> (Heinemann). "Old Brandy."
London <u>Sunday Times</u>, January 22, 1950, p. 3.

LOFTS, NORAH. <u>The Luteplayer</u> (Michael Joseph). "Mauriac
Country." London <u>Sunday Times</u>, November 18, 1951, p. 3.

LONGFORD, ELIZABETH. <u>Wellington. V. 2: Pillar of State.</u>
"Duke After Battle of Waterloo." London <u>Financial Times</u>,
November 2, 1972, p. 30.

LOOS, ANITA. A Mouse is Born (Cape). "Witch-Hunting Today."
London Sunday Times, December 16, 1951, p. 3.

LOTHAR, ERNEST. Return to Vienna (Hodder & Stoughton).
"Character Drawing." London Sunday Times, September 17,
1950, p. 3.

LOWE, ALFONSO. La Serenissima. "Long Colonnades." London
Financial Times, May 16, 1974, p. 14.

LOWRY, MALCOLM. October Ferry to Gabriola. "Wolfe's Clothing."
London Financial Times, September 2, 1971, p. 10.

LUBBOCK, PERCY. The Craft of Fiction (Cape). "Novelists at
Work." London Sunday Times, July 18, 1954, p. 5.

LYONS, F.S.L. Charles Stewart Parnell. "Kitty's Lover."
London Financial Times, June 9, 1977, p. 30.

MCCARTHY, MARY. Birds of America. "Humans without Hope."
London Financial Times, September 30, 1971, p. 36.

_____. Cast a Cold Eye (Heinemann). "A Visit to Turkey."
London Sunday Times, January 13, 1952, p.3.

MCCLEAN, R. Victorian Publishers' Book Bindings in Cloth
and Leather. "Victorian Values." London Financial Times,
April 18, 1974, p. 18.

MCCLELLAN, J.S. The French Right from de Maistre to Maurras.
Edited by J.S. McClellan. "How It All Began." London
Financial Times, March 5, 1970, p. 10.

MCFEE, WILLIAM. Family Trouble (Faber). "Real People."
London Sunday Times, September 11, 1949, p. 3.

MCGRAW, HUGH. The White Cat (Arthur Barker). "Fashion."
London Sunday Times, September 3, 1950, p. 3.

MACINNES, COLIN. June in Her Spring (MacGibbon & Kee).
"Newcomers." London Sunday Times, October 19, 1952, p. 5.

MACKEN, WALTER. I Am Alone (Macmillan). "Sentimental Stories."
London Sunday Times, December 18, 1949, p. 3.

_____. Rain in the Wind (Macmillan). "Laws of Promise."
London Sunday Times, October 1, 1950, p. 3.

MACKENZIE, COMPTON. Hunting the Fairies (Chatto & Windus).
"Two Entertainments." London Sunday Times, May 29, 1949,
p. 3.

MACKENZIE, NORMAN AND JEAN. The First Fabians. "Gradual People." London Financial Times, July 15, 1977, p. 27.

_____. The Time Traveller: The Life of H.G. Wells (Weidenfeld & Nicolson). "H.G. Sees It Through." London Financial Times, June 21, 1973, p. 36, c. 1.

MACKENZIE-GRIEVE, AVERIL. The Brood of Time (Hutchinson). "Love and Hate." London Sunday Times, August 28, 1949, p. 3.

_____. The Waterfall (Heinemann). "A Matter for Pride." London Sunday Times, May 28, 1950, p. 3.

MCLACHLAN, DONALD. In the Chair: Barrington-Ward of 'The Times', 1927-1948. "Establishment Editor." London Financial Times, May 13, 1971, p. 12.

MACLAREN-ROSS, JULIAN. The Weeping and the Laughter. London Sunday Times, May 17, 1953, p. 7.

MCLAVERTY, MICHAEL. The Game Cock (Cape). "Away from Conflict." London Sunday Times, May 15, 1949, p. 3.

MCLEVY, JAMES. The Casebook of a Victorian Detective. "Policeman and Psychopath." London Financial Times, July 24, 1975, p. 12.

MCMAHON, THOMAS. A Random State. "At Los Alamos." London Financial Times, February 4, 1971, p. 12.

MACMANUS, FRANCIS. The Fire in the Dust (Cape). "Puritan Ireland." London Sunday Times, April 16, 1950, p. 3.

MCMULLEN, ROY. Victorian Outsider. "Acting Like Artists." London Financial Times, August 1, 1974, p. 14.

MCWILLIAMS-TULLBERG, RITA. Women at Cambridge. "Those Conquering Heroes." London Financial Times, November 20, 1975, p. 28.

MADAN, SPENCER. Spencer and Waterloo: The Letters of Spencer Madan. Edited by Beatrice Madan. "Blind to Byron." London Financial Times, April 29, 1971, p. 16.

MAILER, NORMAN. Barbary Shore (Cape). "The Ugliest Trend." London Sunday Times, February 3, 1952, p. 3.

_____. A Fire on the Moon. "Mailer's Orbit." London Financial Times, December 4, 1970, p. 10.

MALLABY, GEORGE. Each in His Office: Studies of Men in Power. "Where Power Lies." London Financial Times, March 2, 1972, p. 24.

MANCHESTER JOINT RESEARCH COUNCIL. Industry and Science. "Using Science." New Statesman and Nation, 48, no. 1202 (March 20, 1954) 374.

MANKOWITZ, WOLF. Dickens of London. "The Greatest?" London Financial Times, September 16, 1976, p. 15.

_____. Make Me an Offer (Andre Deutsch). "Antiques With the Lid Off." London Sunday Times, August 10, 1952, p. 3.

MANN, THOMAS. The Holy Sinner (Secker & Warburg). "To Dream Again." London Sunday Times, April 20, 1952, p. 3.

_____. Joseph and His Brethren. Stories of a Lifetime: V. 1, 2. Letters of Thomas Mann, 1889-1942. "Mind of Mann." London Financial Times, December 18, 1970, p. 22.

MANNING, OLIVIA. School for Love (Heinemann). "A Memorable Story." London Sunday Times, September 9, 1951, p. 3.

Marcel Proust, 1871-1922: A Centenary Volume. Edited by Peter Quennell. "Marcel's Way." London Financial Times, August 19, 1971, p. 20.

MARCH, WILLIAM. October Island (Gollancz). "Facts as Well as Fiction." London Sunday Times, June 15, 1952, p. 11.

MARCHAL, LUCIE. The Mesh (Heinemann). "Five Good Stories." London Sunday Times, March 11, 1951, p. 3.

MARCHAND, LESLIE A. Byron. "Blind to Byron." London Financial Times, April 29, 1971, p. 16.

MARQUAND, DAVID. Ramsey MacDonald. "Lad from Lossiemouth." London Financial Times, March 3, 1977, p. 12.

MARQUAND, J.P. Point of No Return (Robert Hale). "Interest Without Art." London Sunday Times, December 4, 1949, p. 3.

MARSDEN, RUTH. Catherine Brooke (MacGibbon & Kee). "Mauriac Country." London Sunday Times, November 18, 1951, p. 3.

MARSHALL, BRUCE. <u>Every Man a Penny</u> (Constable). "Four
Exceptional Novels." London <u>Sunday Times</u>, May 14, 1950,
p. 3.

MARTIN, JAY. <u>Nathaniel West: The Art of His Life</u>. "Mr.
Lonelyhearts." London <u>Financial Times</u>, June 3, 1971, p. 12.

MARTIN DU GARD, ROGER. <u>Jean Barois</u> (Bodley Head). "Murder
Most Foul." London <u>Sunday Times</u>, April 2, 1950, p. 3.

_____. <u>Notes on Andre Gide</u> (Deutsch). "The Case Against
Andre Gide." London <u>Sunday Times</u>, July 12, 1953, p. 5.

MASON, HOWARD. <u>Proud Adversary</u> (Michael Joseph). "Pestilent
Plants." London <u>Sunday Times</u>, August 26, 1951, p. 3.

MASON, PHILIP. <u>The Dove in Harness</u>. "One-Sided Dialogue."
London <u>Financial Times</u>, December 2, 1976, p. 31.

_____. <u>A Matter of Honour</u>. "Ringside Views." London
<u>Financial Times</u>, August 8, 1974, p. 12.

_____. <u>A Shaft of Sunlight</u>. "Colonial Man." London
<u>Financial Times</u>, May 4, 1978, p. 18.

MASSEREENE AND FERRARD, JOHN, SKEFFINGTON, VISCOUNT.
<u>The Lords</u>. "Second Chamber Sallies." London <u>Financial
Times</u>, April 26, 1973, p. 12.

MASTERMAN, J.C. <u>On the Chariot Wheel</u>. "Don's Saga." London
<u>Financial Times</u>, September 26, 1975, p. 16.

MASTERS, JOHN. <u>The Deceivers</u> (Michael Joseph). "Putting
Down the Thugs." London <u>Sunday Times</u>, August 24, 1952, p. 5.

_____. <u>The Nightrunners of Bengal</u> (Michael Joseph). "A
Matter of Pace." London <u>Sunday Times</u>, June 3, 1951, p. 3.

MATRAT, JEAN. <u>Robespierre</u>. "Father of the Revolution."
London <u>Financial Times</u>, September 4, 1975, p. 11.

MAUNY, ERIK DE. <u>The Huntsman in His Career</u> (Lindsay Drummond).
"Love and Hate." London <u>Sunday Times</u>, August 28, 1949, p. 3.

MAURIAC, FRANCOIS. <u>The Dark Angels</u> (Eyre & Spottiswoode).
"Mauriac's Way." London <u>Sunday Times</u>, February 11, 1951,
p. 3.

_____. <u>The Desert of Love</u> (Eyre & Spottiswoode). "Artists
in Contrast." London <u>Sunday Times</u>, November 20, 1949, p. 3.

_____. The Enemy (Eyre & Spottiswoode). "Artists in Contrast."
London Sunday Times, November 20, 1949, p. 3.

_____. A Kiss for the Leper (Genetrix). "More Mauriac."
London Sunday Times, June 11, 1950, p. 3.

_____. The Little Misery (Eyre & Spottiswoode). "Mauriac for
Beginners." London Sunday Times, April 6, 1952, p. 3.

_____. That Which Was Lost (Eyre & Spottiswoode). "Mauriac's
Way." London Sunday Times, February 11, 1951, p. 3.

MEDAWAR, P.B. The Hope of Progress. "Things Do Get Better."
London Financial Times, March 29, 1974, p. 38.

MEERSCH, MAXENCE VAN DER. The Poor Girl (Pilot Press). "Good
Short Stories." London Sunday Times, August 14, 1949, p. 3.

MENDILOW, A.A. Time and the Novel. "The Novelist's Method."
Spectator, 190, no. 6505 (February 27, 1953) 254-56.

MENEN, AUBREY. The Stumbling Stone (Chatto & Windus).
"Captivating Satire." London Sunday Times, November 27,
1949, p. 3.

MEREDITH, ANNE. A Fig for Virtue (Faber). "The Seeing Eye."
London Sunday Times, July 1, 1951, p. 3.

MEYER, MICHAEL. The End of the Corridor (Collins). "Short
and Long." London Sunday Times, March 18, 1951, p. 3.

MICHAELIS-JENA, RUTH. The Brothers Grimm. "Brotherly Love."
London Financial Times, July 2, 1970, p. 12.

MIDDLEMASS, KEITH. The Life of King Edward VII. "Teddy's
Boys." London Financial Times, December 28, 1972, p. 10.

MILLER, MERLE. The Sure Thing (Lehmann). "A Novelist to
Watch." London Sunday Times, February 19, 1950, p. 3.

MILNER-GULLAND, ROBIN. Russian Writing Today. "Inside
Stories." London Financial Times, March 17, 1977, p. 35.

MILTON, RODERICK. The Lightning That Struck Me (Hart-Davis).
"No Loving-Kindness." London Sunday Times, July 29, 1951,
p. 3.

_____. The Magic City (Hart-Davis). "Laws of Promise."
London Sunday Times, October 1, 1950, p. 3.

MITCHELL, MARY. Simple Simon (Methuen). "Antiques With the Lid Off." London Sunday Times, August 10, 1952, p. 3.

MITFORD, NANCY. Love in a Cold Climate (Hamish Hamilton). "Miss Mitford Up to Date." London Sunday Times, July 31, 1949, p. 3.

MITTELHOLZER, EDGAR. A Morning at the Office (Hogarth Press). "Four Exceptional Novels." London Sunday Times, May 14, 1950, p. 3.

_____. Shadows Move Among Them (Peter Nevill). London Sunday Times, April 8, 1951, p. 3.

MIZENER, ARTHUR. The Saddest Story. "Ford the Talent Spotter." London Financial Times, May 11, 1972, p. 29.

MOERS, ELLEN. Literary Women. "Miss Austen Regrets." London Financial Times, July 21, 1977, p. 30.

_____. Two Dreisers: The Man and the Novelist. "Wise, Dumb Ox." London Financial Times, August 6, 1970, p. 8.

MOLLAT, M. AND WOLFF, PHILIPPE. The Popular Revolutions of the Late Middle Ages. "Peasant Power in Turbulent Times." London Financial Times, August 16, 1973, p. 12.

MONNIER, ADRIENNE. The Very Rich Hours of Adrienne Monnier. "When We Were Very Young." London Financial Times, July 9, 1976, p. 29.

MONSARRAT, NICHOLAS. Life Is a Four-Letter Word. V. 2. Breaking Out. "Sweet Smell of Success." London Financial Times, August 27, 1970, p. 8.

MONTHERLANT, HENRY DE. The Boys. "Boys Will be Boys." London Financial Times, April 4, 1974, p. 32.

MOON, PENDERELL. Wavell: The Viceroy's Journal. Edited by P.M. (Oxford University Press). "How We Quit India." London Financial Times, July 5, 1973, p. 39, c. 1.

MOORE, HENRY. Henry Moore Drawings. Selected and introduced by Kenneth Clark. "Dawn of Civilization." London Financial Times, October 17, 1974, p. 23.

MOOREHEAD, ALLAN. Gallipoli (Hamish Hamilton). "Books of the Year-II; Chosen by Eminent Contemporaries." London Sunday Times, December 30, 1956, p. 10.

MORAVIA, ALBERTO. The Conformist (Secker & Warburg). "Unusual Quintet." London Sunday Times, March 9, 1952, p. 3.

_____. Conjugal Love (Secker & Warburg). "Short and Long." London Sunday Times, March 18, 1951, p. 3.

_____. The Woman of Rome (Secker & Warburg). "Robust Realism." London Sunday Times, July 17, 1949, p. 3.

MORGAN, CHARLES. The River Line. London Sunday Times, July 10, 1949, p. 3.

MORGAN, JANET P. The House of Lords and the Labour Government, 1964-1970. "A Look at the Other Place." London Financial Times, May 29, 1975, p. 12.

MORISON, SAMUEL ELIOT. The European Discovery of America: The Northern Voyages A.D. 500-1600. "With the Norsemen to Vinland." London Financial Times, July 22, 1971, p. 10.

MORLEY, CHRISTOPHER. The Man Who Made Friends With Himself (Faber). "Lively Quartet." London Sunday Times, October 30, 1949, p. 3.

MORLEY, ROYSTON. The Desert in the Bed (Methuen). "Quality from America." London Sunday Times, July 9, 1950, p. 3.

MORRIS, JAMES. Heaven's Command. "Imperial Dilemma." London Financial Times, November 7, 1973, p. 40.

MORRIS, WILLIAM. William Morris: Ornamentations and Illustrations. "Victorian Values." London Financial Times, April 11, 1974, p. 18.

MORRISON, N.B. The Hidden Fairing (Hogarth). "Plot or No Plot?" London Sunday Times, January 14, 1951, p. 3.

MORTIMER, JOHN. Answer Yes or No (Bodley Head). "A Matter for Pride." London Sunday Times, May 28, 1950, p. 3.

MORTON, FREDERIC. The Darkness Below (Secker & Warburg). "Rough Stuff." London Sunday Times, January 28, 1951, p. 3.

MOSS, CYNTHIA. Portraits in the Wild: Animal Behavior in East Africa. "Beast Watching." London Financial Times, February 19, 1976, p. 29.

The Most Gracious Speeches to Parliament. Edited by F.S.W. Craig. "No. 10 People." London Financial Times, December 18, 1975, p. 16.

MUDFORD, PETER. Birds of a Different Plumage. "Ringside Views." London Financial Times, August 8, 1974, p. 12.

MUGGERIDGE, MALCOLM. Affairs of the Heart (Hamish Hamilton). "Sentimental Stories." London Sunday Times, December 18, 1949, p. 3.

MULKERNS, VAL. A Time Outworn (Chatto & Windus). "Masks and Faces." London Sunday Times, April 22, 1951, p. 3.

MURASAKI SHIKIBU. The Tale of Genji. "Shining One." London Financial Times, February 17, 1977, p. 28.

MURDOCH, IRIS. The Black Prince (Chatto & Windus). "Woman and Gurus." London Financial Times, March 1, 1973, p. 29.

MURE, DAVID. Practise to Deceive. "Monitoring the Enemy in Wartime." London Financial Times, March 2, 1978, p. 32.

MURRAY, K.M. ELISABETH. Caught in the Webb of Words: James Murray and the Oxford English Dictionary. "Word Men Define." London Financial Times, September 22, 1977, p. 14.

MURRAY, PETER. Architecture of the Renaissance. "Classical Mould." London Financial Times, March 25, 1977, p. 33.

NABOKOV, VLADIMIR. Transparent Things (Weidenfeld & Nicolson). "Poet Maidens." London Financial Times, May 3, 1973, p. 16, c. 1.

NARKISS, BEZALEL. Jewish Art. "Family Ritual." London Financial Times, February 24, 1972, p. 28.

NEILL, ROBERT. Mist Over Pendle (Hutchinson). "Atmospherics." London Sunday Times, May 20, 1951, p. 3.

_____. Moon in Scorpio (Hutchinson). "Salute to a Fine Novelist." London Sunday Times, July 13, 1952, p. 3.

NEUMANN, ROBERT. Insurrection in Poshansk (Hutchinson). "Episode in Siberia." London Sunday Times, June 1, 1952, p. 8.

The New English Bible with the Apocrypha. "The Bible into Modern English." London Financial Times, March 19, 1970, p. 30.

New Oxford Book of English Verse. Edited by Helen Gardner. "Scaling Parnassus." London Financial Times, December 15, 1972, p. 34.

NEWBY, P.H. <u>The Snow Pasture</u> (Cape). "The Visual Gift."
London <u>Sunday Times</u>, January 16, 1949, p. 3.

_____. <u>The Young May Moon</u> (Cape). "Old Brandy." London
<u>Sunday Times</u>, January 22, 1950, p. 3.

NIALL, IAN. <u>Foxhollow</u> (Heinemann). "Real People." London
<u>Sunday Times</u>, September 11, 1949, p. 3.

NICHOL, PETER. <u>Italia, Italia</u>. "Brio and Bayonets." London
<u>Financial Times</u>, February 7, 1974, p. 26.

NICOLSON, NIGEL. <u>Alex: The Life of Field Marshal Alexander
of Tunis</u>. "Stylish Soldier." London <u>Financial Times</u>,
April 5, 1973, p. 32.

NICOLSON, ROBERT. <u>The Gradual Day</u> (Constable). "Conflicts."
London <u>Sunday Times</u>, June 25, 1950, p. 3.

NIEVO, IPPOLITO. <u>The Castle of Fratta</u>. Translated by L.F.
Edwards. London <u>Sunday Times</u>, November 24, 1957, p. 8.

NILIN, PAREL. <u>Cruelty</u> (Foreign Languages Publishing House,
Moscow). "Books of the Year." London <u>Sunday Times Magazine
Section</u>, December 28, 1958, p. 11.

NORTHCOTT, CECIL. <u>David Livingstone</u> (Lutterworth Press).
"Explorer's World." London <u>Financial Times</u>, May 17,
1973, p. 31, c. 1.

NORWICH, JOHN JULIUS. <u>Venice: The Rise to Empire</u>. "Holding
the Gorgeous East in Fee." London <u>Financial Times</u>, December
1, 1977, p. 33.

NUNN, E. WESTBY. <u>The House in Siemenstrasse</u> (Staples).
"Local Knowledge." London <u>Sunday Times</u>, December 30,
1951, p. 3.

O'CONNOR, FRANK. <u>Traveller's Samples</u> (Macmillan). "Stout-
Hearted Stories." London <u>Sunday Times</u>, February 25, 1951,
p. 3.

O'CONNOR, JOSEPH. <u>The Norwayman</u> (Faber). "The Novelist's
Ear." London <u>Sunday Times</u>, October 2, 1949, p. 3.

ODELL, ROBIN. <u>Exhumation of a Murder</u>. "A Drop of Arsenic."
London <u>Financial Times</u>, April 10, 1975, p. 32.

O'DYLEY, ELIZABETH. <u>The Mired Horse</u> (Michael Joseph).
"Witch-Hunting Today." London <u>Sunday Times</u>, December 16,
1951, p. 3.

O'FLAHERTY, LIAM. Insurrection (Gollancz). "Wild Men." London Sunday Times, November 5, 1950, p. 3.

OLDENBOURG, ZOE. The Corner-Stone. London Sunday Times, November 14, 1954, p. 5.

_____. The World Is Not Enough (Gollancz). "An Outstanding Novel." London Sunday Times, January 30, 1949, p. 3.

ONIONS, OLIVER. A Penny for the Harp (Michael Joseph). "A Visit to Turkey." London Sunday Times, January 13, 1952, p. 3.

OPPENHEIMER, J.R. The Flying Trapeze: Three Crises for Physicists. New York Herald Tribune Book Review, November 29, 1964, p. 3.

OUOLOGUEM, YAMBO. Bound to Violence. "Angry African." London Financial Times, July 29, 1971, p. 10.

OZICK, CYNTHIA. The Pagan Rabbi. "Two Discoveries." London Financial Times, July 20, 1972, p. 31.

PACHAI, BRIDGLAL. Livingstone: Man of Africa (Longman). "Explorer's World." London Financial Times, May 17, 1973, p. 31, c. 1.

PAGE, NORMAN. Wilkie Collins: The Critical Heritage. "Seeker After Sensation." London Financial Times, December 19, 1974, p. 10.

PAINTER, GEORGE D. Chateaubriand: V. 1: The Looked for Tempests. "Free Spirit." London Financial Times, November 3, 1977, p. 15.

_____. William Caxton: A Quincentenary Biography. "Master Printer." London Financial Times, October 15, 1976, p. 20.

PAKINGTON, HUMPHREY. Young William Washbourne (Chatto & Windus). "Writing in Exile." London Sunday Times, December 11, 1949, p. 3.

PALEOLOGUE, MAURICE. An Ambassador's Memoirs, 1914-1917 (Hutchinson). "Suicide of the Old World." London Financial Times, September 13, 1973, p. 30, c. 1.

PANOVA, VERA. The Factory (Putnam). "Productivity." London Sunday Times, February 5, 1950, p. 3.

_____. The Train (Putnam). "Action and Analysis." London Sunday Times, January 9, 1949, p. 3.

PARGETER, EDITH. <u>Holiday With Violence</u> (Heinemann). "Salute to a Fine Novelist." London <u>Sunday Times</u>, July 13, 1952, p. 3.

PARKER, DEREK AND PARKER, JULIA. <u>The Compleat Lover</u>. "Boy Meets Girl." London <u>Financial Times</u>, December 7, 1972, p. 32.

PARKER, T.H.L. <u>John Calvin</u>. "Civil Servant of God." London <u>Financial Times</u>, December 31, 1975, p. 13.

PARRY, DENNIS. <u>Fair House of Joy</u> (Hale). "Laws of Promise." London <u>Sunday Times</u>, October 1, 1950, p. 3.

PARTRIDGE, ERIC. <u>A Dictionary of Catch Phrases</u>. "Word Men Define." London <u>Financial Times</u>, September 22, 1977, p. 14.

PASSMORE, JOHN. <u>Man's Responsibility for Nature</u>. "When to Conserve?" London <u>Financial Times</u>, May 2, 1974, p. 28.

PATERSON, NEIL. <u>Behold Thy Daughter</u> (Hodder & Stoughton). "A Remarkable Novel." London <u>Sunday Times</u>, July 23, 1950, p. 3.

PAUL, PHYLLIS. <u>Camilla</u> (Heinemann). "Another Jumbo." London <u>Sunday Times</u>, November 13, 1949, p. 3.

_____. <u>Constancy</u> (Heinemann). "Masks and Faces." London <u>Sunday Times</u>, April 22, 1951, p. 3.

PEARSON, JOHN. <u>Edward the Rake</u>. "Tum-Tum." London <u>Financial Times</u>, May 1, 1975, p. 32.

PEARSON, LESTER B. <u>Memoirs, 1897-1948: Through Diplomacy to Politics</u>. "Dry Canadian." London <u>Financial Times</u>, August 9, 1973, p. 10.

<u>The Pelican Book of English Prose</u>. V. 1, 2. "Our Prose Heritage." London <u>Financial Times</u>, February 5, 1970, p. 24.

PENN, MARGARET. <u>The Foolish Virgin</u> (Cape). "A Charming Heroine." London <u>Sunday Times</u>, March 25, 1951, p. 3.

PEPYS, SAMUEL. <u>The Diary of Samuel Pepys: V. 1-3</u>. Edited by Robert Latham and William Matthews. "Pepys Deciphered." London <u>Financial Times</u>, November 12, 1970, p. 15.

PEROWNE, BARRY. <u>Raffles Revisited</u>. "Raffles Rides Again." London <u>Financial Times</u>, April 3, 1975, p. 34.

PETER, MARGOT. Unquiet Soul. "In Old New York." London
Financial Times, November 7, 1975, p. 14.

PETERS, FRITZ. The World Next Door (Gollancz). "Old Brandy."
London Sunday Times, January 22, 1950, p. 3.

PETTAVEL, JOHN. The Good Samaritan (Hand and Flower Press).
"The Man Behind the Story." London Sunday Times, February
24, 1952, p. 3.

PHILLIPPE, C.L. Marie Donadieu. Translated by Violet Hudson
(Grey Walls Press). "A Minor Classic?" London Sunday Times,
January 8, 1950, p. 3.

PICKERING, GEORGE. Creative Malady. "Happily Ill." London
Financial Times, September 26, 1974, p. 32.

PLATONOV, ANDREI. The Fierce and Beautiful World. "The
White and the Red." London Financial Times, February 12,
1971, p. 27.

PLUMB, J.H. The Making of a Statesman. V. 2: The King's
Minister. "Odour of Man." London Financial Times,
September 28, 1972, p. 14.

_____. Sir Robert Walpole (Cresset Press). "Books of the
Year-II; Chosen by Eminent Contemporaries." London Sunday
Times, December 30, 1956, p. 10.

POE, EDGAR ALLEN. Comic Tales of Edgar Allen Poe. Edited
by Angus Wolfe Murray. "Extravagant Poe." London
Financial Times, January 3, 1974, p. 32.

POPE-HENNESSY, JAMES. Anthony Trollope. "Beyond Barchester."
London Financial Times, November 4, 1971, p. 16.

_____. The Houses of Parliament. "All in Miniature." London
Financial Times, April 17, 1975, p. 16.

PORTER, H.C. Reformation and Reaction in Tudor Cambridge
(Cambridge University Press). "Books of the Year." London
Sunday Times Magazine Section. December 28, 1958, p. 11.

POUND, REGINALD. A.P. Herbert. "Men of Letters." London
Financial Times, September 9, 1976, p. 34.

POWER, CRAWFORD. The Encounter (Eyre & Spottiswoode). "No
Loving-Kindness." London Sunday Times, July 29, 1951, p. 3.

POWYS, JOHN COWPER. <u>Porius</u> (MacDonald). "Pestilent Plants." London <u>Sunday Times</u>, August 26, 1951, p. 3.

PRATOLINI, VASCO. <u>A Hero of Today</u> (Hamish Hamilton). "Stout-Hearted Stories." London <u>Sunday Times</u>, February 25, 1951, p. 3.

_____. <u>A Tale of Santa Croce</u> (Peter Owen). "Facts as Well as Fiction." London <u>Sunday Times</u>, June 15, 1952, p. 11.

PRESCOTT, H.F.M. <u>The Man on a Donkey</u>. Two vols. (Eyre & Spottiswoode). "The Pilgrimage of Grace." London <u>Sunday Times</u>, March 23, 1952, p. 3.

PRICE, DON K. <u>Government and Science: Their Dynamic Relation in American Democracy</u>. "Scientists in America." <u>Spectator</u>, 193, no. 6576 (July 2, 1954) 29-30.

PRIESTLEY, J.B. <u>The Magicians</u>. London <u>Sunday Times</u>, February 21, 1954, p. 5.

_____. <u>Thoughts in the Wilderness</u>. London <u>Sunday Times</u>, November 17, 1957, p. 8.

PROKOSCH, FREDERIC. <u>Storm and Echo</u> (Faber). "Real People." London <u>Sunday Times</u>, September 11, 1949, p. 3.

PROLE, LOZANIA. <u>Our Dearest Emma</u> (Museum Press). "Eye on the Ball." London <u>Sunday Times</u>, December 25, 1949, p. 3.

PRYCE-JONES, DAVID. <u>Unity Mitford: A Quest</u>. "Adolf's Admirer." London <u>Financial Times</u>, November 11, 1976, p. 14.

PUDNEY, JOHN. <u>The Accomplice</u> (Bodley Head). "A Gifted Writer." London <u>Sunday Times</u>, November 19, 1950, p. 3.

_____. <u>Hero of a Summer's Day</u> (Bodley Head). "Collapse in Burma." London <u>Sunday Times</u>, December 2, 1951, p. 3.

QUENEAU, RAYMOND. <u>Pierrot</u> (Lehmann). "A Gifted Writer." London <u>Sunday Times</u>, November 19, 1950, p. 3.

QUENNELL, PETER. <u>The Marble Foot</u>. "Vanishing I." London <u>Financial Times</u>, September 30, 1976, p. 14.

RAMUZ, C.-F. <u>When the Mountain Fell</u> (Eyre & Spottiswoode). "A Varied Trio." London <u>Sunday Times</u>, June 19, 1948, p. 3.

RANSOME, ARTHUR. <u>The Autobiography of Arthur Ransome</u>. Edited by Rupert Hart-Davis. "Men of Letters." London <u>Financial Times</u>, September 9, 1976, p. 34.

RAPHEL, CHAIM. A Feast of History. "Family Ritual." London Financial Times, February 24, 1972, p. 28.

RATHBONE, IRENE. The Seeds of Time (Faber). "Living People." London Sunday Times, November 30, 1952, p. 5.

RAY, GORDON N. H.G. Wells and Rebecca West. "The Invisible Woman." London Financial Times, November 28, 1974, p. 30.

RAYMOND, ERNEST. The Chalice and the Sword (Cassell). "Inside Hollywood." London Sunday Times, December 14, 1952, p. 5.

_____. Gentle Greaves (Cassell). "Sentimental Stories." London Sunday Times, December 18, 1949, p. 3.

READ, DONALD. Edwardian England, 1901-1915. "Teddy's Boys." London Financial Times, December 28, 1972, p. 10.

REDINGER, RUBY V. George Eliot: The Emergent Self. "On The Floss." London Financial Times, April 29, 1976, p. 37.

REED, V.S. New Day (Heinemann). "English, French, Jamaican." London Sunday Times, March 5, 1950, p. 3.

REES, GORONWY. A Chapter of Accidents. "Friend to Burgess." London Financial Times, February 17, 1972, p. 22.

REITH, J.C.W. R. The Reith Diaries. Edited by Charles Stuart. "Wrath of Reith." London Financial Times, September 18, 1975, p. 16.

REMARQUE, ERICH MARIA. Spark of Life (Hutchinson). "A Rising Reputation." London Sunday Times, September 21, 1952, p. 5.

RICHARDSON, JOANNA. Enid Starkie. "Restless Spirit." London Financial Times, August 23, 1973, p. 26.

_____. Verlaine. "Bohemian and Bourgeois." London Financial Times, May 20, 1971, p. 12.

_____. Victoria and Albert. "Victoria's Loves." London Financial Times, May 26, 1977, p. 10.

RIDLEY, JASPER. Lord Palmerston. "Pam's Progress." London Financial Times, November 19, 1970, p. 14.

ROACH, J.P.C. The Victoria History of the County of Cambridge. V. 3: The City and the University of Cambridge. "Lessons from Cambridge." New Statesman, 57 (March 21, 1959) 406-08.

ROBBINS, LORD. Autobiography of an Economist. "Classical Virtues." London Financial Times, September 16, 1971, p. 10.

RIEFF, PHILLIP. Fellow Teachers. "Parochial Spires." London Financial Times, February 27, 1975, p. 32.

RITCHIE, CHARLES. The Siren Years: Undiplomatic Diaries, 1937-1945. "World Ago." London Financial Times, January 16, 1975, p. 11.

ROBERTS, J.M. The Hutchinson History of the World. London Financial Times, January 7, 1977, p. 19.

ROBERTS, KENNETH. Captain Caution (Collins). "Action and Analysis." London Sunday Times, January 19, 1949, p. 3.

ROBEY, KINLEY. The King, the Press and the People. "Tum-Tum." London Financial Times, May 1, 1975, p. 32.

ROBINSON, GEOFFREY. Hedingham Harvest. "Rustic Joys." London Financial Times, December 23, 1977, p. 13.

ROBINSON, HENRY MORTON. The Cardinal (Macdonald). "Short and Long." London Sunday Times, March 18, 1951, p. 3.

ROBINSON, KENNETH. Wilkie Collins. "Seeker of Sensation." London Financial Times, December 19, 1974, p. 10.

ROE, IVAN. The Green Tree and the Dry (Heinemann). "A Matter for Pride." London Sunday Times, May 28, 1950, p. 3.

ROMILLY, GILES. Christina Claimed. "A Matter of Pace." London Sunday Times, June 3, 1951, p. 3.

ROOKE, DAPHNE. A Grove of Fewer Trees (Cape). "Short and Long." London Sunday Times, March 18, 1951, p. 3.

ROSE, KENNETH. The Later Cecils. "Solidarity and Single-Mindedness of the Cecils." London Financial Times, July 3, 1975, p. 10.

ROSKILL, STEPHEN. Hankey: Man of Secrets. V. 1: 1877-1918. "Inside the Cabinet." London Financial Times, April 16, 1970, p. 8.

_____. Hankey: Man of Secrets. V. 3: 1931–1936. "Public Servant's Private Face." London Financial Times, May 31, 1974, p. 38.

ROSSI, JEAN BAPTISTE. The False Start (Secker & Warburg). "A Home Disrupted." London Sunday Times, July 15, 1951, p. 3.

ROSTEN, LEO. People I Have Loved, Known or Admired. "Sentiment and Sarcasm." London Financial Times, August 5, 1971, p. 10.

ROTHENBURG, GUNTHER. The Art of Warfare in the Age of Napoleon. "Under Fire." London Financial Times, February 9, 1978, p. 28.

ROTHSCHILD, LORD. Meditations of a Broomstick. "Sweeping Mind." London Financial Times, September 15, 1977, p. 35.

ROWDON, MAURICE. The Fall of Venice. London Financial Times, March 12, 1970, p. 12.

ROWSE, A.L. Appeasement: A Study in Political Decline, 1933–39. "All Souls and Appeasement." Listener, 65 (April 27, 1961) 747.

_____. Appeasement: A Study in Political Decline, 1933–39 (Norton). "Englishmen of Power and Place on the Road That Led to Munich." New York Times Book Review, December 24, 1961, p.

_____. Matthew Arnold: Poet and Prophet. "Celtic Arnold." London Financial Times, December 23, 1976, p. 10.

ROY, GABRIELLE. Where Nests the Water Hen (Heinemann). "Putting Down the Thugs." London Sunday Times, August 24, 1952, p. 5.

RUDE, GEORGE. Robespierre. "Father of the Revolution." London Financial Times, September 4, 1975, p. 11.

RUESCH, HANS. Top of the World (Gollancz). "Character Drawing." London Sunday Times, September 17, 1950, p. 3.

RUNBECK, MARGARET LEE. Time for Love (Davies). "Reflected Glory." London Sunday Times, August 20, 1950, p. 3.

SACKVILLE-WEST, E. Simpson (Weidenfeld & Nicolson). "A Novel Revised." Spectator, 187, no. 6422 (July 27, 1951) 136–38.

SALISBURY, H.E. The 900 Days; The Siege of Leningrad (Harper & Row). New York Times Book Review, January 26, 1969, p. 1.

SALTER, ELIZABETH AND HARPER, ALLANAH. Edith Sitwell.
"When We Were Very Young." London Financial Times,
July 9, 1976, p. 29.

SANDERSON, MICHAEL. The Universities in the Nineteenth
Century. "Parochial Spires." London Financial Times,
February 27, 1975, p. 32.

SANSOM, WILLIAM. The Face of Innocence (Hogarth). "Masks
and Faces." London Sunday Times, April 22, 1951, p. 3.

SAROYAN, WILLIAM. The Assyrian, and Other Stories (Faber).
"Mauriac's Way." London Sunday Times, February 11, 1951,
p. 3.

SARTON, MAY. Shadow of a Man (Cresset Press). "To Dream
Again." London Sunday Times, April 20, 1952, p. 3.

SARTRE, J.P. Iron in the Soul (Hamish Hamilton). "Intelligent
Mr. Sartre." London Sunday Times, August 6, 1950, p. 3.

SAYRE, ANNE. Rosalind Franklin and DNA. "The Corridors of
DNA." New York Review of Books, 22, no. 18 (November
13, 1975) 3-4.

SCHEINFELD, AMRAM. You and Heredity. "The Truth of Genetics."
Discovery, N.S., 2, no. 21 (December 1939) 617-19.

SCHILPP, ARTHUR PAUL. Albert Einstein, Philosopher-Scientist.
"The Moral Grandeur of Einstein." New Statesman, 59,
no. 1515 (March 26, 1960) 453-54.

SCHMIDT, MICHAEL AND LINDOP, GREVEL. British Poetry Since
1960: A Critical Survey. "Scaling Parnassus." London
Financial Times, December 15, 1972, p. 34.

SCHOENBAUM, S. Shakespeare's Lives. "Shakespeare." London
Financial Times, January 1, 1971, p. 10.

SCOTT, J.D. The End of an Old Song. "Novels of 1954:
Counter-Revolution." London Sunday Times, December 26, 1954,
p. 5.

_____. The Margin (Pilot Press). "Miss Mitford Up to Date."
London Sunday Times, July 31, 1949, p. 3.

_____. The Way to Glory (Eyre & Spottiswoode). "Summer in
Paris." London Sunday Times, May 18, 1952, p. 9.

SCOTT, J.M. The Touch of the Nettle (Hodder & Stoughton). "Local Knowledge." London Sunday Times, December 30, 1951, p. 3.

SCOTT, RACHEL. A Wedding Man is Nicer than Cats, Miss. "Yorkshire Pakistanis at School." London Financial Times, November 25, 1971, p. 14.

SCOTT, WARWICK. The Doomsday-Story (Davies). "Episode in Siberia." London Sunday Times, June 1, 1952, p. 8.

_____. Image in the Dust (Davies). "The Seeing Eye." London Sunday Times, July 1, 1951, p. 3.

SEALE, PATRICK AND MCCONVILLE, MAUREEN. Philby: The Long Road to Moscow (Hamish Hamilton). "Mind of a Spy." London Financial Times, July 26, 1973, p. 33, c. 1.

SEARLE, JOHN. The Campus War. "Boys and Girls and Bricks." London Financial Times, August 24, 1972, p. 14.

SEBASTIAN, ANNA. The Dreams (Cape). "Productivity." London Sunday Times, February 5, 1950, p. 3.

SECHANT, OLIVIER. The Dead Won't Know (Hart-Davis). "A Visit to Turkey." London Sunday Times, January 13, 1952, p. 3.

SEGRE, EMILIO. Enrico Fermi: Physicist. "Elder Scientists." London Financial Times, March 16, 1972, p. 24.

SERGE, VICTOR. The Case of Comrade Tulayev (Hamish Hamilton). London Sunday Times, April 8, 1951, p. 3.

SEWELL, ELIZABETH. The Dividing of Time (Chatto & Windus). "Games of Hide and Seek." London Sunday Times, August 12, 1951, p. 3.

SHAW, G.B. The Bodley Head Bernard Shaw: Collected Plays with their Prefaces. V. 1. "Chaos of Clear Ideas." London Financial Times, June 25, 1970, p. 8.

_____. Shaw: An Autobiography, 1856-1898. Selected from his writings by Stanley Weintraub. "Chaos of Clear Ideas." London Financial Times, June 25, 1970, p. 8.

SHAW, IRWIN. The Troubled Air (Cape). "Witch-Hunting Today." London Sunday Times, December 16, 1951, p. 3.

_____. The Young Lions (Cassell). "Another Jumbo." London Sunday Times, November 13, 1949, p. 3.

SHEEAN, VINCENT. A Certain Rich Man (Cassell). "Real People." London Sunday Times, September 11, 1949, p. 3.

SHERIDAN, JACK. Mamie Brandon (Home and Van Thal). "Good Short Stories." London Sunday Times, August 14, 1949, p. 3.

SHUTE, NEVIL. A Town Like Alice (Heinemann). "More Mauriac." London Sunday Times, June 11, 1950, p. 3.

SIMENON, GEORGES. Chit of a Girl (Routledge & K. Paul). "Simenon's Best Yet." London Sunday Times, June 26, 1949, p. 3.

_____. The House by the Canal (Routledge & K. Paul). "The Pilgrimage of Grace." London Sunday Times, March 23, 1952, p. 3.

_____. Maigret and the Black Sheep. "Digging Up Clues." London Financial Times, February 5, 1976, p. 16.

_____. Maigret on Holiday (Routledge & K. Paul). "In the Jungle." London Sunday Times, December 3, 1950, p. 3.

_____. Three Beds in Manhattan. "Digging Up Clues." London Financial Times, February 5, 1976, p. 16.

SIMEONS, A.T.W. The Mask of a Lion (Gollancz). "Newcomers." London Sunday Times, October 19, 1952, p. 5.

SIMON, EDITH. The Golden Hand (Cassell). "Most Musical, Most Melancholy." London Sunday Times, June 29, 1952, p. 5.

SINCLAIR, UPTON. One Clear Call (Werner Laurie). "Cult of the Atrocious." London Sunday Times, October 16, 1949, p. 3.

SINGH, KHUSHWANT. The Mark of Vishnu (Saturn Press). "Laws of Promise." London Sunday Times, October 1, 1950, p. 3.

SLUNG, MICHELLE B. Crime on Her Mind. "Digging Up Clues." London Financial Times, February 5, 1976, p. 16.

SMITH, GODFREY. The Flaw in the Crystal. "Novels of 1954: Counter-Revolution." London Sunday Times, December 26, 1954, p. 5.

SOMMERFIELD, JOHN. The Adversaries (Heinemann). "The Man Behind the Story." London Sunday Times, February 24, 1952, p. 3.

SPACKS, PATRICIA MEYER. The Female Imagination. "Second Sex." London Financial Times, September 23, 1976, p. 13.

SPEAIGHT, ROBERT. George Eliot. "George Eliot's Return." London Sunday Times, January 17, 1954, p. 5.

SPEER, ALBERT. Inside the Third Reich. "Architect of Evil." London Financial Times, October 15, 1970, p. 30.

_____. Spandau: The Secret Diaries. "Twenty Years Inside." London Financial Times, March 23, 1976, p. 15.

SPENCE, JONATHAN D. Emperor of China: Self-Portrait of K'ang Hsi. "Magnificent Manchu." London Financial Times, December 12, 1974, p. 12.

SPEWACK, SAMUEL. The Busy, Busy People (Macmillan). "Robust Realism." London Sunday Times, July 17, 1949, p. 3.

SPURLING, HILARY. Ivy When Young: The Early Life of Ivy Compton-Burnett, 1884-1919. "Maiden Lady." London Financial Times, March 15, 1974, p. 30.

STANDISH, ROBERT. Gentleman of China (Davies). "Love and Hate." London Sunday Times, August 28, 1949, p. 3.

_____. Storm Centre (Davies). "Games of Hide and Seek." London Sunday Times, August 12, 1951, p. 3.

STANSKY, PETER AND ABRAHAM, WILLIAM. The Unknown Orwell. "Orwell Up for Air." London Financial Times, October 19, 1972, p. 28.

STEELE, MAX. Debby (Secker & Warburg). "Plot or No Plot?" London Sunday Times, January 14, 1951, p. 3.

STEGNER, WALLACE. Angle of Repose. "Humans Without Hope." London Financial Times, September 30, 1971, p. 36.

_____. The Big Rock Candy Mountain (Hammond, Hammond). "Quality from America." London Sunday Times, July 9, 1950, p. 3.

_____. The Preacher and the Slave (Hammond, Hammond). "A Matter of Pace." London Sunday Times, June 3, 1951, p. 3.

_____. The Women on the Wall (Hammond, Hammond). "Millionaire Among the Miners." London Sunday Times, May 4, 1952, p. 6.

STEINBECK, JOHN. Steinbeck: A Life in Letters. Edited by Elaine Steinbeck and Robert Wallsten. "Success Saga." London Financial Times, May 7, 1976, p. 12.

STEINER, GEORGE. In Bluebeard's Castle: Some Notes Towards the Redefinition of Culture. "Steiner's Manifesto." London Financial Times, October 14, 1971, p. 14.

STEINER, ZARA S. Britain and the Origin of the First World War. "Under Fire." London Financial Times, February 9, 1978, p. 28.

STERN, FRITZ. Gold and Iron: Bismarck, Bleichroder, and the Building of the German Empire. "Golden Outsider." London Financial Times, April 15, 1977, p. 37.

STERN, G.B. Ten Days of Christmas (Collins). "In the Jungle." London Sunday Times, December 3, 1950, p. 3.

STEVENSON, FRANCES. Lloyd George: A Diary by Frances Stevenson. Edited by A.J.P. Taylor. "Political Heroine." London Financial Times, August 26, 1971, p. 8.

STEWART, GEORGE R. Earth Abides (Gollancz). "Bees in the Bonnet." London Sunday Times, July 16, 1950, p. 3.

_____. Fire (Gollancz). "A Charming Heroine." London Sunday Times, March 25, 1951, p. 3.

STOLL, DENNIS GRAY. Memory is the Scar (Gollancz). "The Novelist's Ear." London Sunday Times, October 2, 1949, p. 3.

STORR, ANTHONY. The Dynamics of Creation. "Perchance Not to Dream." London Financial Times, September 7, 1972, p. 12.

STOUT, REX. A Family Affair. "Exit Nero." London Financial Times, July 22, 1976, p. 12.

STRACHEY, ISOBEL. The Younger Sister (Cape). "Rough Stuff." London Sunday Times, January 28, 1951, p. 3.

STRACHEY, JULIA. The Man on the Pier (Lehmann). "A Memorable Story." London Sunday Times, September 9, 1951, p. 3.

STRONG, ROY. Nicholas Hilliard. "All in Miniature." London Financial Times, April 17, 1975, p. 16.

STUFFS, JEAN. Dear Laura. "Crop of Crimes." London Financial Times, April 12, 1973, p. 37.

SULZBERGER, C.L. The Last of the Giants. "Our Man on the Spot." London Financial Times, April 27, 1972, p. 34.

SUMPTION, JONATHAN. Albigensian Crusade. "Heretics Committed to the Flames." London Financial Times, April 6, 1978, p. 28.

SUPERVIELLE, JULES. The Survivor (Secker & Warburg). "Collapse in Burma." London Sunday Times, December 2, 1951, p. 3.

SUTHERLAND, J.A. Fiction and the Fiction Industry. "Feast or Famine." London Financial Times, April 13, 1978, p. 18.

SUYIN, HAN. The Morning Deluge: Mao Tse-Tung and the Chinese Revolution, 1883-1954. "Mao Then and Now." London Financial Times, November 9, 1972, p. 29.

SWARTHOUT, GLENDON. The Shootist. "Case for the Cliffhanger." London Financial Times, May 15, 1975, p. 18.

SWINNERTON, FRANK. The Doctor's Wife Comes to Stay (Heinemann). "Captivating Satire." London Sunday Times, November 27, 1949, p. 3.

_____. Master Jim Probity (Hutchinson). "The Love Story of Lydia." London Sunday Times, October 5, 1952, p. 5.

SYKES, CHRISTOPHER. Evelyn Waugh. "Handfuls of Dust." London Financial Times, October 1975, p. 16.

_____. Nancy. "Tempestuous Lady." London Financial Times, October 5, 1972, p. 14.

SYKES, JOHN. The Romantic Wife (Werner Laurie). "Inside Hollywood." London Sunday Times, December 14, 1952, p. 5.

SYLVESTER, A.J. Life with Lloyd George. Edited by Colin Cross. "In and Out of the Wilderness." London Financial Times, June 5, 1975, p. 34.

SYMON, JULIAN. Bloody Murder: From the Detective Story to the Crime Novel: A History. "Little Gray Cells." London Financial Times, April 6, 1972, p. 24.

TAYLOR, A.J.P. Beaverbrook. "Absentee Presence." London Financial Times, June 29, 1972, p. 33.

TAYLOR, ELIZABETH. <u>Blaming</u>. "Second Sex." London <u>Financial Times</u>, September 23, 1976, p. 13.

TEILHET, HILDEGARDE. <u>Rim of Terror</u> (Gollancz). "Reflected Glory." London <u>Sunday Times</u>, August 20, 1950, p. 3.

TEMPLETON, EDITH. <u>The Island of Desire</u> (Eyre & Spottiswoode). "Salute to a Fine Novelist." London <u>Sunday Times</u>, July 13, 1952, p. 3.

TERRAINE, JOHN. <u>The Road to Passchendaele</u>. "Under Fire." London <u>Financial Times</u>, February 9, 1978, p. 28.

THEROUX, PAUL. <u>The Family Arsenal</u>. "Son of Burr." London <u>Financial Times</u>, April 1, 1976, p. 28.

_____. <u>Fong and the Indians</u>. "Son of Burr." London <u>Financial Times</u>, April 1, 1976, p. 28.

THIRKELL, ANGELA. <u>County Chronicle</u> (Hamish Hamilton). "Character Drawing." London <u>Sunday Times</u>, September 17, 1950, p. 3.

THOMAS, GWYN. <u>Now Lead Us Home</u> (Gollancz). "Millionaire Among the Miners." London <u>Sunday Times</u>, May 4, 1952, p. 6.

_____. <u>The World Cannot Hear You</u> (Gollancz). "Florentine Summer." London <u>Sunday Times</u>, June 17, 1951, p. 3.

THOMPSON, R.W. <u>Churchill and Morton</u>. "Strange Bedfellows." London <u>Financial Times</u>, August 12, 1976, p. 10.

THOMSON, DAVID. <u>Scott's Men</u>. "Polar Peril." London <u>Financial Times</u>, August 4, 1977, p. 8.

THOMSON, GEORGE MALCOLM. <u>Sir Francis Drake</u>. "El Draque." London <u>Financial Times</u>, April 13, 1972, p. 36.

THURLEY, GEOFFREY. <u>The Dickens Myth: Its Genesis and Structure</u>. "The Greatest?" London <u>Financial Times</u>, September 16, 1976, p. 15.

THWAITE, ANN. <u>Waiting for the Party: The Life of Frances Hodgson Burnett</u>. "Causes of Mirth." London <u>Financial Times</u>, June 6, 1974, p. 30.

TILSLEY, FRANK. <u>The Jungle of Your Heart</u> (Eyre & Spottiswoode). "Conflicts." London <u>Sunday Times</u>, June 25, 1950, p. 3.

TOFFLER, ALVIN. Future Shock. "Never Before." London Financial Times, October 8, 1970, p. 26.

TOLSTOY, LEO. The Law of Love and the Law of Violence. "Tolstoy at 80." London Financial Times, February 13, 1970, p. 26.

TOMALIN, CLAIRE. The Life and Death of Mary Wollstonecraft. "Radical Wife." London Financial Times, September 5, 1974, p. 13.

TOOLE, MILLIE. Farewell to the Family (Dent). "Home Disrupted." London Sunday Times, July 15, 1951, p. 3.

_____. The Man at the Door (Dent). "Summer in Paris." London Sunday Times, May 18, 1952, p. 9.

TOULMIN, STEPHEN AND GOODFIELD, JUNE. The Fabric of the Heavens. "The Universe of Modern Man." Observer, January 22, 1961, p. 28.

TOURVILLE, ANNE DE. Jabadao. Translated by Mervyn Savill (Britannicus Liber). "Newcomers." London Sunday Times, October 19, 1952, p. 5.

TOYNBEE, ARNOLD. Cities on the Move. "World's Eye View." London Financial Times, September 3, 1970, p. 8.

TRAVEN. B. The Rebellion of the Hanged (Hale). "First Novel Success." London Sunday Times, January 27, 1952, p. 3.

TREFUSIS, VIOLET. Pirates at Play (Michael Joseph). "Conflicts." London Sunday Times, June 25, 1950, p. 3.

TREVELYAN, RALEIGH. Princes Under the Volcano. "Sicilian Splendours." London Financial Times, January 19, 1973, p. 12.

TREVOR, MERIOL. The Arnolds. "House and Its Head." London Financial Times, April 19, 1973, p. 39.

TREVOR, WILLIAM. Elizabeth Alone (Bodley Head). "Boer Blockbuster." London Financial Times, November 22, 1973, p. 30, c. 1.

TRICKETT, RACHEL. The Return Home (Constable). "Divided Households." London Sunday Times, July 27, 1952, p. 5.

TROLLOPE, THOMAS ADOLPHUS. What I Remember. Edited by
Herbert van Thal. "Background to Trollope." London
Financial Times, January 31, 1974, p. 25.

TROYAT, HENRI. Gogol. "Impossible Gogol." London Financial
Times, March 20, 1975, p. 30.

_____. My Father's House (Macmillan). "Living People."
London Sunday Times, November 30, 1952, p. 5.

TRUMAN, MARGARET. Harry S. Truman (Hamish Hamilton). "Man
From Missouri." London Financial Times, September 6, 1973,
p. 19, c. 1.

TUOHY, FRANK. Fingers in the Door. "Snapshot Album."
London Financial Times, May 14, 1970, p. 12.

TUTUOLA, AMOS. The Palm-Wine Drinkard (Faber). "Episode in
Siberia." London Sunday Times, June 1, 1952, p. 8.

VAIZEY, JOHN. Capitalism. "Generous Social Critic." London
Financial Times, December 9, 1971, p. 12.

_____. Social Democracy. "Generous Social Critic." London
Financial Times, December 9, 1971, p. 12.

VANSITART, PETER. A Verdict of Treason (Bodley Head).
"Antiques with the Lid Off." London Sunday Times, August
10, 1952, p. 3.

VAUGHAN, MATTHEW. The Discretion of Dominick Ayres. "Exit
Nero." London Financial Times, July 22, 1976, p. 12.

VAUGHAN, RICHARD. Moulded in Earth (Murray). "Short and
Long." London Sunday Times, March 18, 1951, p. 3.

The Victorian Public School. Edited by Brian Simon. "Those
Conquering Heroes." London Financial Times, November 20,
1975, p. 28.

VIDAL, GORE. Burr. "Fallible Father." London Financial
Times, March 21, 1974, p. 15.

_____. 1876. "Son of Burr." London Financial Times, April
1, 1976, p. 28.

VILMORIN, LOUISE DE. Julietta (Harvill Press). "Episode
in Siberia." London Sunday Times, June 1, 1952, p. 8.

WAIN, JOHN. Samuel Johnson. "Sam the Strong." London Financial Times, December 5, 1974, p. 34.

WALKER, PATRICK GORDON. The Cabinet. "Inside the Cabinet." London Financial Times, April 16, 1970, p. 8.

WALL, JOSEPH FRAZIER. Andrew Carnegie. "Man of Steel." London Financial Times, March 11, 1971, p. 14.

WALLENSTEIN, MARCEL. Tuck's Girl (Constable). "Rough Stuff." London Sunday Times, January 28, 1951, p. 3.

WALTARI, MIKA. Michael the Finn (Putnam). "Wild Men." London Sunday Times, November 5, 1950, p. 3.

_____. Sinuhe the Egyptian (Putnam). "Artists in Contrast." London Sunday Times, November 20, 1949, p. 3.

WARD, MARY J. The Professor's Umbrella (Cassell). "Eye on the Ball." London Sunday Times, December 25, 1949, p. 3.

WARNER, REX. Men of Stones (Bodley Head). "Captivating Satire." London Sunday Times, November 27, 1949, p. 3.

WARREN, KATHLEEN. Intruder in the House (Faber). "A Home Disrupted." London Sunday Times, July 15, 1951, p. 3.

WATKINS, ERNEST. Prospect of Canada. "Phase of Expansion." Spectator, 193, no. 6588 (October 1, 1954) 406.

WATNEY, JOHN. The Unexpected Angel (Collins). "Action and Analysis." London Sunday Times, January 9, 1949, p. 3.

WATSON, COLIN. Snobbery with Violence. "Raffles, Wimsey and Co." London Financial Times, July 15, 1971, p. 28.

WATSON, GEORGE. The English Ideology. Studies in the Language of Victorian Politics (Allen Lane). "Sages and Plagues." London Financial Times, March 22, 1973, p. 34, c. 1.

WAUGH, EVELYN. The Diaries of Evelyn Waugh. Edited by Michael Davie. "Temporary Captain." London Financial Times, September 2, 1976, p. 23.

WEDGWOOD, C.V. Oliver Cromwell (Duckworth). "The Protector." London Financial Times, June 7, 1973, p. 17, c. 1.

WEIDMAN, JEROME. The Price is Right (Hammond, Hammond). "Conflicts." London Sunday Times, June 25, 1950, p. 3.

WEINTRAUB, STANLEY. Whistler. "Acting Like Artists." London
Financial Times, August 1, 1974, p. 14.

WELCH, DENTON. A Voice Through a Cloud (Lehmann). "A Brave
Talent." London Sunday Times, March 19, 1950, p. 3.

WELTY, EUDORA. The Golden Apples (Bodley Head). "Fashion."
London Sunday Times, September 3, 1950, p. 3.

WENDT, STEPHEN. Pray Love, Remember (Secker & Warburg).
"A Charming Heroine." London Sunday Times, March 25, 1951,
p. 3.

WEST, ANTHONY. On a Dark Night (Eyre & Spottiswoode). "Cult
of the Atrocious." London Sunday Times, October 16, 1949,
p. 3.

WEST, REBECCA. Rebecca West: A Celebration. Selected from
Her Writings. "West Way." London Financial Times,
December 15, 1977, p. 29.

WHARTON, EDITH. The Age of Innocence. "A Writer of Quality."
Spectator, 190 (March 27, 1953) 384-85.

_____. The House of Mirth. "A Writer of Quality." Spectator,
190 (March 27, 1953) 384-85.

WHITE, ANTONIA. The Sugar House (Eyre & Spottiswoode).
"Divided Households." London Sunday Times, July 27, 1952,
p. 5.

WHITE, MAX. The Man Who Carved from Wood (Hamish Hamilton).
"Murder Most Foul." London Sunday Times, April 2, 1950,
p. 3.

WIENER, NORBERT. I Am a Mathematician. "The Mind of the
Mathematician." New Statesman and Nation, 52, no. 1328
(August 25, 1956) 219-20.

WILDE, OSCAR. The Artist as Critic: Critical Writings of
Oscar Wilde. Edited by Richard Ellmann. "Wilde's
Importance." London Financial Times, March 26, 1970,
p. 12.

WILLIAMS, DAVID. George Meredith. "Victorian Masters."
London Financial Times, September 1, 1977, p. 14.

WILLIAMS, DUNCAN. Trousered Apes: A Study in the Influence
of Literature on Contemporary Society. "Calling a Halt."
London Financial Times, July 1, 1971, p. 12.

WILLIAMS, JOHN. Stoner (Allen Lane). "Good Men and Foes."
London Financial Times, May 24, 1973, p. 20, c. 1.

WILLIAMS, RAYMOND. Culture and Society, 1780-1950 (Chatto &
Windus). "Books of the Year." London Sunday Times Magazine
Section, December 28, 1958, p. 11.

WILLIAMS, TENNESSEE. The Roman Spring of Mrs. Stone (Lehmann).
"A Playwright's Novel." London Sunday Times, December 17,
1950, p. 3.

WILLINGHAM, CALDER. End As a Man (Lehmann). "The Ugliest
Trend." London Sunday Times, February 3, 1952, p. 3.

WILSHIRE, LEWIS. Spring Song. "Five Good Stories." London
Sunday Times, March 11, 1951, p. 3.

WILSON, ANGUS. The Strange Ride of Rudyard Kipling: His Life
and Works. "Triumph or Despair." London Financial Times,
November 10, 1978, p. 28.

_____. Such Darling Dodos, and Other Stories. "A Remarkable
Novel." London Sunday Times, July 23, 1950, p. 3.

_____. The World of Charles Dickens. "Salute to Dickens."
London Financial Times, June 4, 1970, p. 12.

WILSON, EDMUND. Upstate. "Two Critics." London Financial
Times, April 20, 1972, p. 14.

WILSON, HAROLD. The Governance of Britain. "High Office
Hindsight." London Financial Times, November 4, 1976,
p. 27.

WILSON, JOHN. A Life of Sir Henry Campbell-Bannerman.
"Good-Living P.M." London Financial Times, February 1,
1973, p. 14.

WILSON, MITCHELL. A Passion to Know. "As If John Gunther
had Written 'Inside Science'." New York Times Book Review,
June 18, 1972, p. 4.

WITTKOWER, RUDOLF. Palladio and English Palladianism. "Long
Colonnades." London Financial Times, May 16, 1974, p. 14.

WODEHOUSE, P.G. The Old Reliable (Jenkins). "Masks and Faces."
London Sunday Times, April 22, 1951, p. 3.

WOLFF, GEOFFREY. Black Sun: The Brief Transit and Violent
Eclipse of Harry Crosby. "Harry Boy." London Financial
Times, January 13, 1977, p. 29.

WOLFF, ROBERT LEE. Gains and Losses: Novels of Faith and Doubt in Victorian England. "Victorian Masters." London Financial Times, September 1, 1977, p. 14.

WOLLASTON, NICHOLAS. The Tale Bearer. "Two Discoveries." London Financial Times, July 20, 1972, p. 31.

WOODHAM-SMITH, CECIL. Queen Victoria: Her Life and Times. V. 1: 1819-1861. "Victorian Will Power." London Financial Times, October 12, 1972, p. 16.

Words. By Kingsley Amis. . . . [and others] "English as She Is Spoke." London Financial Times, December 4, 1975, p. 29.

Working-Class Stories of the 1890's. "The Likes of Us." London Financial Times, June 17, 1971, p. 24.

WOROSZYLSKI, WIKTOR. The Life of Mayakovsky. "Blissful Dawn." London Financial Times, January 27, 1972, p. 12.

WORSLEY-GOUGH, BARBARA. The Sly Hyena (Michael Joseph). "Games of Hide and Seek." London Sunday Times, August 12, 1951, p. 3.

WORSTHORNE, PEREGRINE. The Socialist Myth. "Romantic Hawk." London Financial Times, April 22, 1971, p. 30.

The Writer's Dilemma. "The Pressures of Society." Times Literary Supplement, no. 3093 (June 9, 1961) 391.

WYATT, WOODROW, ed. English Story. 9th Series (Collins). "Good Short Stories." London Sunday Times, August 14, 1949, p. 3.

WYDENBRUCK, NORA. Placidia's Daughter (Lehmann). "A Rising Reputation." London Sunday Times, September 21, 1952, p. 5.

WYKES, ALAN. Abroad: A Miscellany of English Travel Writing, 1700-1914. "The English on Tour." London Financial Times, January 17, 1974, p. 8.

_____. The Pen-Friend (Duckworth). "A Playwright's Novel." London Sunday Times, December 17, 1950, p. 3.

WYNDHAM, JOHN. The Day of the Triffids (Michael Joseph). "Pestilent Plants." London Sunday Times, August 26, 1951, p. 3.

YEATS, W.B. Ah, Sweet Dancer: W.B. Yeats, Margot Ruddock; A Correspondence. Edited by Roger McHugh. "Poet's Last Dance." London Financial Times, July 23, 1970, p. 22.

_____. Memoirs. Edited by Denis Donoghue. "Come Into the Garden, Maud." London Financial Times, January 11, 1973, p. 10.

ZIEGLER, PHILIP. Melbourne: A Biography of William Lamb, 2nd Viscount Melbourne. "Lord Dalliance." London Financial Times, August 26, 1976, p. 10.

ZOLA, EMILE. Nana. "Great Robust Girl." London Financial Times, June 22, 1972, p. 14.

ZUCKMAYER, CARL. A Part of Myself. "Zuckmayer's Zest." London Financial Times, November 5, 1970, p. 14.

Writings about Snow

Books

B1   HOFF, HARRY SUMMERFIELD. Young People, [by] William Cooper
[i.e. H.S. Hoff]. London: Macmillan, 1958. 359 pp.
        A novel of English provincial life. Its hero,
Swan, is reputedly a portrait of the younger Snow.

B2   _____. C.P. Snow [by] William Cooper [i.e. H.S. Hoff].
London: Published for the British Council by Longmans
Green, 1959. 39 pp.
        One of the earliest books about Snow. Written by
an old friend. Includes critical remarks on Snow's
works up to The Affair as well as a brief discussion
of Snow's concern with the "Two Cultures" problem.
(Bibliographical series of supplements to British
Book News on Writers and their Work, no. 115.)

B3   GREACEN, ROBERT. The World of C.P. Snow. With a bibliography
by Bernard Stone. Lowestoft, Suffolk: Scorpion Press,
1962. 64 pp.
        Greacen's study on pp. 9-39. Stone's bibliography:
pp. 41-64. Includes coverage of the Snow-Leavis affair,
and critical remarks on Snow's works up to and including
The Affair and Science and Government. Stone's bibliography has been superseded both by the work of
Rabinovitz (B251) and Stanton (B328).

B4   HOFF, HARRY SUMMERFIELD. C.P. Snow [by] William Cooper
[i.e. H.S. Hoff]. Rev. ed. London; New York: Longmans,
Green, 1962, 39 pp.
(Bibliographical series of supplements to British
Books News on Writers and their Work, no. 115.)

B5   LEAVIS, FRANK RAYMOND. Two Cultures? The Significance of
C.P. Snow. With an Essay on Sir Charles Snow's Rede
Lecture by Michael Yudkin. London: Chatto & Windus,

1962, 45 pp.
   Reprints of B101, B123.

B6   GREACEN, ROBERT. The World of C.P. Snow. With a bibliography by Bernard Stone. New York: London House &
   Maxwell, 1963, 64 pp.
      Reprint of B3.

B7   HUXLEY, ALDOUS. Literature and Science. New York: Harper,
   1963, 118 pp.
      Huxley, ectomorphic aesthete, untouched by the
   Snovian vision ("bland scientism") and unmoved by
   the Leavisite rejoinder ("one-track, moralistic
   literarism") joyfully sets himself a high agenda:
   "What is the function of literature, what is its
   psychology, what the nature of literary language?
   And how do its function, psychology and language
   differ from the function, psychology and language of
   science?. . . . What would it be profitable, artistically
   speaking, for a twentieth century man of letters to do
   about twentieth-century science?" He concludes that
   literary men would most profit from the study of biology
   and psychology.

B8   KARL, FREDERICK ROBERT. C.P. Snow: The Politics of
   Conscience. With a preface by Harry T. Moore.
   Carbondale: Southern Illinois University Press, 1963.
      One of the early, serious and sustained studies
   on Snow. It should probably be read in conjunction
   with Rabinovitz (B251-B154). See also Karl's later
   writings on Snow as a novelist. (Crosscurrents:
   modern critiques)

B9   LEAVIS, FRANK RAYMOND. Two Cultures? The Significance of
   C.P. Snow. Being the Richmond Lecture. With a New
   Preface for the American Reader. And an Essay on
   Sir Charles Snow's Rede Lecture by Michael Yudkin.
   New York: Pantheon Books, 1963. 64 pp.
      Reprints of B101, B123. See also: B5.

B10   CORNELIUS, DAVID KRAUSE, comp. Cultures in Conflict;
   Perspectives on the Snow-Leavis Controversy [by]
   David K. Cornelius and Edwin St. Vincent. Chicago:
   Scott Foresman, 1964. 179 pp.
      CONTENTS: The Two Cultures [excerpt] by C.P.
   Snow.--Two Cultures? The Significance of C.P. Snow
   [excerpt] by F.R. Leavis.--A Certain Judo Demonstration,
   by John Wain.--Snow vs. Leavis, by Hilary Corke.--
   The Two Cultures: An Editorial [in Spectator].--From
   the Top Drawer and the Bottom, by Anthony West.--

Grounds for Approval, by Richard Wollheim.--The Voice
of Sir Charles, by William F. Buckley.-- A Literary
Defense of the Two Cultures, by Martin Green.--Science,
Literature and Culture; A Comment on the Leavis-Snow
Controversy, by Lionel Trilling.--The New Science, by
Sir Francis Bacon.--Preface to Lyrical Ballads, by
William Wordsworth.--The Four Ages of Poetry, by
Thomas Love Peacock.--On Machine Labour, by John
Ruskin.--Science and Culture, by Thomas Henry Huxley.--
Literature and Science, by Matthew Arnold.--What
Science Is, by Stuart Chase.--How Does a Poem Mean?
by John Ciardi.--The Appreciation of Science as an
End in Itself, by John R. Baker.--Whatever Hope We
Have, by Maxwell Anderson.--Science as an Element in
Culture, by Bertrand Russell.--Why do We Teach Poetry?
by Archibald MacLeish.--Is Life Becoming Happier? by
H.G. Wells.--The Industrial Magnate, by D.H. Lawrence.
--Mechanism and Culture, by James T. Shotwell.--
"1984" Can Be a Good Year, by J. Bronowski.--The Sane
Society, by Erich Fromm.--The Machine Stops. by E.M.
Forster.

B11   GREEN, MARTIN BURGESS. Science and the Shabby Curate of
       Poetry; Essays about the Two Cultures. London:
       Longmans, 1964. 159 pp.
            "His book consists of nine essays written during
       the course [of a self-imposed study of science by a
       literary man], some of them previously published in
       scholarly journals or given as talks on the BBC. Two
       essays are criticisms of the Leavis Richmond Lecture,
       [see B130] and the Trilling counterattack in Commentary.
       Two others survey the literature of science. One
       discusses the teaching of liberal studies in colleges
       of technology. . . . The book also contains a thoughtful
       essay on how the teacher of English or liberal studies
       in technical colleges can fuse literature and science."
       --Simpson, Mary S. "The Two Cultures Revisited."
       Bulletin of the Atomic Scientists, 21, no. 7 (September
       1965) 31-32.

B12   DAVIS, ROBERT GORHAM. C.P. Snow. New York: Columbia
       University Press, 1965.
            (Columbia essays on modern writers, no. 8.)

B13   GREEN, MARTIN BURGESS. Science and the Shabby Curate of
       Poetry; Essays about the Two Cultures. First American
       ed. New York: Norton, 1965.

B14   KARL, FREDERICK ROBERT. C.P. Snow. Carbondale: Southern
       Illinois University Press, 1965. Pbk. 162 pp.
            Reprint of B8.

B15   THALE, JEROME. <u>C.P. Snow</u>. New York: Scribner, 1965. 160 pp.
           CONTENTS: Life and early works.--Snow and the
       Liberal Context.--The "Strangers and Brothers" Sequence.
       --Snow's Art.--Other writings.--Snow and His Critics.
       [Includes critical comments up to and including <u>The
       Corridors of Power</u>.]

B16   *<u>AIKAMME KAKSI KULTUURIA</u>. Toimittanut Eero Saarenheimo.
       Puheenvuorot: Heikki Brotherus [et al.] Provo: W.
       Soderstrom, 1967.
           Not examined.

B17   *KREUZER, HELMUT [et al.] <u>Literarische und Naturwissen-
       schaftliche Intelligenz: Dialog uber die "Zwei Kulturen"</u>
       Stuttgart: Klett, 1969. 273 pp.
           Not examined.

B18   GRAVES, NORA CALHOUN. <u>The Two Culture Theory in C.P. Snow's
       Novels</u>. Hattiesburg: University and College Press of
       Mississippi, 1971. 95 pp.
           "In this study I have tried to present C.P. Snow's
       Two Culture Theory and the two culture reflections to
       be found in his fourteen novels. Despite my conviction
       that the two culture thinking pervades Snow's fiction,
       I am not insinuating that such a scheme was part of his
       original design or that he manipulated his creative work
       for that specific purpose. Such mechanical employment
       would confine the writer in a vise! But the idea of
       two cultures seems inherent in Snow's work and emerges
       in character portrayals, in structure, and in theme."
       --Pref. [Includes comments on Snow's work up to and
       including <u>Last Things</u>.] (University & College Press
       of Mississippi series--humanities).

B19   LEAVIS, FRANK RAYMOND. <u>Nor Shall My Sword; Discourses on
       Pluralism Compassion and Social Hope</u>. New York:
       Barnes & Noble, 1972. 232 pp.
           CONTENTS: Introductory.--Two Cultures? The
       Significance of Lord Snow.--Luddites? or There is
       Only One Culture.--'English', Unrest and Continuity.
       --'Literarism' versus 'Scientism': The Misconception
       and the Menace.--Pluralism, Compassion and Social
       Hope.--Elites, Oligarchies and an Educated Public.

B20   TASKER, JOHN. <u>The Richmond Lecture: Its Purpose and
       Achievement</u>. Swansea: Brynmill Pub. Co., 1972. 32 pp.

B21   *ANIKIN, GENNADIFI VIKTOROVICH. <u>Anglifiskifi roman 60-kh</u>
        [i.e. Shestideskilatykh] <u>godov</u> [i.e. dvadktlsatogo] <u>veka</u>.
        Moskva: Vyssh. shkola, 1974. 102 pp.
            (Sovremennakila zarubezhnakila literatura). Not
        examined.

B22   JOHNSON, PAMELA HANSFORD. <u>Important to Me</u>. New York:
        Scribner, 1975 [c1974]. 254 pp.
            Not an autobiography, but a series of autobiographical
        sketches on her marriage to Snow, delivery of the Godkin
        Lectures at Harvard, their stint as Fellows at Wesleyan
        University and at Berkeley.

B23   . <u>Important to Me: Personalia</u>. London: Macmillan, 1974.
        254 pp.
            American ed. of B22.

B24   JAKI, STANLEY L. <u>Culture and Science: Two Lectures Delivered</u>
        <u>at Assumption University, Windsor, Canada, on February</u>
        <u>26 and 28, 1975</u>. Windsor, Ontario: University of
        Windsor Press, 1975. 52 pp.
            CONTENTS: A hundred years of two cultures.--
        Knowledge in an age of science. [Reprint, in book form,
        of B319.]

B25   SHUSTERMAN, DAVID. <u>C.P. Snow</u>. Boston: Twayne Publishers,
        1975.
            CONTENTS: Preface.--Chronology.--Boy from the
        Midlands.--Two Controverseries.--Snow's Literary Outlook.
        --Early Novels.--"Strangers and Brothers": The Early
        Novels of Direct Experience.--"Strangers and Brothers":
        The Novels of Observed Experience.--"Strangers and
        Brothers": The Last Novel of Direct Experience.--<u>The</u>
        <u>Malcontents</u> and Conclusion. (Twayne's English Authors
        Series, 179). 161 pp.

B26   RAMANATHAN, SUGUNA. <u>The Novels of C.P. Snow: A Critical</u>
        <u>Introduction</u>. New York: Scribner, 1978. 125 pp.
            "I started reading the novels of C.P. Snow over
        ten years ago, long before this book was ever thought of.
        With each volume that I read, Baudelaire's phrase 'mon
        semblable, mon frere' would pass through my mind. . . .
        I have included all his novels from <u>The Search</u> to <u>In</u>
        <u>Their Wisdom</u> in this study, omitting his two earlier
        works, <u>Death Under Sail</u> (a detective story) and <u>New Lives</u>
        <u>for Old</u>. . . .
            CONTENTS: Sensibility and Form.--The Social
        Setting.--The Examined Life.--Groups and Enclaves.--
        The Darkening Vision.--Characterisation and Style.

Dissertations

B27 GOODWIN, DONALD R. "The Fiction of C.P. Snow." Thesis, Iowa, 1966. Dissertation Abstracts, V. 27 (1967) 3009A. Order no.: 67-2622.

B28 GRAVES, NORA C. "The Two Cultures Theory in C.P. Snow's Novels." Thesis, University of Southern Mississippi, 1967. Dissertation Abstracts, V. 28 (1967) 1434A-35A Order no.: 67-12,378.

B29 GULLIVER, ANTONY F. "The Political Novels of Trollope and Snow." Thesis, Connecticut, 1969. Dissertation Abstracts International, V. 30 (1969) 684A. Order no.: 69-12,738.

B30 NOVACK, ROBERT L. "The New Man, the Lewis Eliot Man: A Study of the Narrator in C.P. Snow's Novel Sequence, Strangers and Brothers." Thesis, University of Oklahoma, 1972. Dissertation Abstracts International, V. 33 (1972-73) 1175A-76A. Order no.: 72-23,104.

B31 NEUMAN, ROBERT ROLAND. "Structure and Meaning in the Strangers and Brothers Novel Sequence of C.P. Snow." Thesis, Marquette University, 1973. Dissertation Abstracts International, V. 34 (1973-74) 2646A. Order no.: 73-27513.

B32 MULLAN, JAMES FRANCIS. "Resonance in the Strangers and Brothers Novel Sequence by C.P. Snow." Thesis, Fordham University, 1976. Dissertation Abstracts International, V. 37, no. 5 (1976) p. 2899A. Order no.: 76-25,742.

B33 WALSH, RUTH MURPHY. "C.P. Snow: Poet of Organizational Behavior." Thesis, University of South Florida, 1976. Dissertation Abstracts International, V. 37, no. 3 (1976) p. 2207A. Order no.: 76-23,744.

Articles, Essays, Etc.

B34 JOHNSON, PAMELA HANSFORD. "With Prejudice." Windmill, v. 1, no. 1 (1944) 1-10.
    [A survey of contemporary novelists. Includes a discussion of Snow's George Passant on pp. 4-5.] Although she has a taste for the lavish and the golden, for Proust and Joyce, this work is the most striking novel of the last five years. When Snow is finished

dealing with George Passant, the vivisection is absolutely final and complete. We know that, as a result
of the petty financial fraud, George is finished, even
if he will not admit the fact to himself. The novel
includes the essence of the post-war years. "Snow is
a flawless writer of unadorned prose; stylistically,
he might even be considered icily regular and splendidly
null. What matters, however, is whether this scientific
prose is the best medium for setting down the process of
an exploratory operation; and I think it is. He is the
only novelist of under forty years of age of whose
future I am not in the slightest doubt."

B35 _____. "Three Novelists and the Drawing of Character:
C.P. Snow, Joyce Cary and Ivy Compton-Burnett." Essays
and Studies, N.S., V. 3 (1950) 82-99.
[An early essay on George Passant, The Light and
the Dark and Time of Hope. See pp. 82-89.] Snow might
be described as a neo-realist or, better yet, as a
humanist--a man, to use an old definition, with a
profound interest in human nature. Snow's method of
drawing character is Balzacian not Proustian: the
characters are described directly without false or
misdirecting cues. George Passant, Sheila Knight and
Lewis Eliot are the most fully realized characters in
the novels. Passant's gift of self-deception, Sheila
Knight's unremitting cruelty (which still provokes
sympathy!), and Lewis Eliot's arrogance and humility
are conveyed with a constant skill. Only the charm
of Lewis Eliot is left to be inferred from the narrative.
Roy Calvert is a splendid but unapproachable creation--
too far above mere mortals.

B36 NEWBY, P.H. The Novel, 1945-1951. London: Published for the
British Council by Longmans, Green, 1951.
[For a brief appraisal of Snow's writings, see pp.
38-39.] Some excerpts: "C.P. Snow's writing is uneven
in quality but he disdains all the developments in
fiction over the past quarter of a century--so that he
gives an impression of directness and honesty. . . .
Where [Snow] betrays himself is in his scale of values.
The solicitor's clerk, George Passant, is presented as
a 'massive intellect' by Mr. Snow, but it is hard for
the reader to see the justification for such a claim.
In the same way, the central figure of The Light and the
Dark is so inadequate to the theme that the book has,
not unfairly, been called pretentious. But these remarks
do not apply to Time of Hope which contains a very
effective account of the making of a tragic marriage and
sets a standard below which--if it is to justify itself--
the rest of the series cannot afford to fall."

B37   SEIGEL, LEILA. "C.P. Snow." Wilson Library Bulletin,
            v. 28 (January 1954) 404.
                [An early biographical sketch. Also quotes the
            judgments of selected reviewers on Snow's novels
            from Death Under Sail to The Masters.]

B38   BALLIETT, WHITNEY. "[C.P. Snow: A Biographical Sketch]"
            Saturday Review, V. 38, no. 2 (8 January 1955) 9.
                [Biographical sketch which accompanies Harrison
            Smith's review of The New Men in this issue. Describes
            him as a man of quiet, iron practicality, and quotes
            Snow to prove it.]

B39   "SNOW, CHARLES PERCY." In Twentieth Century Authors.
            Edited by Stanley J. Kunitz. First supplement. New
            York: Wilson, 1955, pp. 932-34.
                [Biographical sketch. Includes judgments of some
            early reviewers on Snow's novels from Death Under Sail
            to The New Men.]

B40   WAGNER, GEOFFREY. "Writer in the Welfare State." Commonweal,
            V. 65, no. 2 (12 October 1956) 49-50.
                Snow's attempt to re-introduce old-fashioned
            fictional values has failed. His novels are proof of
            the fact. The characters, including Lewis Eliot, fail
            to develop. Further, Lewis Eliot, Snow's alter ego,
            is obnoxious. He is guilty of the most tedious self-
            praise. The narrative passages are banal, mininfor-
            mation appears, and grammatical lapses occur. The
            war passages reflect the cliché of British phlegm and
            sang-froid and, in fact, the other characters are well-
            worn stereotypes. Snow is no Proust; he is not even a
            Galsworthy. Snow's critical theory is misguided.
            ". . .Snow has clearly identified himself with the
            managerial class that suspects art and art has revenged
            itself upon him."

B41   CALISHER, HORTENSE. "Can There Be an American C.P. Snow?"
            Reporter, V. 15 (1 November 1956) 39-43.
                Tries to answer the question why novel sequences,
            so common in England, are rare in the United States.
            Part of the answer is that the American author, who
            writes enormous (but discontinuous) books, must
            identify "some homogeneous pattern before he can sit
            down to describe it." These observations are followed
            by Snow's method (the repetition of one initially
            sounded note), and the themes of friendship and
            ambition in Snow's novels. Homecomings, Snow's
            latest novel, demonstrates that Lewis Eliot is a
            virtuoso in describing public matters, but uncommonly

reticent and close-mouthed in his private affairs.
"The autobiographical element in a writer's work is
of more oblique interest only when its transmutation
seems incomplete" and it is possible Snow would have
been better advised to write the sequence in the third
person.

B42   TINDALL, WILLIAM Y. "The Stream of Consciousness," in his
       Forces in Modern British Literature. New York: Vintage,
       1961, p. 210.
              [A one paragraph summary of Snow's article entitled
       "Story-tellers for the Atomic Age," New York Times Book
       Review, 30 January 1955, p. 1. [See: A243.] In it,
       Snow argued against the "mindless and unreadable" novels
       of Joyce, Woolf and Dorothy Richardson and against the
       stream of consciousness technique.]

B43   TRILLING, LIONEL. "The Novel--Alive or Dead," in his A
       Gathering of Fugitives. Boston: Beacon Press, 1956,
       pp. 125-32.
              [Reprint of B435.]

B44   COOPER, WILLIAM. "World of C.P. Snow." Nation, v. 184,
       no. 5 (2 February 1957) 104-105.
              Snow is a moral force both as a writer and a man,
       and he commands the respect of the younger novelists who
       must, of necessity, participate in society in just the
       fashion Snow enjoins: they can no longer earn their
       living by writing novels. Snow has set them an example
       of a man who has combined the careers of artist and
       practical man of affairs. These younger writers also
       observe that in the chaotic and splintered contemporary
       society, the scientists and non-scientists fail to
       communicate, highbrow art is divorced from popular art,
       and social ossification is a feature of the Welfare
       State. "It is to slow down, arrest, reverse this
       process that Snow devotes himself, by the activities
       of his practical life and through the message implicit
       in his novels. As litterateur, scientist, businessman,
       adviser on this and that to people and organizations,
       he acts as go-between, as integrator of a divided
       society. That is what makes his voice, as a writer,
       seem one of the sanest and most lucid of the present
       day."

B45   HARTLEY, ANTHONY. "The Inevitable Oligarchy." Twentieth
       Century, 162, no. 968 (October 1957) 303-08.
              Oligarchies are inevitable; the role of the current
       British oligarchy is to administer, not govern. Includes
       fleeting references to Snow's "new men" and to a Snovian
       (?) "committee of hard-faced men." Also quotes Trilling

on Snow's novels: ". . . .one of the curious things about their depiction of a power-elite world is a lack of impulse to blame."

B46   PROCTOR, MORTIMER R. "The Cult of Oxford," in The English University Novel. Berkeley: University of California Press, 1957, pp. 150-81.
         For a brief discussion of The Light and the Dark and The Masters see pp. 179-81.

B47   ANON. "The Two Cultures." Times Literary Supplement, 22 May 1959, p. 305.
         [A Times leader, or editorial.] The study of the history of science, music and religion can all be viewed as means of bridging the gap between the cultures of science and the arts.

B48   "Experience of a Life-Time." Times Literary Supplement, 23 May 1958, p. 345.
         Lawrence Durrell, Doris Lessing, Anthony Powell and C.P. Snow are all writing romans fleuves. The practice of all these writers, with the possible exception of the first, suggests a rejection of James Joyce's Flaubertian dictum that the artist "like the God of Creation remains within or behind or beyond or above his handiwork, invisible, refined out of existence, indifferent, paring his fingernails." These authors not only tell a story, but comment on it, and the quality of the novelist's mind is everything. The real-life equivalent of Snow's The Masters is found in Mark Pattison's Memoirs.

B49   STANFORD, RANEY. "Personal Politics in the Novels of C.P. Snow." Critique; Studies in Modern Fiction, v. 2, no. 1 (Spring-Summer 1958) 16-28.
         Examines The Masters and The New Men to demonstrate that Snow undertakes to expose and condemn a typically modern but immoral tendency: to create a caricature of a man by means of abstraction and then to pass judgment on the caricature rather than the man. So Jago is judged, on non-existent grounds, to be a supporter of the Nazi regime. So Sawbridge, the spy, simultaneously perceives his colleagues as friends and as Fascist lackeys. So Martin Eliot, the cold climber, is willing to profit from the caricature when he sets out to break Sawbridge down. Against this tendency to false judgment Snow opposes, in the person of Lewis Eliot, a "set of rather old-fashioned notions about loyalty and generosity."

B50   WEBSTER, HARVEY CURTIS. "Sacrifices of Success." Saturday
          Review, v. 41, no. 28 (12 July 1958) 8-10.
                A brief biographical sketch of Snow followed by
          observations on the characters ("Predominant, and this
          at first seems curious, are the relative failures.")
          and typical themes of Snow's Strangers and Brothers
          novel sequence.

B51   HOGGART, RICHARD. "The Unsuspected Audience." New
          Statesman, v. 56, no. 1434 (6 September 1958) 308-10.
                Certain British readers like American fiction
          because it is more demotic and less class-defined than
          the British. [Snow is mentioned, very much in passing,
          as one of the British authors who can communicate to
          a defined and civilized audience.]

B52   "Audience for Decision." Time, v. 72, no. 13 (29 September
          1958) 55.
                [Digest and popularization of A259.]

B53   GREACEN, ROBERT. "Profile of C.P. Snow: Novelist and
          Scientific Humanist." New Humanist, v. 73 (October
          1958) 9-11.
                [A biographical sketch. Includes appreciative
          summaries of The Masters, The Conscience of the Rich,
          and provides a synopsis of Snow's article entitled
          "Man in Society," an early appearance of Snow's "Two
          Cultures" thesis.]

B54   IVASHEVA, V. "The English Novel of the Fifties."
          Inostrannaja Literatura, no. 1 (1958) 211-17.
                [In Russian.]

B55   KAZIN, ALFRED. "A Gifted Boy from the Midlands." Reporter,
          v. 20, no. 3 (5 February 1959) 37-39.
                . . . one of the striking aspects of the novels
          is their perceptive and sensitive description of
          "intellectuals on the make." There is an emphasis on
          the will to rise, counteracted by the "sometimes tragic
          mystery of personality, which often unmakes the career
          that the will has made." Although Snow has objected
          to an "excessive personal sensibility in fiction, "
          his best device is the Jamesian one of the "central
          character who unites all strands of a story in his
          central consciousness." AES, V. 2, no. 4 (April 1959)
          114.

B56   "Two Western Cultures." Time, v. 74, no. 1 (6 July 1959)
          59.
                A brief account of the "Two Cultures" lecture
          preceded by a biographical sketch which describes

Snow's credentials to discuss the issue.

B57   READ, HERBERT. "Mood of the Month--X." <u>London Magazine</u>,
       v. 6, no. 8 (August 1959) 39-43.
           The Rede lecture misstates the issue. Scientists
       and literary intellectuals are not in opposition.
       Instead, the typical intellectual is suspicious of
       technology because it destroys sensuous discrimination
       and formative imagination.
           Defends Yeats, Pound, Eliot, and Wyndham Lewis
       insofar as these eminences attacked the prevailing
       money system. "It is still possible to maintain, with
       reason and scientific proof, that usury has been one
       of the major causes of the misery in the modern world
       . . . ." He goes on to attack the science of economics.
       Scientists, Snow claims, are "tough and good and deter-
       mined to fight it out at the side of their brother
       men." Read: "Yes, one knows the type, and that is why
       so many of them become, and even remain, communists."
       The peasant who exchanges the peaceful contemplation
       of cow-dung for the dark satanic mills of industry will
       lead a life of social neurosis, threatened by ulcers,
       cancer and syphilis. "I am. . . . an intellectual
       Luddite. . . I believe that the technological revolution
       is a disaster that is likely to end in the extermination
       of humanity." The reason: industrialization destroys
       "sensuous perception and imaginative experience."
       [For Snow's reply to Sir Herbert Read, see <u>London
       Magazine</u>, V. 6, no. 10 (October 1959) 57-59. For H.
       Read, battling back, see <u>London Magazine</u>, V. 6
       (November 1959) 73-74. Reprinted in B193.]

B58   "The Two Cultures; A Discussion of C.P. Snow's Views."
       <u>Encounter</u>, v. 13, no. 2 (August 1959) 67-73.
           [Brief comments on the issue by various authors.]
       Walter Allen cites an example of the mutual incompre-
       hension of the two cultures, and comments that the
       British situation would be different if Marxism rather
       than anti-industrial socialism had led to the British
       Labour Party. A.C.B. Lovell warns that the relentless
       drive, efficiency and priority of Russian science will
       break the pattern of existence as we know it, and wants
       the universities to lead, rather than frustrate, the
       scientific revolution. J.H. Plumb observes that
       younger humanists are willing to cross the divide,
       but that the scientists seem unwilling to do so. He
       also comments on the class basis of the literary culture,
       and considers the neglect of the arts due to the defi-
       ciencies of its practitioners and the elevation of false
       literary gods. David Riesman finds that the cultural
       gap divides the sexes, calls on the West to go on a

campaign of sacrifice to industrialize the poor nations. Bertrand Russell agrees with Snow's recommendations, and provides examples of communication between the arts and sciences in past centuries. Sir John Cockcroft feels the communication between the cultures is best served by residential colleges rather than potted courses, and provides statistical comparisons of scientific, technological and research growth in the United States, U.S.S.R. and Britain. Michael Ayrton finds that the painter, once closely connected with science or literature, has been removed to anti-intellectual limbo, and calls for the return of intellect.

B59   SHARP, JOHN. "What Is Wrong with Secondary Schools?" Listener, v. 62, no. 1589 (10 September 1959) 383-84, 393.
        Observes that Snow's "Two Cultures" lecture is "easily the most important statement about English education since the Hadow Report of 1926." Considers the present nature of intensive British educational specialization, and outlines a curriculum that includes science, mathematics, foreign languages, history and literature.

B60   BANTOCK, G.H. "A Scream of Horror." Listener, v. 62, no. 1590 (17 September 1959) 427-28.
        Prompted by The Two Cultures and the Scientific Revolution. Cites Auden, Day Lewis, Koestler, Orwell and Spender to weaken or refute the charge that the literary culture is afflicted by a reactionary syndrome. Doubts if, ipso facto, scientists and literary men can have much in common. He defends the literary distrust of applied science: it is based, Bantock believes in a rooted "distaste for the stimulation of the assertive will." Quotations from Women in Love are cited to elaborate the point. [For Snow's reply, see Encounter, V. 14, no. 2 (February 1960) 64-68.]

B61   POLANYI, MICHAEL. "The Two Cultures." Encounter, v. 13, no. 3 (September 1959) 61-64.
        Unlike Snow, Polanyi considers science a decisive factor in moulding contemporary attitudes, and he believes scientific rationalism has "corrupted the public life of our century." The article is complicated and difficult to summarize. One recent observer sums it up as follows. "C.P. Snow has spoken of "two cultures" describing the gap between science and the rest of our society. Polanyi has answered Snow by observing that in a deeper sense than Snow considered, we really have one culture, not two. While there is a major disjunction between the knowledge of the general public and the technical knowledge of scientists, the authority of science exerts a comprehensive power over the minds of

most persons today. Science exercises the kind of
authoritative sway that Christian religion once did.
To assert that a person, or his idea, is "unscientific"
is the severest charge. It is in this way that we have
to approach the objective ideal of knowledge. It is
not an ideal directly and explicitly taught, so much as
it is the central dogma of the scientific age. . . .
Events and ideas have combined to convince the modern
world that the objective ideal of knowledge is the
method of science and the hallmark of truth, even
though it is not practiced in science, nor capable of
establishing truth. The attractiveness of the objective
ideal will turn out to be its pseudo-substitution of
fact for responsible commitment, the appearance of
holding knowledge without risk or values."--Gelwick,
Richard. The Way of Discovery; An Introduction to the
Thought of Michael Polanyi, pp. 14-15. New York: Oxford
University Press, 1977.

B62 SYMONS, JULIAN. "Two Cultures, One Missing." Encounter,
v. 13, no. 3 (September 1959) 83-84.
Letter. Snow's account of the traditional literary
culture is grotesquely inadequate, and the claim that
scientists make up or share a common culture is false.

B63 BRADY, CHARLES A. "The British Novel Today." Thought;
(1959-60) 518-46.
[For the discussion of Snow's fiction, see p. 536+.
An early, appreciative evaluation deftly done but without
much depth.] On style: ". . .the Trollopian affinities
literally impose themselves at every point." On the
fictional principle of resonance: power and the many
states of love form two of Snow's main themes. On
priggishness: caused by Snow's conscious moral posture,
the man's self-confessed scientific humanism, but
redeemed by the "old subterranean Christian postulates"
implicit in Snow. On the characters in the series:
Snow neither blames nor judges them, and they become
our intimates through successive shocks of familiarity
and surprise. Snow's work is marked by quiet intensity,
analytic authority objectified in action and conversation,
and a civilized taste for the elusive bouquet of
personality typical of Austen and Trollope.

B64 WADDINGTON, C.H. "Humanists and Scientists: A Last Comment
on C.P. Snow." Encounter, v. 14, no. 1 (January 1960)
72-73.
The scientist who sees an egg turning into a larva,
or observes tracks in a cloud chamber is as adept in the
art of sensuous awareness as the specialist in Ossian.
Modern medicine and nutrition lead to longevity; and,

if the introduction of that and related technologies
brings about a decline in the production of, say,
excellent Nigerian pottery, or hand-colored cloth,
the gains outweigh the losses. The "Two Cultures" gap
is easy to remedy: teach potted science and humanities
subjects to humanists and scientists respectively.
[For Snow's response, see "The Two Cultures Controversy:
Afterthoughts." Encounter, V. 14, no. 2 (February 1960)
64-68.]

B65   CAUTE, DAVID. "A Writer's Prospect-IX." London Magazine,
      v. 7 (February 1960) 40-46.
         [Snow passim.] On the pervasive empirical
      tradition in English fiction and the failure of certain
      younger novelists and dramatists to make constructive
      social statements. One reason for this failure is the
      rarified education of most young writers. Snow's
      statement that a divorce exists between the literary
      and scientific culture is hard to challenge; a similar
      divorce exists between the literary and social-scientific
      culture. Young writers should learn the details of
      working class life and receive a grounding in the sciences.

B66   GREACEN, ROBERT. "The World of C.P. Snow." John O'London's,
      v. 2, no. 18 (February 1960) 126.
         [Review of William Cooper's C.P. Snow published in
      London by Longmans, Green.] Cooper, like his subject,
      is a scientist, novelist and critic. Snow may aptly
      be described as a scientific humanist whose novels are
      concerned with the themes of ambition and the struggle
      for power among men. Cooper observes that the crises
      in Snow's books are essentially tragic, but that the men
      involved in them are irradiated by hope for what lies
      ahead. This central insight makes the book well worth
      reading.

B67   WAGNER, GEOFFREY. "Sociology and Fiction." Twentieth
      Century, v. 167, no. 996 (February 1960) 108-14.
         [Snow passim.] The vogue of the sociological
      novel, currently fashionable in America, and gaining
      ground even in France, leads to lifeless prose; and
      it is, in any case, inferior to sociology taken straight.
      Snow, who has argued against the aesthetic novel "writes
      (as a consequence?) in a style so lame, laboured, and
      insensitive to words and sentence rhythms that his
      roman-fleuve really comes to read like a parody of
      John Marquand parodying a stodgy and inarticulate
      Bostonian writing his class record." If the trend
      continues, "The prose writing of a purely utilitarian
      society is simply going to be C.P. Snow's brand of Soviet

realism, Sartre's 'committed' communication, and
eventually the arid Newspeak of 1984. . . ."

B68   BERGONZI, BERNARD. "The World of Lewis Eliot." Twentieth
          Century, v. 167, no. 997 (March 1960) 214-25.
              William Cooper's study of Snow's work, C.P. Snow,
          (London and New York: Longmans, Green, 1959) leaves no
          doubt about his admiration for the Strangers and Brothers
          sequence of novels. Bergonzi explains how he disagrees
          with Cooper's assessment. AES, V. 3, no. 9 (September
          1960) 426.

B69   SCHUCHART, MAX. "De Romankunst van C.P. Snow." Book van nu,
          v. 13, no. 7 (March 1960) 130-31.
              In Dutch. Snow belongs with that group of authors
          which is returning, as it were, to the art of the
          nineteenth century novelist, and which is passing by
          the psychological-depth-study style of Joyce and Woolf.
          Snow seeks to find the relationship between the
          individual and the powers that surround him, whether
          they be industrial or religious, etc. Snow is not a
          creator of unforgettable characters, but he is a
          recreator of a given reality which he illumines. AES,
          V. 4, no. 5 (May 1961) 172.

B70   DEMPSEY, DAVID. "C.P. Snow." Book-of-the-Month Club News,
          May 1960, p. 4.
              [Biographical sketch which accompanies review of
          The Affair by Gilbert Highet in this issue.]

B71   GRANSDEN, K.W. "Thoughts on Contemporary Fiction."
          Review of English Literature, v. 1, no. 2 (April 1960)
          7.
              Reviewers, out of cowardice or necessity, dodge the
          critical function, and a great many novels are dutifully
          written and dutifully praised but the memory of great
          books (Ulysses, The Ambassadors, The Longest Journal)
          will do much to put down the amiable potboilers.
          Snow passim. He offers both the private and the public
          man. He is probably most successful in the latter role--
          when you prepare a face to meet the faces that you meet.
          Praises Henry Green as a novelist of private sensibility.

B72   MILLGATE, MICHAEL. "Structure and Style in the Novels of
          C.P. Snow." Review of English Literature, v. 1, no. 2
          (April 1960) 34-41.
              Success and love are the major themes developed at
          length in the Strangers and Brothers series, as aspects
          of Lewis Eliot's "inner" and "outer" experiences, which
          are played off against each other. Running through the
          sequence is the "strangers and brothers" theme, seen

in terms of those who do and those who do not give
themselves unreservedly in their personal relationships,
separating those who are on the side of life and those
who are against it. Snow's great strength lies in his
experience of society and his knowledge of men, which
are presented in a deliberately cultivated austerity of
manner which enables the author to "present the human
situation in naked clarity." AES, 4, no. 6 (June 1961)
260.

B73 O'CONNOR, FRANK. "The Girl at the Gaol Gate." Review of
English Literature, 1 (April 1960) 25-33.
[An essay on Irish literature with an aside on
Snow's George Passant on pp. 29-30.] An Irish C.P.
Snow would be an impossibility. Lewis Eliot is pleased
with things as they are, and with his own success. An
Irish Lewis Eliot would never have been able to isolate
Passant's weakness in Snow's fashion.

B74 SAAL, R.W. "Sir Charles P. Snow." Saturday Review, 43
(7 May 1960) 15.
[For annotation, see B521.]

B75 FISON, PETER. "A Reply to Bernard Bergonzi's 'World of
Lewis Eliot'," Twentieth Century, 167 (June 1960)
568-71.
[Defence of Snow's style and themes.] Snow's
style is subtly poetic in parts of The Light and the
Dark but Snow's themes in The New Men are the
Stendhalian ones of power and responsibility, and the
stylistic baldness of Snow's prose does full justice
to the issues. "Eliot's dryness is deliberate, for
even in their private lives, in the relations of Eliot
with Sheila, of Jago to his colleagues, of Calvert
to all his surroundings, Snow's characters seem peren-
nially in committee, and life is made up of the apparently
minute shifts of such relationships." So "let us for
heaven's sake discuss [the style] on its own terms,
and not those of the Proustian epigoni."

B76 IVASHEVA, V. "Illusion and Reality (About the Work of
Charles P. Snow)." Inostrannaja Literatura, no. 6
(June 1960) 198-203.
The series of realistic novels by Charles P. Snow,
Strangers and Brothers, is presumably of an autobio-
graphical nature. At the same time it is a panorama,
though not quite complete, of this or that stratum of
British society at a definite historical period. In
some aspects Snow can be linked to Marcel Proust. But

as a writer he proceeds not from the traditions of
Trollope (as the British critics insist) but rather
from Dickens and Bennett. Evidence of Snow's recourse
to acute social problems is the best novel of the
series, The New Men. AES, 4, no. 1 (January 1961) 14.

B77   TURNER, IAN. "Above the Snow Line; The Sociology of C.P.
        Snow." Overland, no. 18 (August 1960) 37-43.
          In the Strangers and Brothers series, C.P. Snow
        offers "nothing of consolation" but rather a "deeper
        understanding of the men and women we live with, and
        a deeper compassion." The "strongest continuing theme"
        in the series is the drive toward the personal satis-
        faction of power, either "in emotional relationships
        or within the small groups in which men live and work."
        This drive is analyzed within the confines of the
        British intellectual and administrative elite, where
        decisions are found to be based largely on personal
        considerations, rarely on principles. Like every
        elite minority, this one, "hardening in the arteries,"
        is doomed. Outside it, "from London to Leopoldville,
        the millions of strangers and brothers are gathering."
        AES, 5, no. 6 (June 1962) 267.

B78   FARNSWORTH, T.A. "The Future of the Novel is Bright with
        Promise." Forum (South Africa), 9, no. 6 (September
        1960) 25-26.
          The novel is coming back into fashion. Novelists
        like Anthony Powell, C.P. Snow and John Braine have
        repudiated both the Freudianism and the extravagant
        verbal extravaganzas of the twenties, and the modern
        novel is conservative in form, sociological in content
        and popular in its appeal. The trend has its dangers,
        but on the whole it is to be welcomed.

B79   STANFORD, DEREK. "C.P. Snow: The Novelist as Fox." Meanjin,
        19, no. 3 (September 1960) 236-51.
          Snow's books are full of clichés because, since he
        sees existence as clichés, to avoid them would be to
        falsify experience. His interest lies in the mutual
        impact which scientists and the society in which they
        work have on each other. But he also provides a rich
        gallery of portraits and is concerned with psychological
        interrelationships between people. The plan of the
        novels about Eliot reveals true artistic originality.
        Eliot himself, in his lack of moral center, which he
        compensates for with a great show of political morality,
        is characteristic of contemporary British culture. The
        trouble with Snow's books is the thinness of their
        intellectual content; Snow has not thought about the ideas
        he is dealing with. AES, 4, no. 9 (September 1961) 381.

B80 "The Workaday World the Novelist Never Enters." Times
Literary Supplement, 9 September 1960, p. vii.
English novelists rarely, if ever, show an acquaintance with working class life. Their novels rarely, if
ever, show men or women at work. C.P. Snow, like Nigel
Balchin (The Small Back Room) or Roy Fuller (Image of
a Society), is an honorable exception to this rule,
but even he is more concerned with the technicians of
science and law in his novels The New Men and Time of
Hope. As for resonance, "One is safe in saying that
only a small percentage of C.P. Snow's readers have
apprehended this central design, and that only a
fraction of this small percentage finds it significant."
The prime importance of the series is its loving preoccupation with bureaucratic man.

B81 NOON, WILLIAM T. "Satire, Poison and the Professor."
English Record 11, no. 1 (Fall 1960) 53-56.
Charles P. Snow's The Masters is clearly not satire
at all. Evelyn Waugh depicts "the Hilarious absurdities
of English academic communities. . . [and his] control
is that of the traditional moralist in Decline and Fall.
Kingsley Amis' Lucky Jim is a "happy book," not a
"savage one." AES, 4, no. 11 (November 1961) 494.

B82 THALE, JEROME. "C.P. Snow: The Art of Worldliness." Kenyon
Review, 22, no. 4 (Autumn 1960) 621-34.
Snow's critical success can be traced to the
contemporary ideological vacuum in which most novelists
resort to melodramatic intensity or to triviality.
Snow avoids both by his peculiar set of attitudes:
pragmatism, tolerance, worldliness, a secular humanism.
He is allied to the conventional realistic novel rather
than to the experimental; all of his novels treat the
interplay of character and manners or affairs. The
motif of ambition in the early novels of the Strangers
and Brothers is an aspect of the larger unifying theme
of all the novels in the series: possessiveness in social
and personal relations. AES, 4, no. 1 (January 1961) 16.

B83 SLEET, C.P. "The Racket. Part Nine; The Plan Matures;
Chapter 46; Offer of a Cigarette." New Left Review,
no. 5 (September/October 1960) 63-64.
[Parody. The sub-title describes it as "the
seventeenth in the sequence of novels related by Lewis
Elsberger. The complete work, in 30 or 40 volumes,
will have the title Newcomers and Old Timers." The
hero is a jailbird.]

B84   KVAM, RAGNAR. "Ny engelsk prosa." <u>Samtiden</u>, 69, no. 9 (November 1960) 549-57.

        In Norwegian. C.P. Snow's <u>The Affair</u>, Colin Wilson's <u>Ritual in the Dark</u>, and Lawrence Durrell's <u>Alexandria</u> tetralogy reflect, in part, the current antithesis (represented in critical debate by Pamela Hansford Johnson and Philip Toynbee) between the "socially engaged novel with a background of cultural history," and the estheticism of the Bloomsbury school. Snow and Wilson, for all their differences, practice the former; Durrell the latter. AES, 4, no. 7 (July 1961) 301.

B85   "Bring on the Scientists." <u>Time</u>, 76, no. 24 (12 December 1960) 40-43.

        Synopsis, complete with quotations, of the Godkin lecture entitled <u>Science and Government</u>.

B86   "Our New President." <u>Library Association Record</u>, 62 (December 1960) 389-90.

        [Editorial to mark Snow's acceptance of the position of president, British Library Association.] "It is a matter of deep satisfaction that [Snow] should have been offered, and have accepted [the position] for his presence may be regarded as symbolizing the present happy trend in our affairs. Though we are not leaving the humanities behind, we are taking in, to an ever growing degree, the sciences as well."

B87   ROSENBERG, EDGAR. <u>From Shylock to Svengali; Jewish Stereo-types in English Fiction</u>. Stanford, Calif.: Stanford University Press, 1960, pp. 302-04.

        Concludes that "Snow alone in the twentieth century has avoided the stereotypes of presenting the Jew."

B88   "In the Name of Obedience." <u>Nation</u>, 192, no. 1 (7 January 1961) 3.

        [An account of Snow's address before the American Association for the Advancement of Science.] Quotes Snow's advice that the United States should agree to a formal suspension of nuclear tests without the 99.9 percent security against cheating demanded by the Americans. More crimes have been committed in the name of obedience than rebellion.

B89   "Old Boys and Friends." <u>Time and Tide</u>, 42, no. 5 (3 February 1961) 160-61.

        [A brief article.] J.H. Plumb and C.P. Snow are both graduates of Alderman Newton's Grammar School while William Cooper once taught science there. All three have done well.

B90   "People Are Talking About. . . .Sir Charles Snow and Lady
          Snow." Vogue, 137 (1 March 1961) 140-41.
              [Photograph of Snow and P.H. Johnson on p. 140.
          A three hundred word impression of both on p. 141.]

B91   GARDNER, ALAN. "Literary Owl Who Doesn't Give a Hoot."
          Saturday Review, 44, no. 9 (4 March 1961) 53-54.
              [Biographical sketch. Stresses Snow's varied
          career, humble social origin and affable nature.]

B92   WATSON-WATT, SIR ROBERT. "Truth About Churchill's Aide; A
          Rebuttal to the Godkin Lectures by C.P. Snow at
          Harvard." Saturday Review, 44, no. 9 (4 March 1961)
          49-53.
              The novelist in Snow has overpowered the historian.
          Lindemann the man, a freind of Einstein and Churchill,
          was a suave satirist and gentleman. Lindemann the
          scientist read the scientific report which proved the
          feasibility of radar; he did not express any doubts
          about the development of radar to Watson-Watt.
          Lindemann the courtier and friend of Churchill gave
          personal and direct encouragement to the development
          of radar. Lindemann's role in formulating the policy
          of mass bombing is not in dispute, but it is arrant
          nonsense for Snow to argue that "impregnable" calculations,
          compiled by Sir Henry Tizard and others, proved the
          probable failure of Lindemann's policy. First, there
          was no alternative to the policy. Second, no such cal-
          culations can be impregnable in a time of actual or
          theoretical technological progress. [For an exchange
          of letters between Snow and Watson-Watt, see a column
          headed "An Exchange of Knights" in Saturday Review
          44, no. 13 (1 April 1961) 44. Other contributors
          include Jacques Barzun, Alfred C. Harrison, John A.
          Hammer, MacLoubet and James A. Sharat.]

B93   WILLETS, RON. "A World Without a Hero; A Preliminary Comment
          on the Writings of C.P. Snow." Marxism Today, 5, no.
          3 (March 1961) 80-86.
              Includes a biographical sketch of Snow which stresses
          his close connection with society, a fact which marks
          the lives of all the great realists. Quotes, with
          approval, those sections of Snow's The Two Cultures and
          the Scientific Revolution which condemn reactionary
          literary figures, and also those which assert the dis-
          tinction between the tragic individual condition and the
          "untragic" social condition. Provides a brief discussion
          of The Search, and capsule summaries of Snow's novels
          from George Passant to The Affair. The elements of

tragedy are not found in the novels and "those [characters] who are most profoundly realised, to whom are memory most responds, do not assume heroic stature, the depth of tragedy."

B94   COHEN, JON. "The Too Cultured." First Person: A New Concept in Creative Publishing, 1, no. 3 (Spring-Summer 1961) 57-58.
         Youthful satire prompted by The Two Cultures.

B95   PINCK, DAN. "Friends and Sisters." First Person: A New Concept in Creative Publishing, 1, no. 3 (Spring-Summer 1961) 60-63.
         Parody.

B96   JONES, R.V. "Air Defence Clash in Thirties." The Times (London) 6 April 1961, p. 13.
         [A defence of Lindemann's scientific judgment in World War II.] Lindemann's written comments as a member of the Committee for the Scientific Study of Air Defense indicate that he favored a higher (not lower) priority for radar than that committee itself favored. Further, Snow's statement about the impracticality of infra-red detection, a pet Lindemann project, is unjustified; the device is now a commonplace of military hardware. Lindemann also showed his good judgment when he took measures which obliged bomber crews to photograph bombing runs; this step resulted in the adoption of radio aids to navigation. He also insisted on trials for an anti-radar device which resulted in the practical success of operation "Window" in 1943. It is true that, for military (but not moral) reasons, Tizard's objections to the policy of strategic bombing were sound. [For Snow's reply, see letter headed "Scientists at War" in The Times, 8 April 1961, p. 9. See also: B97, B98.]

B97   JONES, R.V. "Fruitless Attempts to Patch Quarrel." The Times (London), 7 April 1961, p. 15.
         [Continuation of B96. For annotation, see B96.]

B98   JONES, R.V. "Complete Change in Bombing Methods." The Times (London), 8 April 1961, p. 9.
         [Continuation of B97. For annotation, see B96.]

B99   "Many-Sided Life of Sir Charles Snow: With Quotations by Snow." Life, 50 (7 April 1961) 134-36.
         [Brief excerpts or adaptations from Snow's published writings compiled by David Snell.] On science in government, the science-culture gap, science

and morality, nuclear testing, World War II bombing,
the academic life, individuals and society, scientific
dictatorship, the novel, angry young men, scientific
discovery and the future.

B100   "The Observer Profile: Sir Charles Snow." Observer, 9 April
       1961, p. 12.
              On Snow as a lecturer and, in his heart, member
       of the literary tribe; the similarities and differences
       between Lewis Eliot and Snow; his work on the scientific
       register and in the Ministry of Labour; relations
       between Snow and his protégé, Harry Hoff [William
       Cooper]; the failure of his scientific research prior
       to writing The Search. Snow's style has its detractors
       and defenders, but Snow's role as the social historian
       of committee rooms, colleges, laboratories and courts
       of law is most secure.

B101   YUDKIN, MICHAEL. "Towards One Culture?" Cambridge Review;
       A Journal of University Life and Thought, 82, no. 2008
       (10 June 1961) 600-05.
              Snow's argument is more tendentious than explicit;
       the definition of culture is unclear; and, if indif-
       ference to literature and the arts defines a culture,
       then there are dozens of cultures. Snow's examples
       of incomprehension—failure to read Dickens on the
       part of scientists, and an inability to define mass or
       acceleration on the part of artsmen—are misleading
       since they imply "an equivalence between an artistic
       experience and a scientific finding." Snow also fails
       to consider that scientists can cross the gulf if so
       inclined, that scientific knowledge is strictly
       useless knowledge to other specialists, and that
       scientific findings cannot naturally be assimilated by
       men in the arts. Snow holds a depersonalized view of
       communication and education, and does not seem to love
       literature. Worse, his call to action in the cause of
       social hope is likely to divert students from the
       arts to the sciences and so further the atrophy of the
       traditional culture one half of him professes to
       admire. [Reprinted: B5, B9.]

B102   WILSON, ANGUS. "If It's New and Modish, Is It Good?"
       New York Times Book Review, 2 July 1961, p. 1.
              The novel of strong social implications which
       eschews formal and verbal experiment in favor of firmly
       constructed narrative and strong plot has made a
       triumphant comeback in England, if not the continent.
       Both Leavis and Snow are responsible for this resurgence
       of the traditional form. However "the conjunction of
       these two streams—of Leavis' criticism asserting a

121

rigid traditional form--seems to me to have dangerous
possibilities both for the writer and for the reader,
above all because both make their demands upon similar
moral and social grounds." The danger of this
[anomalous] alliance is that the West may demand a
form of socialist realism from its writers so that they,
in Stalin's phrase, will become engineers of human
souls, and their novels more "mature, healthier and
more responsible" than is the case in the Soviet Union.
[Reprinted: B116.]

B103   FINKELSTEIN, SIDNEY. "The Art and Science of C.P. Snow."
       Mainstream, 14, no. 9 (September 1961) 31-57.
          [A criticism of Snow's novels, The Two Cultures
       and the Scientific Revolution and Science and
       Government by a self-professed Marxist.] The source
       of Snow's general critical esteem is a tribute to the
       social virtues embedded in the novels. Snow's main
       theme is the search for a social morality and personal
       integrity in a society shot through with duplicity and
       self-serving. Snow's method is not that of the artist,
       but of the scientist testing a hypothesis. [Followed
       by an examination of the issues in Snow's novels from
       George Passant to The Affair: see pp. 35-46.] His
       novels are marred by the exclusion of real life--
       students, workers, labour unions, the big issues of
       World War II. "It is a social picture without society."
       Snow's "Two Cultures" lecture gives a false view of
       the literary and scientific cultures. The literary
       men he condemned were genuinely concerned with the
       misery they saw in society. The scientific men he
       praises work, directly or indirectly, for the big
       corporations and the military. Further, Snow does not
       seem to recognize that it is not science per se that
       gives Russia and the socialist countries the advantage
       in the movement for world peace, but the science of
       society. He regularly and systematically excludes all
       thought of the class struggle from his social thought.

B104   MILLGATE, MICHAEL. "Contemporary English Fiction: Some
       Observations." Venture, 2, no. 3/4 (September-December
       1961) 214-20.
          There are few, if any, great writers in England.
       The old guard--Forster, Huxley, Waugh, and so on--
       have had their day. The mainstream of contemporary
       English fiction is represented by C.P. Snow and those
       who think and write as he does. William Golding and
       Lawrence Durrell stand somewhat apart from the main
       current. The irritations which badgered the "Angry
       Young Men" were mostly of a rather trivial kind

which "provided a strictly limited amount of fictional material." AES, 10, no. 10 (December 1967) 663.

B105   GREACEN, ROBERT. "The World of C.P. Snow." Texas Quarterly, 4, no. 3 (Autumn 1961) 266-74.
        Snow's novels are concerned with the moral problems and dilemmas which ambitious men, struggling for power, must face; the dichotomy between scientists and writers and the personal and societal loss resulting from such a separation; and the ultimate helpfulness--not destructiveness--of science. His world has tragic overtones, but his characters reaffirm the indestructibility of humanity. Includes brief discussions of Homecomings, The Masters, The Conscience of the Rich and The Affair. AES, 6, no. 2 (February 1963) 88.

B106   ROBBINS, RICHARD. "The Bowles Affair." New Republic, 145, no. 15 (9 October 1961) 19-22.
        [Parody.]

B107   FALLERS, LLOYD. "C.P. Snow and the Third Culture." Bulletin of the Atomic Scientists, 17, no. 8 (October 1961) 306-10.
        Although Snow's background is impressive, he makes some elementary and alarming errors in the "Two Cultures." He has moved in scientific and literary circles, but his contact with social scientists has clearly been limited. They could have told him that his simple, rationalist, technocratic faith, shared by Jacobins, Bolsheviks and Chinese Communists, has been proved inadequate and dangerous. The technological progress Snow celebrates has been bought with the lives and liberties of millions. Technocratic millenarianism leads to totalitarian politics. Second, even the progress claimed by the totalitarian planners is open to question. Third, there is evidence that totalitarian control defeats and corrupts the master plan. Further, Snow completely ignores the contributions of intellectuals like Hobbes, David Hume, Adam Smith, Marx, Jakob Burckhardt and Max Weber to the study of society, and social scientists must take steps to remedy the popular ignorance of their subject. [For letters in defence of Snow, see "Readers Score Fallers on Snow," Bulletin of The Atomic Scientists, 18, no. 2 (February 1962) 31-32. The authors include Thomas E. Cooney, William J. Mecham, and C.R. May. Lloyd Fallers defends his views.]

B108   *MACKENZIE, ALASTAIR. "C.P. Snow: Strangers or Brothers?" College Echoes, October 1961, p. 13-20.
        Published by the St. Andrews Committee, Students' Representative Council. [Not examined.]

B109   "Chubb Fellow." New Yorker, 37, no. 44 (16 December 1961)
       44-45.
              [The purpose of a Chubb fellow is to bring
       undergraduates in contact with persons in public life.]
       Here Snow talks about his life as an undergraduate,
       the reception of The Masters in Cambridge, the drama-
       tization of The Affair ("they told me the theatre was
       more jungly than anything I wrote about, so I kept
       away"), fellowships bagged, his writing habits (slow
       and laborious), and pays tribute to his novelist wife
       as the one who knows the apt literary solution to
       technical difficulties.

B110   BLANSHARD, BRAND. "Hamlet Vs. the Laws of Thermodynamics."
       New York Times Magazine, 24 December 1961, pp. 8, 16,
       18.
              Attempts to define the type of education best
       suited for Americans beset by political hocum, specious
       advertising, religious superstition, class and race
       tension, and lopsided partisanship. Science, Blanshard
       asserts, leaves values alone, except the value of truth,
       but men cannot afford to leave the other values alone,
       and therefore a scientific education alone is a
       defective one. As the remark suggests, Blanshard
       comes down uncompromisingly on the side of the human-
       ities in the curriculum.

B111   "Snow, C.P." Current Biography, 22 (December 1961) 28-30.

B112   HEPPENSTALL, RAYNOR. "They Like It Here," in his The
       Fourfold Tradition. London: Barrie & Rockcliff;
       New York: Norfolk, 1961, pp. 224-43.
              [B450, B467, B519 worked into a single article
       by means of revisions and additions.] Includes
       observations on the agnostic element in Lewis Eliot,
       the politics of C.P. Snow, the degree to which the
       various novels can be read independently of the other
       novels and predicts that the remaining two or three
       volumes will be hard to write, and that the Omnibus
       Edition may be a commercial failure. [The tone
       throughout is both respectful and irreverent.
       Heppenstall clearly feels that the series has lost,
       rather than gained power as it nears its end.]

B113   MARTIN, GRAHAM. "Novelists of Three Decades: Evelyn Waugh,
       Graham Greene, C.P. Snow," in The Pelican Guide to
       English Literature, V. 7: The Modern Age. Edited by
       Boris Ford. Baltimore, MD: Penguin Books, 1961,
       pp. 394-414.

Praises Snow's "accurate and painstaking" observation and quotes sample pensées culled from Homecomings, The Light and the Dark and The New Men. Alleges that Lewis Eliot fails to "unify and interpret" the material of the novel sequence. Characters and episodes from The Light and the Dark are examined to prove the point.

B114   PHELPS, GILBERT. "The Novel Today," in The Pelican Guide to English Literature, V. 7: The Modern Age. Edited by Boris Ford. Baltimore, MD: Penguin Books, 1961, pp. 473-493.
        An omnibus review. Snow is discussed in a (largely favorable) aside, only on p. 482.

B115   PUTT, S. GORLEY. "Technique and Culture: Three Cambridge Portraits." Essays and Studies, N.S., 14, (1961) 17-34.
        [Memorable and personal portraits of C.P. Snow, F.R. Leavis and Sir Arthur Quiller-Couch by a former student of all three men.] Attributes Snow's humanitarian hopes to the traditional or literary culture. The supposition that these hopes derive from the scientific culture is strongly rejected. "The scientist in Snow, the critic in Leavis, the worldly wisdom of 'Q' [i.e. Quiller-Couch], all have for us the same lesson: that the enemy of our culture is not another kind of culture, but rather that both cultures of the Rede Lecture are threatened by that drab confusion of ends and means which passes nowadays by the name of technique."

B116   WILSON, ANGUS. "A Plea Against Fashion in Writing." Moderna Sprak, 55, no. 4 (1961) 345-50.
        [Reprint of B102.]

B117   "Deluded Materialists?" Newsweek, 59 (15 January 1962) 20, 23.
        Gropius and Snow criticise aspects of American life. Americans, according to Snow suffer from the delusion that they are invulnerable to attack, that American engineers are the best in the world, and that other races are inferior to the white. America must improve its educational system in order to counter these misconceptions. [Summary and popularization of A282.]

B118   OLSSEN, E.A. "Plato, Sir Charles Snow and the Arts Professor." Comment, 3, no. 2 (January 1962) 12-15.
        Sir Charles Snow's position in The Two Cultures,

that the humanist and the scientist are growing apart, is correct. The solution is for the humanist to insist on the social relevance of his discipline. AES, 5, no. 5 (May 1962) 198.

B119   WILSON, ANGUS. "Fourteen Points." Encounter, 18, no. 1 (January 1962) 10-12.
                In fourteen specific illustrations, Wilson finds that he detests three sins in England today: snobbery, intellectual dishonesty, and the so-called realistic cult of the expedient. Particularly ill-chosen are the dogmatic demands of C.P. Snow and F.R. Leavis for "healthy" themes in literature: such a restriction will not cure the disease, which is mental poverty. AES, 5, no. 4 (April 1962) 154.

B120   NOTT, KATHLEEN. "The Type to Which the Whole Creation Moves? Some Further Thoughts on the Snow Saga." Encounter, 18, no. 2 (February 1962) 87-97.
                Snow's view that the "Two Cultures" should be "unified" suggests that his understanding of "culture" may be lacking an essential element--"values." If culture is only knowledge, then Snow's idea of literary and scientific men instructing each other may be right; but if it includes "values," then its aim is less "unification" than "Gleichschaltung"--a moral question. Snow wants a more scientific underpinning of the social and administrative structure because scientists tend to be future-directed men; yet he also says that they are not always good at making use of "the gift of foresight." Morally and imaginatively, his view of the existing administrative and social structure is "excessively cowed and fatalistic." AES, 5, no. 4 (April 1962).

B121   "A Snow Job?" Newsweek, 59, no. 10 (5 March 1962) 52.
                On Snow's charge that F.A. Lindemann impeded the development of British radar. Passages from Birkenhead's The Professor and the Prime Minister and from a letter to Birkenhead by Watson-Watt are cited to help disprove Snow's assessment.

B122   MARGOLIS, H. "Intellectual Life in England: Leavis Views C.P. Snow; Boothby Views Leavis." Science, 135 (30 March 1962) 1114-15.
                Includes quotations from the lecture by Leavis. Observes that Leavis' lecture is only marginally concerned with the "Two Cultures" but reserves most of its fire for Snow's advocacy of "jam"--the material things that the scientific revolution is bringing to

the masses. Tries to identify exactly what pursuit,
activity, or process Leavis wants us to pursue that
conflict with "jam" and like most commentators, scientist
and non-scientist alike, is baffled by the obscure and
tortuous forms of Leavis' answer.

B123   LEAVIS, FRANK RAYMOND. "The Significance of C.P. Snow."
         Spectator, 208 (9 March 1962) 297-303.
              [This polemic, the Richmond lecture of 1962,
         combined both argument and personal abuse. The argu-
         ments revived the interest of scholarly journals in
         the "Two Cultures" issue; the personal abuse, not quoted
         here, was widely reported in the popular press. Suc-
         ceeding issues of the Spectator denounced Leavis. See
         B124, B125.] The Rede lecture fails to define key terms.
         Snow equates the literary culture with literary intel-
         lectuals--the modish world of the New Statesman and the
         Sunday reviews. Both are enemies of art and life. Snow
         also equates the literary culture with the traditional
         culture which manages the modern world; the equation
         is indefensible. Snow resorts to cliché and debases
         the word culture when he accepts the scientific culture
         as a culture because its members respond without
         thinking. Worse, when Snow asserts that the scientists
         have the future in their bones, he is begging the
         question. Snow's account of the industrial revolution
         is marked by ignorance. His distinction between the
         tragic individual condition and the hopeful social
         condition is illogical. "Where, if not in individuals,
         is what is hoped for--a non-tragic condition, one
         supposes--to be located? Or are we to find the reality
         of life in hoping for other people a kind of felicity
         about which as proposed for ourselves. . .we have no
         illusions?" The value of great literature is that it
         examines human life with an almost religious depth of
         feeling. "What for--what ultimately for? What,
         ultimately, do men live by?" Both Conrad and D.H.
         Lawrence confront the question in their fiction. Snow
         does not do so, and hence he does not know the meaning
         of the novel form. The concern with technological
         progress is not enough, and the study of literature
         in a university where the English School is a center
         of conscience and consciousness can do much to correct
         the abuses and distortions of Snow's crass Wellsianism.
         [Reprinted: B9, B19 (with some revisions).]

B124   "Sir Charles Snow, F.R. Leavis, and The Two Cultures,"
         [by William Gerhardi et al.] Spectator, 208 (16 March
         1962) 329-33.
              [Leavis' attack provoked the following counter-
         attack by Snow's friends and admirers.] William

Gerhardi observes that Leavis is "a sedentary pedent
. . .a teacher of analphabetics. . .a carping footpad
. . .and the Himmler of Literature." Leavis stands
accused of envy and spleen. "Seven times seventy
devils splatter their spleen through one loud orifice."
Leavis, no prince of simple syntax, has a prose style
more choppy than the North Sea in full boil. In the
middle of this discourse, he launches an attack on
D.H. Lawrence. [The attack is reminiscent of Hugh
Kingsmill Lunn's book on D.H.L.--but it is more
heartless and therefore less amusing than Kingsmill's
study of that worthy.] Finally, he defends Snow's
notion of social hope and, in a brief reference to
Snow's fiction, he contributes the view that Snow's
minor comic characters have enough abundant life to
disprove the doctor's charge that Snow cannot create
characters, and make them live on the page. Gerhardi's
contribution is the voice of the bravo. By way of
charming contrast, Dame Edith Sitwell's letter is in the
vein of Lady Circumference, a hunting cry of the
ancien régime. I quote it in full: "I read with an
entire lack of interest, but some surprise, Dr. F.R.
Leavis's non-stop and malevolent attack on Sir Charles
in your last number. I read to the end of this attack
solely because I could not make out what it was all
about, or why Dr. Leavis wrote it. Is it possible
that Sir Charles may have offended Dr. Leavis by the
fact of his great fame, or by the fact that he--Sir
Charles--can write English? Only this can explain such
a silly exhibition." One other contributor, Lord
Boothby--who introduced Snow to the House of Lords when
Snow became a baron and a junior minister in the Labour
government of Harold Wilson--casually compares Leavis
to just the sort of black beetle calculated to earn
the contempt of D.H. Lawrence. The other contributors
include J.D. Scott, Susan Hill, Dennis Lant, Stephen
Toulmin, G. Reichardt, Anthony Storr, G.S. Fraser,
Peter Jay, C.R.O. Jones, M.S. Deol, Sir Oliver Scott,
Arnold L. Haskell and Gavin Ewart. [Snow contributed
nothing to this Schimpflexicon.]

B125   "The Two Cultures." Spectator, 208 (23 March 1962) 365-67.
       [More letters to the editor in response to Leavis'
       attack on Snow's Rede lecture.] J.D. Bernal denounces
       Leavis and defends Snow's reputation as a scientist.
       Snow was, in 1932, a "brilliant physical chemist whose
       work on photo-chemistry in the solid state could easily
       have opened up for him a new field of research." Ian
       Parsons defends Scrutiny and Leavis' reputation.
       Geoffrey Wagner reiterates his protest against the

"utilitarian Newspeak" of Snow's fiction and observes
that the praise of Snow continues to come from the
Barzun-Trilling syndrome and the Book-of-the-Month
Club. Michael Ayrton attacks the Leavis attempt to
find more than squalor in the traditions of the Bushman
or the Indian peasant. Dr. Peter Green spins out the
lively paradox that, in attacking Snow, Leavis actually
attacked the worst sins of Leavis himself. Remington
Rose contributes a scholarly reproof of the logic and
method of William Gerhardi, and asserts that the
reputation of Dr. Leavis is not the "invention of
undergraduates." Other contributors include T.T. Roe,
Sarah Gainham, A.M. Mimardiere, Margot C. Heinemann,
J. Bodington, G.N.A. Guiness, J.F.L. Long, Oswald
Harland and Bernard Miles. Mr. Miles offered Snow the
hospitality of the Mermaid Theatre "on any Sunday evening
during the next six months" to give Leavis a lambasting
in return. Snow did not take up the offer.

B126　"A Question of Brains." Times Literary Supplement, 23 March
1962, p. 201.
On the introduction of the electronic computer
and its use, among other things, in machine translation.
Snow's attempt to bridge the "Two Cultures" is praised
in one paragraph. Leavis' "readable diatribe" is tut-
tutted because it suggests an opposition between C.P.
Snow and the Cambridge School. [Followed by flurry of
correspondance in the pages of the TLS. See March 30,
1962, p. 217 for letters by Joan Bennett, J.H. Kells
and I.C. Robinson. Bennett points out that Leavis
does not speak for all of the Cambridge English School.
Robinson and Kells clarify and defend the Leavis lecture.
See also April 6, 1962, p. 233 for letter by R.H.
Stringer [letter unintelligible or mangled by printer?]
For denunciation of Stringer's style by B.M.G. Reardon,
see April 13, 1962, p. 249. For letter by F.R. Leavis
on Bennett and Stringer, see April 20, 1962, p. 265.
[Note: Dr. Leavis remarks, in his "Literarism' Versus
Scientism'" that the pages of the Spectator and the New
Statesman were charged and swollen with letters from the
intelligentsia who denounced him for his "cruel, gratui-
tous and stupid assault on poor enlightened Snow. . . ."
I have been unable to locate any denunciations of Leavis
in the New Statesman, and assume that Leavis was thinking
of these letters published in the Times Literary
Supplement.]

B127　PANTER-DOWNES, MOLLIE. "Letter from London." New Yorker,
38, no. 5 (24 March 1962) 167-74.
A report of Leavis' "astonishing piece of invective."

The more memorable and defamatory phrases of the
lecture are quoted. A possible clue to the attack:
Snow is not an admirer of D.H. Lawrence.

B128   "Operation Snow Removal." National Review, 12, no. 12
        (March 27, 1962) 194.
            Approving comment on Leavis' "thoughtful criticism
        of the 'Two Cultures' thesis."

B129   WOLLHEIM, RICHARD. "London Letter." Partisan Review, 29
        (Spring 1962) 263-69.
            [See p. 267-69 for a postscript about the Snow-
        Leavis controversy. Wollheim is an impartial critic
        who lambasts both Snow and Leavis.] Of Snow: the
        characterization of the two cultures was inadequate;
        the cultural and educational value of science was not
        established; the attack on the reactionary syndrome
        derived from a superficial conception of art; and Snow
        did not conclusively demonstrate the threat incurred
        by the cultural divide. "Civilization; material
        progress; the cause of the West in the Cold War--all
        these appear momentarily in Snow's lecture as candidates
        for being the ultimate object of his concern. None of
        them is settled for unconditionally. . . ." Of Leavis:
        the intellectual level of the critique of Snow's
        "Neo-Wellsianism" reached a low-water mark in the
        critic's career. "The fact remains that, by failing
        to give [Leavis'] own views [on "jam" or material
        advance] the same serious heavy undivided attention
        that he bestows upon the least of Snow's pretensions,
        he lost the opportunity of raising a notable occasion
        from the level of advertisement to that of argument."

B130   GREEN, MARTIN. "A Literary Defence of The Two Cultures."
        Critical Quarterly, 4, no. 1, (Spring 1962) 155-62.
            Summarizes, with the help of quotations, the
        reasons why Leavis found the tone of Snow's lecture
        offensive. Snow is part of the Wellsian and encyclo-
        pedist movement of the twenties and thirties repre-
        sented by Wells, Russell, Shaw and others, which
        Leavis attacked and subdued in the pages of his
        periodical Scrutiny. That earlier meliorist movement
        has been replaced by an intellectual climate which
        "insists on narrow intense knowledge (insights), on
        the need for personal freedom within the best-planned
        society, on the dangers of modern science and tech-
        nology, and on the irreducibility of artistic and
        religious modes." Green then defends Snow's tone in
        the teeth of Leavis' assertions and accepts, where
        Leavis rejects, the so-called Snovian cliché. Green,
        however, supports Leavis' contention that Snow's

treatment of the historical record of the literary
culture is far too cavalier. "The literary culture
of the nineteenth and twentieth centuries thought
harder and to more purpose than any other group about
the human problems created by the Industrial Revolution."
The point is not greatly elaborated. Green then defends
Snow's reference to parallels between eminent scientists
and creative artists (Rutherford and Eliot) and between
different areas of knowledge (knowing the second law of
thermodynamics and reading Macbeth). The fundamental
issue at stake between Leavis and Snow is the meaning
of the word "culture." For Leavis, the word connotes
certain definite attitudes (see first quotation above).
Snow is proposing to redefine the word by suggesting the
inclusion of scientific virtues and scientific experience and then the idea of culture can "address itself
to contemporary social facts with new energy, and its
future career can be as successful as its past."

B131 MANDEL, ELIAS W. "C.P. Snow's Fantasy of Politics."
      Queen's Quarterly, 69, no. 1 (Spring 1962) 24-37.
      C.P. Snow's various attacks on the literary
      sensibility of this century which surrenders to
      private tragedy and ignores the relation of the
      individual to society prompts one to examine his
      work on the basis of his own terms. Snow's eight
      novels tend to be structured on the basis of a
      disturbance inserted into a "cozy" society and that
      disturbance--"the guilty other"--is driven out as the
      scapegoat. There is only fantasy in a work which
      solves the problems of man's moral nature by excluding
      unpleasant elements from the good society--Passant's
      anarchism, Jago's pride, Martin Eliot's ruthlessness,
      Donald Howard's radicalism. AES, 5, no. 9 (November
      1962) 490-91.

B132 ALLEN, WALTER. "Mr. Leavis Pays His Respects to Mr. Snow."
      New York Times Book Review, 1 April 1962, p. 10.
      Cites some reasons for Leavis' attack on Snow's
      fiction and The Two Cultures. Leavis hates the
      serious newspaper press which has made Snow a pundit.
      He also has a natural tendency to attack the "centers
      of power" and--Leavis' literary influence under
      attack--believes the counterattack to form the best
      defence. Above all, Leavis resents Snow's undermining
      of the dogmatic supposition that English Studies, as
      Leavis understands the term, should form the heart of
      the university curriculum.

B133 NOTT, KATHLEEN. "Whose Culture?" Listener, 67, no. 1724
(12 April 1962) 631-32.
Discussions of culture, it is suggested, are often
conditioned by personal ideologies. Within this frame-
work, Notts examines the notes on culture which have
been advanced by T.S. Eliot, Richard Hoggart (The Uses
of Literacy), Raymond Williams (Culture and Society)
and F.R. Leavis (The Great Tradition). She also believes
that Leavis' writings about moral seriousness suffer
from a certain inconclusiveness. For conclusion, see
Listener, 67, no. 1724 (April 19, 1962) 677-78.

B134 FULLER, EDMUND. "A Question of Brains." Times Literary
Supplement, 13 April 1962, p. 249.
Letter. The attack by Leavis on Snow's "Two
Cultures" lecture is "vindictive, arrogant and sub-
literary." Snow's fiction "is an arena of meaningful
purposeful action in which men are affected by the
chaotic elements in their time but need not inevitably
be engulfed by them." Fuller does not necessarily
endorse the whole of the Rede lecture. "Of course,
Snow is as open to justly considered criticism as any
writer. But anyone who wishes to criticize him should
take up the task in terms of common courtesy, reason,
and demonstration, worthy of the solid, proved, and
widely esteemed body of work for which many of us are
grateful to C.P. Snow."

B135 "Sunny Snow." Time, 79, no. 16 (20 April 1962) 51-52.
Concerned with Snow's detached retina, the attack
by Leavis, the defense by Snow loyalists, and Snow's
election to the post of rector, St. Andrews.

B136 FULLER, EDMUND. "Snow-Leavis Affair." New York Times Book
Review, 22 April 1962, pp. 24-25.
Letter to the editor. The malicious lecture by
Leavis has damaged his reputation as a great literary
critic. Snow's own reputation as a novelist who
eschews breakdown, despair and sickness to concentrate
on a "large, varied, effectively functioning world
peopled by all sorts and conditions of men" remains
intact.

B137 *"C.P. Snurd on Banality." Private Eye, 1 (May 1962) 3.
[Not examined. Described by Derek Stanford in
Month 29, no. 2 (February 1963) as a parody of Snow's
rectorial address, "On Magnanimity," delivered at
St. Andrews.]

B138   "C.P. Snow on American Education." <u>School and Society</u>,
        90, no. 2210 (5 May 1962) 209.
                A summary of Snow's opinions of American primary,
        secondary and university education as broadcast over
        radio station WTIC of Hartford, Conn., January 1962,
        in the series "Yale Reports."

B139   BUCKLEY, WILLIAM F. "The Voice of Sir Charles." <u>National</u>
        <u>Review</u>, 12, no. 20 (22 May 1962) 358.
                A reference to the Snow-Leavis dispute which
        includes the disclosure that Leavis has a reputation
        for always getting his man. This genial forecast is
        followed by an extended attack on Snow's remark that
        he would feel equally at home in the United States
        and the U.S.S.R.

B140   STEINER, GEORGE. "F.R. Leavis." <u>Encounter</u>, 18 (May 1962)
        37-45.
                A sympathetic sketch of the critic's career.
        However, Leavis role in the Snow-Leavis dispute is
        mildly condemned on p. 42-43. [Reprinted: B256.]

B141   WILSON, EDMUND. "An Interview with Edmund Wilson." <u>New</u>
        <u>Yorker</u>, 38 (2 June 1962) 118+.
                Snow's novels are almost completely unreadable,
        but his work has opened up a whole new geography of
        the mind. The "Two Cultures" divide is more pronounced
        in England than the United States. Leavis is a
        dogmatist who makes a moral issue out of reading
        preferences [and he alienates Wilson.] Leavis' one
        real point, that Snow represents technical education
        and development as desirable in themselves, may be
        worth discussing. "This naturally gets Leavis's back
        up, because his interest in literature is passionate
        and moral--almost, I suppose, religious. For Leavis
        Snow, I suppose, is committing the sin against the
        Holy Ghost."

B142   CARR, W.I. "Literature and Society." <u>Caribbean Quarterly</u>,
        8, no. 2 (June 1962) 76-93.
                C.P. Snow's <u>The Two Cultures and the Scientific</u>
        <u>Revolution</u>, sets up a bogus paradigm in describing
        the cleavage between science and literature. The real
        division is between professional social inquiry and
        imaginative understanding, "between conceptualized
        intelligence and the literary critical function."
        The sciences and the arts must, as Snow suggests,
        realize that "each has its peculiar value." AES, 6,
        no. 6 (June 1963) 260-61.

B143   TRILLING, LIONEL.   "Science, Literature and Culture: A
        Comment on the Leavis-Snow Controversy." Commentary,
        33, no. 6 (June 1962) 461-77.
            Snow and Leavis are the modern proponents of
        positions once advanced by T.H. Huxley and M. Arnold.
        After reviewing the attacks on Leavis' Richmond lecture
        in the Spectator, and deprecating the tone of the
        lecture itself ("It is a bad tone, an impermissible
        tone") Trilling remarks that it can properly be under-
        stood only by those who appreciate the extent to which
        Leavis is committed to literature as the criticism of
        life. Leavis' special intensity is understandable
        since Snow's Rede lecture "represents literature as
        constituting a danger to the national well-being, and
        most especially when it is overtly a criticism of
        life." A very competent résumé of The Two Cultures
        is interrupted to defend Orwell's 1984. Attacks what
        he takes to be Snow's logical glissando: the literary
        culture suddenly becomes transformed into the
        traditional culture which manages the Western world.
        A rhetorical question puts paid to this insouciant
        notion. "The actions of parliaments and congresses
        and cabinets in directing the massive affairs of state,
        the negotiations of embassies, the movement of armies
        and fleets, the establishment of huge scientific
        projects for the contrivance of armaments and of
        factories for the production of them. . .these, we
        are asked to believe, are in the charge of the culture
        of literature. Can we possibly take this to be so?"
        Then defends Coleridge, Carlyle, Mill, Dickens, Ruskin,
        Arnold and William Morris. Their efforts "made it ever
        harder for people to be indifferent to the misery
        around them or to the degradation of the national life
        in which they came to think themselves implicated."
        The English writers of the nineteenth century did not
        contract out or shudder away in maidenly disgust at
        machines and soot as Snow alleges. Further, Snow does
        not make a single substantive proposal about education.
        Snow requires scientists to have the right to make
        their own ethos and devise their own criticism of life
        "with no questions asked. The culture of literature
        . . . must now be supplanted." Snow's claims of the
        virtues of scientists plainly overwhelm Trilling. The
        critic is led to suppose that the curtailment of free
        criticism, combined with an almost biological link,
        a mystical brotherhood between scientists, will enable
        Western and Soviet scientists to join together "in an
        entity which will do what governments have not done,
        the work of relieving the misery of the world." Snow's
        lecture "communicates the strongest possible wish that

we should forget about politics" and "politics goes on
living its own autonomous life, of which one aspect
is its massive resistance to reason." Trilling then
takes up the curious fact that the monumental writers
(Proust, Joyce, Lawrence, Yeats, Mann [as novelist]
Kafka, Rilke, Gide [also as novelist] have considered
the liberal ideology as, at best, a matter of indifference. The general acceptance of these writers is
explained on two grounds. One, the radical young
perceive that the novel, the essay, the story, the
poem "is always on the side of their own generous
impulses." Second, the passionate hostility to society
shown by these writers is perhaps an affirmation of what
is actually, as opposed to speciously, good in society.
[? At this point, the argument becomes allusive and
elusive.] Trilling contemplates the sad spectacle of
Snow and Leavis, both Roundheads, both committed to
England, Home and Duty, and to social mobility, at
loggerheads with each other. There follows an extremely
learned adverse criticism of the idea of culture which
Dr. Trilling proposes to replace with the idea of Mind,
and he observes that Faraday was the best scientific
representative of the belief in mind. ". . . there
is cause for surprise and regret that it should be
Charles Snow and Dr. Leavis who have jointly demonstrated how far the cultural mode of thought can go in
excess and distortion." [For discussion, see Commentary,
34, no. 5 (November 1962) 447-48. Reprinted: B190,
B196, B228, B248.]

B144   WAIN, JOHN. "The Conflict of Forms in Contemporary English
       Literature." Critical Quarterly, 4 (Summer 1962) 101.
            The rise of competing technologies (radio,
       television, journalism) has caused the arts to develop
       pure forms (non-representational painting, the concern
       with pure mass and form in sculpture, the pure novels
       of James, Flaubert, Chekhov and Joyce.). Within this
       general framework Snow is mentioned twice: on p. 107
       as a novelist interested in showing how the world
       works, and for whom the Trollopian-Galsworthian tradition
       is perfectly adequate; and on p. 114 where, in an aside
       on the relationship between literary and political
       attitudes, it is argued that it is nonsensical of G.S.
       Fraser to suggest that both the United States and
       U.S.S.R. are blunt and simple giants, or that Snow is
       attempting to teach these giants to understand each
       other.

B145   WAIN, JOHN. "London Letter." Hudson Review, 15, no. 2
       (Summer 1962) 253-58.
            For the section on Snow, see p. 254-58. Wain

suggests that Snow's knowledge of Russian literature
in the original is not intimate, and he believes
Snow's credulity when confronted by the claims of the
Russian bureaucrats in the course of Snow's 1960 visit
to Russia, disqualifies him for the role of teaching
these blunt and simple giants (the United States and
the U.S.S.R.) to understand each other. [Comments
prompted by Gerhardi's and Fraser's defences of Snow
in Spectator. See B124.]

B146 MILLAR, RONALD. "My Relationship With C.P. Snow." Time and
      Tide, 43 (20 September 1962) 16.
          Brief account of the dramatization of The Affair,
      The New Men and The Masters. The success of The Affair
      was due to its topical appeal; it is really a play about
      the Cold War. Neither Snow nor Millar is touchy and,
      once Snow approved the original draft, Millar was given
      a free hand. Leavis' idea that Snow's dialogue is
      unspeakable on the stage is nonsense.

B146a New York Theatre Critics' Reviews, 23, no. 15 (24 September
      1962) 270-72.
          Reprints of B569, B572-574, B577.

B147 MALDONADO DENIS, MANUEL. "'Las dos culturas' de C.P. Snow."
      Asomante, 18, no. 3 (July-September 1962) 20-25.

B148 SISK, JOHN P. "Writers and Scientists: The Two Cultures."
      Ramparts, 1 no. 2 (September 1962) 17-22.
          Briefly examines the anti-scientific, anti-
      mechanistic notions expressed by Wordsworth, Emerson,
      Tennyson, Arnold, Housman, Henry Adams, Melville. "The
      result [of scientific discoveries about the natural
      world] is that especially in the last one hundred and
      fifty years, the literary artist has been. . . fighting
      for a view of the universe that would validate his
      literary vision." Although historically science has
      often threatened the writer's vision, the genuine
      advances of science ought to enrich it. "Nevertheless,
      in its total effect on countless laymen, writers and
      readers alike, science has had a belittling effect on
      the purely personal experience of life, similar to that
      of the first book of Gulliver's travels." Some obser-
      vations on the optimism of scientists and the pessimism
      of literary men culminate in a comparison of Werner
      von Braun's optimistic Life on Mars and Aldous Huxley's
      pessimistic Brave New World. "The writer, in fact, is
      inclined to suspect that the scientist can be optimistic
      largely because he has abstracted himself out of his
      human condition, and this often strikes the literary
      man as a kind of betrayal."

B149   GREEN, MARTIN. "A Literary Defence of The Two Cultures."
       Kenyon Review, 24 Autumn 1962) 731-39.
               [Reprint of B130.]

B150   HAMILTON, KENNETH. "C.P. Snow and Political Man." Queen's
       Quarterly, 69, no. 3 (Autumn 1962) 416-27.
               In rebuttal to E.W. Mandel's article on Snow in
       Queen's Quarterly, "C.P. Snow's Fantasy of Politics,"
       (see B131) it is argued that Snow is dealing with
       substance rather than grasping at shadows, that his
       method is realistic rather than fantastic, and that
       his strength lies in his clearheaded appreciation of
       the nature of political man. His fault lies not in
       his low-toned technique but in his remaining skeptical
       concerning the comfort of faith. AES, 5, no. 10
       (December 1962) 559.

B151   JURCZAK, CHESTER A. "Humanities or Science?" Duquesne
       Review, 8, no. 1 (Fall 1962) 3-11.
               The main theme in Snow's monograph The Two
       Cultures and the Scientific Revolution is the existence
       of two polar groups: literary intellectuals and physical
       scientists. His conception of culture is inaccurate
       because, as defined by anthropologists, the two groups
       are actually sub-cultures. Moreover, he minimizes the
       difficulty of carrying out a scientific revolution.
       AES, 13, no. 7 (March 1970) 443.

B152   RAMIREZ, J. ROLAND E. "The Rich and the Poor: Some
       Observations on C.P. Snow." Duquesne Review, 8, no. 1
       (Fall 1962) 16-21.
               The main issue of the scientific revolution,
       according to Snow, is that the gap between the rich
       and poor is widening: actually it will be closed within
       fifty years at the most. Education will bridge the
       gap provided it is tempered with the acknowledgment
       that it is the purpose of technology to serve man, not
       the purpose of man to serve technology. AES, 13, no.
       7 (March 1970) 443.

B153   SCHREIBER, KURT C. "C.P. Snow and Education for Tomorrow."
       Duquesne Review, 8, no. 1 (Fall 1962) 13-15.
               The second point that Snow discusses in The Two
       Cultures and the Scientific Revolution concerns the
       deficiencies of the educational systems of developed
       nations, especially Great Britain, the United States,
       and Russia. While he offers no specific solution, it
       would seem that adding a variety of additional subject
       areas to the high school curriculum and intensifying
       subject matter in the elementary curriculum would al-
       leviate the problem. AES, 13, no. 7 (March 1970) 443.

B154   STANFORD, DEREK. "Sir Charles and The Two Cultures."
        Critic, 21, no. 2 (October–November 1962) 17-21.
                Snow's novels reveal his "innocent" belief in the
        moral values "life-manship": having taken over whole-
        sale certain popular notions--"decency," "justice,"
        "fairness,"--and given them the same connotation as
        general usage bestows on them, he gives no indication
        of having thought back to the root of these notions.
        In this he reveals the naiveté of the scientist. AES,
        6, no. 2 (February 1963) 54.

B155   HALIO, JAY R. "C.P. Snow's Literary Limitations." Northwest
        Review, 5, no. 1 (Winter 1962) 97-102.
                Snow's sense of structure and psychological
        analysis are fictional strenghts. His notable weaknesses
        are the opacity of his prose style and a deliberate slide
        into repertorial techniques when the situation demands
        drama and heightened expression. These weaknesses are
        probed in a somewhat prolonged examination of The New
        Men. "Lying at the bottom of Snow's inhibited expression
        of those passions may be either the purely technical
        difficulty of the first person narrative method, or (as
        I suspect) the conflict between a severely disciplined,
        repressive ego and a highly sophisticated kind of vanity
        that enjoys such histrionics as the novel can afford."

B156   JOHNSON, GERALD W. "Footnote to a Current Dialogue."
        American Scholar, 32 (Winter 1962-63) 66-72.
                Scientists are now widely distrusted in the
        Republic. They are considered mad or malevolent. Their
        accounts of their high-toned wizardry strain the cre-
        dulity of the demos. Further that same distrust extends
        to political matters so that Russia and the United
        States now threaten each other with atomic bombs.
        Emotion, not intellect, fuels that mutual distrust. The
        people, as Hamilton observed, are a great beast. What
        is needed is a study of ethics to purge the people of
        their proclivity to purges and, if possible, to prevent
        a nuclear exchange which will eliminate Gerald W.
        Johnson from a world where he has been pleasantly
        educated in the mysteries of science by Raymond Pearl,
        biologist and bon-vivant.

B157   STANFORD, RANEY. "The Achievement of C.P. Snow." Modern
        Humanities Review, 16, no. 1 (Winter 1962) 43-52.
                Snow's novel sequence, Strangers and Brothers,
        shows him to be one of the distinguished novelists of
        the twentieth century. Snow's narrator, Lewis Eliot,
        is not a literary man and does not record his experience
        with any degree of wit or perception; hence, isolated
        details or scenes may seem insignificant or dull. But

as Eliot's observations and opinions accumulate throughout the series, they reveal Snow's profound moral
concerns and his search for meaning in the lives of
ordinary men. The Affair, here analyzed in some detail,
is an excellent example of the accrued meaning that
gives Snow's work significance. AES, 5, no. 7 (September
1962) 365.

B158   BUCKLEY, VINCENT. "C.P. Snow: How Many Cultures?" Melbourne
       Critical Review, 5 (1962) 102-07.
            Two thirds of the "Two Cultures" lecture consists
       of truisms while one third, particularly that pertaining
       to the definition of culture, is surprisingly muddled.
       Buckley defines the cultured man as one with access to
       the means of personal growth who uses these means as
       fully as circumstances allow. The greatest literature
       at once represents and enhances life. "Snow is a
       fashionable novelist; yet what must we conjecture about
       the sense he has of his own vocation as a creative
       writer when he ignores all the magnificent and various
       complexity with which English literature has created
       and recreated images both of the human fact and pos-
       sibility, and offers us as examples of literary men only
       the "Luddites" and prattlers of his booklet, and the
       trivial or crippled oddities in his novels?"

B159   FRIED, ALBERT. "The Scientific Culture of C.P. Snow." New
       Politics, 1, no. 4 (1962) 105-10.
            [Cogent comments on science, scientists, industrial-
       ization, and the literary culture by a member of the
       editorial board of New Politics. Also discusses Snow's
       Science and Government as well as The Two Cultures and
       the Scientific Revolution.] The cumulative effect of
       both lectures is to argue for the preeminence of science
       in the curriculum and the dominance of scientists in
       government. Fried then makes these observations.
       Science is amoral, and "Science has become the chief
       means by which massive organizations, creative and
       destructive, totalitarian and democratic alike, obtain
       and exercise power." Scientists, once revolutionaries--
       Galileo, Descartes and Spinoza--are now the servants
       of state and industry. To call for industrialization
       is not enough; the means to industrialization are as
       important as the end. Snow does not prefer "one ideology
       over another. Industrialization transcends all ideologies.
       Snow is as prepared to excuse the crimes of nineteenth
       century capitalism as of twentieth century communism.
       This fact leads him to make particularly crude and unfair
       criticisms of nineteenth century intellectuals who
       opposed the industrial revolution." Fried refers to
       Ruskin, Morris, Emerson and Thoreau. "They, along with

the workers who had been mercilessly driven off the
land by the Enclosure and by the repeal of the Corn
Laws, would have laughed bitterly at Snow's romantic
assertion that 'with singular unanimity, in any country
where they have had the chance, the poor have walked
off the land into the factories as fast as the factories
would take them.'"

B160   BLACKETT, P.M.S. "Science and Government." In Studies of
       War; Nuclear and Conventional. London: Oliver & Boyd,
       1962, pp. 120-27.
           [Reprint of B552.]

B161   FULLER, EDMUND. "C.P. Snow: Spokesman of Two Communities."
       In his Books With Men Behind Them. New York: Random
       House, 1962, pp. 120-27.
           Snow is a cerebral Balzac without Balzac's wide
       social range, sensuousness, erotic tinge and occasional
       melodramatic nonsense. Snow's realism is eminently
       praiseworthy because it concentrates on the normal, not
       the abnormal, on functional behavior—and not on a
       psychological or moral morasse. A pious unbeliever in
       religion, Snow knows, to use the language of Roy Calvert,
       that a man should be appalled at his own nature, and
       must forgive himself to get along. [This sentiment forms
       the chief theme of Fuller's essay, and leads into dis-
       cussions of power and character in Charles March, Martin
       Eliot, Martineau and George Passant.] Snow's "Two
       Cultures" are actually communities rather than cultures.
       Education of the young and popularization of science
       must play a part in reducing the estrangement between
       literature and science. The moral component Snow ascribes
       to science and scientists is denied with vigor. "It is
       the opposite of Snow's qualities—solipsism and self-
       pitying isolation, craven retreats from responsibility
       and denials that life has meaning—that have put one
       large wing of the literary community out of touch with
       the constructive stream of our age, and even with many
       of their fellow artists."

B162   GINDIN, JAMES. "Some Current Fads," in his Postwar British
       Fiction; New Accents and Attitudes. Berkeley: University
       of California Press, 1962, pp. 207-15.
           Optimism explains Snow's popularity among his
       American contemporaries. His work, like that of Lawrence
       Durrell and Colin Wilson, is overrated. The series
       suffers from the moral compromises from Lewis Eliot,
       repetitive plots which overlap different novels, and the
       pervading air of melodrama. "Snow's work seems curiously
       out of date. In addition to the oversimplifications, the
       woodenness, and the melodrama. . . Snow's novels are

limited by perspectives relevant only to the 'twenties
and the 'thirties, perspectives . . . that seem quaint
and superficial when applied to Britain since 1945."

B163   KARL, FREDERICK R. "The Politics of Conscience: The Novels
of C.P. Snow," in his The Contemporary English Novel.
New York: Farrar, Straus and Cudahy, 1962, pp. 62-84.
The whole novel sequence explores the effects of
moral conflicts on decent people, and Lewis Eliot
exemplifies a form of personal self-control alien to
the more brilliant George Passant and Roy Calvert.
Followed by extended commentary on The Light and the
Dark, The Masters, The Conscience of the Rich and The
Affair. The Conscience of the Rich is the best of the
books; it best exemplifies the issue of responsibility
and personal choice in the context of a personal
conflict. The Affair, a thesis novel, suffers from
abstraction and the absence of human interest.

B164   KAZIN, ALFRED. "A Brilliant Boy from the Midlands," in his
Contemporaries. Boston: Little, Brown, 1962, pp.
171-77.
[Revised and expanded version of B55.] Snow's
invocation of science connects him with the new rulers,
the scientists. In the same way, Dickens identified
himself with social reform and Wells with scientific
utopianism. The fascination of Snow's novels derives
from a set of attitudes typical of Lewis Eliot and
traceable to Snow's own history as a poor boy rising
towards the Establishment: a wary, intense probing of
the strengths and weaknesses of his contemporaries.
He is a relentlessly observant Gibbon of intellectuals
on the make. This spectator position, this constant
appraisal, "has permitted Snow to write so many interesting novels at a time when many writers are in despair
about the novel as a form. Despite Snow's strictures
against excessive personal sensibility in fiction, his
own work depends on such sensibility; and what James
called the 'foreground of the observer,' the leading
character who unites all strands of a story in his
central consciousness, is fundamental to Snow's work."

B165   KERMODE, FRANK. "Beckett, Snow and Pure Poverty," in his
Puzzles and Epiphanies. London: Routledge and K. Paul;
New York: Chilmark Press, 1962, pp. 155-63.
[Reprint of B524.]

B166   LEAVIS, FRANK RAYMOND. "Two Cultures? The Significance of
C.P. Snow." Melbourne Critical Review, 5 (1962) 90-101.
Snow is rather ignorant of world civilization,
history, and literature, despite his literary production

and despite his authoritative tone in <u>The Two Cultures</u>
<u>and the Scientific Revolution</u>. This work, the Rede
Lecture of 1959, is repetitious, naive, full of bad
writing, clichés and ideas; it lacks depth. AES, 6,
no. 5 (May 1963) 225.

B167   LEHAN, RICHARD. "The Divided World: <u>The Masters</u> Examined,"
in <u>Six Contemporary Novels</u>. Edited by William O.S.
Sutherland. Austin: University of Texas Press, 1962,
pp. 46-57.
      The principle of resonance can be explained by
tracing the themes of possessive and unrequited love.
The death of Royce, the old Master, is delayed to enable
Snow to make some comments about death and society.
The reasons which guide the characters to vote for Jago
or Crawford are irrational, and Snow's narrative method
is plainly the nineteen century convention of the
omniscient narrator. The novel, for all its undoubted
narrative skill, has its faults. The distinction between
the tragic individual and an "untragic" society seems
untenable. Snow should have learned and applied more
of the techniques pioneered or demonstrated by Henry
James, Faulkner, Joyce and Proust. The suspense is
admirable, but "If the test of a great novel is that
one wants to read it over and over again, then <u>The</u>
<u>Masters</u> is not a great novel. And <u>The Masters</u> is by far
the best novel Snow has written to date."

B168   "Snow, C.P." <u>Current Biography Yearbook</u>, 1961. Edited by
Charles Moritz. New York: Wilson, 1962.
      Brief biographical sketch.

B169   TRILLING, LIONEL. "Science, Literature and Culture: A
Comment on the Leavis-Snow Controversy." <u>Universities</u>
<u>Quarterly</u>, 17 (1962-63) 1-32.
      Reprint of B143.

B170   DOBREE, BONAMY. "The Novels of C.P. Snow." <u>Literary Half</u>
<u>Yearly</u>, 4, no. 1 (January 1963) 28-34.
      If the main object of a novel is to make readers
know about the behavior of people in society, the eight
volume serial novel <u>Strangers and Brothers</u> is most
important. It deals with people in our age in whose
hands our destinies lie--the scientist and those who
inhabit the "corridors of power." Snow is exceptionally
skillful in creating individual characters, in devising
a vast structure, readable in single volumes but
meaningful as a total unit. His books enlarge our
knowledge of humanity and of the structure of the
society in which we have to shape our lives. AES, 6,
no. 8 (October 1963) 449.

B171   STANFORD, DEREK. "A Disputed Master: C.P. Snow and His
           Critics." Month, N.S., 29, no. 2 (February 1963) 91-94.
               C.P. Snow, whose talents both as a novelist and
           as a sage have been hotly disputed, has not succeeded
           in bridging the gulf between the two cultures of science
           and the humanities nor has he interpreted the two areas
           of thought to each other. Because he is not a phi-
           losopher but a man of practical wisdom, he does not
           command a common language for the two disciplines.
           However, he has done more than any other to make readers
           realize that the scientists have ceased to speak to the
           creative writers and critics. AES, 6, no. 7 (September
           1963).

B172   "Pat on the Back." Senior Scholastic, 82, no. 8 (20 March
           1963) 4T.
               Summary of Snow's address in praise of American
           higher education delivered at a banquet in Washington
           University in St. Louis.

B173   MANDEL, ELIAS W. "Anarchy and Organization." Queens
           Quarterly, 70, no. 1 (Spring 1963) 131-41.
               Reply to article by Kenneth Hamilton. [See B150]
           Hamilton is wrong when he holds C.P. Snow's convictions
           to be sane although he writes in a faulty style.
           Actually, Snow "simply cannot conceive of the signif-
           icance of the individual tragedy in the social context."
           His proposed social hope contains a view of life full
           of complete inhumanity. Snow's charge that twentieth
           century literature represents political irresponsibility
           of the worst sort is "preposterous" and really charac-
           terizes his own work with its superficial humanity and
           its brotherhood of coziness. AES, 6, no. 8 (October
           1963) 462.

B174   CORKE, HILARY. "Dog That Didn't Bark." New Republic,
           148, no. 15 (13 April 1963) 27-30.
               Review of Leavis' Two Cultures? The Significance
           of C.P. Snow (New York: Pantheon, 1963). A biographical
           note on Snow and a temperate assessment of Snow's
           fiction ("a conscientious writer of the second rank"
           and mind ("wide but comparatively shallow") are followed
           by remarks on Yudkin's criticism of Snow ("the honors
           are pretty well even") and cruel remarks on the cruelty
           of Dr. Leavis. Corke accuses Leavis of literary fascism,
           smugness, a self-vaunting self-importance, and envy.
           It is suggested that the motive for Leavis' attack on
           Snow has its foundations in the belief that Snow was one
           of those Cambridge adversaries who delayed Leavis'

election to a Cambridge Fellowship. [No proof of this
contention is adduced. For discussion of the review,
see New Republic, 148 (4 May 1963) 36-37.]

B175   KIRK, RUSSELL. "Can We Apprehend Science?" Teachers College
        Record (N.Y.), 64, no. 7 (April 1963) 536-44.
                [An attack on Snow's scientism advanced with the
        help of rhetoric and long quotations from Orwell,
        Oakeshott and Loren Eiseley.] Snow is a follower of
        the Francis Bacon who said that knowledge is power, and
        he sounds like Wells before the onset of the Wellsian
        disillusionment. Quotes from Orwell's The Road to
        Wigan Pier part of the twenty page digression which
        alleges that the philosophers of scientism are little
        fat men who reduce the world to a place in which nothing,
        theoretically, goes wrong. Then Orwell: "But in a world
        in which nothing went wrong, many of the qualities which
        Mr. Wells regards as 'godlike' would be no more valuable
        than the animal faculty of moving the ears." Further,
        the cult of scientism leads to shoddy history. The
        apparent predilection of the poor for life in the
        factories owes more to the decline of infant mortality
        at the end of the seventeenth century than to the
        seductiveness of the factories themselves. The poor
        had to work in the factories or starve. Oakeshott shows
        that the rationalist (i.e. Snow) has an ominous interest
        in education, but that his interest lies in technique,
        training and technical knowledge. "If the 'scientific
        culture' of Snow . . . means the destruction of our
        intellectual inheritance . . . if 'science' is under-
        stood to mean an all-embracing ideology which supplants
        established modes of politics and the traditions of
        civility, if the object of science is the realizing of
        a future in which everyone will be just like everyone
        else" it is no wonder that Snow has found few disciples.
        Gives reasons why science attracts more students than
        philosophy or English. Suggests that following
        Whitehead's recommendations will lead to a strict,
        lively and harmonious study in real science and
        genuinely humane subjects.

B176   SIMPSON, M.S. "Snow Affair." Bulletin of the Atomic
        Scientists, 19 (April 1963) 28-32.
                [A superb set of summaries. The works digested
        include Two Cultures? The Significance of C.P. Snow,
        some letters in the March 16, 1962 issue of Spectator
        which denounced Leavis; Lionel Trilling's "Science,
        Literature and Culture: A Comment on the Leavis-Snow
        Controversy," and Science and Government, by C.P. Snow.
        Those without access to, or time for, the original
        texts, should refer to this article.]

B177   WOHLSTETTER, ALBERT. "Scientists, Seers and Strategy."
        Foreign Affairs, 41 (April 1963) 466-78.
                [An essay on Snow's Science and Government. Based
        on a 136 leaf monograph of the same title delivered at a
        conference of the Council of Atomic Age Studies at
        Columbia University.] Questions of military policy do
        not normally fall only within the technical competence
        of scientists. The question of the efficacy of a given
        bombing policy is not answered in a textbook on physics.
        The statistical methods used in assessing complex
        military operations are, as Blackett has observed,
        closer to those of biology or economics than physics.
        These methods are, given time, well within the grasp
        of the intelligent administrator. Snow's claim that
        the physicist or scientist possesses a special prescience
        is probably false. Prescience is no substitute for long
        and detailed study. Snow's derision of Lindemann's
        pet scheme of infrared detection reflects a lack of
        knowledge: the principle is used in the Sidewinder
        missile.

B178   SHAPIRO, CHARLES. "The Civil War of Sir Charles." Saturday
        Review, 46, no. 20 (18 May 1963) 28-29.
                Review of Two Cultures? The Significance of C.P.
        Snow, by F.R. Leavis; and C.P. Snow; the Politics of
        Conscience, by Frederick R. Karl.

B179   WAGNER, GEOFFREY. "In Search of the Snow of Yesteryear."
        Commonweal, 78, no. 10 (31 May 1963) 285.
                [Review of The World of C.P. Snow, by Robert
        Greacen; C.P. Snow, by Frederick Karl; and Two Cultures?
        The Significance of C.P. Snow, by F.R. Leavis.] Greacen's
        book is nothing more than an "uncritical piece of slip-
        shod journalism by the Daily Telegraph hack." Karl's
        book is serious. It demonstrates that Snow's material
        is not matched by his style, that Lewis Eliot is a
        master of deceit, and Snow's literary conservatism
        makes him no more than a bad British Marquand rather
        than a superior Galsworthy. Snow's "recipe for the good
        life becomes the repression of ambition, a secular
        attitude, and the acceptance of the second rate." Leavis
        is rather wonderful; his attack contains an immense
        amount of sense. It demonstrates his seriousness about
        literature and his demand that the novelist should write
        on the highest plane of intelligent existence.

B180   HALL, WILLIAM F. "The Humanism of C.P. Snow." Wisconsin
        Studies in Contemporary Literature, 4, no. 2 (Spring-
        Summer 1963) 199-208.
                The forms of Snow's novels are somewhat old-
        fashioned, but his moral assumptions are neither

old-fashioned nor shallow, as some critics maintain. He
rejects modern literary humanism for its over-emphasis
on individualism which leads to "crystallization," and
he rejects scientific humanism which stops at "predes-
tination." His sequence, Strangers and Brothers
traces the search for a viable union between individualism and social responsibility which is both complex
and forward-looking. AES, 13, no. 2 (October 1969) 110.

B181   STRICKLAND, GEOFFREY. "The Question of Tone: Reflections
        on the Snow-Leavis Controversy." Delta; The Cambridge
        Literary Magazine, no. 30 (Summer 1963) 16-21.
            [A defence, by a disciple, of Dr. Leavis' tone.
        The article, badly proofread, lacks some opening
        quotation marks, and at first gives the opposite im-
        pression.] The tone of Leavis' lecture was entirely
        apt. Snow appeals to various attitudes, uncritical,
        snobbish and presumptuous, that should be cause for
        regret. For example, Snow's writing about scientists,
        both in The Masters and in the Rede Lecture, invites
        us, by its reassuringly familiar details, to take the
        intellectual distinction of his famous scientists on
        trust. In a similar way, when Snow writes about the
        comparative politics of pure scientists and engineers,
        he is guilty of unverifiable and meaningless statements.
        [Concludes by quoting Leavis on Snow as a would-be
        genius, the presence of cliché in his style and thought,
        and the self-satisfied nature of Snow's social life.]

B182   PUTT, S. GORLEY. "The Snow-Leavis Rumpus." Antioch Review,
        23, no. 3 (Fall 1963) 299-313.
            The furor created by F.R. Leavis' attack on the
        views in Snow's The Two Cultures and the Scientific
        Revolution, may be compared to a high-spirited, old-
        time "internecine doctrinal rumpus." Despite the
        strong feelings aroused, and for all the petty sniping
        of commentators, no one denies that both men were
        impelled to the lectern by their concept of duty; nor
        can the sincerity of their appeals for social commitment
        be questioned. However regrettable the vitriol of
        Leavis' attack, even worse are a bland indifference to
        the real issues involved and the reaction of "alien
        cynicism." AES, 8, no. 3 (March 1965) 119.

B183   GREENBERG, D.S. "Reaction to Snow: Scientists' Role in
        Public Affairs Draws Increasingly Heavy Criticism."
        Science, 142, no. 3588 (4 October 1963) 34-35.
            Robert M. Hutchins, former president of the
        University of Chicago, wittily observed: "My view,
        based on long and painful observation, is that professors
        are somewhat worse than other people, and that scientists

are somewhat worse than other professors. . . . The
narrower the field in which a man must tell the truth,
the wider the area in which he is free to lie. This
is one of the advantages of specialization." Comments
that scientists, as a group are no better or worse
than lawyers, admirals or architects, and that the
scientific community is not monolithic. It includes
its Edward Tellers and Linus Paulings. [For a letter
by Thomas J. Scheff "Scientists, Lawyers and Admirals"
see Science, 143, no. 3601 (3 January 1964) 7.]

B184   "Scientific Nightingale." Spectator, 211, no. 7058 (4
       October 1963) 406-07.
            [Review of Aldous Huxley's Literature and Science.]
       After an "impressive and continuously entertaining
       demonstration of Mr. Huxley's literary and scientific
       knowledge" we are told somewhat lamely that the songs
       of the nightingale demonstrate territoriality and with
       this pious conclusion he withdraws from the discussion.
       The true issue is scientism, the belief that science
       has a general validity divorced from philosophy or
       "that stock of humane ideas which has traditionally
       directed the direction of Western civilization."

B185   GREEN, MARTIN. "Lionel Trilling and The Two Cultures."
       Essays in Criticism, 13, no. 4 (October 1963) 375-85.
            Trilling's recent article [Universities Quarterly,
       17 (1962-63) 9-32] misrepresents Sir Charles Snow's
       argument in The Two Cultures and the Scientific
       Revolution, by trying to detect hidden preoccupations
       and unconscious drives. His argument wavers, and is
       inconsistent with his earlier statements that modern
       literature attacks the life of society. He defines
       science as a non-humane intellectual discipline,
       although there is no lack of substantive proposals for
       humanizing scientific education. Snow's obvious truths
       have flung both Leavis and Trilling (as representatives
       of literature) into panic. AES, 7, no. 2 (February
       1964) 66.

B186   VOGEL, ALBERT W. "The Academic World of C.P. Snow."
       Twentieth Century Literature, 9, no. 3 (October 1963)
       143-52.
            The academic world, as it is usually portrayed in
       modern fiction, lacks strong drama. Although the
       academic theme is not the most important one in the
       Strangers and Brothers series, Snow does call "our
       attention to the imperfectness of human nature, which
       when set against an equally imperfect society, can

still manage to come out as a net gain for man if man
is willing to put human values first." AES, 7, no. 10
(December 1964) 571.

B187　MAYNE, RICHARD.　"The Club Armchair."　Encounter, 21, no.
5 (November 1963) 76-82.
　　　　C.P. Snow's novels have the comfort of a club chair
and his characters are suitable inhabitants of it.
deriving, as they do, from the pre-war detective story;
his own, Death Under Sail, anticipates several themes
of his later work.　While inadequacies exist in both
Snow's "people first and foremost" and his "people in
society" groups of the Strangers and Brothers sequence,
they show a certain nobility in attempting to fill an
omission in today's serious literature, "the world in
which large numbers of literate people live and work."
AES, 7, no. 2 (February 1964) 61-62.

B188　"Two Cultures Reaffirmed."　Scientific American, 209, no. 6
(December 1963) 67.
　　　　Excerpts from "The Two Cultures: A Second Look."
Times Literary Supplement, 25 October 1963, pp. 839-44,
in which Snow reaffirms and expands the views first
aired in The Two Cultures and the Scientific Revolution.
For the full text, see A293.

B189　IVASHEVA, V.　"Meeting Charles Snow."　Soviet Literature,
no. 8 (1963) 180-82.
　　　　Within the past year or so, translations of The
Affair (100,000 copies) and Time of Hope (75,000 copies)
have been published in the Soviet Union, and The Search
and Homecomings will be issued soon.　Soviet readers
admire Snow for his realism, his humanism, his portrayals of society, but especially for eschewing the
"philosophy of death and despair" which marks so much
Western writing.　AES, 7, no. 4 (April 1964) 182.

B190　LEVINE, GEORGE AND THOMAS, OWEN (Eds.)　The Scientist Vs.
the Humanist.　New York: Norton, 1963.
　　　　CONTENTS:　The Two Cultures, by C.P. Snow [The
text is that of the New Statesman and Nation, 52
(6 October 1956) 413-14]--What Science Is, by H.J.
Muller.--Gulliver's Travels: A Voyage to Laputa, by
Jonathan Swift.--The Rambler, Number IX, by Samuel
Johnson.--Hard Times [i.e. Thomas Gradgrind's inter-
rogation of the school children] by Charles Dickens.--
Literature and Science, by Matthew Arnold.--Science
and Culture, by Thomas Henry Huxley.--Science, Literature
& Culture, by Lionel Trilling.--Charles Darwin, The
Anesthetic Man, by Donald Fleming.--William Butler
Yeats, by Edmund Wilson.--When I Heard the Learn'd

Astronomer, by Walt Whitman.--Those Skilled Barbarians, by William Barry Furlong.--Reason, by Isaac Asimov.-- Who Am I and Who Are You? by Erwin R. Steinberg.-- Scientist and Humanist: Can the Minds Meet? by I.I. Rabi.--The Tree of Knowledge, by Robert Oppenheimer.-- The Humanities and the Common Reader, by Howard Mumford Jones.--Quo Vadis, by P.W. Bridgman.

B191   O'CONNOR, FRANK. "The Girl at the Gaol Gate," in his The Lonely Voice; A Study of the Short Story. Cleveland; New York: World Pub. Co., 1963, pp. 202-13.
          [Reprint of B73.]

B192   PETELKIN, G. AND SIMKIN, JA. Carl'z Persi Shou, pisatel' i celovek. Rostov: University Press, 1963.

B193   READ, SIR HERBERT. "The Great Debate," in his To Hell With Culture; And Other Essays on Art and Society. New York: Schocken Books, 1963, pp. 178-85.
          [Reprint of B57.]

B194   SHESTAKOV, DMITRI. "Dva romana Carl'za Shou." Novyi mir; literaturno-politicheskii i nauchnyi zhurnal (Moscow) 39 (1963) 262-65.

B195   SPENDER, STEPHEN. "The Modern Imagination," in The Struggle of the Modern. London: H. Hamilton, 1963, pp. 55-67.
          [A comment on the "Two Cultures" lecture by a poet.] Snow is for the scientists and against the poets. But his case is lopsided: he gives the scientists' case against the poets, but not the poet's case against the results of science--which can be good or bad. In any case, the notion of progress resides in the literary, not the scientific culture. Further, the poet judges man, not in a statistical context, but as an individual. Too much science can harm the poet. Witness the case of Coleridge. Snow's two-dimensional characters may inadvertently and uncon-sciously echo Eliot's line "We are the hollow men." To say that scientists, those morally neutral midwives of technology, should be unimpeded by the views of literary men is to prepare the way for a Stalin. There is beauty in the Second Law of Thermodynamics and Keats' Ode to a Nightingale, but the beauty is of a different nature and degree.

B196   TRILLING, LIONEL. "Science, Literature and Culture: A Comment on the Leavis-Snow Controversy," in The Scientist Vs. the Humanist. Edited by George Lewis Levine and Owen Paul Thomas. New York: Norton, 1963.
          [Reprint of B143.]

B197   WEST, PAUL. The Modern Novel. London: Hutchinson, 1963.
        Snow passim.

B198   HODGSON, P.E. "Culture and Subculture." Month, 217 (March
        1964) 177-81.
                Kenneth Richmond's Culture and General Education
        makes some important points about the "Two Cultures"
        division relevant to education in general and Catholic
        education in particular. Tests reveal that the most
        intelligent students of both cultures can cross the
        divide. Further, the students in the sixth forms make
        the most consistent progress in scores, and stagnation
        occurs in the university years and during the onset
        of middle age. The indifference and antagonism of
        Catholic schools and the Church towards the teaching
        of scientific subjects is highly regrettable.

B199   WALL, STEPHEN. "The Novels of C.P. Snow." London Magazine,
        4, no. 1 (April 1964) 68-74.
                C.P. Snow has neither the vision of a major
        writer nor the technical resources to convey such a
        vision if he did have it. Seemingly unable to dwell
        on his material, he resorts to summary because he
        cannot substantiate. So, though a man of many parts,
        his narrator (Lewis Eliot) remains a splintered man,
        and reveals that Snow has in fact a crudely simple
        view of human nature. Indeed, at every level in this
        "white elephant of a work," one meets an inadequacy
        which mocks its pretensions. AES, 7, no. 7 (September
        1964) 353.

B200   EISELY, LOREN. "The Illusion of the 'Two Cultures'."
        American Scholar, 33, no. 3 (Summer 1964) 387-99.
                [A defence of imagination and art by a scientist.]
        "Today's secular disruption between the creative aspect
        of art and that of science is a barbarism that would
        have brought lifted eyebrows in a Cro-Magnon cave. It
        is a product of high technical specialization, the
        deliberate blunting of wonder, and the equally delib-
        erate suppression of a phase of our humanity in the
        name of an authoritarian institution: science, which
        has taken on, in our time, curious puritanical
        overtones."

B201   ALLEN, WALTER. "C.P. Snow." Book-of-the-Month Club News,
        August 1964, p. 4-5.
                [Biographical sketch which accompanies John Mason
        Brown's review of Corridors of Power in this issue.]
        Snow has had a varied career, and his novels have
        given him an international reputation. "There are
        times when it seems you are almost as likely to glimpse
        his burly figure, with its great bespectacled dome of

a head, and hear his grunts and barks of delighted laughter, in Moscow as in New York." He can justly be compared to Trollope, and his rapid success has made him the subject of attack by critics. He has borne these attacks with admirable dignity.

B202 SCHENCK, HILBERT. "Revisiting the 'Two Cultures'," The Centennial Review of Arts and Science (Michigan State) 8, no. 3 (Summer 1964) 249-61.

Yeats, Pound, Eliot and Wyndham Lewis do not in fact represent the literary culture. Second, they did not aid or encourage the Nazi movement. The traditional culture, not the scientific, has the moral component to relieve the squalid conditions of the world's poor countries. The logic of science, left to itself, produces the profligate and foolish twenty-forty billion Apollo project. Snow's description of the scientific culture is flattering but largely untrue. To say that the scientific culture is democratic and free of racial feeling is largely misleading: the Civil Rights movement had its source in the traditional culture. Few scientists took part. The moral component of science simply reflects the need to report accurate results. This honesty does not imply larger, more expansive virtues, and the record of scientists on many difficult and controversial issues has been simply disgraceful. "Unless the traditional culture [advances the cause of the poor] with the most profound humanistic arguments of which it is capable, we will see increasingly more and more scientific effort put where it pays off quickly, excitingly, and without ideological difficulties. Great craft will fly to the planets, monster ships will dive into the deepest ocean canyons, and people will starve in half a hundred countries."

B203 FIEDLER, LESLIE A. "Poetry, Science and the End of Man." Tri-Quarterly (Fall 1964) 7-14.

The "Two Cultures," wickedly philistine but negligible in itself, is symptomatic of the confusions which saddle scientists as a group. It represents more evidence of "left-colored phillistinism" based on hoary nineteenth century platitudes, a mere naive impulse towards a New Totalitarianism. The fact is that, on one level, poetry (defined as imaginative use of language in verse or prose) serves as a corrective to the hubris and dehumanization of science. On another level, both poetry and science (in its great, startling, offensive moments--the Copernican revelation, the Newtonian synthesis, Darwinism, Freudianism) combine to rout mere complacency, and prove that "anguish and disquiet rather than self-satisfaction and repose are the proper human condition."

151

B204   JAFFA, HERBERT C.   "C.P. Snow: Protrait of Man as an Adult."
        Humanist, 24, no. 5 (September-October 1964) 148-50.
               In the modern world, the typical adult knows that
        ignorance kills. He must exercise judgment beyond the
        narrow bounds of his vocation. Both in his non-fiction
        and in his fiction Snow exemplifies this principle and
        process. His fiction is not only devoted to public
        issues; it also incessantly asks the question of what
        men and women want from each other. Snow's novels
        are superior to Upton Sinclair's World's End series, but
        Snow is essentially a good and not a great writer.

B205   "Familiar and Unfamiliar; Some Faces of Labor." Newsweek,
        64 (2 November 1964) 51.
               Portraits and very brief biographical sketches of
        Frank Cousins, Snow and others.

B206   "Two Cultures in the Corridors." Time, 84, no. 21 (20
        November 1964) 102.
               An account of Snow's decision to join the Ministry
        of Technology along with verdicts on his novel,
        Corridors of Power, by Conservative politicians Sir
        Edward Boyle, Iain Macleod and Quintin Hogg. The
        assessment of the novel by these Tory leaders and the
        critic, F.R. Leavis, is bleak. [For reviews by Boyle,
        Hogg and Macleod, see B631, B644, and B650.]

B207   ADAMS, ROBERT. "Pomp and Circumstance: C.P. Snow."
        Atlantic Monthly, 214, no. 5 (November 1964) 95-98.
               A bilious look at the politics of Corridors of
        Power ("It is not hard to portray liberals as wise and
        prudent men when one systematically ignores the problems
        which liberalism cannot solve") is followed by a
        judgment of Snow's fictional aim of resonance (not
        effective), and irreverent but appreciative notes on
        the courtship of Margaret and Lewis in Homecomings,
        the sole novel of the series in which Lewis Eliot's
        "nagging, corrupting sense of moral responsibility" is
        for once not allowed to prevail against the "voice of
        instinct, the voice of tragic need." [The remaining
        half of this elegant essay belabors Snow's The Two
        Cultures and the Scientific Revolution.] Specialization
        is inevitable. Socialist realism is detestable. "The
        culture [loosely defined as the weight of all knowledge
        and moral demands] presses on us, huge, intricate and
        demanding: most of it we shall have to ignore; of some
        small part we can be peripherally aware; and within a
        tiny area of their choice, a few men in each generation
        have a bare chance of knowing what they are talking
        about."

B208 ALLEN, WALTER. "War and Post-War: British," in his
Tradition and Dream: The English and American Novel
from the Twenties to Our Time. London: Phoenix House,
1964, pp. 248-251.
Snow's knowledge of one part of human ecology, the
public relations of men with other men, and the conflicts
between conscience and ambition, comes to its finest
fruition in The Masters. Moral agnosticism, the
reluctance to make moral judgments, is another of his
fictional attributes; and it is a mistake to think that
his work is solely concerned with public men wearing
public faces. Witness Homecomings and its tribute to the
mute incommunicability of human suffering. The series
is pervaded by a humility and largeness of mind which
more than compensate for Eliot's pomposities and pre-
tentiousness.

B209 BARZUN, JACQUES. "One Culture, Not Two," in his Science:
The Glorious Entertainment. New York: Harper & Row,
1964, pp. 9-30.
Culture no longer connotes cultivation of mind.
It refers to a discrete object of study, the mental and
material workings of a people and, considered in this
light, there is only one culture: the scientific culture
of the Western world in the twentieth century. Its
influence parallels the theological culture of the
Middle Ages. Traces the process by which the pre-eminence
of science was established, from the pre-scientific,
purely technological discoveries produced by artisans and
clever workmen, to the publicity about all the sciences
which followed the debates attending Darwin's Origin of
the Species. The later peculiarity of science, which
now bedevils modern man, is the loss of the ability to
communicate scientific processes or results in mere words.
The grim deficiency of the scientific culture stems from
the fact that science and the results of science are not
with us an object of contemplation. The paradox is that
science is equated, by many of its most eminent practitioners, as the activity of science; and the curse of the
modern world is "specialism" which is withdrawing subject
after subject from "direct, unscholarly, unpedantic
enjoyment, discussion, and criticism." The effect of
specialism is the destruction of a public culture, with
the consequent laments of isolation, loss of community,.
etc. The challenge confronting scientists is to make
science an object of contemplation.

B210 CORNELIUS, DAVID K. AND ST. VINCENT, EDWIN (Eds). Cultures
in Conflict; Perspectives on the Snow-Leavis Controversy.
Chicago: Scott, Foresman, 1964.
CONTENTS: The Two Cultures [excerpt] by C.P. Snow.

153

--Two Cultures? The Significance of C.P. Snow [excerpt]
by F.R. Leavis.--A Certain Judo Demonstration, by
John Wain.--Snow vs. Leavis, by Hilary Corke.--The Two
Cultures: An Editorial [in Spectator].--From the Top
Drawer and the Bottom, by Anthony West.--Grounds for
Approval, by Richard Wollheim.--The Voice of Sir Charles,
by William F. Buckley.--A Literary Defense of the Two
Cultures, by Martin Green.--Science, Literature and
Culture; A Comment on the Leavis-Snow Controversy, by
Lionel Trilling.--The New Science, by Sir Francis Bacon.
--Preface to Lyrical Ballads, by William Wordsworth.--
The Four Ages of Poetry, by Thomas Love Peacock. On
Machine Labor, by John Ruskin.--Science and Culture, by
Thomas Henry Huxley.--Literature and Science, by Matthew
Arnold.--What Science Is, by Stuart Chase.--How Does a
Poem Mean? by John Ciardi.--The Appreciation of Science
as an End in Itself, by John R. Baker.--Whatever Hope We
Have, by Maxwell Anderson.--Science as an Element in
Culture, by Bertrand Russell.--Why Do We Teach Poetry?
by Archibald MacLeish.--Is Life Becoming Happier? by
H.G. Wells.--The Industrial Magnate, by D.H. Lawrence.
--Mechanism and Culture, by James T. Shotwell.--1984
Can Be a Good Year, by J. Bronowski.--The Sane Society,
by Erich Fromm.--The Machine Stops, by E.M. Forster.

B211   CAZAMIAN, LOUIS AND RAYMOND LAS VERGNAS. "The Twentieth
        Century," in A History of English Literature (Modern
        Times: 1660-1963). Revised ed. New York: Macmillan,
        1964, pp. 1391-92.
            "Books such as The Masters or The Affair are
        remarkable pictures of the rivalries, manoeuvres and
        ambitions that mar relationships between members of the
        teaching and administrative staffs. They form a power-
        ful study in depth of the workings of justice within
        a closed circle of intellectuals." Lewis Eliot is truly
        a man of today. "The fact remains that C.P. Snow,
        despite the recent and vehement attacks by F.R. Leavis,
        is regarded by many Britons as one of the most important
        novelists of today."

B212   LINDEGREN, CARL C. "He Is no Scientist But an Administrator."
        Humanist, 84, no. 3 (1964) 91-92.
            [A review of C.P. Snow: The Politics of Conscience,
        by F.R. Karl. The review is a springboard for some
        literary criticism by a scientist.] Sheila Eliot sym-
        bolizes science. She "gives all her gifts to others,
        and witholds them from Lewis Eliot [i.e. C.P. Snow]."
        Argues that there is no difference between creative
        activity in science and the arts. Objects to the pre-
        sentation of scientists in Snow's novels. "None of

Snow's creative scientists are balanced individuals.
They are headed for suicide or they are belittled by
gross sensuality or other asocial behaviors." Also
grumbles at Snow's preoccupation with scientific
fraud in his fiction.

B213   VAN HAITSMA, GLENN. "Coleridge's Idea of Culture."
Wisconsin Studies in Contemporary Literature, no. 1
(1964) 27-36.
Coleridge's concept of culture helps to clarify
the fundamental issues (semantic and socio-moral) in
the C.P. Snow-F.R. Leavis debate, in which Snow argued
that scientific culture should replace literary culture
because the latter has become morally irrelevant. A
means of resolving the Snow-Leavis conflict may also
be seen in Coleridge's concept of culture and the "law
of Bicentrality" underlying it. This law enables one to
take an inclusive view of culture and to regard science
and literature both as having a necessary autonomy and
as being related in their mutual dependence upon an
ultimate moral reality. AES, v. 13, no. 3 (November 1969)
154.

B214   WEST, ANTHONY. "From the Top Drawer and the Bottom," in
Cultures in Conflict, edited by D.K. Cornelius and
Edwin St. Vincent. Chicago: Scott, Foresman, 1964.
[Reprint of B578.]

B215   MORGAN, JOHN. "London Diary." New Statesman, 69, no. 1771
(19 February 1965) 273.
[A socialist scolds Snow for sending his son to
Eton rather than to a comprehensive school.]

B216   QUOODLE [pseud.] "The Two Cultures." Spectator, 214 no.
7130 (19 February 1965) 225.
[A paragraph in "Spectator's Notebook."] Snow, the
public advocate of comprehensive schools, has exploded
his reputation by blurting out the fact that his son
attends Eton.

B217   HOLLIS, CHRISTOPHER. "Snows of Tomorrow Year." Spectator,
214, no. 7131 (26 February 1965) 254.
A satirical poem. Snow the advocate of comprehensive
schools, has sent his son to Eton, "where the chaps are
nice to know."

B218   NICOLSON, MARJORIE. "Resource Letter SL-1 on Science and
Literature." American Journal of Physics, 33, no. 3
(March 1965) 175-83.

A bibliography of writings on the theme of the "Two Cultures." Ninety six items. Chronological arrangement under broad subject headings. Brief annotations.

B219   BERNARD, KENNETH. "C.P. Snow and Modern Literature." University Review (Kansas City), 31, no. 3 (Spring 1965) 231-33.
　　　　　Prompted by The Two Cultures: and A Second Look (1964). Snow fails to define the "modern" literature hostile to a scientific revolution represented by better food and health and a longer lifespan. Snow misrepresents Orwell's 1984, a dystopia opposed, not to the future, but to a very particular future. The modern writer, Bernard suggests, is opposed to the empty, desiccated, hopeless automaton produced by industrial society. These writers have faced and explored the existential discontents of industrialized life and if, in the process, they have also rejected a middle class tradition which has provided no answer or anodyne to the terrible desperation of modern man in the face of nothingness, they are less than conservative.

B220   "Can Science Save Britain's Industry?" Business Week, no. 1862 (8 May 1965) 112-21.
　　　　　Examines the problems of British industry, names some members of the newly created Ministry of Technology, and observes that the Ministry's main preoccupations lie with computers, machine tools, telecommunications and electronics. Snow, appointed Parliamentary secretary to the Ministry six months before the article was written, is the subject of a brief biographical sketch. Some of his comments about the job, and the state of British industry, are quoted. Known as an idea man, his current concern is an improvement in the status of British engineers.

B221   MARSDEN, DENNIS. "Lord Snow's Middle-Class Dilemma." Twentieth Century, 173, no. 1025 (Spring 1965) 6-14.
　　　　　On British educational institutions and the social classes they serve. When Snow admitted, in the House of Lords, that his son was attending Eton "He should, according to precedent, either have praised the virtues of boarding as such, or he should have told the old joke about Eton being one of the first comprehensives."

B222   WATSON, KENNETH. "C.P. Snow and The New Men." English, 15, no. 88 (Spring 1965) 134-39.
　　　　　This novel stands the test of close and detailed reading; its parts have "a relevance beyond themselves and echo from different points in the whole work."

There is skill in the use of detail, in characterization, and in the consistency of style which, though it appears too flat to convey the novels's intensity of feeling, it is nevertheless appropriate: the deeper the emotion, the more limited the expression must be. The level style also fits the public-man character which predominates in the novel. AES, 10, no. 5 (May 1967) 298.

B223   PICKREL, PAUL. "Two Novelists: Outsider and Insider."
        Harper's, 230, no. 1381 (June 1965) 116–18.
            Review of Dreiser, by W.A. Swanberg, and C.P.
        Snow, by Jerome Thale. The two novelists are not, to
        use the sinister phrase, compared and contrasted in any
        strict academic sense.

B224   "Technology and Humanism." Times Literary Supplement, no.
        3309 (29 July 1965) 641–42.
            After some ponderous maneuvers which set loose,
        along the way, some amorphous innuendoes, the writer
        discusses the confrontation between Leavis and Snow.
        It is suggested that the fundamental issue between
        Leavis and Snow "is more than a question of priorities.
        It is a conflict of needs--starved inwardness and
        spiritual poverty on the one hand, physical misery
        and insecurity on the other. The food, as one might
        put it, of the inner and the outer man. Which comes
        first?" Leavis makes his stand for the inner man;
        Snow is adamant that humanity and the future are on
        his side when he opts for the outer man. The signifi-
        cance of Leavis' attack on Snow's fiction is the clear
        implication that Snow can make machine tools, but
        "he scarcely has it in him to take us beyond that."
        The remaining five paragraphs are given over to cold
        pensées on the novel sequence in general (Snow "tends
        to set out his feelings as if they were minutes . . .
        Snow's instinct seems to be to clarify, to depersonalize")
        and culminate in the observation that Snow deserves praise
        for practicing what he preaches and for possibly bringing
        the creative writer back into public life.

B225   ROBERTS, CATHERINE. "Nightingales, Hawks, and The Two
        Cultures." Antioch Review, 25, no. 2 (Summer 1965)
        221–38.
            A comment on the "Two Cultures" controversy which
        makes frequent references to natural history and Aldous
        Huxley's Literature and Science.

B226   SMITH, LEROY W. "C.P. Snow as Novelist: A Delimitation."
        South Atlantic Quarterly, 64, no. 3 (Summer 1965) 316–31.
            There are two reasons why Snow does not rank as a
        major English novelist: a limitation of moral vision,

and artistic inadequacy. The first is attributable to
his belief that the individual condition is tragic,
but that the social condition offers hope. The net
result of the dichotomy is that Snow neglects or turns
away from the fundamental questions of human existence.
On this issue, Leavis was more optimistic and more
nearly right than Snow. Snow's artistic failures are
the result of his unwillingness or inability to observe
the truth of Leavis' dictum in The Great Tradition--
"that the intensity of art is in proportion to the
artist's command of the dramatic mode of representation."
Although Snow the novelist is warm, full of insight and
compassion, Lewis Eliot the narrator is finally too
intrusive, omniscient and given to expository summary.
[Numerous examples of these alleged faults are cited.]
Snow's narrative method of combining enactment and
commentary sacrifices drama.

B227 KARL, FREDERICK R. "C.P. Snow: The Unreason of Reason," in
      his Contemporary British Novelists. Edited by Charles
      Shapiro. Carbondale: Southern Illinois University Press,
      1965, pp. 114-24.
          [Karl, author of books and articles about Snow, here
      qualifies his former, favorable views about Snow's
      fiction.] The code of Snow's novels is "progressive
      scientific liberal humanitarianism." Unfortunately,
      this code is completely inadequate to the twentieth
      century, and it does not result in interesting fiction.
      Snow's novels are not about people, but about processes
      and things. This concentration on the surface of life
      entails many sacrifices, notably the private life of the
      inner man. "Public roles--the sum and substance of
      C.P. Snow's world--ultimately become meaningful to us
      only as they reflect private beings. The novelist must
      recognize that man has many faces, only one of which
      he wears in his work; and that the face at work is often
      the least, not the most, interesting." The fiction
      proper to our century must be shot though with hatred
      controlled by satire, irony and wit. Lewis Eliot, an
      anal figure, is incapable of this virtuoso performance.

B228 TRILLING, LIONEL. "The Leavis-Snow Controversy," in his
      Beyond Culture; Essays on Literature and Learning.
      New York: Viking, 1965, pp. 145-77.
          Also published under title: "Science, Literature
      and Culture: A Comment on the Leavis-Snow Controversy."
      Reprint of B143.

B229 MURRAY, BYRON O. "C.P. Snow: Grounds for Reappraisal."
      Personalist, 47 (January 1966) 91-101.
          [A discussion of the "Two Cultures" lecture.]

Both Leavis and Trilling, in their different ways,
commented on the Rede lecture; but it has been insuf-
ficiently noted that Snow qualified his indictment of the
literary culture in a way which permits it to be read,
not as an attack on literature "but upon a certain
dominant mood in twentieth century criticism. . . .
It might have been more to the point [for Snow] to
have named T.S. Eliot, Pound, I.A. Richards and T.E.
Hulme as setting the critical stage for a literary
sensibility which wilfully ignores much of the literature
of the nineteenth century. Literature, widely defined,
is the criticism of life. "And it is time for the
critics to recognize the possibility of creativeness
in that writing which, like Snow's, presents life from
the viewpoint of more or less normal people moving about
among the problems of a recognizably normal society. . ."

B230   STONE, PETER. "The Cousins Anti-Climax." Statist (London),
        190, no. 4584 (14 January 1966) 78-79.
            Criticizes the organization of the Ministry of
        Technology under Frank Cousins. Too many civil servants
        are on the 5,000 member staff. Suggests specific ways
        in which the Ministry can perhaps improve its performance.
        The article refers to Snow twice: once as a man who hopes
        to hire 600 engineers "of the right quality" to work with
        the machine tool industry, and once as a man who defends
        the presence of the civil servants. "Lord Snow told
        the Statist. . . it is impossible to take on a man from
        one company without arousing suspicions of partnership
        among the others."

B231   DIXON, JOHN R. "Two Semantic Cultures." ETC: A Review of
        General Semantics, 23, no. 1 (March 1966) 77-83.
            A mechanical engineer considers 1) the semantic
        issue inherent in the "Two Cultures" debate; 2) the
        possible emergence of a purely scientific morality;
        and 3) the problem of communication between the two
        cultures. The semantic issue is troublesome. The
        language of science is distinguished by clarity: the
        use of operational definitions, objective terms and
        quantitative symbols. The literary artist, as Aldous
        Huxley observes in Literature and Science, "expresses
        himself not by simplyifying and jargonizing but by
        deepening and extending, by encircling with allusive
        harmonics, with overtones of association and undertones
        of sonorous magic." Engineers, in Dixon's experience,
        are deaf to these Circean melodies. Huxley's assertion
        that literary men must absorb and use technical and
        scientific knowledge is unconvincing. Second, in an
        age when science and technology are destined for

preeminence, a purely scientific morality, "objective, operational, humanizing," is well on the way. Witness Science and Human Values by Bronowski and Science in the Cause of Man by Gerard Piel. Third, communication between the two cultures, at any rate between legislators and men of science, is currently accomplished by bringing the latter onto advisory committees. Communication in a wider sense, between the cultures of science and literature, will become possible when literary men "produce the novels, plays, and poems which personalize the relationship of individuals to the scientific-technical world." For its part, the scientific-engineering culture "might learn to read literature more effectively." Given the semantic impasse, Dixon is skeptical; he doubts that his own prescription will reconcile the cultures.

B232 FAULKNER, PETER. "William Morris and The Two Cultures." Journal of the William Morris Society, 2, no. 1 (Spring 1966) 9-12.

In 1959, C.P. Snow delivered a Rede Lecture entitled "Intellectuals as Natural Luddies," arguing that literary intellectuals have never tried to understand the industrial revolution, much less accept it. "Plenty of them shuddered away. . . . some, like Ruskin and William Morris . . . . tried various kinds of fancies, which were not in effect more than screams of horror." In 1962, F.R. Leavis, in the same tradition as Morris, contested the view that benefits of industrialism lead to happiness, saying that literature maintained culture and showed us what we really believe. AES, 10, no. 6 (June 1967) 357.

B233 "Personalities of the Week." Illustrated London News, 248 (9 April 196) 13.

B234 MCELHENY, V.K. "Snow Returns to Writing." Science, 152, no. 3723 (6 May 1966) 745.

Announces Snow's departure from the Ministry of Technology. Quotes Snow's remarks in the House of Lords ("It seems to me that if you are living in a fairly prosperous home it is a mistake to educate your child differently from the mass of people you know socially") when Lord Eccles pointed out that Snow was sending his son to Eton although the official Labour government policy favored a policy of comprehensive high schools. "This was frank but not good politics. For one reason or another, very little was heard from Lord Snow after this exchange, although he made an excellent impression during his recent visit to the

United States." Includes an account of personnel changes in other and related government departments.

B235 COUSINS, NORMAN. "Third Culture." Saturday Review, 49, no. 19 (7 May 1966) 42.
Lack of communication is not the besetting problem of the two cultures. The true issue is the failure of the two cultures to serve the requirements of world peace, and a third culture, not concerned with merely parochial, specialist issues, is needed to deal with this momentous issue.

B236 DOWNS, HUGH. "Let's All be Eggheads." Science Digest, 59, (May 1966) 90-93.
[An article prompted by Snow's lecture before the Franklin Institute of Philadelphia.] Science will remedy the inequalities between rich and poor nations. The unknowable repercussions of some scientific discoveries should not be allowed to inhibit the process of scientific investigation. The layman should develop an intelligent, if amateur, interest in scientific knowledge.

B237 MACDONALD, ALASTAIR. "Imagery in C.P. Snow." University Review (Kansas City), 32, no. 4 (June 1966) 303-06.
The imagery of Snow's novels reflects their expression of conflict: violent physical movement, light and dark, comfort and desolation, confinement and freedom, physical solidity and muscularity, flux and haze. His style is based upon colloquial modern conversation. See also: B238 below. AES, 13, no. 6 (February 1970) 383.

B238 MACDONALD, ALASTAIR. "Imagery in C.P. Snow, II." University Review (Kansas City), 33, no. 1 (Autumn 1966) 33-38.
Much of Snow's imagery is visual, involving sound and motion. Situation and theme are often supported by images of "energy, tension and violence," these sometimes adequately balancing the situation, though not usually doing so exactly, being sometimes inadequate, sometimes excessive. Yet when overstating, his imagery compensates for restraint. Sometimes his imagery becomes symbolic--e.g., that involving light, windows, and cricket, all suggesting security and comfort, though the window may occasionally have an opposite or different meaning: sometimes his images reflect the violent and chaotic. Snow's imagery suggests that no compromise is possible between the individual spirit and the "world of affairs," though

Snow seeks one. The weakness of his novels lies in
his tendency to deny "the tragic vision"; by least
denying it, The Light and the Dark may be great. AES,
13, no. 9 (May 1970) 577.

B239　BICANIC, SONIA. "Svijet C.P. Snowa." Forum (Zagreb), 5,
no. 7-8 (July-August 1966) 618-29.

B240　HAND, HARRY E. "The Paper Curtain: The Divided World of
Snow and Leavis Revisited." Journal of Human Relations
14, no. 3 (Third Quarter, 1966) 351-63.
The division between the "Two Cultures" is
negligible in United States. American artists have
been influenced by "Outer space, our environment as
seen through scientific instruments, such as the
telescope and the electron microscope, inner space
(or the unconscious, the subconscious, the id), shock
waves, stress and strain, fragmentation of matter and
optics." [No evidence is cited to support this
position.] The creative scientist and artist share
similar personality traits: these include "resistance
to conformity, independence of judgment, a marked
preference for complexity and disorder, and a great
respect for the irrational forces in themselves and
others." Snow believes in the integrity of scientists
and their power to save the human race, but when the
scientist leaves the laboratory for the world of
action, he is confronted by all the confusion, clamor
and passion of politics; and one of the objections to
scientism is man's basic nature, inadequately conveyed
by Snow's reference to the tragic individual condition.
"There is always the beast within." Defends the right
of literary men to contract out of society for the
sake of a balanced perspective, and gives some reasons
why, in America, scientists and humanists realize
common concerns, values and problems.

B241　KETELS, VIOLET B. "Shaw, Snow and The New Men." Personalist,
47, no. 4 (Autumn 1966) 520-31.
No one since George Bernard Shaw has more constructively measured the dynamics of the ship of power in the
hands of responsible and educated men than C.P. Snow.
The analogies between the writers illuminate the vital
contemporary question of values and their relation to
power in a society in which atom smashers have frag-
mented the old gods. In his Shavian combination of
moral vision and practical judgment, Snow has focused
on the "new men" to give his writing a "significance
beyond literary merit which has not yet been closely
studied or adequately praised." AES, 10, no. 6
(June 1967) 385.

B242　KRESS, PAUL F.　"Self, System and Significance: Reflections
　　　　on Professor Easton's Political Science." Ethics,
　　　　77, no. 1 (October 1966) 1-13.
　　　　　　[An essay on Easton. Only marginally concerned
　　　　with Snow the political novelist.]

B243　FOWLER, ALBERT.　"The Negative Entropy of C.P. Snow."
　　　　Approach, no. 58 (Winter 1966) 7-13.
　　　　　　Discusses the interpretations of the laws of
　　　　thermodynamics stated by Sadi Carnot and J.P. Joule.
　　　　Norbert Wiener uses the concept of negative entropy
　　　　to describe the eventual death of the universe, and
　　　　the term has invaded literary criticism, economics and
　　　　sociology. It is a little known fact that some
　　　　physicists dissent from Wiener's conclusions. The
　　　　prestige of science prompts scientists to make pro-
　　　　nouncements on matters of language, literature,
　　　　philosophy, ethics and religion--all fields in which
　　　　they have no special competence. Snow's division
　　　　of society into two cultures demonstrates a point of
　　　　view perhaps derived from negative entropy.

B244　BEKER, MIROSLA.　"Svijet C.P. Snowa." Forum (Zagreb), no.
　　　　7-8 (1966) 618-28.

B245　ENRIGHT, D.J.　"Easy Lies the Head: C.P. Snow and the
　　　　Corridors of Power," in his Conspirators and Poets.
　　　　Chester Springs, Pa.: Dufour, 1966, pp. 106-110.
　　　　　　[Reprint of B640.]

B246　FIETZ, LOTHAR.　"Cambridge und die Diskussion um das
　　　　Verhaltnis von Literatur und Naturwissenschaft." In
　　　　Literatur-Kultur-Gesellschaft in England und Forschungs-
　　　　Beitrage. Friedrich Schubel zum 60. Geburtstag, edited
　　　　by Horst Mueller and Hans Joachim Zimmermann. Frankfurt:
　　　　Diesterwieg, 1966, pp. 113-27.

B247　SHESTAKOV, DMITRI.　"What C.P. Snow Means to Us." Soviet
　　　　Literature, no. 1 (1966) 174-79.
　　　　　　Snow explores the common destiny of his contem-
　　　　poraries, not their individual fates, because he feels
　　　　that the important decisions of life are made in a
　　　　social context. This approach, while it provides
　　　　nothing new for an age that thrives upon the new, does
　　　　remain true to the essential foundations of human life.
　　　　AES, 12, no. 2 (October 1969) 91.

B248　SYMONS, JULIAN.　"Of Bureaucratic Man," in his Critical
　　　　Occasions. London: Hamish Hamilton, 1966, pp. 68-74.
　　　　　　[Reprint of B434.]

B249   TRILLING, LIONEL. "Science, Literature and Culture: A
        Comment on the Leavis-Snow Controversy," in The
        Commentary Reader; Two Decades of Articles and Stories.
        Edited by Norman Podhoretz. New York: Atheneum, 1966,
        pp. 467-88.
            Reprint of B143.

B250   BORK, ALFRED M. "Resource Letter Co1R-1 on Collateral
        Reading for Physics Courses." American Journal of
        Physics, 35, no. 2 (February 1967) 71-78.
            A bibliography of writings on the subject of the
        "Two Cultures." "The present list is restricted to
        articles which are not the raw material of science
        itself. In most cases specific articles rather than
        full books are listed, since we wish to confine
        ourselves to relatively short selections that lend
        themselves to assignment as collateral reading."
        113 items. Chronological arrangement under broad
        subject headings. Brief annotations.

B251   RABINOVITZ, RUBIN. "C.P. Snow, b. 1905: [a Bibliography],"
        in his The Reaction Against Experiment in the English
        Novel, 1950-1960. New York; London: Columbia University
        Press, 1967, pp. 196-211.
            Includes books (to 1964) articles, essays, reviews
        (to 1963?) and books, articles and essays about Snow
        (to 1965).

B252   _____. "C.P. Snow versus the Experimental Novel."
        Columbia University Forum, 10, no. 3 (Fall 1967) 37-41.
            In the London Sunday Times in 1949-1951 and else-
        where later, Snow attacked "moment by monent fiction"
        because, he said, it had nearly killed the form and
        because its practitioners were reactionaries. He
        shaped English taste in the fifties with his liking
        for popular, realistic novels about moral and social
        problems. AES, 11 (1968) 296.

B253   _____. "C.P. Snow as Literary Critic," in his The Reaction
        Against Experiment in the English Novel, 1950-1960.
        New York: Columbia University Press, 1967, pp. 97-127.
            [The most complete and scholarly examination of
        Snow's critical writings to date. It is supported by
        a formidable bibliographical apparat of 113 footnotes.]
        Examines Snow's social and literary criticism of the
        experimental movement (Eliot, Yeats, Wyndham Lewis,
        Dorothy Richardson, Pound, Joyce and Virginia Woolf).
        Occasionally disagrees with Snow's assessments and
        shows a tendency to point out Snow's inconsistencies
        as well as a willingness to defend James Joyce. Collects
        and assembles Snow's references to realism, his praise

of realistic writers and examines the similarities and differences between the Marxist critic, Georg Lukacs, and C.P. Snow. Snow's critical evaluations of American authors demonstrate Snow's extreme distaste of all traces of the stream of consciousness technique and lead him into the mistake of giving high critical opinions of Cozzens, Lewis Auchincloss and Wallace Stegner at the expense of Faulkner, Hemingway and Dos Passos. Snow's newspaper reviewing in the London Sunday Times suffers from imprecise jargon, but it undoubtedly encouraged the emerging neo-realistic novelists.

B254   . "C.P. Snow as Novelist," in his The Reaction Against Experiment in the English Novel, 1950-1960. New York: Columbia University Press, 1967, pp. 128-65.
        [In which Rabinowitz shows himself to be an uncompromising member of the anti-Snow faction.] On the pervasiveness of suspense in Snow's novels, his use of common words in combination with obscure tongue-twisters, his rejection of modern psychology, deter-minism in Snow's work, absence of irony, his adherence to a theory of humours and the unconvincing speech habits of the American, Dr. Rubin. Snow has a tendency to summarize; he does not substantiate. The actual resonance is that between the life of Lewis Eliot and the career of C.P. Snow--which leads Rabinovitz to point out the autobiographical elements in Snow's fiction. Lewis Eliot is guilty of much self-praise; he is also guilty of hypocrisy. Discusses the presence of positivism, and the absence of existentialism, in Snow's novels, and the worldly success of second-rate men. Ultimately, Snow's novels flatter bureaucrats in the United States and the U.S.S.R. and make their appeal to the mediocre self-satisfied professional classes.

B255   SEEHASE, GEORG. "Kapitalistische Entfremdung und humanistische Integration. Bemerkungen zum Englischen proletarischen Gegenwartsroman." Zeitschrift fur Anglistik und Amerikanistik, 15, no. 4 (1967) 383-400.
        In German. Alienation from capitalism and ensuing humanistic integration is an important theme of the contemporary English novel. It appears in various forms: predominance of alienation without any real solution (Iris Murdoch, Durrell, Waugh, Golding); attempted solution by humanistic integration (Aldridge, Snow, Greene); and predominance of humanistic inte-gration in the works of proletarian writers or writers

of the "New Left" bourgeoisie (Margot Heinemann, Lindsay, Sillitoe, Lambert, Chaplin, Allen, Williams and Sommerfield).

B256 STEINER, GEORGE. "F.R. Leavis," in his Language and Silence: Essays on Language, Literature, and the Inhuman. New York: Atheneum; London: Faber, 1967, pp. 221-38.
        [Reprint of B140.]

B257 BUTLER, JOHN. "Snow in the Tropics." Transition, 7, no. 34 (December-January 1968) 31-33.
        Parody.

B258 DALLMAYR, FRED R. "Political Science and The Two Cultures." Journal of General Education, 19, no. 4 (January 1968) 269-95.
        Examines the old problem of the organization and relationship of various branches of knowledge, and discusses the contributions of Plato, Aristotle, various scholastic philosophers, Vico, Bacon, Descartes, Kant, Compte, Spencer, Dilthey, Wilhelm Wundt, Wilhelm Windelband, Heinrich Rickert, Erich Becher and others on this subject. Then clarifies the position of political science within the hierarchy of the arts and sciences. "Clearly our discipline cannot meet Snow's challenge if it is merely an adjunct of natural science." [A long, complicated article.]

B259 MILLAR, RONALD. "The Play of the Book." Times Literary Supplement, no. 3473 (19 September 1968) 1053.
        The dramatist describes how The Affair, The New Men and The Masters were adapted for the London stage.

B260 "State of Siege." Time, 92, no. 21 (22 November 1968) 17.
        [Excerpts from the John Findley Green lecture at Westminster, Mo.] Two experts, Emil Mrak and Harrison Brown, agree with Snow's Malthusian pessimism while Addeke Boerma and Robert McNamara disagree.

B261 "Glum Snow Job?" Senior Scholastic, 93, no. 12 (6 December 1968) 23.
        An account of Snow's warning entitled "State of Siege" delivered at Westminster College, Fulton, Mo. Snow warns that a sea of famine will sweep the earth by the year 2,000. Many scientists do not agree with his views.

B262 "Snow's War." Nation, 207, no. 20 (9 December 1968) 612.
        Approving capsule comment on the John Findley Green lecture entitled "State of Siege."

B263   "Spector of Famine." Commonweal, 89, no. 11 (13 December
        1968) 367–68.
            [Editorial.] Snow's suggestion that youth adopt
        the cause of the food-population collision is impractical.
        In fact, the issue should be entrusted to the United
        Nations.

B264   GROGER, ERIKA. "Der burgerliche Atomwissenschaftler im
        Englisch-Amerikanischen Roman von 1945 bis zur
        Gegenwart." Zeitschrift fur Anglistik und Amerikanistik,
        16, no. 1 (1968) 25–48.
            After Hiroshima, a new theme and a new character
        appear in English and American fiction: the danger of
        misuse of atomic energy and the nuclear scientist. Four
        groups of relevant works may be discerned: atomic utopias,
        atomic thrillers, peace-movement novels, and serious
        (mostly tragic) novels, especially C.P. Snow's The New
        Men, Masters' The Accident, and Wilson's Meeting at a
        Far Meridian. The theme gives a new twist to the
        relationship between literature and science and
        literature and social reality. AES, 12, no. 1 (September
        1969) 53.

B265   IVASHEVA, V. "V koridorakh vlasti [In the Corridors of Power]."
        Raduga (Moscow), 8 (1968) 159–74.

B266   KASHCHEEVA, V. "Ranee tvorchestvo Ch. P. Snou; Roman 'Poiski
        [Early Works of C.P. Snow; His Novel The Search]."
        Moskovskii gosudarstvennyi pedagogicheskii institut
        imeni Lenina (Moscow), 304 (1968) 170–88.

B267   LENGYEL, EMIL. "The Two Cultures and the Abyss in Between,"
        in The Humanities in the Age of Science. Edited by
        Charles Angoff. Rutherford, N.J.: Farleigh Dickinson
        University Press, 1968, pp. 101–15.
            Includes comments on the rapid advance of science,
        quotes from Jungk's Brighter Than a Thousand Suns,
        gives an account of an interview with Einstein, who
        remarks that a unified field theory of mankind includes
        art, science and ethics; quotes scientists who believe
        that the only way out of the nuclear dilemma is to
        create a world government. Snow appears only on p. 112
        as a believer in the value of education. Education is
        not enough; an ethical component is needed.

B268   ARSENESCU, ADINA. "C.P. Snow." Orizont (Timisoara,
        Rumania), no. 2 (February 1969) 51–54.

B269   ALLEN, WALTER. "Recent Trends in the English Novel."
        English, 18, no. 100 (Spring 1969) 2–5.

The novel is a paradigm of man's life in society.
Past works (<u>Tom Jones</u>, <u>Emma Domby & Son</u>, <u>Nostromo</u>,
<u>Ulysses</u>, <u>The Rainbow</u>, <u>Finnegans Wake</u>) form extended
and completely satisfying metaphors for the life of
the time at its most significant. The new world picture
is marked by Nazi death camps and the bomb: it is
irreconcilable with art. More, it leads to attitudes
"tentative, temporary, provisional." The rise of
<u>romans fleuves</u>, including Snow's <u>Strangers and Brothers</u>
sequence, in which novelists speak only for themselves,
without the implicit magisterial generalization about
the nature of society as reflected in Victorian
novelists, is hauled in to prove the point that current
society is splintered, disoriented, unclassic. [The
brief lucubration on Snow is mainly devoted to the
subtle observation that Snow's fictional work is
autobiographical in whole or in part.]

B270   BANON, B.A. "Authors and Editors." <u>Publishers Weekly</u>,
       195, no. 15 (14 April 1969) 25-27.
          Resume of <u>State of Siege</u>. Includes comments.

B271   BROGAN, DENIS. "Inequality and Mr. Short." <u>Spectator</u>,
       222, no. 7347 (18 April 1969) 505.
          [A sardonic defense of Snow against the short
       view of Mr. Short, the Minister of Education and
       Science. Short denounced Snow's views on the genetic
       basis in education as "reminiscent of Dr. Goebbels in
       <u>The Times</u> of April 9, 1969, p. 1.] "Lord Snow is not
       a bit like Dr. Goebbels. For one thing Dr. Goebbels
       was an effective orator, and Lord Snow is not an
       effective orator. Also, up to the end Dr. Goebbels
       had a very great political talents, and Lord Snow
       has demonstrated how easy it is to get lost in the
       corridors of power when he moved from fiction into
       fact."

B272   SMITH, PETER J. "The Gene Drain." <u>Spectator</u>, 222, no.
       7349 (18 April 1969) 502.
          "Lord Snow was quite in order to wonder publicly
       why Jewish achievement is disproportionately high;
       and to ask, quite non-rhetorically, whether this has
       anything to do with genetic quality is a perfectly
       legitimate question. The truth is that there is little
       evidence either way." The remainder of the article
       considers the effect on Britain of emigration of
       professional and managerial classes.

B273   "Why Are Jews Successful?" <u>Christianity Today</u>, 13, no. 15
       (25 April 1969) 31.
          A report of Snow's remarks at the New York School

of Hebrew Union College-Jewish Institute of Religion.
Snow drops the blockbuster that, in his view, there
is a genetic basis for Jewish intellectual ability.

B274 SHAHAK, ISRAEL. "The Gene Drain." Spectator, 222, no.
7349 (2 May 1969) 596.
Letter. Imputes Jewish achievement over the last
150 years to the abandonment of cramped, superstitious
and repressive Orthodox Judaism. The resulting freedom
is the spur to achievement.

B275 WREN-LEWIS, JOHN. "Ten Years Under Snow." New Statesman,
78, no. 2010 (19 September 1969) 386.
[A comment on the "Two Cultures" lecture 10 years
later.] The alienation from science and technology
on the part of youth, while superficially a symptom
of disaffection, is really a new expression of the
experimental spirit which was first enunciated in the
seventeenth century. "If, and only if, we take the
new culture seriously as Snow asked us to do, we shall
find that it abolishes all the traditional distinctions
between 'art' and 'science', between 'humanities' and
'technics', between 'Eastern' inwardness and 'Western'
activism, by seeing human life in terms of creative
action (in which the inner continually seeks expression
in the outer) instead of in terms of conformity (in
which the inner and the outer remain at odds unless
inner spontaneity is completely abandoned). For
realising this, Snow deserves, in my view, to be ranked
a major prophet of our time."

B276 BURSTYN, HAROLD L. "Tradition and Understanding: The Sciences
and the Humanities." School and Society, 97, no. 2320
(November 1969) 419-24.
"The purpose of this paper will be to look directly
at education and to develop Snow's insight into the two
cultures, so as to clarify its implications for education." Science is cumulative and incorporative; the
present absorbs the past. The present-day physicist
need not consult Newton. The humanities are not incorporative in the same sense at all. The contemporary
student of the humanities must read Shakespeare, about
the causes of the French Revolution, World War I, etc.
So it appears logical to suggest that "The ultimate
meaning for education of this analysis of the two
cultures into a scientific and a humanist tradition--
the one of method, the other of content--is that both
scientific method and humanist content are necessary
for the educated man or woman."

B277   RICHARDSON, KENNETH RIDLEY. "Snow, C.P." Twentieth Century
        Writing: A Reader's Guide to Contemporary Literature.
        London: Newnes Books, 1969, pp. 571-74.

B278   "Snow, C.P." Contemporary Authors; A Bio-bibliographical
        Guide to Current Authors and Their Works. V. 5-8.
        Edited by Barbara Harte, Carolyn Riley. Detroit:
        Gale Research Corporation, 1969, pp. 1073-76.

B279   "Snow, C.P." 200 [i.e. Two Hundred] Contemporary Authors.
        Detroit: Gale, 1969.

B280   DAVENPORT, WILLIAM H. "Resource Letter TLA-1 on Technology,
        Literature, and Art since World War II." American
        Journal of Physics, 38, no. 4 (April 1970) 407-14.
            A bibliography of writings on the subject of the
        "Two Cultures." "This resource letter lists materials
        for collateral reading in classes in physics and other
        sciences as well as in new cross-discipline courses;
        it also offers professors and students alike an
        opportunity to see how modern science and technology
        appear to artists and writers--in other words, to see
        themselves as others see them." 111 items. Chrono-
        logical arrangement under broad subject headings.
        Brief annotations.

B281   DAVIS, ROBERT MURRAY. "Market Depressed and Unstable:
        Surveys of the Recent English Novel." Papers on
        Language and Literature, 6, no. 2 (Spring 1970) 211-23.
            [Review of The Reaction Against Experiment in the
        English Novel, 1950-1960 by Rubin Rabinovitz.] The
        work shows diligence. Angus Wilson comes off best.
        Kingsley Amis' self-conscious philistinism is scored.
        C.P. Snow's literary principles are the object of
        a crushing indictment, and Snow gets the most unfa-
        vorable treatment. The book may seem desiccated and
        old-fashioned, but its substantial content may make
        it valuable to future readers.

B282   LEAVIS, FRANK RAYMOND. "Literarism versus 'Scientism'--The
        Misconception and the Menace." Times Literary Supplement,
        23 April 1970, pp. 441-44.
            [An attack on grossly quantitative evaluations
        and endorsements of education. Leavis proposes a
        qualitative function of education, a reason for living,
        to the unthinking poets and sages of the Gross National
        Product. The method of the article, a gossippy casti-
        gation of the real or imagined sins of hack journalists
        writing in the Times Literary Supplement, is clever.

It suggests that his opponents, Lord Annan and Snow among them, aim at a form of education that produces these suspect sages, these blank cartridges. For replies by Snow and Annan, see Times Literary Supplement, 16 July 1970, p. 774; 23 July 1970, pp. 814-15.]

B283   RAY, CYRIL. "Letter to the Editor." Times Literary Supplement, 30 April 1970, p. 478.

     Mr. Ray, employed by Spectator, describes Snow's pre-publication reaction to Leavis' Richmond Lecture entitled "The Significance of C.P. Snow." Snow laughed a lot; his wife, Pamela Hansford Johnson, was more indignant and less amused. Mr. Ray obtained Snow's permission to publish the lecture, or diatribe, without any cuts.

B284   GALE, GEORGE. "Saying the Unsayable." Spectator, 225, no. 7413 (25 July 1970) 65-66.

     An article which favors the disinterested investigation of differences between various races. Snow's remarks on the genetic basis of Jewish ability are noted in one paragraph. These remarks, it is observed, created a fuss because Arthur Jensen published his views on the genetic basis of intellectual ability two weeks before the address.

B285   BERGONZI, BERNARD. "Looking Backward," in The Situation of the Novel. Pittsburgh: University of Pittsburgh Press, 1970, pp. 133-48.

     Describes Snow's anti-modernist critical views and considers him a lesser Trollope. His novels are sociological activities unrelieved by art. The aim of resonance is not achieved: the flat style is incapable of expressing nuances of feeling and the first person narrative involves Snow in difficulties. The early chapters of Time of Hope convey an **authenticity of** feeling which makes the thinness and shallowness of the later volumes so much more apparent, although the elusive character of Sheila Knight is realized. Roy Calvert is described in the stock epithets of serial fiction for women. He compares unfavorably to Powell's Charles Stringham. The charm and magnetism of George Passant are not communicated. The Masters, and parts of the other novels in which Snow depicts intrigue and a struggle for power, show him to best advantage, and he is capable of effective portraits of old men. The series as a whole suffers from fragmentation.

B286   DAVENPORT, WILLIAM H. "Selected Bibliography: Readings in **Relationships between Science, Technology, and Engineering and Humanities, Social Sciences, and Fine**

Arts," in his The One Culture. New York: Pergamon Press, 1970, pp. 170-76.

A bibliography of writings on the subject of the "Two Cultures." 140 items. Includes books and articles. Approximate cut-off point: 1968. Alphabetical arrangement by author. No annotations, but the works are extensively discussed in the text.

B287   . The One Culture. New York: Pergamon Press, 1970, 182 pp.

"This book is designed to be of use to any student or layman who is interested in or concerned about the state of culture, particularly American culture, in this Age of Technology. It is not an attempt to match the style of C.P. Snow (Lord Snow), the acerb retorts of F.R. Leavis, or the aplomb of Lionel Trilling, the first being the celebrated scientist and novelist who wrote The Two Cultures and the latter pair his most prominent critics."--Preface.

B288 RAMAKRISHNAIAH, C. "Possessive Love in Strangers and Brothers: A Study of Snow's Use of the Principal of Resonance in Developing the Theme." Indian Journal of English Studies, 11 (1970) 112-21.

Snow regards possessive love as the "one-sided devotion" bestowed upon its subject by a parental figure, foredoomed to be rejected by the subject who feels "claustrophobic" until an open clash occurs. The consequent emotional crisis leads the suffering giver toward self-comprehension. The iterative treatment of this theme is achieved through "resonating devices" such as verbal echoes and flashbacks that induce a mood of reminiscence. With the momentary insight that follows, the principal characters comprehend the significance of their past experiences. As a structural device, "resonance" is responsible for the "cyclical" or cumulative nature of the novels, as Cooper has shown in C.P. Snow (London: Longmans, Green, 1959). Functionally, this device is analogous to the physical phenomenon of resonance, and its use in shaping a novel shows Snow to be a highly original novelist whose art is deeply influenced by his identity as a scientist. AES, 16, (1972) 246.

B289 SIEGMUND-SCHULTZE, DOROTHEA. "Zur Diskussion des Begriffes der Kultur in Gross-Britannien." Zeitschrift fur Anglistik und Amerikanistik, 18, no. 2 (1970) 118-30.

In German. The contributions of Raymond Williams' Culture and Society, 1780-1950 (New York: Harper & Row, 1958) and C.P. Snow's The Two Cultures: and a Second Look (Cambridge: Cambridge University Press, 1964) to the

172

discussion of the term "culture" in Great Britain
adapt the old bourgeois concept of "one nation, one
culture" to the new conditions of twentieth century
capitalism but do not add anything fundamentally new.
Both authors use the term "culture" in a normative
sense as if there were a "common tradition" for the
whole nation and thus ignore that "there are two
cultures in each national culture" (Lenin), for the
basis of culture is the antagonism of classes. AES,
14, no. 4 (December 1970) 209.

B290   "Snow, C.P." The Blue Book: Leaders of the English-Speaking
World, 1970. Chicago: St. James Press, 1970.

B291   TROCSANYI, MIKLOS. "C.P. Snow." In Az angol irodalom a
huszadik szazadban (Budapest: Gondolat, 1970) 2, p. 57-76.

B292   WEBSTER, HARVEY CURTIS. "C.P. Snow: Scientific Humanist,"
in his After the Trauma: Representative British Novelists
Since 1920. Lexington: University of Kentucky Press,
1970, pp. 168-90.
        Includes sympathetic accounts of Snow's literary
criticism. Argues that the novelists of personal
sensibility, Virginia Woolf, Henry James and James Joyce
deliberately led limited lives which may have circumscribed their knowledge of the social world. Observes
that Death Under Sail shares similarities with Corridors
of Power, lists many of Snow's fictional characters,
divides them into failures and successes, and briefly
refers to the undogmatic morality that is the basis for
Snow's scientific humanism.

B293   GRAVES, NORA C. "Literary Allusions in Last Things." Notes
on Contemporary Literature, 1, no. 1 (January 1971) 7-8.
        [A response to Rubin Rabinovitz who observed that
Snow, a student of science, did not receive a liberal
education and so lacked classical allusions.] Snow
makes literary allusions to ancient and medieval writers.
The more recent nineteenth and twentieth century writers
get a heavier emphasis. Examples are given.

B294   FRY, PHILLIP, AND JAMES W. LEE. "An Interview in Austin
with John Lehmann." Studies in the Novel, 3, no. 1
(Spring 1971) 80-96.
        Lehmann discusses the relationship of Virginia
Woolf to the "transformation of poetry into the prose-
form of the novel," power as a theme in the British
novel since World War II, and Leonard Woolf's treatment
of him and his relationship with the Hogarth Press in

The Journey Not the Arrival Matters (Hogarth, 1969). He
also comments on the influence of C.P. Snow and the
literary characteristics of such writers as Alan
Sillitoe, Christopher Isherwood, Edward Upward and the
Auden group. AES, 15, no. 5 (January 1972) 307.

B295   SCOTT-KILVERT, IAN. "English Fiction 1969-1970." British
Book News, June 1971, pp. 425-30.
        British fiction of 1969-70 was notable for diversity
rather than for experimentation or originality. Many
novelists produced nothing. C.P. Snow and Anthony Powell
continued their cycles with, respectively, Last Things
(Strangers and Brothers) and Books Do Furnish a Room
(Music of Time) series. Some established writers changed
direction, including Graham Greene with the conscience-
less woman in Travels With My Aunt and John Fowles with
the dual hero and the dual ending of The French Lieu-
tenant's Woman. Experimental writing included Lawrence
Durrell's disappointing Nunquam, a philosophical romance.
Regional, historical and documentary novels also appeared.
AES, 17, no. 2 (October 1973) 112.

B296   STEINER, GECRGE. "Imagining Science." Listener, 86, no. 2255.
(18 November 1971) 686-88.
        Only the creative writer can give insight into the
mentality of the scientist. Wordsworth in the Preface
to Lyrical Ballads saw poetry exhibiting the "central
energies of the science of his time." Coleridge thought
of the epic poet's task as including an understanding
of the sciences. Novelists like George Eliot, C.P. Snow
and Vladimir Nabokov have understood the scientist's
predicament. But much contemporary writing is dull,
because creative writers are lazily ignoring the need
to grapple with and communicate the essence of scientific
life and thought. [Includes a passing reference to
Snow's The Search.] AES, 17, no. 5 (January 1974) 277.

B297   PARKHILL-RATHBONE, JAMES. "The 'Gravitas' of C.P. Snow."
Books and Bookmen, 17, (November 1971) 6-8.
        Snow's novels include simple but evocative poetic
passages and while his characters may seem devoid of
feeling, may resemble people briefly glimpsed from trains
and cars, their feelings almost certainly can be inferred.
The "gravitas" of the novels derives from the fact that
power is not conspiratorial but a fine, slow tango with
that siren, compromise. "C.P. Snow may be said to be
indebted in some measure to William Gerhardi's maxim
that it is the very ordinariness of ordinary things that
makes them so extraordinary."

B298　FRASER, G.S.　"C.P. Snow," in The Politics of Twentieth
　　　　Century Novelists.　Edited by G.A. Panichas.　New York:
　　　　Hawthorne Books, 1971, pp. 124-33.
　　　　　　　[Fraser ostensibly sets out to explore the politics
　　　　of The Masters, The New Men, The Affair and Corridors of
　　　　Power.　He devotes about a sentence to each of the four
　　　　novels mentioned.　He decides all four novels are about
　　　　"pure" politics--defined as the process of making deci-
　　　　sions which inevitably entails some compromise.　The
　　　　only substantial allegation about Snow's politics to
　　　　emerge is that Leicester is a decent sort of place;
　　　　therefore, C.P. Snow who lived there for some twenty
　　　　years, is a decent sort of man.　Fraser's forte is
　　　　impressionistic literary criticism, not the announced
　　　　theme, and so he compares Snow, with varying degrees
　　　　of rigor, to Angus Wilson, Anthony Powell, Stendhal,
　　　　Tolstoy, Dickens, Thackeray and Proust.]

B299　LODGE, DAVID.　The Novelist at the Crossroads, and Other
　　　　Essays on Fiction and Criticism.　Ithaca, N.Y.: Cornell
　　　　University Press, 1971.
　　　　　　　[For Snow, see pp. 18-19, 205, 219n, 281.]　Snow's
　　　　assertion that there was no literary development between
　　　　Painted Roofs and Finnegan's Wake or The Sound and the
　　　　Fury does not survive the most cursory examination.

B300　KARL, FREDERICK R.　"The Politics of Conscience: The Novels
　　　　of C.P. Snow," in his A Reader's Guide to the Contemporary
　　　　English Novel.　Revised ed.　New York: Farrar, Straus and
　　　　Giroux, 1972, pp. 62-84.
　　　　　　　[Reprint, with revisions, of B163.　In the 1962
　　　　ed. Snow is said to be emerging as a "major literary
　　　　figure."　The 1972 reading is "firm literary figure."]

B301　　_____.　"C.P. Snow: Postscript: 1960-1970," in The Contemporary
　　　　English Novel.　Revised ed.　New York:　Farar, Straus
　　　　and Giroux, 1972, pp. 346-49.
　　　　　　　The sequence lost its impetus long before the
　　　　publication of the last three volumes.　When Snow became
　　　　a technological messiah, he was lost to literature, and
　　　　his novels became mere moral outposts.　In Corridors of
　　　　Power, he pretends that reason and decency can mediate
　　　　political issues.　In The Sleep of Reason, he deals with
　　　　torture and murder in a style as "nonchalant as a
　　　　travelogue about surfing in New Zealand."　F.R. Leavis
　　　　feared that literature would lose its religious fervor
　　　　in the hands of Snow; those fears have been confirmed.

B302　MORRIS, ROBERT K.　"C.P. Snow.　Strangers and Brothers:
　　　　The Morality of History," in his Continuance and Change;
　　　　The Contemporary British Novel Sequence.　Carbondale:

Southern Illinois University Press; London: Feffer &
Simons, 1972, pp. 93-122.

Includes comments on the resonance technique, the
effectiveness of Roy Calvert as a character (Ivan
Karamazov, grown up in the Midlands, with a degree in
philosophy), the quest for truth, the treatment of
time, and the role of morality and reason in the series:
"Little wonder that Lewis Eliot, pinned down over eleven
volumes by a murderous crossfire of reason, is a
creature with all passion spent . . . Living within a
controlled society may provide the sole key to historic
order, may buffet the chaotic forces of time or change.
Yet is this not a terrible price to pay if individuality,
freedom, the demonic, creative, even self-destructive
urge is totally absorbed into a strong, saving, uniform,
but equally horrifying morality?"

B303   POOLE, ROGER C. "Life Versus Death in the Later Criticism
of F.R. Leavis." Renaissance and Modern Studies,
16 (1972) 112-41.

The resolute service of life and its moral values
is Leavis' criterion for judging the excellence of art
and for including a novelist in The Great Tradition
(London:Chatto & Windus, 1948). In his early criticism,
the concept of "life" was an extremely vague ideal
defined largely negatively by its utter exclusion of
scholarship, technology, and materialism. His attack in
1962 on The Two Cultures and the Scientific Revolution,
resulted in the honing of his concept of Life into a
more precise ideal. After this point, he increasingly
viewed life as a teleological circuit of energy which
permits interpretation and evaluation of the ends of
society. This bias makes of Leavis' later criticism a
radically realist criticism of life which demands of the
novel a total fidelity to reality. AES, 17, no.4
(December 1973) 214.

B304   ROUSSEAU, G.S. "Are There Really Men of Both Cultures?"
Dalhousie Review, 52 (1972) 351-72.

[A historical review intended to identify those
individuals genuinely at home in the scientific and
literary cultures.] Considers Leonardo, Goethe, Sir
Peter Medawar, Dr. William Whewell, the Huxley family,
Hegel, Julian Huxley, Ludwig von Bertalanffy, J.D.
Bernal, Cyril Darlington, Conrad Waddington, William
Harvey and George Bernard Shaw. He concludes that art
and science are distinct and separate; the one does not
nourish or assimilate the work of the other and, in
fact, the one displaces the other in areas to which
they both lay claim. Future technology will be trium-
phant, but art will endure--and we must "shed any

sentimental or nostalgic notion of science and the arts
magically fusing into some hermaphroditic whole."

B305   SEEHASE, GEORG. "Humanistische Moglichkeiten im kritischen
       Realismus von Charles Percy Snow." Zeitschrift fur
       Anglistik und Amerikanistik, 20, no. 1 (1972) 119-30.

B306   "Snow, Charles Percy," in Contemporary Novelists. Edited
       by James Vinson. London; Chicago: St. James Press,
       1972, pp. 1151-55.
           Includes a chronology (to 1964), a short list of
       Snow's books (to 1972) and an appreciation by Walter
       Allen. Reprinted with minor revisions: B322.

B307   ASHTON, T.L. "Realism and the Chronicle: C.P. Snow's cinema
       verite." South Atlantic Quarterly, 72 (Autumn 1973)
       516-27.
           [This article is abstract, opaque, characterized by
       quotations from various 100 proof pundits on this and
       that, and stupendously unintelligible. One sentence
       in every hundred makes sense. As near as I can make out,
       it attempts to praise Snow's fictional realism by refer-
       ence to certain abstractions cited at strategic moments
       in the text.] Snow's work is two-dimensional; it is
       reminiscent of cinema verite, and the restrained
       chronicle leads to "moral consciousness predicated on
       the ethics of realism."

B308   KARL, FREDERICK R. "Conrad, Wells, and the Two Voices."
       Publications of the Modern Language Association, 88,
       no. 5 (October 1973) 1049-65.
           [A fascinating article which describes the
       differences in the aesthetic credos of H.G. Wells and
       Joseph Conrad. Wells's credo of social realism, it is
       suggested, was later echoed by that Wellsian, Snow,
       for socially desirable ends.]

B309   SWINDEN, PATRICK. "The World of C.P. Snow." Critical
       Quarterly, 15, no. 4 (Winter 1973) 297-313.
           Snow is clearly a novelist of remarkable ability.
       Over and above the virtues implied in Trilling's
       sketch (see B435)--intelligence, grasp of affairs,
       weighty common sense and sheer doggedness--he posseses
       remarkable powers of narrative, knows the value of
       suspense, and his themes, the sociological content
       of his novels, are widely acknowledged to have some
       redeeming value. The sequence demonstrates, not only
       Snow's own attitude toward the Soviet Union, but the
       influence of Russian writers on his work. He is a
       Russian Balzac and, in the Russian fashion, his

readers are educated into responsibility. The three
themes of Lewis Eliot's life are the love of ambition,
the pursuit of love, and the struggle for a better
world. In the course of developing these themes, or
in asides, Snow suggests that human life is tragic;
but he simultaneously maintains that social life is
not tragic. In the first instance he sounds like
Conrad; in the second like D.H. Lawrence. The
characters in the novels who live continuously with
this tragic self, Passant, Calvert, Paul Jago, Rubin
are singularly uninteresting. They are incapable of
taking on life within the confines of Snow's plots,
and all his remarkable narrative skill is powerless to
give them interest commensurate with their own insight
and supposed suffering. The fundamental problem is that
Snow is a committed realist, and a presentation of the
tragic nature of human life calls for a less than
realistic plot, and so the tragic vision in Snow's
sequence remains "muddled and blurred."

B310 BRADBURY, MALCOLM. "C.P. Snow's Bleak Landscape," in his
Possibilities; Essays on the State of the Novel. New
York: Oxford University Press, 1973, pp. 201-210.
[Revised and expanded version of a review of
Last Things first published in New Statesman. See
B748.] Snow "has made his peculiar mixture of the
reasonable, neo-scientific, positivistic literary
imagination into a kind of test case, a radical
opposite to literary despair." It is true that the
public life of Snow's characters is towards optimism
and progress. Witness, for example, Snow's treatment
of his New Men, the meritocratic class, which makes
him seem like the exact heir of Wells. Witness also
Snow's concern with the life of the family, a social
repository of the forces of reason and growth. Still,
the overall movement of the cycle is from public
optimism to private despair. Lewis Eliot, once a
man of affairs, full of ceaseless attention and moral
energy, now finds the big world shrivelling, and Last
Things is "an epic of ungracious survival." This
movement, this reduction of Eliot from public man
to private emperor of angst, is prefigured in the early
novels of observed experience: the emotions observed
there are typically those that lie outside order and
pull in the direction of desperation. "The circle
is rounded off with the fading of the hope that let
that dense, substantiated fictional world of the early
novels take on such compelling power, the power of
being a culture co-existent in time and fiction. For
a writer who, it is often said, has no gift to move
us, it is a terrible story."

178

B311   SEYMOUR-SMITH, MARTIN. "British Literature," in Funk &
        Wagnalls Guide to Modern World Literature. New York:
        Funk & Wagnalls, 1973, pp. 286-88.
            Snow's fictional practise is inadequate and
        obscurantist. It is not a literary achievement. He
        lacks imagination. Lewis Eliot is a flattering self-
        photograph. The series is "as drab as Monday morning
        at the Ministry of Social Security. . . ." [Quotes
        various adverse judgments of Snow by Geoffrey Wagner,
        Rubin Rabinovitz and from Frederick R. Karl's
        "Postscript."] "Let us grant Snow's good intentions
        . . . . His enormous yarn . . . demands an answer of the
        same magnitude. The answer is that it is reprehensible
        . . . to treat human beings as objects in any kind
        of games--even in office games . . . . Members of
        Parliament can read Snow with pleasure; one cannot
        imagine their having much time for Powell."

B312   LEVENSTON, E.A. "Interrupted and Interruption Sentences."
        English Studies, 55, no. 5 (October 1974) 414-20.
            [A technical work on Snow's sentence structure
        in Last Things.] The text of Snow's narrator includes
        parenthetical information--sometimes set off by dashes--
        occasionally by parentheses and commas. The effect
        of these interruptions is to "take the reader into the
        narrator's confidence. They create a feeling of
        intimacy, of companionship almost, between writer and
        reader that is difficult to obtain with more orthodox
        sentence structure. You can trust a narrator who stops
        in mid-sentence to correct a misunderstanding, or
        allows you to share his self-doubt." 3000w

B313   BRADBURY, MALCOLM. "The Novel," in The Twentieth Century
        Mind, edited by C.B. Cox and A.E. Dyson. Oxford:
        Oxford University Press, 1974, pp. 337-39.
            The effect of the attacks against mannered
        experimentalism, and the critical move towards more
        traditional and more provincial sources for literature
        "was to produce more interest in society than sensi-
        bility, to restore a stronger sense of the public
        language of reference, of shared common sense, and
        shared recognitions available to the novelist. . . ."
        Also provides brief synopses of The Search, Strangers
        and Brothers (i.e. George Passant), The New Men, The
        Masters, and The Sleep of Reason.

B314   "Snow, C.P." The International Who's Who, 1974-75. London:
        Europa Publications; Detroit: Gale, 1974.
            [Biographical sketch.]

B315 "Snow, C.P." <u>The New Encyclopaedia Britannica</u>. 15th ed.
      Chicago: Encyclopaedia Britannica, 1974.
      [Biographical sketch.]

B316 DAVENPORT, WILLIAM H. "Resource Letter TLA-2: Technology,
      Literature, and the Arts, Contemporary." <u>American</u>
      <u>Journal of Physics</u>, 43, no. 1 (January 1975) 4-8.
      A bibliography of writings on the subject of the
      "Two Cultures." Updates B280. 84 items. Chronological
      arrangement under broad subject headings. Brief
      annotations. Includes music.

B317 "Snow, C.P." <u>A Library of Literary Criticism; Modern British</u>
      <u>Literature</u>. V. 4. Compiled and edited by Martin Tucker,
      Rita Stein. New York: Ungar, 1975, pp. 486-92.
      [Excerpts from the work of literary critics.]

B318 ESTALL, H.M. "The Snows of Yesteryear." <u>The Humanities</u>
      <u>Association Review (La Revue de l'Association des</u>
      <u>Humanites)</u> 26 (1975) 1-9.
      Examines the historical precedents of the arts v.
      sciences controversy in the writings of Swift and
      Henry Adams, then focusses his attention on Snow's
      "Third Culture" of social scientists and tries to
      answer the question of how, if at all, the methods of
      this "Third Culture" differ from predecessors (Herodotus,
      Thucydides, Plato, Aristotle), protests that social
      scientists must recognize the distinction between a
      problem and a "mystery," observes that ends, as opposed
      to means, lie outside the range of sociological inquiry.

B319 JAKI, STANLEY L. "A Hundred Years of Two Cultures."
      <u>University of Windsor Review</u> (Windsor, Ont.), 11, no.
      1 (Fall/Winter 1975) 55-79.
      Recapitulates the dispute between T.H. Huxley and
      Matthew Arnold, and suggests that an extreme devotion
      to the methods of science in the affairs of men [i.e.
      scientism] produces automata, not men. Snow's Rede
      lecture includes a number of faults. The word culture
      is not properly defined. As it stands, Snow's purely
      behavioristic definition can apply equally to the
      Hitlerjugend, the Komsomol, and the Red Guards. The
      attribution of special virtues to scientists is unsound.
      The backbone of the lecture is a strong prejudice in
      favor of scientists, but especially applied scientists.
      Further, the lecture's "explanations of culture and
      society in terms of industrial production have a
      curiously Marxist ring" and Snow is silent about the
      various defects of Soviet society. Other apostles of
      scientism (Huxley, Wells, Bertrand Russell) expressed
      their later disillusionment, and it is possible that

Snow will do so. Includes some comments on Leavis',
Trilling's and Aldous Huxley's criticisms of Snow's
lecture. "While it may sound a truism, it cannot be
repeated often enough that for scientific investigation
of nature the esthetic beauty in nature is largely
irrelevant" and illustrates the assertion by quotations
from Wordsworth and E.E. Cummings. [For conclusion
of article, see University of Windsor Review, 11, no.
2 (1976) 81-103. The conclusion has little or no bearing
on Snow. Reprinted: B24.]

B320   WIDDOWSON, PETER J. "C.P. Snow's Strangers and Brothers
       Sequence: Lewis Eliot and the Failure of Realism."
       Renaissance and Modern Studies (University of Nottingham),
       19 (1975) 112-28.
            Snow championed the role of the reflective intel-
       ligence in his criticism, and embodied his own precept
       in his fiction, but Lewis Eliot resorts to mere analysis
       and eschews the dramatic presentation of character, and
       this technique reduces Snow's novels to reports. Eliot,
       who issues reports about his own character both as a
       young and as a mature man, cannot himself be judged since
       the novels provide no dramatized actions which would
       make such judgments possible. Snow has expressed his
       admiration of Percy Lubbock's The Craft of Fiction but
       he has significantly disregarded some of Lubbock's
       recommendations. The result is a confusion in point of
       view. The deficiencies of Snow's narrative technique
       are best shown in The Sleep of Reason and Last Things,
       in which the "devitalized presentation of character is
       at its most extreme." Snow's technique does not
       successfully evoke character. It piles abstraction on
       abstraction, a fact evident in the portrayals of Roy
       Calvert and Dr. Jago. The talk of different characters
       in different novels conveys a "flatly prosaic similarity
       of tone."

B321   KIRVAITIS, GRAZVYDAS. "Problema konflikta mezdu licnoj i
       obscestvennoj sovestkju v romanax C.P. Snou."
       Literatura, 18, no. 3 (1976) 77-83.

B222   "Snow," in Contemporary Novelists. 2d ed. Edited by James
       Vinson. London; Chicago: St. James Press, 1976,
       pp. 1262-65.
            Reprint, with minor revisions, of B306.

B323   DAVIS, ROBERT GORHAM. "C.P. Snow," in Six Contemporary
       British Novelists. Edited with an introduction by
       George Stade. New York: Columbia University Press, 1976,
       pp. 57-114.
            [An introductory survey of The Search and all the

novels in the Strangers and Brothers sequence.] Snow
the novelist and Snow the polemicist are different
creatures; there is, for example, very little science
in Snow's books. After some introductory comments on
the literary cultures (not reactionary), Snow's
fictional method, the sneers of Dr. Leavis and Snow's
affinities with Trollope, the essay discusses The Search
(p. 67-), Time of Hope (p. 72-), Homecomings (p. 76-),
George Passant (p. 79-), The Light and the Dark (p. 81-),
The New Men (p. 84-), The Conscience of the Rich (p. 87-),
The Masters (p. 90-), The Affair (p. 92-), Corridors of
Power (p. 94-), The Sleep of Reason (p. 100-), The
Malcontents (p. 104-), Last Things and In Their Wisdom
(p. 106). Snow's novels are circumscribed. They
include little of the scientific experience, Hemingway's
life of action, the elegant Proustian touches or Tolstoy's
vast human and geographical scope. It may be inferred
that they intend to celebrate the joys of science, sex
and success. Snow's popular success is possibly due to
his use of classic humoral psychology. [Davis' discussions of Snow's later novels are pointedly
unfavorable.]

B324   HAYMAN, RONALD. Leavis. London: Heinemann; Totowa, N.J.:
        Rowman and Littlefield, 1976.
            For a brief account of the "Two Cultures" dispute
        told from the point of view of Dr. Leavis, see pp.
        52, 57, 111-13, 117-18.

B325   PALMER, HELEN H. "Snow," in English Novel Explication.
        Hamden, Conn.: Shoestring Press, 1976, pp. 207-08.
            [Attempts to steer readers to criticism of Snow's
        novels. Very sketchy and incomplete.]

B326   TRILLING, LIONEL. "The Novel--Alive or Dead," in his A
        Gathering of Fugitives. Uniform edition. New York:
        Harcourt, Brace Jovanovich, 1977, pp. 135-42.
            [Reprint of B435.]

B327   TASK, JOHN. "Uncompromising Critic." New York Times,
        18 April 1978, p. 42.
            [An obituary of F.R. Leavis, who died on April 14,
        1978. Describes the famous critic's influence and
        career. Includes a 300 word summary of his quarrel with
        Snow in 1962.]

B328   STANTON, ROBERT J. "Charles Percy Snow," in his A
        Bibliography of Modern British Novelists. V. 2. Troy,
        N.Y.: Whitston Pub. Co., 1978, pp. 807-993.
            A bibliography--and a tribute to the energy of its

compiler. It supersedes Rabinovitz (B251) as
Rabinovitz superseded Bernard Stone (B6). Includes
Snow's works and translations of these works, Snow's
articles, both literary and scientific (chronological
order), book reviews in the London Financial Times
and elsewhere (but not from London Sunday Times) and
book reviews of Snow's works. Brief selective
annotations.

Book Reviews

Death Under Sail. 1932.

B329   ANDERSON, ISAAC. "New Mystery Stories." New York
      Times Book Review, 16 October 1932, p. 21.
      [Chiefly plot summary.] It "is a baffling mystery
and an excellent story of how men and women behave under
the strain of mutual suspicion."

B330   ANON. "New Novels." New Statesman and Nation, 4, no. 75
      (30 July 1932) 134.
      "Mr. Snow's story is a straight detective story
farsed, as is the modern method, by some hard character-
drawing, a little farce and some very tedious humour.
There is ingenuity in the book, and after the first
three chapters, Mr. Snow's style improves; but his story
would have been much better had all his characters been
men—rarely even in detective fiction have quite such
unlikely feminine marionettes pirouetted for our in-
credulity."

B331   ANON. Review of Death Under Sail. Times Literary
      Supplement, 11 August 1932, p. 570.
      "This novel by a young Cambridge don was written
as a relaxation from a long period of important bio-
chemical research. It is clearly the work of an acute
and analytical mind. . . . An intellectually stimulating
and satisfying story." 180w

B332   ANON. Review of Death Under Sail. New York Herald
      Tribune Book Review, 8 September 1932, p. 10.
      "Naturally Finbow finds the fiend, largely by means
of questions and answers. You'll enjoy it more if you
care for the people."

B333   BREMNER, MARJORIE. Review of Death Under Sail.
      Twentieth Century, 167 (January 1960) 91.
      "Interesting as the first published fiction by

Snow, but dullish on its own merits." 70w

B334   PARTRIDGE, RALPH. "Detection and Crime." New
       Statesman, 58, no. 1494 (31 October 1959) 600.
           [Omnibus review.] The yarn is "just sufficiently
       ingenious to bear re-issue now that the author is a
       famous novelist. The plot is artifically contrived and
       the characters a set of dummies; but there are a few
       minutes when each one of them must be closely scrutinised
       to solve the chess-problem." 50w

B335   PYM, CHRISTOPHER. "It's a Crime." Spectator, 203, no.
       6850 (9 October 1959) 494.
           Finds that the book is typical of the "puzzle stories
       of the early thirities, but the Knoxes and Milnes of those
       days had more wit and charm than this Snow of yesteryear."
       45w

New Lives for Old. 1933.

B336   ANON. Review of New Lives for Old. Times Literary
       Supplement, 10 August 1933, p. 536.
           [Snow's only anonymous book. It has never been
       reprinted.] "'By one of our younger scientists,' says
       the dust-cover, and there are touches which hint that
       he does not write of age from the inside. And if he
       had consulted Bock [a fictional statistician in the
       book] about suicide, it seems likely that Callan would
       not have been the only person in the book who did not
       want the extra thirty years—and even he changed his
       mind by Pilgrim's death-bed. Taking the sexual side
       alone (as the author seems inclined to), a prospect
       of the recurrence of a desire with as few chances as
       ever to gratify it (perhaps fewer) would of itself almost
       counterbalance the instinctive clinging to life." 500w

The Search. 1934.

B337   ANON. Review of The Search. Times Literary Supplement,
       6 September 1934, p. 602.
           The theme, the choice of a career for the complete
       man, calls for the handling of certain abstractions
       difficult to assimilate and reproduce with the appeal
       associated with the novel form. The egoistic, ambitious,
       truth-loving and moderately hedonistic hero, Arthur Miles,
       is typical of modern youth and "as such a rebel and
       contemptuous of all established institutions." His two

women seem to represent science and social progress.
Although it is described as a long novel with a serious
purpose, the reviewer believes that Dr. Snow "has not
overtaxed his powers in undertaking it." 300w

B338 ANON. "A Crystallographic Arrowsmith." Nature, 134,
(8 December 1934) supplement p. 890.
Compares the novel to Sinclair Lewis' Arrowsmith
and suggests they belong side by side. The nature of
Arthur Miles second enthusiasm, the psychological and
political education of mankind, is vague: "his aims seem
so mild and moderate, so Lowes-Dickensonian, so L.N.U."
But "We have in The Search a really important study of
human life as it is lived in the world of science. If
Mr. Snow can push on along this line, we are not willing
to suggest bounds for his possible achievement. But
it will need a more definite socio-political outlook,
and all the understanding that the closest and most
sympathetic observation of human behaviour can give. The
results of such a life are certainly no less valuable
than a hundred papers in Proceedings and Transactions."
[Signed: J.N. & D.N.] 800w

B339 ANON. "Sin Among the Scientists." Time, 73, no. 1 (5
January 1959) 87-89.
Lord Rutherford may have disapproved of the erotic
content of this novel but the sex life, described in
a flat and dogged style, is more reminiscent of Kinsey
than Ovid. The central theme, a scientist's devotion
to his subject, follows the familiar pattern of a
pietistic tract--from first vocation to final serenity
of soul. The maneuvers for the direction of the
research institute recall Trollope. The characters,
judged on a traditional basis, may amuse or alarm the
non-scientist.

B340 ANON. Review of The Search. Publishers' Weekly, 192,
no. 3 (1 September 1967) 71.
[Brief review of the Scribner paperback ed.] "The
book was first published in 1934; this edition is that
of the author's revision of 1958." 50w

B341 BENET, WILLIAM ROSE. "A Scientist's Story." Saturday
Review of Literature, 11, no. 39 (13 April 1935) 622.
The novel is concerned less with emotional and
physical matters than with the intellect. The novels
by Wells combined intellect and emotion, but Snow is
no Wells! His style is marked by a praiseworthy clarity,
but it is too dry and wordy. It does, however, possess

an integrity of purpose. The hero's analysis of his attitude towards science is the most interesting part of the work. "The book is somewhat cluttered with disquisition, but the scientific matters are so outlined for the layman as to appear quite clear. Also one feels a general lack of buncombe about this novel, where so much modern work is sensational." 900w

B342   BIEN, PETER. "Novel of Scientist in the Twenties." New York Herald Tribune Book Review, 18 January 1959, p. 5.
It is a novel of traditional narrative technique, but devoid of Victorian stuffiness. Its true value lies in its dissection of normal character. Snow's "uniqueness is that he smashes the myth of the rational man without invoking the sub-conscious, and without introducing degenerate types." The committee scenes give us the triumph of Snow's technique, and Snow can communicate the joy of scientific discovery, but not the contentment of a happy marriage, or the course of a love affair. Its cry for human values in a technological world is prophetic.

B343   GRANSDEN, K.W. "People and Power." Encounter, 11, no. 6 (December 1958) 91.
Omnibus review. It is a remarkable first novel [The Search is Snow's third published novel] and Arthur Miles strongly resembles the Lewis Eliot of the later novels. Considers this novel, and apparently some other novels of the series, as a clash between the rebel and the mediocre time-servers. To make his way in the world the rebel must bow to the mediocrities. This inter-pretation of the novels "also explains the self-made hero's obsession with knowledge as a means of power and success, the constant, niggling, measuring-up of one's contemporaries, the determination to palm himself off on them as sound, solid chap while reserving the right to see through them which belongs properly to the artist." 300w

B344   HAMILTON, ALEX. Review of The Search. Books and Bookmen, 10 (March 1965) 35.
[One sentence reference to Snow's "unexciting first novel." The Search was Snow's third published novel.]

B345   KIEFER, H.C. "Review of The Search." Arizona Quarterly, 15, no. 4 (Winter 1959) 363-64.
The novel foreshadows themes later used with more accuracy and perceptiveness in The Masters and The New Men. Snow's prefatory note, which observes that the

book gives an account of a scientist's working life, raises false expectations. Arthur Miles "always conscious of his lower-class origins, shrewd in affairs to the point of dishonesty, superior to even good scientists but neither dedicated nor profoundly gifted" is a special case, not a typical scientist.

B346 KILEY, FREDERICK S. Review of The Search. Clearinghouse, 35, no. 6 (February 1961) 379.
[Review of Signet paperback edition of 1960. Brief and vague 100 word plot summary.]

B347 MCDONOUGH, JAMES P. "Review of The Search. Best Sellers, 18 (January 1959) 401-02.
The book will not initiate readers into the scientific experience. They will, however, soon learn that scientists at play are irreligious, amorous, envious and sometimes mendacious. When the scientists are shown at work, and not at their fine play, details are insufficient to interest the reader. "It is a mistake to assume that the non-scientific reader cannot understand what the scientist is driving at." 400w

B348 O[WEN], I.M. Review of The Search. Tamarack Review, 12 (Summer 1959) 101-02.
Snow's preface describes the book as a false start, but the Snow of today is much like the Snow of yesteryear. His descriptions of the working life and the struggle for power are brilliantly alive. It conveys the motives and excitements of research with total success. The scenes of personal, domestic or sexual relations sound stilled to the point of self-parody. "But this is a fine piece of work, and the best possible introduction to C.P. Snow."

B349 RAVEN, SIMON. "Three Out of Four." Spectator, 201, no. 6789 (10 October 1956) 496-97.
Omnibus review. It is a tremendously exciting book as an account of scientific research. It parallels Snow's later success, in the Strangers and Brothers series, in depicting characters in their professional processes. 250w

B350 SHERMAN, BEATRICE. "The Search and Some Other Recent Works of Fiction." New York Times (Daily), 14 April 1935, p. 6.
The title refers to a search for the important things in life. Quotes some epigrams from the book ("He had the endearing property that when he did anyone a bad turn he bore no resentment afterward") and

considers it "a meaty, stimulating novel which deserves
and demands a careful reading . . . The book produces
some clear thinking and some interesting discussion.
It is an extraordinarily provocative piece of work
which raises more questions than it decides. It would
be more satisfying and complete as a novel if Miles's
rejection of science were more clearly motivated. As
it is, the shifting of his search to a rather vague
sort of writing on economics seems an unsatisfactory
way out of his disillusion." 700w

B351   TILDEN, DAVID. "Some Recent Leading Fiction: The Search."
        New York Herald Tribune Books, 28 April, 1935, p. 12.
            ". . . throws a sharp beam of light on the lives
        and careers of many of us. It is not wholly a
        comfortable book for that reason. It is also a trifle
        pedestrian in manner, and most of its characters are
        bookish and shadowy. For all that, it undoubtedly
        presents a true picture of the pains and pitfalls that
        await the ambitious scientists or, for that matter, the
        personally ambitious man of any kind today."

George Passant. 1940.

B352   ANON. Review of Strangers and Brothers. Times Literary
        Supplement, 26 October 1940, p. 541.
            The characters are not an interesting cross section
        of English life. On the contrary, they are as shadowy
        at the end as at the beginning of the book. George
        Passant gives the impression of a "vague and crude
        busybody, whose ventures into a sort of exalted moral
        libertinism are those of mawkish adolescence." After
        Passant's trial for fraud, Snow's opinion of Passant's
        character is still not made clear: is he weak or strong,
        right or wrong, admirable or despicable? The imaginative
        treatment is too flat to convey the novelist's purpose.

B353   ANON. Review of Strangers and Brothers. Kirkus, 28
        (15 July 1960) 576.
            "It provides a slowly, closely pursued examination
        and rationale and an enlightened discussion of questions
        of conscience and conduct and commitment. And as such,
        if within a narrower margin, it is filled with the
        concerns which are so fundamentally and essentially a
        part of this writer's work and have attracted a firm
        following."

B354   ANON. "Ventures in Fiction: As Six Tales are Told."
        Newsweek, 56, no. 14 (3 October 1960) 88.
            It has all the faults and few of the virtues of
        The Affair, and the trial of George Passant is of
        interest only to lawyers, accountants and professors
        of ethics. The characters are unrelievedly earnest,
        the conversations interminable and all in all "reading
        it is like watching a horse learn how to knit." 150w

B355   ANON. Review of Strangers and Brothers. Booklist, 57
        (1 November 1960) 147.
            An understanding portrayal, by Lewis Eliot, of
        George Passant and his circle.

B356   ANON. Review of Strangers and Brothers. Books and
        Bookmen, 18 (May 1973) 124.
            [Twenty word notice to mark publication of the
        Penguin ed.]

B357   ANON. Review of Strangers and Brothers. Christian
        Century, 78, no. 2 (11 January 1961) 51.
            "Why must idealists have flaws? Passant reveals in
        himself the dichotomy of character and personality
        that is both Pauline and painfully contemporary in
        essence." It is a pity the work was published out of
        its proper sequence "for it describes Lewis Eliot's
        origins and motivations and makes more understandable
        his subsequent career in London and Cambridge." 140w

B358   CHAMBERLAIN, JOHN. "Reading for Pleasure: The Uncertain
        Rebels." Wall Street Journal, 11 November 1960, p. 6.
            Snow's Strangers and Brothers sequence, a
        "Balzacian panorama of impressive proportions" began
        with this book which describes the forces that led
        to the overthrow of Britain's Edwardian leadership. In
        this first book of the series, Snow does not show the
        moralizing impulse. He does not say that the Edwardians
        suppressed men of talent like George Passant. He also
        does not accuse the rebels of moral blindness that
        saddled England with inertia and aimlessness. "The
        reader is left to judge for himself that Passant's
        battle for freedom, while it was justified by the
        circumstances, was a battle fought in darkness." 500w

B359   DAVIS, ROBERT GORHAM. "Facing One's Self is Part of the
        Trial." New York Times Book Review, 25 September 1960,
        p. 5.
            This work is in many respects superior to The Affair.
        The characters are younger; they are more open to

experience and emotion; they are more open to the mysteries, excitement, dangers and hope of sex. The character of George Passant is immensely appealing. ". . . his story is told with an imaginative acceptance which makes him a peculiarly haunting and sympathetic figure and which creates a mood quite different from that of the later novels." 600w

B360   DOBREE, BONAMY. "Fiction." Spectator, 165, no. 5863 (8 November 1940) 486.
        The function of Passant is to radiate energy, and dispense virtue "so as to redeem the depressed half-educated classes, and rouse them to defeat the snobs and the vested interests." But it is hard to believe in Passant's supposed power. The analysis does not cut deep enough. "The ingredients are good enough, there are elements of a novel here, but Dr. Snow has failed to imagine it creatively, and so to write it convincingly." 200w

B361   GEISMAR, MAXWELL. "The Birth of a Sequence." Saturday Review, 43, no. 40 (1 October 1960) 19.
        "What is the secret of these sparse, flat, sometimes almost meager novels, whose concern for social justice and for the rights of the individual is tempered by a hard realism that knows the way of the world? What makes them important--and what is lacking in them?" Snow's importance is partly due to his uncompromising honesty and his practice of stripping away the illusions of his characters. This work is a good novel, but not a great one, and the "series as a whole is good literature but not very good literature. . . .Perhaps Snow's present vogue is due mainly to the fact that he fills the place of the old-fashioned novelist who both entertained and edified us in a very decent way. He is also one of the most civilized novelists now writing-- and that may come close to his central limitation." Snow sees and describes the world in terms of power even when his subject is sexual pleasure. ". . .the world of C.P. Snow is one of invisible and yet prevailing inhibition. . . . It may be that for major fiction the high note of morality and civilization, like honesty, is not enough." 1250w

B362   HARDING, WALTER. "Snow Novel Thought-Provoking Yet Entertaining." Chicago Sunday Tribune Book Review, 2 October 1960, p. 8.
        The genius of C.P. Snow has been unjustly neglected in the U.S. This novel, with its revelations of strengths and weaknesses in the character of George Passant, will stir the reader into making his own analysis of his

motives. Snow's work does not provide answers, but
it asks the questions which will compel re-thinking the
major moral problems of our day. 310w

B363 HAWKINS, DESMOND. "Home and Away." New Statesman and
Nation, 20 (23 November 1940) 520.
George Passant is a pompous, humorless, self-
righteous, tin-pot messiah whose interminable whines
of self-pity deserve the pitiless eyes of Dostoevsky
writing about Stavrogin, or Conrad about Lord Jim.
"To leave Passant untouched by irony, by satire, even
by simple ridicule, is no kindness; at least it is the
mistaken kindness of a sentimentalist." Dr. Snow
mistakenly all but calls Passant a great man and treats
him with great respect. [Excellent brief plot summary.]

B364 HUTCHENS, JOHN K. Review of Strangers and Brothers.
New York Tribune, 27 September 1960, p. 25.
Snow's many and loyal readers debate whether The
Masters, The Conscience of the Rich, or The Affair is
the best of his books. This loyalty equals that of
the adherents of Trollope, and "Sir Charles, like the
old master of Barsetshire, paces along on an even,
satisfying note, neither soaring nor slumping, creating
a world so real that you can reach out and touch it,
and peopling it with men and women who breathe." In
Strangers and Brothers, Snow is revealed as a shrewed
but reticent observer of mankind. This work marks the
beginning of a Comedie Humaine Trollopian in tone but
Balzacian in tradition.

B365 _____. "A Bookman's Notebook: Early C.P. Snow Novel
Makes Its U.S. Debut." San Francisco Chronicle,
13 October 1960, p. 37.
[Slightly condensed version of B364.]

B366 KLEIN, MARCUS. "The Pride of Power." New Leader, 44,
no. 1 (2 January 1961) 26.
In this work, the attractive figure of the young
radical, George Passant, shrivels when subjected to
Snow's massive searchingness and clarity. Someone else
should have written this book "Someone more given to
chances, to reaching for what in humans can't be known,
to lyricism and the zest of personality." The "Two
Cultures" divide is far less true in the United States
than in Great Britain. Snow has an inordinate political
sense of the conflict of individuals within society.

B367   NORDELL, ROD. "Serious Novels: Snow and Hersey Raise
        Some Questions." <u>Christian Science Monitor</u>, 29 September
        1960, p. 11.
            [Reviews this novel and contrasts it with <u>The
        Affair</u>--then still on the best-seller lists.] The
        characters in <u>George Passant</u> are young and unformed and
        concerned with little but themselves; therefore they
        are less worth caring about than the characters of <u>The
        Affair</u>. "Is there a double standard of morality, less
        rigid in matters of sensuality than in matters of
        finance? Is an erring individual 'a child of his time'
        --or personally responsible for his acts? These are two
        of the questions that ultimately become more interesting
        than the characters raising them."

B368   PRESCOTT, ORVILLE. "Books of the Times: <u>Strangers and
        Brothers</u>." <u>New York Times</u> (Daily), 30 November 1960,
        p. 35.
            The central character, George Passant, is pitiful
        and exasperating, and none of the other characters are
        likable or appealing. Still, Snow's manner and
        aesthetic credo remain unchanged over time. Why, then,
        is the book less rewarding than <u>The Affair</u>, <u>The Masters</u>,
        or <u>The New Men</u>? The psychological malaise of George
        Passant is probably not worth a book. Second, the
        setting is drab and ordinary compared to the later
        works, and it represents a less happy choice of subject.
        800w

B369   SPECTOR, ROBERT DONALD. "No. 1 in a Modern Master's
        Chronicle." <u>New York Herald Tribune Book Review</u>,
        27 September 1960, p. 5.
            The concern for the dignity of the individual in
        this work is appropriate. It recalls a time [1940]
        when the existence of all mankind was in jeopardy. The
        dramatic values of the work derive from the complexity
        of its characters, and Snow's solutions are never simple.
        Due to the growth of the characters as the series
        progresses, it is best to begin the sequence at the
        beginning. This work "is the achievement of a man
        whose scientific and humanistic training has made him
        the foremost moralist of the English writers of our
        time."

B370   WALSH, WILLIAM J. Review of <u>Strangers and Brothers</u>.
        <u>Best Sellers</u>, 20 (15 October 1960) 263-64.
            At his best, Snow shares the talent of Austen and
        George Eliot: he communicates the essence of man's
        social experience in a telling gesture, remark or
        detail. The novel, first published in 1940, wears
        well. It illustrates Snow's theme that every intimate,

or brother, is potentially capable of revealing depths of corruption along with nobility, that man is not a seamless vial of virtue or vice. "Recommended to all interested in what one of England's best creative minds has turned up in the course of a sensitive investigation of how men--in this case one of the godless elite--are reacting to the forces that shape the world we live in."

B371   WERMUTH, PAUL C. Review of <u>Strangers and Brothers</u>. <u>Library Journal</u>, 85, no. 16 (15 September 1960) 3106.
    "Like all the novels in the series [it is] distinguished by virtue of its analysis of motive and character and its anatomization of a world in which a smooth mediocrity is the greatest virtue." 230w

<u>The Light and the Dark</u>. 1947.

B372   ALLEN, WALTER. "New Novels." <u>New Statesman and Nation</u>, 34, no. 874 (6 December 1947) 456.
    Omnibus review. Lewis Eliot is extraordinarily garrulous. He gives us the inside dope on senior common rooms, the Manichean heresy, English aristocracy, Monte Carlo, Berlin in 1938 and the higher ranks of the Civil Service. "God takes his place among all these. Unfortunately, Roy Calvert carries rather less conviction than a Ouida guardsman. How can he do otherwise when we are never allowed into his mind, but must always approach it through the all-knowing narrator?" Finds the novel pretentious: "it attempts the most serious subject a novelist can tackle without the necessary sensibility or adequate technique." 250w

B373   ANON. "The Steerforth Tradition." <u>Times Literary Supplement</u>, 8 November 1947, p. 573.
    Roy Calvert is reminiscent of Steerforth, and the tone of worried admiration shown by Lewis Eliot for his friend reminds the critic of the adulation shown by Bunny for Raffles. It is "a painstaking and readable account of university life seen from high table. With personal relationships the author is less at home. Rosalind and Joan never come to life, and the Bostocks [i.e. Boscastles] become "more than a little improbable, picnicking on moselle and strawberries before indulging in archery on the grounds of their Palladian mansion facing the sea." 400w

B374   ANON. "Briefly Noted." New Yorker, 23, no. 98
        (21 February 1948) 90.
                Plot summary. "Nothing very much, unless you can
        bring yourself to accept the author's somewhat mystical
        explanation for the hero's eccentric conduct." 150w

B375   ANON. "Modern Polonius." Time, 77, no. 6 (3 February
        1961) 78.
                "C.P. Snow is devoted to the top-secret novel.
        His characters do not meet, they rendezvous. Even
        their platitudes are guarded. They discuss the time
        of day as if it were classified information. This
        conspiratorial mode apparently suits Snow who seems
        to view life as a vast intrigue in which men endlessly
        scheme for everything, from women and wealth to
        positions of academic bureaucratic and managerial
        power." Followed by plot summary which culminates in
        the observation that The Light and the Dark is a
        "thesis novel designed to prove that a man's nature
        predestines his end." Snow's popular fictional success
        is attributed to the evocation of the '20s and '30s,
        and to the psychology implicit in the novels, life as
        a conspiracy in quest of power." [Also reviews Time
        of Hope.]

B376   ANON. Review of The Light and the Dark. Books and
        Bookmen, 18 (May 1973) 124.
                [Twenty word notice to mark publication of Penguin
        ed.]

B377   CHAPMAN, HESTER W. "Fiction." Spectator, 179, no.
        6230 (21 November 1947) 662-63.
                Roy Calvert's wit, lusts, fascination and ideals
        are not believable. Calvert is ostensibly an
        intellectual; but Snow has given him nothing interesting
        or provocative to say. The treatment of university
        intrigue in the first part of the novel is convincing.
        250w

B378   CHASE, JOHN W. "A Special Melancholy." New York
        Times Book Review, 29 February 1948, p. 16.
                Considers it an intensely serious and adult
        book. Enunciates an early aim of the series, perhaps
        derived from Snow himself: "How much of a person's
        fate is due to the accidents of class and time, and
        how much to the essence of his nature?" Includes
        these critical phrases: "unusual maturity of
        observation. . .sincerity of purpose. . .lacks
        ability to create credible character." The mere

reiteration of Roy's psychological dilemma is not
enough. The dominant characters "are essentially
sterile." 490w

B379   ELMAN, RICHARD M. "C.P. Snow's Disconcerting Narrator."
       New Leader, 44, no. 14 (3 April 1961) 24-25.
            Eliot tells the story of the suicidal Roy Calvert
       with the same tone and dialect used in other novels
       of the series. The brilliant Roy, described by the
       imperturbable Eliot, becomes opaque and less credible
       than when perceived directly. "In the end one simply
       cannot evaluate Roy's actions properly because one has
       only known of him through Lewis Eliot."

B380   FARRELLY, JOHN. "Love Affair." New Republic, 118,
       no. 8 (23 February 1948) 24-25.
            The novel is the description of a lover in which
       the emotion always exceeds the given facts. The facts
       about the erratic Calvert are buried by Snow's enthu-
       siasm for his atmosphere and the result is the safety
       and dignity of dullness. 200w

B381   FELD, ROSE. "Doomed Young Scholar." New York Herald
       Tribune Book Review, 22 February 1948, p. 4.
            The gifted and charming Roy Calvert is beset by
       two fears: a periodic melancholy that turns his days
       and nights into a tortured hell, and a conviction
       that, while God exists, he alone cannot find him.
       The prose is keen and polished, and Calvert's drift
       toward madness is Snow's explicit theme, but the work
       is marred by obscurities that leave the reader restless.
       Eliot's personal tragedy is deliberately witheld, and
       it seems incredible that Eliot does not consult a
       physician about Calvert's condition. 575w

B382   JONES, HOWARD MUMFORD. "Doubting Don." Saturday
       Review, 31 (27 March 1948) 17.
            Admires Snow's ability to write the proper university
       novel—slowly and richly, without partisanship or
       fanaticism. Calvert, the brilliant young don, is a man
       "from whose soul something has been cruelly left out—
       that instinctive faith in the meaning of the universe
       by which most of us live." Calvert is eminently
       believable; Lewis Eliot is less so. Admires the
       deliberate unhurried pace of this novel of academic
       life. 400w

B383   PHILLIPSON, JOHN S. Review of The Light and the Dark.
       Best Sellers, 20 (15 February 1961) 438.
            In this eighth [i.e. fourth] volume of the
       sequence we have a detached and carefully drawn

character-study of a prominent orientalist who tries
to find meaning in the life of scholarship, bibulosity
and carnality. The chapter entitled "Absolute Calm"
is reminiscent of the "Center of Indifference" in
Carlyle's Sartor Resartus but it leads Calvert to no
period of affirmation; it merely confirms him in his
fate. The hero is a memorable figure who reminds us,
in his extreme suffering, of a condition all men must
share in different degrees. "Mr. Snow has produced
a fine novel, restrained in its presentation but
forceful in its tragic impact."

B384   WASSON, DONALD. Review of The Light and the Dark.
Library Journal, 73 (15 February 1948) 337.
"The story includes interesting comments on English
university politics and a segment of British aristoc-
racy, but on the whole it is vague and has little point."
90w

Time of Hope. 1949.

B385   ANON. "A Provincial Childhood." Times Literary
Supplement, 30 September 1949, p. 629.
The fictional account of Eliot's childhood is
convincing; the same can be said for the early struggles
of the penniless young barrister. Certain passages
and characters in the book are memorable (Eliot's
father, the mother's deathbed scene, and the scoundrel,
Getliffe). We get no clear idea of Eliot's character.
Eliot "as an adolescent and as a young man is less
interesting, and in a bad sense more 'literary' than
his childhood and professional struggles. Certainly
the vague account of his conversion to Socialism and of
his long-drawn love affair is the least convincing of
this uneven but notable novel." 300w

B386   ANON. "The Bookshelf: New Summer Novels." Christian
Science Monitor, 22 July 1950, p. 8.
The description of Eliot's fascination with
Sheila, and her inadequacies verges on the clinical
realism of Somerset Maugham. "Yet there are
differences. Dr. Snow is perhaps less finished because
he has his eye not only on his characters as persons,
but also on the times in which they live. It is here,
when he moves tentatively into the larger areas of
society, that he is least successful. George Passant
. . . is the least adequately realized character in
the book." The other characters, egocentric and not in
the least admirable, are all memorable. 300w

B386a   ANON. Review of <u>Time of Hope</u>. <u>New Yorker</u>, 26, no. 23
(29 July 1950) 64.
          The calamitous marriage of Lewis Eliot reminds the
reviewer of Philip Carey in Maugham's novel. "The story
is told in leisurely and impeccable prose, out of which
rises, at intervals, a faint but perceptible whine of
self-pity, leading one to suspect that the results would
have been much the same had the young man stayed home and
tackled a less high-flown program." 150w

B387   ANON. "Modern Polonius." <u>Time</u>, 77, no. 6 (3 February
1961) 78.
          "Then [Lewis Eliot] tackles a case too tangled for
any brief. Sheila is a shimmeringly lovely, self-centered
neurotic. The pain of their dissonant relationship becomes his joyless pleasure. Yet at the novel's end, un-
happiness binds them ever more tight, having awakened a
mutual profound pity." [Also reviews <u>The Light and the
Dark</u>. See also B375.]

B388   ANON. "Fiction." <u>Saturday Review</u>, 49, no. 48 (1 April
1966) 40.
          [Review of paperback ed.] The reticent Lewis
"Eliot's own account of his early years in provincial
England where he struggled to find his place and, like
Stephen Dedalus, to shift his love for his mother from
that for other women." 60w

B389   ANON. Review of <u>Time of Hope</u>. <u>Publishers' Weekly</u>, 189,
no. 26 (27 June 1966) 102.
          Brief review of the Scribner paperback edition.
Critics of the 1950 hardback edition, it is suggested,
all thought highly of the writing; but some were absorbed
while others found it too detached and bleak. 100w

B390   ELMAN, RICHARD M. "C.P. Snow's Disconcerting Narrator."
<u>New Leader</u>, 44, no. 14 (3 April 1961) 24-25.
          The novels should have been compressed into one or
two substantial novels to avoid awkward repetitions and
the elaborate cross-referencing of characters and inci-
dents from one novel to the next. [Snow did precisely
that later. The result was the Omnibus edition of 1972.]
Snow's account of English society is incomplete, and Lewis
Eliot's failure to make public his private experience
leads to "bewilderment, boredom and disbelief." <u>Time of
Hope</u> is a better novel than <u>The Light and the Dark</u> because
it comprises Lewis Eliot's direct experience. He is an
intelligent man with serious difficulties that command
sympathy. Snow should have retained the traditional omniscience of the social novelist and avoided the first
person narrative method. "One is left with the uncomfortable feeling that Snow has chosen to write through

Eliot because he finds it so easy to mimic him, and that
what started out to be another <u>Comedie Humaine</u> has ended
up as an extremely private view of things, interesting and
skillfully written, but for the most part hopelessly
discursive and neutral."

B391   GARRIGUE, JEAN. "Fiction Parade." <u>New Republic</u>,
        123, no. 16 (16 October 1950) 21.
            "The title is ironical. There is no time of hope
        for any of Snow's people. . . . And though [Lewis
        Eliot] tells his story with gloves on, and not quite
        enough of the analysis goes underground, his portrait
        of the ambivalent mysteries of such an obsession and
        of the woman whose heart has been unnaturally shrunken
        is haunting because of its detailed accuracy." The
        melancholy gives an impression of somber charm and
        excellence. 270w

B392   GERHARDI, WILLIAM. "English Odyssey." <u>Spectator</u>,
        183, no. 6327 (30 September 1949) 438-40.
            "The author's insight, shrewd and delicate,
        working as it does in the human medium of pathos,
        is the true comedic delineation of character, thus
        sharply thrown into relief." The portrait of Eliot's
        father is worthy of Wells. The theme is that Eliot
        cannot at once receive and give love, and so he
        fatefully fixes his attention on a "deracinated beauty
        who, exasperating enough without it, adds total sexual
        frigidity to her already formidable lack of matrimonial
        talents." 550w

B393   HASS, VICTOR P. "Novel Charms Even a Chilled, Aching
        Critic." <u>Chicago Sunday Tribune Magazine of Books</u>,
        6 August 1950, p. 3.
            It is a solidly built contemporary book lavishly
        studded with brilliant lesser characters apart from
        the magnificently rendered Lewis Eliot. The theme
        is depressing and it has its turgid moments, but it
        is a novel in the eighteenth century tradition with
        the faults and compelling virtues of the genre.

B394   HILTON, JAMES. "Englishman, Born in 1905." <u>New York
        Herald Tribune Book Review</u>, 16 July 1950, p. 10.
            It evokes a Wellsian social world, and the account
        of Eliot's apprenticeship under Getliffe is extremely
        well done. The bondage of Lewis Eliot to Sheila Knight
        is human enough, but the tragedy does not quite achieve
        importance. Possibly it is more true to life than
        fiction. Still it is clearly the work of a good writer,
        but it does not provide the intellectual and emotional
        excitement of <u>The Search</u> published some 16 years before.

B395   MOODY, PHILLIPPA. "In the Lavatory of the Athenaeum:
        Post War English Novels." Melbourne Critical Review,
        6 (1963) 83-87.
            Snow cannot be taken seriously as a writer, and
        he explodes his own pretensions. His dismissal of the
        stream-of-consciousness technique, his mistrust of
        language, convey the fatal limitation in his art.
        Greene's realism was enriched by the novels of James
        and Joyce; Snow's prose lies dead and inert on the
        page. [Moody selects a passage from Homecomings about
        the daydreams of the young Lewis Eliot, and compares
        it to a somewhat analogous passage from Sillitoe's
        Loneliness of the Long Distance Runner. Sillitoe is
        considered a far better artist.] Snow's literary
        technique is to follow a general statement with a
        particular example. But this is the mode of commentary,
        not of creation." Snow's claims for the reflective
        intelligence is unconvincing; his own work shows only
        a lumbering Polonius-like quality.

B396   SCOTT, J.D. "New Novels." New Statesman and Nation,
        38, no. 970 (8 October 1949) 402-04.
            Omnibus review. Snow, who previously published
        Strangers and Brothers, a very good book, and The Light
        and the Dark, not quite so good, has here surpassed
        himself. "In a book which is marked by an astonishing
        cumulative weight and vividness of characterisation,
        the character of Sheila Knight stands out because of
        the menacing demand which it makes upon our apprehension
        and our sympathy." The end, which marks the end of
        the time of hope, and Eliot's failure to achieve
        his ambitions, demonstrates that "Mr. Snow has eliminated
        his weaknesses, extended his creative power, and
        established himself. . . in an eminent and conspicuous
        position among contemporary English novelists."

B397   SIGGINS, CLARA M. "Review of Time of Hope." Best
        Sellers, 20 (15 February 1961) 438-39.
            The novel obeys Faulkner's dictum that the writer
        should show the human heart in conflict with itself.
        Lewis Eliot develops, boy and man, into a complex
        personality whose compulsion is creditably not credited
        to a single cause or motive. The character of Sheila
        Knight is astonishing. "Not since Sue Bridehead
        ruined obscure Jude's life have I read of such a
        capricious, unreasonable, odd, perplexing, pathologically
        cruel, colossally inconsistent and unpredictable women."
        Snow displays a great measure of spiritual insight and
        a sensitive awareness of the tragic potentialities
        latent in man. 450w

B398   SMITH, HARRISON. "Ardent, Tortured Barrister."
Saturday Review, 33, no. 28 (15 July 1950) 11-12.
    The brilliant novel called The Light and the Dark
is now succeeded by this work, part of a series, which
impressively reveals the supreme importance of individuals in modern society. The style is deliberate,
persuasive and curiously personal and its final effect
is almost overwhelming. Eliot reveals all his capacity
for devotion, love and jealousy in his relations with
the frigid, unstable and sadistic Sheila Knight.
"The pages illuminating Eliot's inner nature are
magnificent portrayals of an ardent nature tortured
by love. They can stand with . . . Rousseau and
Emma Bovary." The cumulative effect of the main
story and the brilliant gallery of other characters
have a massive effect. 750w

B399   SPACKS, BARRY. "Implacable Hopes." Saturday Review,
44, no. 13 (1 April 1961) 18.
    "The result is an extraordinarily concentrated
study of desire and despair; of ambitions achieved,
abandoned, or deferred; of hope as the central human
passion, ennobling, destructive, implacable. . . .
Nowhere more movingly than in the present evocation
of the private essence of his hero-narrator do we
see the essence of Snow's vision, his glorification
of maturity, his sense of controlled vitality as the
center of the business of living."

B400   WEST, HERBERT F. "Sensitive Youth." New York Times
Book Review, 16 July 1950, p. 18.
    The account of Lewis Eliot's psychosomatic illness,
and his struggle to become a solicitor, are masterfully
done. The characters, Percy the law clerk, Getliffe
the lawyer and Aunt Milly, are three-dimensional.
"I found this an absorbing book, a novel in the grand
manner made of the stuff that dreams and life are
made of."

B401   WILLIS, KATHERINE TAPPERT. Review of Time of Hope.
Library Journal, 75 (July 1950) 1181-82.
    It is a brilliantly drawn portrait of the '30s.
Snow's theme is the impact of spiritual values on
individuals, and Lewis Eliot is praised as a clever,
shrewd and sensitive character. 130w

The Masters. 1951.

B402   ANON. "Mantle of the Masters." <u>Times Literary</u>
        <u>Supplement</u>, 20 July 1951, p. 449.
             Snow reminds the reviewer of Trollope and Hugh
        Walpole. The realism is insistent; in fact, the
        unexciting preoccupations of certain characters are
        likely to cause tedium. The fictional portrait of
        the don has changed in recent years. Once conservative,
        vague, eccentric, oddly dressed and snobbish, he is
        now snobbish, left-wing, small minded and grasping.
        "The book closes in an atmosphere of sadness and
        failure; but there can be no doubt that <u>The Masters</u>
        gives an excellent account of at least one side of
        university life, upon which Mr. Snow is to be warmly
        congratulated."

B403   ANON. Review of <u>The Masters</u>. <u>Booklist</u>, 48, no. 3
        (15 October 1951) 58.
             "It has little action and much talk but, for the
        reader who delights in a subtle examination of character
        and detail of setting and atmosphere, it will be a
        gratifying experience."

B404   ANON. Review of <u>The Masters</u>. <u>New Yorker</u>, 27, no. 39
        (10 November 1951) 160.
             "Mr. Snow's writing is slow, sure, and shrewd, and
        powerful enough to draw the reader entirely into his
        closed, almost airtight world of scholars and their
        families." 150w

B405   BARR, DONALD. "Fellows of Cambridge." <u>New York Times</u>
        <u>Book Review</u>, 15 December 1951, p. 17.
             "It has a neat little plot, neat little characters,
        wit, contrivance and insight. It is a story of academic
        politics . . . . The central characters are the Fellows
        of a Cambridge college; and for all their learning and
        their teaching, for all their thinking and sneering
        and thundering, their actions are mocked by a faint
        but besetting littleness." Lewis Eliot is soggy with
        understanding, shapeless with British reticence. The
        novel, although it has its Lilliputian grace, and is
        a neat demonstration of human nature, is dull because
        it lacks satire, or possibly because Snow sets up his
        characters as if they were materials in a Zolaesque
        experiment. 370w

B406   BERNT, H.H. Review of The Masters. Library Journal,
        76, no. 16 (15 September 1951) 1421.
             "It is very English in style and approach, which
        on the one hand will limit appeal for American reader,
        on the other hand give him excellent insight into
        English college faculty life. Strength lies more in
        individual characterization than in movement of general
        plot. Recommended for sophisticated readers."

B407   BLOOMFIELD, PAUL. Review of The Masters. Manchester
        Guardian, 27 July 1951, p. 4.
             "In spite of its unevenness and rather photographic
        quality this may be the most impressive English novel
        since L.P. Hartley's The Boat. . . The dons' talk is so
        well done that one remembers what it is that might
        make some of them snatch at an opportunity of being
        dropped from an aeroplane behind enemy lines a long
        way from their common room." 130w

B408   DOWNING, FRANCIS. Review of The Masters. Commonweal,
        55 (21 December 1951) 283-85.
             Snow's work is characterized by an almost Victorian
        delicacy, decent reticences, and a recognition of the
        complexity of life and men. It "fills us with delight;
        and we are made quiet, calm, subtle and reflective,
        detached and wise, and touched fugitively with brilliance
        --all qualities which we have stolen from this novelist
        while he was giving us, for a while, the radiance of
        his urbanity and grace." 700w

B409   JONES, HOWARD MUMFORD. "Academic Power Politics."
        New York Herald Tribune Book Review, 28 October 1951,
        p. 5.
             Eliot's analysis of the meager events in this novel
        is slow, relentless and sympathetic, and the work
        recalls the clean, bare structure of French classical
        tragedy. The choice of the next Master, a contest
        which leaves the buzzing and booming outside world
        unmoved, is a theme which permits Snow to propound his
        thesis that the realistic pursuit of power often
        involves strands of personality that are far from
        realistic. "You can also argue that The Masters is too
        blatantly a thesis novel. But it is because Mr. Snow
        has the courage to be the moralist of a civilized and
        cultured group that he seems to me important."

B410   LASKI, MARGHANITA. Review of The Masters. Spectator,
        187 (20 July 1951) 187.
             If these demi-gods, these giants of the intellect
        conduct their internal politics "on the level of addle-
        pated women jostling for the chairmanship of the society

bazaar," what is a mere woman to make of this work? "It is certain that The Masters is beautifully constructed, and that to hold the reader's attention for so long a book on a single issue so esoteric and remote is a major achievement. The intention of the book I doubt my capacity to evaluate, and must urge each reader to judge for himself." 360w

B411   LATHAM, EARL. "The Managerialization of the Campus." Public Administration Review, 19, no. 1 (Winter 1959) 45-57.
[Omnibus review of some novels with an academic setting, including Mary McCarthy's The Groves of Academe and Randall Jarrell's Pictures from an Institution.] Includes some brief asides about Snow's book. "In The Masters, the faculty are important men with high professional prestige and social position (it is as well to remember that this is England, another culture). . . ."

B412   RODGER, IAN. "Cambridge and Celts." Listener, 60, no. 1534 (21 August 1958) 281.
[Review of radio version of the novel.] Complains that the cuts made in the novel favour Dr. Jago and the humanists of the Old Guard. The same cuts transform Dr. Crawford into a brusque Scot with little to recommend him to humanists. The actors' performances are praised.

B413   SCOTT, J.D. "New Novels." New Statesman and Nation, 42, no. 1065 (4 August 1951) 134.
Everything not absolutely relevant to the task of electing a successor to the dying master has been cut out. "The work has been written with the economy of a short story; to a remarkable degree it gives the impression of being the product of a single pulsation of energy, and it is only in retrospect that one realized that it is not a short book but quite a long one." While it is not quite as impressive as Time of Hope, it "stands out boldly as an achievement; lucid, compelling, ironical rather than tragic, generous in its fullness. . . ." 600w

B414   SMITH, HARRISON. "The Problems of Intellect." Saturday Review of Literature, 34, no. 44 (3 December 1951) 17.
Suggests that the merit of the Strangers and Brothers novels lies in their personal nature, the fight of one man against a hostile world while the overall thesis is the behavior of the intelligent individual in an increasingly Socialist society. 700w

The New Men. 1954.

B414a   ANON. "New Fiction: Science and Politics." The Times
(London), 1 May 1954, p. 8.
        This novel about the doubts and dilemmas of British
scientists and administrators involved in the development of the atomic bomb occasionally produces suggestive
and subtle effects. "The lightly articulated refine-
ments of Mr. Snow's analysis [in dealing with the
marriage between Martin and Irene Eliot], however,
matter less than his spare but lively sketches of the
community of physicists, chemists, and engineers at
Barford and the telling illustrations of their
individual responses to questions of policy and
security." 250w

B415   ANON. [i.e. W.H.] Review of The New Men. Twentieth
Century, 156 (July 1954) 96.
        The book evades the issue of fixing moral respon-
sibility. The characters in Barford fail to fire the
imagination in the way of Nigel Balchin's novel. The
woman, Irene, has a two-dimensional quality. "An
indication of the rather chilly climate of the
book lies in the fact that one leaves it having made
scarcely a new acquaintance, far less a friend or an
enemy in its pages." 300w

B416   ANON. Review of The New Men. Booklist, 51, no. 10
(15 January 1955) 226.
        "Readers who have no previous acquaintance with
the characters and their personal philosophies may
feel a disconcerting incompleteness here." 50w

B417   ANON. Review of The New Men. Kirkus, 22 (15 December
1954) 813.
        "For the thoughtful reader, the complex here of
ideas and ideals, the duality of progress, towards
destruction, forms an abstraction which is handled
with intelligence." 190w

B418   ANON. Review of The New Men. New Yorker, 30, no. 50
(29 January 1955) 88.
        Snow should have kept close to the human side of
his problem. "Between the brothers and their bond, on
one side, and the discussion of war and its ramifi-
cations, on the other, Mr. Snow's novel disintegrates."
70w

B419   ANON. "Life Among the A-Scientists." <u>Nation</u>, 180,
        no. 10 (5 March 1955) 206.
            The reader who knows the mystery and fear sur-
        rounding the lives of atomic scientists may be startled
        by Snow's unimpassioned approach. These scientists
        reveal petty jealousies and ambitions as well as
        patriotism. They show none of the facile uniformity
        expected of military men and political bureaucrats.
        240w

B420   ASHE, GEOFFREY. "Neutralism." <u>Commonweal</u>, 61, no. 18
        (4 February 1955) 485-86.
            Americans may be bewildered by this fictional
        account of the response of British scientists to the
        dropping of the bombs. These scientists are filled with
        horror. All of them ask the question posed by Norman
        Thomas: why drop the bomb on a city and without warning?
        After the bomb, Snow's fictional scientists carry on
        their research in strangely apolitical fashion. "And
        if one trusted Mr. Snow's picture of moral repugnance
        and half-articulate neutralism, not merely as existing
        but as normal, it would be difficult to regard British
        science as a resource to be counted on in any
        hypothetical war." 240w

B421   BERRYMAN, JOHN. "Days of Crisis in the Great
        Experiment." <u>New York Times Book Review</u>, 9 January
        1955, pp. 4-5.
            The two themes, possessive love and the relations
        between Whitehall and the atomic energy project, are
        not closely related. The minor characters come up to
        Snow's high standard. Learning and pains have gone
        into the description of the women. However, Martin
        Eliot is not pleasantly or unpleasantly engaging; he
        does not compare favorably with Roy Calvert. The
        personal negotiations in <u>The Masters</u> were better done
        than here. Still, the work "does not much weaken my
        feeling that its author is one of the half-dozen most
        substantial living English novelists. . . .Yet this
        novel clearly fails to achieve either the vivacity or
        the intensity of its immediate predecessors." 600w

B422   CRANE, MILTON. "This Age of A-Men, of Power."
        <u>Chicago Sunday Tribune Magazine of Books</u>, 9 January
        1955, p. 3.
            Snow is a man of affairs as well as a novelist, and
        in this account everything, from the atom bomb research
        to the construction of the bomb, Hiroshima and Nagasaki,

atomic spies, rings true. His theme is power, and
the transformation of Martin Eliot from a competent
assistant into a shrewd opportunist and brilliant
manipulator is appallingly convincing. "Snow's
authoritative and moving book is in every sense the
first serious novel about the major fact in the
modern world."

B423   HOBSON, HAROLD. "The Saga of Lewis Eliot." Christian
        Science Monitor, 13 January 1955, p. 7.
            "The scope of this series is vast, its mastery
        sure. . . ." The style is sometimes considered bare
        and spare, but a million words of rich rhetoric would
        cloy and "Dr. Snow's simplicity never wearies." The
        book moves with splendid assurance and Snow probes
        the hearts of his men and women with deceptive simplicity.
        "Dr. Snow has a fine classical restraint; he neither
        preaches nor fulminates; he just shows his people in
        terms of their essential values and ideals. The breadth,
        impartiality, and generosity of his vision are indeed
        remarkable." 550w

B424   HODGART, PATRICIA. Review of The New Men. Manchester
        Guardian, 4 May 1954, p. 4.
            "As a documentary it is fascinating. . . The first-
        hand descriptions of atomic scientists at work are
        exciting enough, but the main characters, although
        their social behaviour in the power game is nicely
        observed, fail to be interesting as human beings.
        This from Mr. Snow is slightly disappointing; such
        a controversial theme demands a less platitudinous
        treatment." 120w

B425   KRUTCH, JOSEPH WOOD. "Moral Dilemma of the Atomic
        Scientist." New York Herald Tribune Book Review,
        9 January 1955, p. 4.
            In this propaganda novel, highly acclaimed in
        Britain, Snow tells us that British scientists would
        have devised, but not dropped, the bomb. Americans
        are given the blame for dropping the bomb on Japanese
        cities, but he neglects to point out that the British
        killed many German civilians with TNT and napalm.
        Science and technology have devised new weapons for
        millenia, and the question of when to stop making, or
        using, these weapons is not easy to answer. Snow,
        somewhat like Bevan, who called the United States a
        greater danger to the world than the U.S.S.R., is
        clearly one of those Englishmen who believes that
        the United States is unfit to wield its great power.
        650w

B426   METCALF, JOHN. "New Novels." <u>Spectator</u>, 192, no.
        6568 (14 May 1954) 600.
            The style and approach recall Stendhal, Stevenson
        and Maddox Ford. The characters are whole and plausible;
        the atmosphere is convincing and authentic. Irene
        Eliot is contrived and literary, while Martin Eliot's
        rejection of the Barford job appears incredible given
        the facts about him. Still the series "begins to
        shape impressively."

B427   PICKREL, PAUL. "Outstanding Fiction." <u>Yale Review</u>,
        44, no. 3 (March 1955) 479.
            The work "has no passion, the central emotional
        situation is not very compelling, bureaucratic telephone
        calls often take the place of action. But it is an
        impressive work nonetheless, because it is presided
        over by an informed, mature, humane intelligence that
        shrewdly analyzes and wisely comments on the men con-
        cerned in the most dramatic and fearful undertaking of
        the age." It may not be exciting fiction, but it is
        an excellent book.

B428   P.[RICE], R.G.G. Review of <u>The New Men</u>. <u>Punch</u>,
        236, no. 5931 (26 May 1954) 649.
            Although Martin Eliot's careerism and the clash
        of ideologies among scientists are interesting, they
        are not <u>very</u> interesting; and the reason is due to a
        thinness of texture. For working out of his themes,
        Snow needed a longer book to pile up detail and
        complications.

B429   RETTGER, T.L. "Troubled People." <u>Chemical and
        Engineering News</u>, 33, no. 26 (27 June 1955) 2764.
            Describes it as a serious and excellent novel.
        Itemizes Snow's qualifications for writing a work
        about nuclear physicists. Quotes an excerpt which
        argues that the engineers are conservative and
        apolitical while the scientists are "rebellious,
        protestant, curious for the future, and unable to
        resist shaping it." Concludes that "This is a mature,
        intellectual and penetrating novel. . . nothing
        extraneous to his purpose is admitted. . . The depth
        of his insight is matched by his human understanding. . .
        it is a calm study of the new men of this era, but it
        offers no easy answers." 570w

B430   ROLO, CHARLES J. "Three Novels." <u>Atlantic</u>, 195, no. 2
        (February 1955) 84-85.
            Asserts that Snow is an artist concerned with
        particular truths rather than a journalistic novelist
        intent on dramatizing political issues. "He has

presented their conflicts of ambition, loyalty, and
responsibility in all their complexity, and with a
calm understanding of the different attitudes which
emerged--an understanding which extends even to the
motives of the traitor. The New Men handles a fateful
new theme with challenging insight and impressive
moral sensitivity." 290w

B431   ROMILLY, GILES. "New Novels." New Statesman and
        Nation, 47, no. 1208 (1 May 1954) 573.
            Omnibus review. "Mr. Snow minutes with masterful
        elegance the intricacies of this shifting material
        [some of the book's themes]. The unforced virtuosity
        of his performance is itself a satisfaction." Further,
        the novel is unprecedentedly clear of that topic of
        dreadful allure--the treacheries of atomic spies--
        which leads to well-meant hysteria by keen but common-
        place minds. Quotes passages from the novel which
        convey the discomfort of Mountenoy at the demands of
        wartime security. "The workings of the love of power
        are the fulcrum that here moves a mass incomparably more
        formidable than the donnish squabbles of The Masters
        . . . [the merits and themes of the novel include] the
        hearty acceptance of the role of ambition, the ability
        to conduct a scene with easy vigour as if it were an
        interview and to turn it off naturally, the undisparaging
        admission of power-drives in women (which incidentally
        animates them here remarkably), the robust but supple
        differentiation of closely related emotions." 600w

B432   SMITH, HARRISON. "Morality Vs. the Atomic Monster."
        Saturday Review, 38, no. 2 (8 January 1955) 9.
            Introduces Snow as England's most distinguished
        living novelist, finds it an enigma that Snow is not
        read in the United States since all those Americans who
        read Trollope should logically read Snow. "There is,
        it is true, a vast amount of argument between
        scientists, politicians, and Government leaders in
        The New Men. It will not be read with pleasure by
        anyone who is addicted to violence and romance in
        fiction. It is a cerebral novel, perhaps, but that
        does not mean that C.P. Snow is not a writer of the
        first rank, that his characters are not three-dimensional,
        living figures, that he does not deal with the most vital
        issues facing mankind today." 550w

B433   SMITH, STEVIE. "New Novels." London Observer, 2 May
        1954, p. 9.
            "It is a fascinating war-time story of human

bewilderment and of guilt for Hiroshima passing to forgetfulness." The presence of irony, the absence of grammatical lapses, and the absence of the contrived novelist's ending would all have made this good book a better one.

B434   [SYMONS, JULIAN] "Of Bureaucratic Man." Times Literary Supplement, 7 May 1954, p. 296.
It is fascinating, the work of a brilliantly gifted reporter; unfortunately Snow's unimpassioned prose cannot convey the conflict or crises in or between human beings, and it mutes even powerful personalities like George Passant and Walter Luke. "The style is that of a lucid and uncommonly honest recorder, rather than of an artist. . . .Mr. Snow may well be regarded as the most faithful recorder of the figure to whom his work is really devoted, the corporate individual, the harassed and virtuous administrator, the bureaucratic man." 2850w [Reprinted: B248.]

B435   TRILLING, LIONEL. "The Novel Alive or Dead." The Griffin (Reader's Subscription, New York), 4, no. 2 (February 1955) 4-13.
[A humorous and imaginary sketch leads in to a review of The New Men. The sketch, in which Snow bets a clubman that the novel is not dead, and takes stock of his talents for the enterprise, has been widely quoted in the literature.] Snow, it appears, has "no great gifts of language, of course. 'I am a plain man,' said Mr. Snow. No new theory of the novel. 'Just begin at the beginning and go on to the end is the only way I know.' No strange or violent or beautifully intense vision of life. No new notions about the moral life--on the contrary, a set of rather old-fashioned notions chiefly about loyalty and generosity. The best he could muster under the moral head was a belief that it was quite hard to live up to even these simple notions. 'It is not much to make a novel with,' Mr. Snow thought." Snow, not a Trollope, has a sense of social fact, a sense of the difference between the present and the recent past and an interest in public matters (man in committee). The New Men does not have the unity of The Masters and Snow's scientists are "peculiarly susceptible to the moral imperatives around which the Communist ideology is built," and one of Snow's personal qualities is the generous lack of an impulse to blame. That generous impulse goes perhaps too far in its view of Snow's "progressive" scientists, but it is essential to Snow's enterprise--and liberating. 2000w [Reprinted: B43, B326.]

B436 WALBRIDGE, EARLE F. Review of <u>The New Men</u>. <u>Library Journal</u>, 80, no. 1 (1 January 1955) 69-70.
It is a thoughtful, muted novel about scientists and government officials responsible for the construction of a British Bomb. It is also a pioneer example of the real, unvarnished science fiction of the here and now. 130w

B437 no entry

Homecomings. 1956.

B438 ANON. Review of <u>Homecomings</u>. <u>The Times</u> (London), 13 September 1956, p. 13.
The passages that deal with the war-time civil service are notable for their uncommon seriousness and subtlety. Snow subdues the melodramatic events of this work with an urbane neo-Trollopian calm. Snow's method is triumphantly successful in his account of Lewis Eliot's marriage to Sheila Knight, but Eliot's passion for Margaret is harder to accept. Eliot's main characteristic, a smug, far-sighted caution, is not very compatible with a passionate love affair.

B439 ANON. Review of <u>Homecomings</u>. <u>Kirkus</u>, 24 (15 September 1956) 4.
"An inordinately objective observer, C.P. Snow's leisurely narrative has a cumulative validity; it is also impressive in its breadth and control."

B440 ANON. Review of <u>Homecomings</u>. <u>Booklist and Subscription Books Bulletin</u>, 53, no. 3 (1 October 1956) 94-95.
"Crisp, carefully fashioned prose; for the discriminating."

B441 ANON. "Galsworthy's Ghost." <u>Time</u>, 68, no. 15 (8 October 1956) 116-18.
Snow reminds the critic of Galsworthy. His middle classes suffer troubles, not tragedies; and those troubles are described in a tone decorously genteel to the point of inaudibility. "The anatomy of power excites Author Snow (himself a sometime physicist and civil servant) in the same way that the very rich fascinated Scott Fitzgerald, and he is at his best in scenes in which two or three top civil servants measure out other men's job futures in judicious mumbles." The scent of the novel is Yardley Soap opera. 550w

B442   ANON. "Briefly Noted." New Yorker, 32 (3 November
        1956) 196-97.
        [Plot summary redeemed by a passionate concern for
        appraising and judging the two main characters, their
        courtship and marriage.] Objects that Lewis Eliot and
        Margaret Davidson have no surprises in them; they share
        the same toneless intimacy discolored by too much
        analysis. "This is a sad, gray story, too real for
        comfort and much too well written to be forgotten. One
        scene stands out. . .in it Eliot, middle-aged now and
        married again and complacent in his recent fatherhood,
        observes the childless marriage of two of his contem-
        poraries and describes what he sees with a malevolence,
        deadly and comic, that he shows nowhere else in the
        book." 360w

B443   BREMNER, MARJORIE. Review of Homecomings. Twentieth
        Century, 160 (December 1956) 582-85.
        Although well planned and contructed, the novel is
        somewhat flat and uneven. The description of the
        Civil Service is excellent, but marred by a certain
        mistiness. Sheila Knight, her parson father and the
        scoundrelly publisher are good portrayals of character,
        but the Eliot-Margaret affair is unconvincing. "The
        author's great ability is never in doubt even when--
        as in Homecomings--he writes a book below his highest
        standard." 900w

B444   COSMAN, MAX. "Voices of Power." Nation, 183, no. 23
        (8 December 1956) 504-05.
        Alleges that Lewis Eliot's assurance and authority
        occasionally play hob with motivation of action; both
        causes lead him to substitute ingenuity for insight.
        Detects in the book Lewis Eliot's hail and farewell to
        the theme and fascination of power. ". . .Mr. Snow the
        man of letters no longer intends to truckle to the man
        of affairs. Homecomings, among other things, is notice
        to that effect."

B445   CRANSTON, MAURICE. "The Immediate Sense of Ordeal."
        New Republic, 135, no. 15 (8 October 1956) 18.
        Briefly recapitulates the rise of Lewis Eliot
        in the earlier novels in which hope is the leitmotif.
        The style, which Cranston describes as often dazed,
        hesitant and bleak, is intended to show, not tell us,
        the nature of Lewis Eliot's feelings. "The literary
        craftsmanship by which [Snow] succeeds in conveying
        the immediate sense of ordeal is, I think, quite
        formidable." Snow is not good at describing scenes

of sexual passion or excitement, but he is a masterly
historian of sexual frustration, and Cranston finds
that Snow's preoccupation with technique, his zeal for
fact, steady accumulation of detail as well as his
thoroughgoing scientific humanism recall the figure of
Thomas Mann. 950w

B446   ENGLE, PAUL. "A Story of Three Loves." Chicago Sunday
Tribune, 7 October 1956, p. 4.
        Snow's prose is attractive and flexible, and it is
the suitable instrument of his subtle insights. The
bright and hopeful ending of this book is made to seem
right and sensible. "Oddly enough, home and children
are offered as substantial values in the later chapters,
which is about as original as a modern novelist can get
. . . .The highest praise of this novel is to say that
I would like to read all of the others."

B447   FLINT, R.W. "The Undying Apocalypse." Partisan Review,
24, no. 1 (Winter 1957) 142.
        Omnibus review. "This is H.G. Wells's world grown
ripe and professional. . . .we have something rather
French in feel; a shrewd, unblinking, original, slightly
but not annoyingly sentimental study of life in the
upper echelons of the British civil service. . . .Lewis
Eliot in love is a tinkerer, an anguished sheep-dog;
Lewis Eliot in Whitehall is quite another story." 250w

B448   GEORGE, DANIEL. "New Novels." Spectator, 197, no. 6690
(14 September 1956) 362.
        Omnibus review. This bleak novel is characterized
by realism, but it is marred by pomposity, Eliot's
grammatical lapses, and his occasional outlandish
diction. [The reviewer's criticisms are made in the
form of a humorous aside addressed to Lewis Eliot.]
400w

B449   GLAUBER, R.H. "C.P. Snow's Number Six." New York
Herald Tribune Book Review, 7 October 1956, p. 2.
        "This is an impressive story, moving, profound and,
perhaps best of all, mature in its thoughtful approach
to the 'problem of pain.'" 430w

B450   [HEPPENSTALL, RAYNOR] "Corridors of Power." Times
Literary Supplement, 7 September 1956, p. 524.
        A review of Snow's novel with incidental references
to the Forsytes of Galsworthy. Snow has annexed a
fictional world formerly the subject of ridicule and
scorn: the workaday world of dons and civil servants.
In fact, Snow threatens to go to the opposite extreme
of suggesting that these academic and civil service

heroes, with their manly struggles of conscience and
elevated scruples, form the true subject of fictional
reality. Praises The Masters and The Light and the Dark
as the best books in the series. This novel is marred
by the presence of Lewis Eliot and George Passant.
Eliot's faults and peccadilloes are the mere result of
novelistic contrivance. For all the emphasis on Eliot's
ruthless selfishness, he remains a vague figure; the
same can be said of Margaret. The marriage between the
two lacks detailed circumstance, and Snow's style,
whatever its merits in other contexts, is not sensual.
In this novel, the style also lacks precision, and the
reviewer dutifully regrets some of Snow's stylistic
ticks, including especially his use of the word "fibres."
George Passant, once an interesting figure, will not
bear the weight of Snow's continuing scrutiny; and
Passant's East Anglian background shows up only in his
addiction to the word "sunket." "One carps, it may
be, because Mr. Snow has sometimes written so wonder-
fully well and one is furious when he falls short of
his best. There is no disabling clash between him and
his time. It is not too late to hope for a perfect
recovery." 2700w [Reprinted, with changes and revisions,
in B112.]

B451   KING, CARLYLE. "Fiction Chronicle." Tamarack Review,
       2 (Winter 1957) 70-71.
            Snow is the most distinguished practitioner of the
       traditional English novel today. The first part of the
       book, in which Eliot is transformed from the generous
       but detached protector of a schizoid wife to a man
       who repudiates his godlike detachment and is prepared
       to let people help him, is excellent. The last part
       of the book reads as if it were contrived to make a
       point. The Masters is the better novel, but this is
       a rewarding book.

B452   MADDOCKS, MELVIN. "In the Corridors of Power."
       Christian Science Monitor, 11 October 1956, p. 11.
            Most novelists deal with people in their most
       personal and private aspects. Snow is most often
       concerned with official relationships between bureau-
       crats, lawyers, academics and businessmen. In this
       book, Snow has failed in describing personal relations.
       The romance between Eliot and Margaret is second rate,
       and Margaret herself is bad for the book; she invites
       Snow to try his hand at descriptions of love and tender-
       ness and "When Mr. Snow leaves the fluorescent brightness
       of the office for the candlelit softness of the tete-a-
       tete, his plotting becomes ordinary, his insights into

situations fuzzy; and after five o'clock his characters
. . .virtually fade away like wraiths."

B453   MAYNE, RICHARD. "Snow: Major Read Ahead!" New
Statesman and Nation, 52, no. 1332 (22 September 1956)
350.
        "All this is told in a comfortable, patient style,
adroitly weaving in and out, cutting from scene to
scene with a kind of leisurely tenseness; Trollope, it
might be, re-written by Robert Penn Warren. The
characters inhabit a Trollope world, a man's world of
power in high place, clubs, dinner-parties, political
manoeuvring; and while the marital problems are deeply
and movingly explored, the women seemed to me to take
second place, decorative screens for the projection of
their men's emotions. . . .it seemed to me to limit
Dr. Snow's achievement." 430w

B454   P.[RICE] R.G.G. Review of Homecomings. Punch, 231,
no. 6057 (3 October 1956) 415.
        Snow is a more careful writer and more intelligent
man than Trollope, but he shares all the latter's
unpartisan curiosity. "The struggle for power in
laboratories and colleges and companies and ministries
is as constant, as entertaining and as frightening as
it was in Barchester, and, as in Barchester, it is not
necessarily disastrous." 150w

B455   SHRAPNEL, NORMAN. "Long Snow." Manchester Guardian,
11 September 1956, p. 4.
        "Many who would be scared away from a brilliant
innovator's back garden as though it were surrounded
by electrified wire feel happily at home in this writer's
traditional acres, a fact that would be unremarkable if
his admirers did not include readers of taste and critics
of discernment." In this work, it is not the story that
explains the devotion of Snow's readers. It is also
not the setting, the 15 years after Munich, which is
described with a restraint that does not guarantee the
success of chronicle novels. Snow's success can be
explained by his serious devotion to character--and to
the fact that he is so serious a moralist.

B456   SMITH, HARRISON. "Love and Precision." Saturday Review,
39, no. 41 (13 October 1956) 15.
        Considers Joyce Cary and Snow the two enduring
novelists of present day England. Followed by running
plot summary. "Homecomings is an engaging book for anyone who can be stimulated by intelligence, accurate
prose and entertaining characters." 800w

B457 STEWART, J.I.M. Review of <u>Homecomings</u>. <u>London</u>
<u>Magazine</u>, 4 (January 1957) 71-73.
Compares Snow's sequence to Spenser's <u>Faerie</u>
<u>Queene</u>. [Stewart achieves the near impossible and
makes this comparison appear quite reasonable.] Eliot,
in this book, remains the spectator of his own suffering.
"His final stature will depend on the extent to which, in
books yet to be written, that suffering finds issue in
action." In various pithy dicta, Stewart then pays
tribute to Snow's realism. ". . . Mr. Snow's writing
won't let us down. . . . No; contemporary men, women
and institutions really are like this. The tycoons and
the permanent secretaries, the womanists and the virgins,
the stuffed shirts and the prima donnas do tick just as
Mr. Snow says they do; it is thus that careers are made
and broken. . . . So we read and learn. Our instructor
is extremely knowledgeable, and not a crackpot as so
many writers are. . . . His world remains very liveable
in and readable about."

B458 SYKES, GERALD. "Portrait of a Public Man." <u>New York</u>
<u>Times Book Review</u>, 7 October 1956, pp. 3, 44.
The novel throws light on the Establishment; witness
for example, the chapter which shows a Cabinet Minister
interrupted by a tycoon who wants part of the atomic
bomb business. <u>Homecomings</u>, however, is directly concerned with "the initiation of a public figure into the
mysteries of feeling." This public figure "carries so
many public responsibilities that he is almost unaware
of his real private requirements. Emotionally he is a
boy. . . .He is exceptionally articulate about everything
save that which concerns him most." Snow has "written
an astonishingly revealing record not only of the inner
government of Britain but of the inner secrets of the
governors." 600w

B459 WAIN, JOHN. "New Novels." London <u>Observer</u>, 9 September
1956, p. 12.
Snow brings the imagination of a born novelist to
the description of successful men, the natural holders
of authority. In this work, Snow has worked out the
emotional journey of Lewis Eliot with subtlety and
authority.

<u>The Conscience of the Rich</u>. 1958.

B459a ANON. Review of <u>The Conscience of the Rich</u>. <u>Kirkus</u>, 25
(1 December 1957) 877.
The novel is "leisurely, intelligent and incisive."

B460   ANON. "<u>The Conscience of the Rich</u>." <u>Booklist</u>, 54, no.
15 (1 April 1958) 445.
The novel "demonstrates anew that precise prose and
phychological [sic] insight are prerequisites for explor-
ing the nuances and fluctuations of human behavior."
120w

B461   BREMNER, MARJORIE. Review of <u>The Conscience of the Rich</u>.
<u>Twentieth Century</u>, 163, no. 976 (June 1958) 586-88.
The emotional tone as retailed by Lewis Eliot is
grey and dull. The characters are not sympathetic, and
the intelligence of the elder March is open to question.
His son, Charles, after all "wants to be a doctor, not
a burglar," and it is probably pathological of the old
man to oppose medical study, but this pathology is
never explored. The old man's abuse of his daughter
Katherine, when she announces her plan to marry a gentile
("Of course, I wish you'd never been born") seems merely
mechanical, and in any case, the erring daughter soon
earns forgiveness. The conflicts and claustrophobia of
the March family are not felt; they are merely and
vaguely intimated by Snow's mechanical description.

B462   COSMAN, MAX. "Wealth and Rebellion." <u>Nation</u>, 186,
no. 11 (15 March 1958) 240.
Snow's liberalism is evident in his depiction of the
Jews: the novel is marked neither by anti-semitism nor
by an effort to curry Jewish favor. Ann Simon, who
topples the patriarch of the clan, proves the existence
of an overtly Freudian element in Snow's work. The
moral of the novel is a warning to all plutocrats that
they are subject to egalitarianism (here termed 'homo-
geneity'), conflict between generations, and eventual
loss of prestige. 700 w

B463   CURRAN, CHARLES. "The Two Worlds of C.P. Snow."
<u>New Republic</u>, 138, no. 22 (2 June 1958) 17-18.
Minimal plot summary. After describing Snow's
education, and the source of Snow's power as a Civil
Service Commissioner, Curran finds Snow uniquely
equipped for his novelistic role. "These novels are
like nothing else in English; they are a unique contribution to the practice, as distinct from the theory
of government." The book, while not one of genius, is
a magnificent novel. "There is a queer fascination
about it. <u>Tout comprendre c'est tout pardonner</u> is only
a half-truth for Snow. He understands but he does not
forgive. He sits, a sleepless spider, at the center of
his web; and he appraises his characters rather as a

spider might sum up the flies. He is as cold as the
frosty Caucases, as pitiless as Rhadamanthus. He
dissects human motives like a surgeon manipulating
the muscles of a cadaver before an audience of medical
students." Snow is a fascinated and fascinating student
of the British governing class. 950w

B464   DAVIS, ROBERT GORHAM. "The Marches of London." New
York Times Book Review, 23 February 1958, p. 4.
    Plot summary generously interspersed with praise of
Snow's novel.

B465   GARDNER, HELEN. "The World of C.P. Snow." New
Statesman, 55, no. 1411 (29 March 1958) 409-10.
    [A review frequently cited in academic critical
writings about Snow.] The author defends Snow's style,
his moral seriousness, and finds a parallel between Snow
and Proust. The Conscience of the Rich, the novel under
review, gets short shrift. Gardner herself knows similar
rich Jewish families and, by comparison with her own
memories, Conscience of the Rich lacks immediacy and
imaginative veracity. But she found the central chapters
of Homecomings moving and unforgettable. This fact led
her to re-appraise the series. She concluded, in part,
that "Snow is attempting. . . . a panoramic novel
which accepts fully the limitations of narration in the
first person. If we complain that the worlds presented
seem grey, colourless, and rather muted, we are com-
plaining of the limitations of the personality of Lewis
Eliot." Lewis Eliot's ceaseless analysis of the
characters of his friends and associates is an attempt
to understand his own nature. The parallel with Proust
can be justified in terms of theme, if not style.
"Professional success plays the same kind of part in the
whole as the cult of social success plays in Proust."
Proust's work is morally cold; Snow's novels appeal to
the conscience and moral experience.

B465a GLAUBER, ROBERT H. "No. 7 in C.P. Snow's Notable Series."
New York Herald Tribune Book Review, 23 February 1958,
p. 5.
    A Snow novel is an almost certain guarantee of an
"engrossing story about intelligent and sensitive people
told with great emotional restraint, sharp personal
insights, and a polished literary style that is a joy
to read." This work, with its penetrating examination
of power from a personal point of view, is no exception.
It is the story of Charles March, a man learning to

stand on his own two feet, and in it Snow seems to be asking how many of us are even mildly interested in being honest with ourselves or with others. 400w

B466 GREENE, JAMES. "Two Generations Between the Two Wars." Commonweal, 68, no. 13 (27 June 1958) 332.
Describes the conflict between the old and young generation typical of the 'thirties. Mostly plot summary. "The real excellence of Snow's book lies in its characters. A more engaging, more complete, character than Leonard March would be difficult to recall. His presence in the beginning is over-powering; it is only at the expense of his superb identity that, in the closing pages of the book, his children emerge from the shadows." 1050w

B467 [HEPPENSTALL, RAYNER] "A Question of Creeds." Times Literary Supplement, 28 March 1958, p. 165.
The novel is praised ("the most beautifully composed of all [Snow's] books") but the reviewer has some criticisms. ". . . the peculiar quality of all these books has come out of some tension between an essentially feminine sensibility and a deep and extensive knowledge of several worlds of masculine endeavour, the masculine 'drives' which early ambition generates being checked by a moral code designed to satisfy the most exacting of noncomformist consciences." Briefly mentions the resonances: love of power, renunciation of power and possessive love. Suggests that Snow would not do well on an examination of Jewish thought. The evidence: Mr. March and his daughter Katherine both refer freely to original sin. The March family, despite its supposed Jewishness, is reminiscent of the Forsyte clan. 750w
[Reprinted: B112 with changes and additions.]

B468 KERMODE, FRANK. "Sophisticated Quest." Spectator, 200, no. 6772 (11 April 1958) 464.
In this tragedy of possessive love, the portrait of Charles March is probably a failure, but that of his father, Leonard March, gradually becomes a "fundamentally comic figure of the utmost seriousness and power. . . ." But "One has to ask why this deeply serious undertaking, for all its magnanimity and justice, for all its humane and devoted craftsmanship, is so clearly hindered by some serious loss of power." One answer lies in the low, unemphatic tone of narration. It makes no compromises with the truth, but "The price is too high; too much is, as it were, lost in the dark." 700w

B469   KIEFER, H.C. Review of The Conscience of the Rich.
        Arizona Quarterly, 14 (Autumn 1958) 261-64.
            Snow is one of the few novelists who responds to the
        fact of change, especially classlessness, as the central
        quality of contemporary civilization. His work, while
        different in intention and detail from that of William
        Faulkner, involves a high degree of craftsmanship and
        interwoven complexity. The title is apt. Snow is
        exploring the notion that conscience should be divorced
        from environment and the heritage of the past. The
        inflexibility of Leonard March in matters of conscience
        reflects family tradition, wealth, migration, nationality
        and race. By contrast, Lewis Eliot's conscience is more
        flexible, or at least more capable of dealing with
        flexible moral situations. He can, for example, associate
        himself with Ann March's Marxism and Roy Calvert's
        Fascism, in terms that suggest that pity is more important
        than ideological commitment. His style is pure, simple
        and direct "and his work has the prospect of greatness."

B470   LARNEN, BRENDAN. Review of The Conscience of the Rich.
        Best Sellers, 17 (March 1958) 408.
            The blurb states that the Marches provide fascinating
        fictional material, that it is a powerful Jewish family,
        and that the story is complex. It is wrong on all three
        counts. Charles March's sensitivity, intelligence and
        crisis of conscience are not significantly displayed.
        In a similar vein, the March family loyalty and pride are
        commented upon but not communicated. The only unequivocal
        attitude to emerge is Ann March's loyalty to Communism.
        The faults of the novel lie in making Eliot merely a
        sympathetic observer and commentator on the action.

B471   MADDOCKS, MELVIN. Review of The Conscience of the Rich.
        Christian Science Monitor, 27 February 1958, p. 11.
            "The father is the most memorable and affecting
        character in the book. . . . At marvellously described
        family dinner parties he wills a kind of ceremonial
        unity and through anecdotes of total recall he stakes
        out the past as sacred and inviolate while the present
        breaks up around him." A sober, nostalgic but not
        despairing novel of the disintegration of a social
        pattern.

B472   PODHORETZ, NORMAN. "England, My England." New Yorker,
        34, no. 12 (10 May 1958) 143-46.
            [A long review which deals directly with the novel
        at hand, and discusses it in terms of possessive love.]
        Asserts that Snow sees the conflict between Charles and
        Leonard March as the source of comedy, not tragedy.

Snow "refuses to make too much of what is, after all, the standard battle of the generations." Comments that coldness and cruelty animate the apparently noble and heroic final decision of Charles March. Observes that Snow deliberately avoids the temptation to create suspense, or add drama and color to the basic plot. "The result is that his books are quiet, low-pressure and frequently on the edge of becoming pedestrian, and the fact that they hardly ever topple over the edge is a tribute to his intelligence and the keeness of his observations." 2500w

B473 PRESCOTT, ORVILLE. "Books of the *Times*." *New York Times* (Daily), 21 February 1958, p. 21.
"C.P. Snow has worked out a complicated situation deftly. He has made his people seem completely real. He has explored the special customs and life of a very rich Jewish family with all the authority he customarily displays no matter what the subject. But, unfortunately, his Marches are only mildly interesting and their story seems somewhat slow and static."

B474 P.[RICE], R.G.G. Review of *The Conscience of the Rich*. *Punch*, 234 (23 April 1958) 554.
One of the most continuously interesting novels of the series. It is refreshing that Snow accepts the struggle for power in the world, and does not hide the fact in a cloud of imagination.

B475 QUIGLY, ISABEL. "A Problematic Lot." *Encounter*, 11, no. 1 (July 1958) 92.
Omnibus review, and Snow's novel is called the 'giant' of the lot. Mostly plot summary. "The scandal that results [from the conflict of loyalties and generations in the novel] is not very explosive: just the dismissal of an elderly minor politician, the faint but unjust smearing of an honourable name. A novelist less sure of his subject would have followed drama with counter-drama: a suicide, or at least a family row. Sir Charles makes mere disappointment far more moving." 250w

B476 REDMAN, BEN RAY. "The Complexities of Sir Charles." *Saturday Review*, 41, no. 8 (22 February 1958) 19.
Suggests that the intricate exploration of complex human character is the distinguishing mark of Snow's novels. He is a moralist, but one who witholds judgment; it is also suggested that Arthur Brown's outlook ("Brown loved his friends, and knew they were only men") is

shared by Snow. The Conscience of the Rich is discussed
in one paragraph. Then: "As always, the Snow style is
plain and unvarnished. . . . But he is a novelist of
real merit, who brings to his fiction a remarkably varied
experience of life. . . ." 550w

B476a RIBALOW, HAROLD U. Review of The Conscience of the Rich.
Chicago Jewish Forum, 17, no. 3 (Spring 1959) 178-79.
Three major characters, Charles and Katherine March
and Ann Simon, are troubled by their Jewish heritage.
"The entire novel deals with the March family, and
although the author considers them representative Jews
of England, the portrait he draws of them, while favorable, gives little substance to them as Jews." Despite
this insubstantiality, the novel is continuously
interesting and well worth Snow's effort.

B477   ROLO, CHARLES. "The Recording Novel." Atlantic, 201,
no. 4 (April 1958) 94-95.
The book is an example of the recording novel which,
in the words of one commentator, describes the timeless
struggles of the human heart as they existed under a
certain set of conditions. Mostly plot summary followed
by this judgment: "Leisurely in pace, the novel is one
in which milieu, characterization and atmosphere are
solidly realized. And in Leonard March, Snow has
achieved a masterly portrait of a remarkable type--the
great Anglo-Jewish gentleman." 280w

B478   SHRAPNEL, NORMAN. "Whose Day and Age?" Manchester
Guardian, 1 April 1958, p. 4.
"C.P. Snow drifts constructively on, and what he
has given us already has the look of something solid
and even permanent." In this work, partly by virtue
of the setting, partly by reason of the old-fashioned
chapter headings, Snow does not always seem contemporary.
The chapter headings breed "a certain unease, as though
a splendid Fabian aunt were suddenly to affect a coy
old lady's ribboned bonnets."

B479   WALBRIDGE, E.F. "The Conscience of the Rich." Library
Journal, 83 (15 February 1958) 609.
"Able work, but rather coldly intellectual."

B479a WOOD, FREDERICK T. Review of The Conscience of the Rich.
English Studies; Journal of English Letters and
Philology, 41, no. 1 (February 1960) 51.
"Indeed there is a sincerity, an understanding and

an honesty of presentation about all the characters
that makes the story a study of the complexities of
human nature on the one hand and of ideals and loyalties
on the other."

B480   WYNDHAM, FRANCIS. Review of The Conscience of the Rich.
London Magazine, 5 (June 1958) 70-72.
        The book is somewhat marred by the pervasive
presence of Lewis Eliot, and the characters are hard to
visualize, including Mr. L., who is slightly more
palpable as a result of an attempt to turn him into a
character in the superficial sense; but Snow's characters
exist in the moral sense or not at all; and, once the
moral dilemma is glimpsed in this novel, the characters
have drama and life. Snow the humanist emerges almost
naked in the book and the basis of his fictional
practice emerges in the musings of young Swan in Cooper's
Young People: "Passing moral judgments seems to me to
be the chief intellectual recreation of the human race
. . . . The first moral compulsion ought to be to
understand. . . passing moral judgments should be open
to you only when you understand what you're judging, not
before." 700w

B481-
B484   no entry

The Two Cultures and Scientific Revolution. 1959.

B485   [ALLEN, WALTER?] "Shorter Review: The Two Cultures and
the Scientific Revolution." New Statesman, 57, no. 1473
(6 June 1959) 806.
        "Snow's thesis is not likely to be easily contro-
verted, and its exposition is marked by humanistic
passion as generous as it is urgent." Literary intellectuals from Arnold to Eliot have been natural Luddites;
the question is, how were they able to have their own
way in the face of the Huxleys and H.G. Wells? [Review
signed W.A.] 350w

B486   ANON. Review of The Two Cultures and the Scientific
Revolution. Virginia Quarterly Review, 36, no. 4
(Autumn 1960) cxxviii.
        "The lecture is characterised by a solemnity, or
even over-solemnity, which is perhaps not always absent
from the lecturer's novels. At the same time, the
calculated grim note on which the lecture ends is
doubtless salutory and not unwarranted." 200w

B487   ANON. "Attack on the 'Two Cultures' of C.P. Snow:
        Work Criticized by Dr. Leavis." The Times (London),
        1 March 1962, p. 12.
            [Not a review but a summary of Leavis' Richmond
        lecture entitled "Two Cultures? The Significance of
        C.P. Snow."]

B488   BARNETT, H.G. "Reappraisal." Northwest Review, 3, no.
        3 (Summer 1960) 95-98.
            Observes that, apart from the literary and scientific
        culture, there is a third culture of social scientists
        perhaps more qualified than scientists and technologists
        to help the poor nations. "The history of technical
        assistance to underdeveloped countries offers ample
        evidence that technicians and scientists as popularly
        understood have too little understanding and sympathy
        with the people with whom they are required to work."

B489   BEER, JOHN. "Pools of Light in Darkness." Cambridge
        Review, 7 November 1959, pp. 106-09.
            Snow's lecture justifies the endowment of lecture-
        ships. His condemnation of ignorance in various branches
        of science and technology (machine tools, button manu-
        facture, the second law of thermodynamics) is justified--
        even though ignorance of all these topics is not equally
        reprehensible; but it is well to point out that teaching
        science involves the instruction of students into new
        patterns of thought. Further, a case can be made against
        technological expansion: it subordinates the individual
        to the community; leads to a depersonalized view of man;
        and promotes great weapons without great increases in
        human wisdom. One passage of the lecture ("Those
        triumphs of life are pools of light we make for ourselves
        while the edge of the road is black") can well be applied
        to Snow's novels, and the passage demonstrates that
        Snow's fictional analysis points to a "background not of
        sunlight or half-light, but of darkness."

B490   CLARKE, GEORGE A. Review of The Two Cultures and the
        Scientific Revolution. Ethics, 71 (October 1960) 72-73.
            "Snow has consciously oversimplified his two
        cultures and seems to underestimate the problem of
        poverty, but the way he links these two issues is highly
        suggestive. His distinction between man's individual
        and social condition is not only practically helpful;
        it also throws light into the Cartesian chasm between
        fact and value." 220w

B491   COLLINS, FREDERIC W. "Where There Is No Understanding."
       New Republic, 142, no. 15 (11 April 1960) 17–18.
           [Primarily an exposition of Snow's thesis with
       little or no comment.] "But it is not the warnings
       and proposals of Sir Charles that interest us as the
       insight from which they take off, the definition of
       the two cultures and the meaning, in time of scientific
       revolution, of the division between them. From that
       insight, one can take off on his own thinking, and
       perhaps add to what Sir Charles here offers." 1100w

B492   DAVENPORT, BASIL. Review of The Two Cultures and the
       Scientific Revolution. Book-of-the-Month Club News,
       June 1960, pp. 10–11.
           The warning that failure to close the gap between
       the scientific and literary cultures, and between the
       rich and poor nations, will lead to disaster, is one
       that Snow is unusually fitted to give by virtue of his
       varied experience. "In a time when there is a widespread
       feeling that our education system should be drastically
       revised, the views set forth in this book should be of
       the widest interest."

B493   GREEN, MARTIN. "The Great Threat." Commonweal, 71,
       no. 20 (12 February 1960) 552.
           Snow "offers us three ideas, any one of which could
       cause a revolution; every one of which almost certainly
       will." The three ideas: members of the literary and
       scientific cultures do not understand each other, and
       exhibit a good deal of mutual hostility; the literary
       culture has not accepted the industrial, much less the
       scientific revolution; the gap between the rich and
       poor nations grows greater and, unless the West agrees
       to industrialize the poor nations, the Russians, who
       have the trained engineers and scientists to do the job,
       and are not afflicted with two opposed cultures, will
       do the job themselves. Snow's message is inflammatory,
       but his prose is cool. The essay achieves a "lightness
       of touch with no implications of flimsiness, a personal
       and polite tone married to a prophetic idea as enormous
       as anything in, say, Carlyle."

B494   JENSEN, JAY. Review of The Two Cultures and the
       Scientific Revolution. Journalism Quarterly, 37, no. 4
       (Autumn 1960) 608.
           A fifty word exposition of the ideas of this
       "brief but provocative book."

B495   MARCUS, STEVEN. "Intellectuals, Scientists and the
        Future." Commentary, 29 (2 February 1960) 165-69.
            Snow's description of the nature of the cultures
        includes errors of observation and judgment. The
        literary culture is not mainly Luddite, and Orwell's
        dystopia, 1984, is not an expression of Luddite sym-
        pathies projected to the future; it is a non-fulfilling
        prophesy intended to avert a specific, damnable
        future. Writers are, by choice and inclination, tied
        to "particular material, temporal and spiritual circum-
        stances." As a group they take their epigraph from
        Thoreau: "I came into this world not chiefly to make it
        a good place to live in, but to live in it, be it good
        or bad." Snow may believe he is requiring only that
        writers be disinterested, but in fact he is asking
        that they be abstract. Shelley is an example of the
        literary man with a mania for the abstract; the virtue,
        or the fault, explains his intense, humane belief in an
        unrealized future. Snow's novels are specific descrip-
        tions of the professional life; but they tend to become
        abstract in other, larger areas of experience. The
        scientific culture is a culture only in an anthropological
        sense. Applauds the second half of the lecture, which
        deals with the industrial revolution and the extension
        of technology to benefit the poor, but also endorses all
        of Snow's own qualifications and doubts.

B496   MINER, EARL. "C.P. Snow and the Realistic Novel."
        Nation, 190, no. 26 (25 June 1960) 554-55.
            "What annoys me most is the lecture's fundamental
        anti-intellectualism in either the literary or scientific
        sense. There is disturbing Wellsian worship of tech-
        nology which diminishes his case and the issues involved
        . . . and if Sir Charles thinks technologists the salt
        of the earth, he finds in them a savor no one else dis-
        cerns. None the less, we must take the charge to action
        seriously, not shirking home truths simply because they
        are obvious." Snow's novel The New Men, gives a more
        convincing and satisfying treatment of the "problems
        of integrating our civilization." See also: B531.

B497   MORRIS, MAX. Review of The Two Cultures and the
        Scientific Revolution. Marxism Today, 3, no. 12
        (December 1959) 374-80.
            Snow's 'Two Cultures' lecture is considered in the
        context of specialized British education. Quotes
        sections from the higher education policy of the
        Communist Party. Argues that the historical predom-
        inance of non-scientific courses in British education

is the work of the British upper class, which devised
a traditional education of religion and literacy--a
prelude for a "life of labor in the service of others."
The role of British public schools is to ensure upper
class social cohesion. The relative neglect of science
in Britain is due to two factors: 1) the comfortable
British lead in the industrial revolution and 2)
imperialism--which ensured an adequate return on capital
and so discouraged further scientific education. Finally,
Morris gives some of the reasons why the Russians have,
as Snow claims, the right educational emphasis on science
and technology.

B498   SIEPMANN, CHARLES. "Judgment Day for the Modern Mind."
       Saturday Review, 43, no. 5 (30 January 1960) 22.
          Snow alleges that ignorance of the experiments of
Yang and Lee at Columbia, the failure to define a
machine tool, and an ignorance of button manufacture
is part of that split between the two cultures which
leads to the impoverishment of contemporary literature
and to a general inability to appreciate the scientific
edifice of the physical world. All these allegations are
half true, half false. "If, to be educated, we need to
know the 'social organization' that goes to making
buttons. . . we are indeed in a parlous state."
Oppenheimer's "Prospects in the Arts and Sciences" is
a deeper and better written work on the same theme. On
the other hand, Snow's remarks on the necessity imposed
on the West to transform the economies of the Third
World countries are "massive, well deployed, and ominous."
850w

B499   SUMNER, W.L. Review of The Two Cultures and the
       Scientific Revolution. Nature, 184, no. 4684 (8 August
       1959) 411-12.
          A series of brief excerpts from the lecture preceded
by a short introduction.

B500   WILHELMSON, FREDERICK D. "Man and the Scientific Age,
       I: The Sorcerer's Apprentice." National Review, 8,
       no. 9 (27 February 1960) 144-45.
          [Observations made from the perspective of a
philosopher.] The true issue is the relation that
should prevail between science and man. The conflict
between modern science and human values must, where it
exists, be decided in favor of the latter. "The
scientific revolution, itself capable of altering the
very fabric of human personality, must be disciplined
according to the moral and intellectual and even psychic
demands of the human substance." For the rest of

Snow's proposal "What is needed is a heroism that will give machines to men who need them and deny machines to men who have too many already." 900w

B501   WILSON, J. TUZO. "Two Worlds of the Modern Mind that Seldom Meet." New York Times Book Review, 3 January 1960, pp. 3, 14.

International cooperation to deal with the threats of atomic war, overpopulation and poverty may be idealistic but it is probably the most practical path. The comments on the two cultures of science and the humanities appear to be less soundly based, and they ignore the contributions of Sir Eric Ashby and Arthur Koestler on this theme. To say that literary intellectuals are Luddites is an exaggeration, and to say that only Ibsen understood the Industrial Revolution is in the same category. Consider, for example, the remarks of the capitalist Undershaft in Shaw's Major Barbara. 1000w

B502   WOLLHEIM, RICHARD. "Grounds for Approval." Spectator, 203, no. 6841 (7 August 1959) 168-69.

Science gets too low a place and prestige in contemporary British culture, and science is essential for British economic development. It is also essential to deal with the "appalling squalor and disease and overpopulation in Africa and Asia. . . ." But Snow clearly intends more than these boring and acceptable truisms. He is stating that culture 1) pays inadequate attention to science and 2) that culture should assimilate the results of science. The practical effect of 2) will no doubt bore certain people. "Why must they swallow their boredom, or else be deprived of education and denied creativity?" It is possible that Snow's underlying assumptions are 1) in an egalitarian but meritocratic society, the study of science shows the individual differences of merit most clearly and 2) in any modern society, the prevailing spirit must be that of science and "any form of poetry or painting that does not share in this overruling concern of the age is an anachronism. . . ." Snow observes that modern literary culture is ignorant of scientific progress; it might be more true to say that the bitter hostility shown to science by the greatest artists indicates a relation between art and agression. [These remarks are offered as theories that may support or controvert Snow's thesis.]

The Affair. 1960.

B503   ANON. "Review of The Affair." The Times (London),
        14 April 1960, p. 13.
             In this novel, as in his other works, Snow explores
        men who make momentous spiritual decisions which have
        comparatively trifling practical results. The problem
        of the forged photograph is never clearly stated, and
        the degree of innocence and stupidity attributed to
        Howard is almost inconceivable. The scale of values
        that leads Snow to make a comparison between this novel
        and the Dreyfus affair is faulty. "The perfect seri-
        ousness that seems here misapplied--the dons are seen
        as reverentially as Galsworthy saw his Forsytes--has
        else-where been C.P. Snow's greatest strength as a novelist
        . . . [But this work, though flawed, has a] narrative
        that is driven forward with force and subtlety."

B504   ANON. "The Corridors of Power." Time, 75, no. 20
        (16 May 1960) 103-04.
             Plot summary which pays more attention than most
        to the conflict between the political right and left
        in this novel. Includes a biographical sketch ("Snow
        throws parties conspicuously free of fellow novelists")
        which suggests, in passing, that the novels of Snow's
        wife, Pamela Hansford Johnson, are less ambitious but
        better crafted than her husband's. Quotes Snow on
        Lawrence Durrell: "A bit like eating a box of soft
        chocolates." Remainder of review quotes opinions and
        phrases from Snow's Rede lecture. 1300w

B505   ANON. Review of The Affair. New Yorker, 36 (28 May
        1960) 141-42.
             Plot summary followed by this judgment. "Mr.
        Snow's characterization is acute and authoritative, and
        the separate personalities of his men and women are
        impressed on the reader from their first introduction.
        His men, as a group, are very consciously gentlemen.
        His women, as a group, are aggressive, and inclined
        to speak up instead of just speaking."

B506   ANON. Review of The Affair. Booklist, 56 (1 June
        1960) 602.
             "The interplay of personalities, the revelation
        of rival factions--particularly in connection with the
        forthcoming election of a new Master--and the impersonal
        passion for justice are of dominant interest as the

academic group slowly and deliberately deals with the case. Will be appreciated most by readers of the earlier books in the sequence but will also introduce new readers to the older books."

B507 ANON. Review of The Affair. Virginia Quarterly Review, 36, no. 3 (Summer 1960) lxxvi.
    The twists and turns of the plot mark this work as one of the best plotted of Snow's novels. "It would be interesting to know whether any reader introduced to Snow through this book would be able to avoid running to library or bookstore to procure and greedily read all of the others."

B508 ANON. "For Special Attention." English Journal, 49, no. 6 (September 1960) 439-40.
    Substantial plot summary. Followed by brief but enthusiastic praise for plot and characters.

B509 BERGONZI, BERNARD. "All Decent." Spectator, 204, no. 6877 (15 April 1960) 394-95.
    The novel shows Snow's talents to best advantage. It excludes characters like George Passant and Roy Calvert, love affairs, and the embarrassing events which afflict the young, rising Lewis Eliot. It is an accomplished piece of writing. The prose is taut, and the tension is well-maintained. Unlike The Masters, which focussed on the intrigue itself, in The Affair "A moral theme of some profundity dominates the whole work; it is, inescapably, a meditation on the nature of justice. . . ." 1050w

B510 BREMNER, MARJORIE. Review of The Affair. Twentieth Century, 168, no. 1001 (July 1960) 89-90.
    Snow's novels describe elites; they withold comment on the moral values to be found in these elite groups.

B511 BRYANT, DONALD C. Review of The Affair. AAUP Bulletin, 47, no. 1 (March 1961) 70.
    Discusses the novel in terms of Snow's "Two Cultures" dichotomy. The younger scientists stand for impersonal justice; the older scientists and non-scientists alike favor the Establishment, conservative religion and politics. Can the passion for disinterested justice prevail in this setting? "The answer, not altogether uncluttered by uncertainties, is: Yes, if that society is controlled by physicists." Praises both Snow's narrative and Snow's narrative touches. "In sum, The Affair is an artistic novel, engaging, diverting, on a theme of moment both within and without the AAUP."

B512 BUTCHER, FANNY. "Trouble on an English Campus."
      Chicago Sunday Tribune Magazine of Books, 8 May, 1960,
      p. 22.
          A leisurely work, remarkable for the absence of
      women and a "revealing, affectionate picture of life in
      a great English university, with its customs, its
      secrecy and its spirit."

B513 CLANCY, JOSEPH P. "The Corridors of Power." Commonweal,
      72, no. 7 (13 May 1960) 184-86.
          "C.P. Snow is the best living British novelist."
      The novels explore aspects of personal and social power.
      Snow's ability to introduce complications in his
      fictional narrative, and to avoid bromides on the scale
      of "power corrupts" merits much praise. The book "moves
      slowly and with surface brilliance, gaining its strength
      from its trueness to the ways of men in society. . . ."
      Quotes and praises a paragraph which sums up Martin
      Eliot's character. Snow's theme is the intelligence,
      not the subconscious, of his characters; he judges, and
      does not merely depict, experience. "C.P. Snow is
      tough-minded, compassionate, always aware of the mystery
      of the persons involved in the politics. These are
      rare gifts in any novelist, and the ones which lay most
      claim to our attention and our applause."

B514 CRANSTON, MAURICE. "Foreword." London Magazine, 7,
      no. 8 (August 1960) 7-9.
          In his novels, not his pamphlets, Snow treats his
      right-wing characters with sympathy and occasional
      indulgence. One of the lessons of The Affair is that
      traditional radicals do not support the victims of the
      Establishment. "Indeed a reader would have to look far
      among living practitioners of political science, so-
      called, for anyone with Snow's acute awareness of those
      shifting patterns of interest and ideology, of romantic
      and calculating motives, of public spirit and personal
      ambition which govern our common destinies."

B515 DAVIS, ROBERT GORHAM. "Up for Trial Was Justice Itself."
      New York Times Book Review, 8 May 1960, pp. 1, 24.
          Substantial plot summary. The central theme is
      that intelligent men, especially scientists, are pre-
      disposed toward honesty and justice. Includes brief
      comments on the imagery of light and dark. Compares
      The Affair to Trollope's The Last Chronicle of Barsett.
      Suggests that Snow's fiction is not building an imagin-
      ative bridge between literature and science. Snow's
      work does not represent an "imaginative advance beyond
      the work of those writers (Yeats, Pound, Wyndham
      Lewis) whom he condemns."

B516   DERRICK, CHRISTOPHER. "Power and Glory." Tablet, 214
        (23 April 1960) 394.
            "Justice is done by a narrow margin and, as for
        Dreyfus, too late; things are not made easier for them
        by the esoteric nature of the central problem, and the
        book is partly an essay or a warning parable about the
        twoness of the two cultures, and far from an impartial
        one, Sir Charles being always very ready to point a
        moral derived from his faith in the saving merits of
        steam and the electric telegraph." 250w

B517   DIDION, JOAN. "Inadequate Mirrors." National Review,
        8, no. 27 (2 July 1960) 430.
            [Omnibus review. More judgment--brisk, brightly
        phrased, and unfavorable--than plot summary.] Snow's
        novels constitute "the literature of the National Health
        Service, and celebrate a world of committees, compromise,
        decisions and revisions, a world in which Civil Service
        Hamlets Behave Well in Difficult Situations." The novel
        is sophomoric: liberal and speculative novelists like
        Snow are perpetually surprised by the fundamental
        depravity of mankind.

B518   GLASS, BENTLEY. Review of The Affair. Science, 133,
        no. 3465 (26 May 1961) 1698-99.
            "The strength of the novel, as in The Masters,
        lies in Snow's ability to deal with human motives and
        psychological problems. Its weaknesses are those
        already marked in previous Snow novels: the shadowy
        character of his females and the exclusively intel-
        lectual level on which his protagonists seem to live."
        The motivations of certain characters are weak, obscure
        or unexplained: the reasons for the (putative) fraud
        of Palairet, the malignity of Nightingale, and the lust
        for the mastership by Getliffe remain unexplained.
        Those critics who see a reflection of Snow's preoc-
        cupation with the 'Two Cultures' lecture in the novel
        are mistaken. [Reasons for this view are given.]
        Briefly compares Snow's novel with Eleazar Lipsky's
        The Scientists.

B519   [HEPPENSTALL, RAYNOR]. "Old Friends in New Roles."
        Times Literary Supplement, 15 April 1960, p. 237.
            It took boldness and complacency on Snow's part
        to publish a book which invites comparison with the
        Proustian treatment of the Dreyfus affair. The
        punishment inflicted on Donald Howard, teaching in a
        grammar school, is not remotely comparable to the
        dreadfulness of Devil's Island. The work lacks suspense.

231

However, the "pace is beautifully even." Objections
to Snow's diction follow. "People still feel things
in their fibres, and on occasion the fibres speak."
Eliot's Latin genders show signs of decay. Margaret
Eliot has no fictional career commensurate with her
splendid attitude and obvious talents. The gap of
five years between the end of Homecomings and this work
is disconcerting. "A total structure seemed to be
gaining in depth. One now has a feeling that the
structure has in some obscure but quite real sense been
abandoned." Intimates that the work is lifeless.
1100w [Reprinted, with additions and revisions, in
B112.]

B520   GOLD, HERBERT. Review of The Affair. New Leader, 43,
no. 20 (16 May 1960) 28.
". . . . a climactic moment in one of the most
impressive imaginative constructions of the century."
In this account of the joys and perils of virtue in
action, Snow displays a tenderness towards his
characters, but he never abdicates the power of judgment.
The style is non-rhetorical and matter-of-fact, but this
manly, sturdy style reveals all Snow's intelligence,
confidence and high purpose. "Vice interests all
novelists. In addition, and to an extent unique in
contemporary letters, C.P. Snow has succeeded in making
the active pursuit of virtue a matter of magic, suspense
and passion."

B521   HICKS, GRANVILLE. "A Matter of Justice." Saturday
Review, 43, no. 19 (7 May 1960) 15, 66.
Favorable plot summary. The best novelists convey
a sense of the mystery of human personality. The
emphasis in Snow's fiction is on intelligence. Inset
biographical sketch of Snow by Rollene W. Saal is
notable chiefly for its short description of The
Devoted--a novel which was never published. According
to Snow, quoted here, this work described the "life
of quite lowly clerks, secretaries, the floating
population of a great city. . . ."

B522   HIGHET, GILBERT. "Report on C.P. Snow's The Affair."
Book-of-the-Month Club News, May 1960, pp. 1-3.
Describes the differences between a college in the
U.S. and a College in Cambridge or Oxford and remarks
that in such a closed society there is much room for
ardent rivalries and poisonous feuds. "Perhaps [Snow's]
chief virtue as a novelist is that he can show us men

and women caught in difficult problems of right and
wrong--some lying almost without knowing it, some
searching for the truth almost without wishing to find
it, some doing right for the wrong reasons--and still
make us feel a deep sympathy for them all."

B523   HOLLANDER, JOHN. "Two Worlds, Two Generations." New
       Republic, 142, no. 22 (30 May 1960) 17-19.
            The Affair may replace The Masters as prototypical
       Snovian novel of closed politics. Hollander evidently
       relishes Snow's moments of calm, non-epigrammatical
       insight, and he gives two examples, one from The Affair,
       the other culled from George Passant, and quotes them
       in full. A long paragraph is devoted to Lester Ince,
       who not only makes noisy flourishes, but studies
       Nostromo word by word. Finds Ince somewhat of a
       caricature. His remaining critical belief is a short
       polemic in favor of the novels of direct experience,
       Time of Hope and George Passant, the characters found
       in them (George Passant, Roy Calvert, Sheila Knight)
       and the tense but lyrical experience in these early
       novels.

B524   KERMODE, FRANK. "Beckett, Snow, and Pure Poverty."
       Encounter, 15, no. 1 (July 1960) 76-77.
            Snow, like most scientists, is probably at least
       a meliorist. In his fictional judgments Snow displays
       the typical confidence of the scientist who can assess
       the achievement of a fellow scientist with precision.
       Examples of these judgments are cited. Women, unlike
       men, are "mostly spectators here, but are often assessed
       by a different measure, their sexual activity, or what
       can be inferred of it." Snow, unlike D.H. Lawrence,
       has no interest in the "last naked him"--an essential
       naive core of innocence typical of man but not of man
       the social animal. "Sub specie temporis [Snow's]
       Combination rooms say more to us than Beckett's wet
       and windy plains, his grovelling exiles. (Let's leave
       eternity out of it.) And he's also, it must be said,
       a great deal easier and more pleasant to read."
       [Reprinted: B165.]

B525   KIEFER, H.C. Review of The Affair. Arizona Quarterly,
       16, no. 3 (Autumn 1960) 276-77.
            The issue is resolved in terms that are human and
       cloudy rather than theoretical and clear-cut. The
       past, despite Eliot's disclaimer, impinges on the present.
       Observes that the cycle achieves rhythm in E.M. Forster's
       sense of the word, and briefly differentiates Snow's
       series from the work of Durrell, Romains, Faulkner,
       Proust and Powell.

B526   LODGE, ROBERT A. Review of The Affair. Best Sellers,
        20 (1 June 1960) 90.
            "The Affair. . . demonstrates in a delightful
        and gripping way his deep understanding of the thoughts,
        feelings, and aspirations of man in an age when moral
        values apparently are being completely depreciated."

B527   MATTHEWS, GEOFFREY. "Two 'Committed' Novelists."
        Stand, 4, no. 2 (1960) 42-44, 46.
            Observes that Snow's wide and varied experience
        does not necessarily make him a better novelist. This
        novel, while readable, sane and anchored in actual
        human problems, is totally devoid of irony and humor,
        and the resulting flatness leads the reader into moral
        dilemmas, notably when Howard is expressly cautioned
        by Lewis Eliot not to make insinuations against
        Nightingale, and yet Lewis Eliot later dogtrots out
        these same insinuations. The fundamental problem is
        the character of Donald Howard. He is described as
        despicable and incompetent, and this depiction makes
        the "comfortable injustice" of the final verdict less
        relevant to the problems of our time. "Ultimately the
        bland assumption of worldly maturity and tolerant
        wisdom that pervade this book covers up a fundamental
        artistic cowardice."

B528   MERCIER, VIVIAN. "Sex, Success and Salvation."
        Hudson Review, 13, no. 3 (Autumn 1960) 450-51.
            Omnibus review. Scientists, particularly British
        scientists, can measure success by decorations,
        fellowships, Masterships, knighthood. "Lewis Eliot
        in The Affair might well measure his present status
        by the fact that he can defend a falsely accused young
        scientist, who is probably a Communist, without
        seriously endangering his own career." Followed by
        brief plot summary. "Things turn out, as always in
        Snow's books, worse than one had hoped, but better
        than one had feared." Snow presents a valid attitude:
        play the success game for all it is worth. 350w

B529   MILLER, NOLAN. "Of the Many, a Few: A Fiction Summary."
        Antioch Review, 20, no. 2 (Summer 1960) 255.
            Omnibus review. Snow is a latter-day Galsworthy.
        "Snow's characterization is old-fashioned, heavy-
        handed; he writes with the nineteenth century novelist's
        panoramic view of the sources of tradition in English
        society. . . .But Snow is impersonal; he lacks the
        'character' of a point of view, a necessary human vigor,
        always found in Dickens or Thackeray. . . . Fortunately,

the insights are always there; he is more than intelligible, that is, 'readable'; he has a respected direction
of detached intelligence." 300w

B530 MILLGATE, MICHAEL. "Strangers and Brothers." Commentary,
30, no. 1 (July 1960) 76-79.
[A long and leisurely review by a critic favorably
disposed to the whole Strangers and Brothers sequence.]
Millgate gives synopses of other novels in the sequence.
He defines (with one example) the notion of 'resonance,'
or sympathetic vibrations between what Lewis Eliot sees
and what he feels. Millgate notes those qualities which
make a fictional character a 'stranger' or 'brother' in
Snow's eyes. He is also acquainted with Snow's critical
writings on the novel form, and observes that the
deliberate emphasis in Snow's fiction is on the strength
and clarity of narrative line rather than on a richness
of texture. "When the sequence is rounded off it will
unquestionably be the most comprehensive, the most
informative and, all in all, the most impressive portrait
of modern England that any novelist has yet given us."

B531 MINER, EARL. "C.P. Snow and the Realistic Novel."
Nation, 190, no. 26 (25 June 1960) 554-55.
A review of C.P. Snow (London: Longmans Green, 1959)
by William Cooper; The Two Cultures and Scientific
Revolution (Cambridge: Cambridge University Press, 1959)
by C.P. Snow; and The Affair by C.P. Snow. Miner's
comments and judgments apply to the whole series. The
Affair gets praise but that praise is brief and fleeting.
He believes the novels of direct experience are dull;
the novels of observed experience are interesting. The
Conscience of the Rich is the best of the lot: it has,
"at times, a Dickensian vitality in a Jamesian social
world." The Affair is preferable to The Masters: the
issues are better defined, and it integrates the personal
and social lives of its characters with greater success.
He also defines realism, compares Snow to Trollope and
Ivy Compton Burnett and, like P.H. Newby in a very early
assessment, praises Snow's unblinking honesty. Miner's
objection to Snow's series centers on the limited stock
of fictional techniques; more variety is in order.
"Questions about his 'place' in the fiction of our time
can wait. It is enough to say that he has harmonized--
sometimes imperfectly, sometimes brilliantly, always
interestingly--an almost forgotten Augustan concern with
the social life of man and the familiar post-Romantic
concern with realizing individuality. The future will
decide how to weigh the rather old-fashioned technique
in balance with the new and convincing realism." 1000w

B532   NELSON, BRYCE E. Review of <u>The Affair</u>. <u>Audit/Poetry</u>,
        1, no. 10 (March 1961) 11–15.
            Snow's fictional world is detached and analytical,
        and his descriptions of nature are rarely sensuous.
        The words 'passion' and 'passionate' occur frequently
        in the series; but Lewis Eliot is far from a passionate
        man. His novels are worth reading because Snow, follow-
        in Malraux's dictum, has turned the widest possible
        varied experience into a subject for conscious thought
        and because he tells us so much about people and their
        motives.

B533   NORDELL, ROD. "C.P. Snow's New Novel: A Question of
        Justice Among Men of Affairs." <u>Christian Science Monitor</u>,
        12 May 1960, p. 8B.
            Plot summary filled with praise. One small reser-
        vation is expressed. Lewis Eliot is somewhat insuf-
        ferable from time to time when he catalogs the achieve-
        ments of his associates. Quotes comments by Lewis
        Eliot on hypocrites, making choices, the sheltered
        and cossetted egos of tycoons and Civil Service bosses
        compared to the vulnerable position of the artist in
        a critical no-man's land. "Most novelists these days
        seem to be dealing with the disreputable or abnormal
        and/or abstracting the individual from society; Snow
        performs the valuable service of elucidating the ways
        of the rich, the influential, the gifted. . . .
        Whatever the ultimate rank of this sequence as
        literature it can hardly fail to have lasting interest
        as a sensitive picture of an important segment of our
        times."

B534   O[WEN], I.M. Review of <u>The Affair</u>. <u>Tamarack Review</u>,
        no. 17 (Autumn 1960) 75–76.
            Snow deals best with his themes of the acquisition
        and manipulation of power in a small college setting,
        and this work shows the change from left-wing agnosticism
        to religious Toryism among the Fellows.

B535   PICKREL, PAUL. "A Fellow Needs a Friend." <u>Newsweek</u>,
        55, no. 19 (9 May 1960) 114.
            "Snow, who has a quiet mastery of human complex-
        ities and crotchets, can have marvellous fun, for
        instance, with a fatuous 96-year old Icelandic scholar
        who still wants to get into the scientific act; he
        reveals the modest, kind heart at the core of a wonder-
        fully suave lawyer. He has an almost uncanny grasp of
        inter-human loathing and liking." 300w

B536   _____. "People with Power." Harper's, 220, no. 1321
(June 1960) 97-98.
        Substantial plot summary. Praises Snow's ability
"to locate the living nerve in the mass of manipulation"
typical of a committee meeting; Snow's fairness to the
moral complexity of the issues; and Snow's skill in
sensing and describing the human limitations of his
characters.

B537   PRESCOTT, ORVILLE. "Books of the Times." New York
Times (Daily) 9 May 1960, p. 27.
        "Snow writes with extraordinary penetration and
admirable narrative skill. . . . [Snow's] approach is
objective, intellectual, detached--with enough sympathy
to be likable, but without much emotional commitment.
The result is an intellectually brilliant novel and a
marvelous entertainment for moderately tough-minded
readers."

B538   PRICE, R.G.G. "New Novels." Punch, 238, no. 6238
(13 April 1960) 530.
        Snow has a curious narrative power, and he often
tells poor stories very well. His novels are enjoyable,
original and impressive. This work, nearly as gripping
as The Masters, is one of the best.

B539   PRICE, MARTIN. "Some Novels from Abroad." Yale Review,
N.S., 49, no. 4 (June 1960) 620-22.
        "In The Affair C.P. Snow provides a notable instance
of a form which he has virtually created and has perhaps
begun to exhaust. Snow's interest is in the professional
man, and his subjects are the sense of vocation, the
nature of careers, the use and cost of power, the
politics of work and the work of politics." Followed by
astute and precise comments on Arthur Brown, Sir Francis
Getliffe, Nightingale, Eliot, Jago. ". . . .these
personalities are explored only as such exploration is
required by the need to predict or control." 1000w

B540   SNYDER, ROSS. Review of The Affair. Christian Century,
77, no. 40 (5 October 1960) 1156-58.
        "Somewhere in the course of this novel the shrewdly
paradoxical remark is made that the world would be much
more pleasant if only the good and noble were victimized
by the perverse workings of justice." Substantial plot
summary follows. Ends with a rebuke to the blurb
writer who added two years to the life of the 'delightful'
M.L.H. Gay, and also committed the cardinal sin of
misspelling Icelandic. 340w

B541   STANFORD, DEREK. "Postscript." [to his article
"C.P. Snow: The Novelist as Fox"] Meanjin, 19, no. 3
(September 1960) 247-51.
   [A flamboyant, balanced review which is a pleasure
to read.] Avoids detailed plot summary but gives a
reasonable intimation of the book's contents. Memorably
sketches some of the younger Fellows in the novel. "I
am filled, turn by turn, with irritation and deep
satisfaction; with a sense of the author's fine observation coupled with a detection of prejudice disguised
as judiciousness." Praises Snow's presentation of the
man-woman relationship. Denounces the morality of
Snow's fiction. "For all [Snow's] penetration into
character—for all his radical sympathies—he does
himself ultimately believe that the tactics of 'life-
manship' provide us, in the long run, with the soundest
moral values. . . . Somehow it is as if Lewis Eliot
had received his moral notions from Samuel Smiles or
Martin Tupper, de-Christianized them, and then given
them a 'Top People' dressing. Perhaps this is another
way of saying that Lewis Eliot's school of morals is
that of Darwin and the struggle for survival. The
Victorian cult of independence, industry, and success,
has married the twentieth century Common Man's ethic of
'decency', 'fair play' and 'justice.'" Suggests that
Snow's morality derives from his scientific education.
Briefly laments the thin intellectual content of Snow's
books. His final judgment, despite these objections,
is favorable. ". . . no other living British novelist
has quite his weight, his enduring interest, a sense
of continuing familiar excitement." 2200w

B542   STEINER, GEORGE. "The Master Builder." Reporter, 22,
no. 12 (9 June 1960) 41-43.
   Refers to Balzac, Proust and Stendhal in a discussion of Snow's fictional oeuvre. Steiner praises the
dialogue, the comedic touches (M.L.H. Gay) and the
conclusion of The Affair. "In Snow, intellectual and
moral argument has a lucid immediacy that is nearly
sensual. . . .The claims of justice are met; but the
claims of behavior and humane good taste are also met."
Steiner then returns to his main theme. "Snow conducts
The Affair with such majestic ease largely because he
has moved nearer than ever before to identifying himself
personally with the narrator. Lewis Eliot has Snow's
career behind him, and he has the complex worldliness
of Snow's thought, and his ability to bridge the literary
and scientific." This advantage is attended by dis-
advantages: the fictional range is narrowing, the style

shows a metallic precision, and there is an absence of a vital, fluid element of experience often found in music and the best of the world's fiction. Throughout The Affair "the comparison with Proust is openly invoked, and it is a mark of Snow's excellence that it can justly be made." 2000w

B543   WARD, FERDINAND. Review of The Affair. Extension; The National Catholic Monthly, 55, no. 5 (October 1960) 6.
        "The Affair abounds in good sketches of people like Arthur Brown, the senior tutor; the persistent Laura Howard and her unpleasant husband, Nightingale, the Bursar of the college, who might have destroyed the photo, and others concerned with the case. Not every one will care for Snow's latest novel, for he writes for discriminating readers. His story is well written!"

B544   WATERHOUSE, KEITH. "New Novels." New Statesman, 59, no. 1518 (16 April 1960) 566.
        [Plot summary.] "The warm, Talbot Baines Reed atmosphere of The Masters is disappearing. . . . [The novels of observed experience induce] a feeling of cosiness followed by one of acute claustrophobia. Is the little world really symbolic of the big world? Is the microcosmic justice of the Howard affair really symbolic of macrocosmic justice outside? Snow has recorded changes within the groups and families and closed-circuit society which he describes--his London clubs are letting women in to dine--but what he has not described satisfactorily enough for me is how, in the context of the world outside, the groups themselves have shifted to a new position." 480w

B545   WEBB, W.L. "Chronicler of the Intelligentry." Manchester Guardian Weekly, 21 April 1960, p. 11.
        Here the important Lewis Eliot, who might be Home Secretary, or the head of M.I. 5 (to judge by his self-important air), sets out to pursuade the college government that a young man accused of scientific fraud may be innocent. On the level of a psychological thriller, the novel is good; but Snow's high grade substitute for art is in evidence. It consists of rounding off every scene with atmosphere--and usually involves some comment on the weather. This technique coats the action with a rich, even patina of cozy melancholy. Eventually, the technique is recognized as the literary cosmetic that it is, and Lewis Eliot's carefully nursed angst and sentimentality about certain

characters leads to the "curious glamour with which
Snow invests his world." If Snow were to rid himself
of nostalgia, and deal with the donnish scene as it is
today, his next novel might be valuable.

B546 WEEKS, EDWARD. "A Study in Justice." Atlantic, 205,
no. 6 (June 1960) 166.
    Snow brings to mind the thoroughness and crafts-
manship of Galsworthy. Snow's forte: depicting the
motives, vanities, and subtle resourcefulness of men of
intellect. These remarks are followed by plot summary,
and a selection of three peppery phrases pleasing to
Weeks. Sample: "she asked after our child, but with
the touch of impatience of people who haven't any."
Conclusion: "For its vitality and excellence, I should
put this book beside The Masters, which up until now
has been Mr. Snow's best." 350w

B547 WERMUTH, P.C. Review of The Affair. Library Journal,
85 (15 March 1960) 1144.
    "The tangle of motives, prejudices, kindnesses
and hatreds represents Snow at his best. For as a
novelist he is interested in power, and in the character
of men who have it. No other current writer writes so
well or so perceptively about human politics in its
widest sense: in fact, C.P. Snow is one of the best
novelists writing today. Highly recommended for all
libraries."

Science and Government. 1961.

B548 ANON. "A Partial View." Times Literary Supplement,
14 April 1961, p. 226.
    Snow's argument is based on "a perusal of a small
fragment of Sir Henry Tizard's private papers." Snow's
conclusions as a result of this reading are 1) that
Lord Cherwell, if put in Tizard's shoes, would not have
prepared the British radar chain in time for the Battle
of Britain and 2) that Tizard, if put in Lord Cherwell's
position, would have advised against the policy of
strategic bombing. To present this case, Snow fails
to mention one of Tizard's failures and one of Cherwell's
successes. On the great bombing debates of 1942 Snow's
"analysis. . . is of little value because in this
matter C.P. Snow loses sight of, or does not know, the
facts." Tizard did not oppose the bombing policy; he

disputed the amount of probable damage inflicted. Bomber
Command made a major contribution to the Allied victory.
Snow's lectures, incisive and brilliantly written, should
not be mistaken for the final historical record. [For
Snow's reply, which alleges misrepresentation of his
intentions, and cites statistics which question the
policy of strategic bombing, see Times Literary Supplement,
21 April 1961, p. 249.] 1300w

B549   ANON. Review of Science and Government. Booklist, 57,
no. 16 (15 April 1961) 514.
"Short, but provocative, the material was first
presented as a group of lectures at Harvard in 1960."
50w

B550   ANON. Review of Science and Government. New Yorker,
37, no. 10 (22 April 1961) 179-80.
[Excellent exegesis.] "This tiny book is a masterly
contribution to one of the most important discussions in
the world." 180w

B551   BARRACLOUGH, GEOFFREY. "Salesmen in Power." Spectator,
206, no. 6929 (14 April 1961) 521.
"It is superlatively well done, a brilliant thought-
provoking essay." Lindemann's policy of strategic
bombing added at least six months to World War II.
Crucial decisions which must be made in secret for
reasons of security or on grounds of their inherent
abstruseness, are difficult. Snow's suggested solution,
the active participation of scientists in all levels
of government, could be very misleading. Non-scientists,
after all, questioned the merit of strategic bombing as
well as the Suez invasion. The true battle must be
directed against the terrible simplificateurs, the
Lindemanns, of modern democratic society. 800w

B552   BLACKETT, P.M.S. "Books; C.P. Snow's Account of the
Role of Two Scientists in Government." Scientific
American, 204, no. 4 (April 1961) 191-95.
Gives some reasons why Snow, the "novelist of
committees and court politics in this scientific age"
is singularly well-equipped to describe and comment on
the role of scientists in government, and endorses Snow's
analysis and comment. "By various accidents I was
personally involved in both conflicts, and I can vouch
for the fundamental truth of Snow's account of what went
on." [Blackett, Director of Operational Research at
the Admiralty during World War II, then discloses in

some detail the results of the bombing campaign in the
light of the statistical findings of the post-war U.S.
Strategic Bombing Survey, and condemns the ill-advised
Western reliance on nuclear weapons at the expense
of conventional land-based forces. Reprinted: B160.]

B553   CALDER, RITCHIE. "Clash of Titans." Nation, 192, no.
       15 (15 April 1961) 323-24.
           [A long summary of Snow's contentions complete with
       references to Watson-Watt's defense of Lindemann (see
       B92) by the former British Director of Plans of
       Political Warfare.] Calder parts company with Snow on
       two details: 1) Lindemann would not have impeded the
       development of British radar if Churchill had been
       in a position to influence events, and 2) the British
       war-time Cabinet included at least two men with
       scientific training. The bombing policy made no political,
       much less military contribution to winning the war.
       Agrees with Snow's assessment that "committee politics,
       hierarchial politics and Eminence Grise politics are
       dangerous and that, in a world socially dominated by
       science, the sooner men of wisdom equip themselves with
       enough science to cope with the 'experts,' the better.
       It is well said." 2250w

B554   COWEN, ROBERT C. "C.P. Snow on Natural Science and
       Public Policy." Christian Science Monitor, 6 April
       1961, p. 9.
           Gives the essence of Snow's argument in the book;
       suggests that the favorable treatment of Tizard, and
       the unfavorable description of Lindemann indicate Snow's
       emotional involvement, if not parti pris; and briefly
       cites the opinions of Robert Watson-Watt and Lewis L.
       Strauss that Snow's Lindemann is totally unlike the
       Lindemann they knew. 1100w

B555   CROSSMAN, R.H.S. "Secret Decisions." Encounter, 16,
       no. 6 (June 1961) 86-90.
           Snow's three brilliant lectures on decision-making
       in the twentieth century State complement Galbraith's
       The Affluent Society and Williams' The Long Revolution.
       Crossman restates the Lindemann position that massive
       bombing would destroy fifty percent of German working
       class houses, the disagreements of Tizard and Blackett
       with this high estimate, and describes his experience
       as the director of Political Warfare against the Enemy
       when it was concluded that bombing would increase, not
       decrease, German working class morale. He cites the
       decision to develop the H-bomb as the third momentous

secret decision of this century. Crossman endorses the
sensible, if somewhat obvious, morals Snow draws from
his war-time narratives; but he goes on to argue the
case for Socialist central planning of the peacetime
economy as the sole means of winning the Cold War.
[For correspondance between Crossman and Robert Strausz-
Hupe, see Encounter, 17, no. 2 (August 1961) 85-86.]

B556   DEININGER, WHITAKER T. "Unsilent Snow." Christian
Century, 78, no. 23 (June 1961) 712-13.
      Summary. "Science and Government makes a fasci-
nating book. More than any other, it can convey to the
man in the street the urgency of the problem of
scientists in government." 480w

B557   HARRISON, GORDON. "Scientific Duel and Its Moral."
New York Tribune Lively Arts, 9 April 1961, p. 29.
      "Behind its deadpan title, Science and Government
is part history, part political speculation, part human
observation and all C.P. Snow--a kind of closeup of a
warm and subtle mind. . . .It is Sir Charles' contention,
based largely on a study of Tizard's personal papers,
that Tizard more than any other single man was responsible for pushing the development of Britain's radar air
defense system so that it was ready in 1940 for the
Battle of Britain. It is also his contention that
Lindemann labored to frustrate Tizard. . . Twice. Sir
Charles believes, Lindemann was disastrously wrong. Had
he twice prevailed, Britain might have lost the war.
Maybe so. Such hypotheses are unprovable and largely
profitless. In any case the feud makes a good story of
conflict between powerful and complex personalities for
high stakes. . . Sir Charles's suggestions. . . are
debatable and incomplete but they are provocative."
700w

B558   JENKINS, OWEN. "Two Dialects of Non-Discussion: Science
and Government." Carleton Miscellany, 2 (Summer 1961)
104-09.
      Observes that Snow's method of argument, or dialectic
is marked by the same faults in the 'Two Cultures' essay
as well as Science and Government. Snow presents one
problem, develops the problem so that it permits no
choice, and then proceeds to expound only one solution.
In both books, Snow begs the question; that is, he
assumes the truth of that which is to be proved.

B559   JOHNSON, PAUL. "Jupiter Complex." New Statesman, 61,
no. 1569 (7 April 1961) 549-50.
      Snow's brief but brilliant book argues that scien-
tists should participate in major governmental decisions,

but it does not answer the question: what is a scientist? The question is not a quibble; Lindemann was an eminent scientist but his decisions were guided by emotion, not by the dispassionate application of scientific methods. So, what is needed is men distinguished by scrupulous adherence to scientific method, and those latter-day commentators who talk about the bomb as a 'deterrent' and the Polaris submarine as the 'absolute weapon' are surely guilty of scientific nonsense. 1000w

B560   JONES, MERVYN. Review of Science and Government. Science and Society; An Independent Journal of Marxism, 26, no. 1 (Winter 1962) 58-63.
        [Also reviews I.I. Rabi's My Life and Times as a Physicist.] Rabi advocates the narrow view that science should be represented by a minister at the Cabinet level, while Snow argues, more broadly, that scientists are needed in government because they have the quality of foresight. Examines the limitations and dangers of Rabi's proposal of bringing scientists directly into government, and endorses Snow's position that scientist-administrators must have a vision of the future society to play a useful role in government.

B561   LEKACHMAN, ROBERT. "Book Notes." Political Science Quarterly, 81, no. 3 (September 1961) 465.
        This book, like the provocative The Two Cultures and Scientific Revolution, gives rise to more questions than it answers. "How are the scientifically ignorant politicians to distinguish between the good and bad scientists? How does a Harry Truman adjudicate the argument between a Robert Oppenheimer and an Edward Teller. How, on the other hand, can physicists and mathematicians understand that wily beast the politician? Exactly what sort of jobs should scientists be doing?" 260w

B562   LEWIS, JOHN D. Review of Science and Government. American Political Science Review, 55, no. 4 (December 1961) 912.
        [Review of three books on the subject of science and government.] Appreciates some of Snow's inferences from the Tizard-Lindemann conflict, but wonders if Tizard's commitment to radar was not "a desperate commitment to a new gadget." Snow establishes a strong case against reliance on court politics, "in this case the support of Churchill, and Lindemann's consequent freedom from effective criticism by other scientists."

B563   MOON, ERIC. Review of <u>Science and Government</u>.
        <u>Library Journal</u>, 86, no. 9 (15 May 1961) 1894.
        "The story has a moral and purpose. We need more
        scientists and scientific foresight in government. We
        need to know how to use them. Nobody does this sort
        of thing better than Snow, or with such simplicity
        or economy. One of the books of the year (already!) for
        all libraries." 150w

B564   PERLMAN, DAVID. Review of <u>Science and Government</u>. <u>San</u>
        <u>Francisco Chronicle</u>, 16 April 1961, p. 22.
        "Perhaps because it was written to be spoken, the
        book has the lucidity and flow of an easy conversation;
        it also has the same deft phrasing and brilliant flash
        of personal detail that mark Snow's novels. Altogether,
        in its brief pages, it is a most important essay." 850w

B565   PRESCOTT, ORVILLE. Review of <u>Science and Government</u>.
        <u>New York Times</u> (Daily), 3 April 1961, p. 31.
        "But Sir Charles does not indicate how any govern-
        ment is to recruit wise scientists like Tizard rather
        than misguided ones like Lindemann. How is the career
        politician or civil servant to tell the difference?"
        Snow also does not specify in what departments of
        government scientists should be deployed. Should they
        be given purely political or administrative tasks?
        Snow himself, in the 'Two Cultures' appears not to
        think so. 1100w

B566   ROBERTS, HENRY L. Review of <u>Science and Government</u>.
        <u>Foreign Affairs</u>, 39, no. 4 (July 1961) 697.
        [Listed as part of a bibliography of recent books
        with a forty word summary.]

B567   STRAUSS, LEWIS L. "Who Should Have Power to Decide? The
        Scientist and Public Policy are Examined by Sir Charles
        Snow." <u>New York Times Book Review</u>, 2 April 1961, pp. 1,
        14.
        Quotes passages and phrases from Snow's anti-
        Lindemann invective, and makes a number of corrections
        and observations. First, the inventor of radar was Sir
        Robert Watson-Watt, not Sir Henry Tizard. Second,
        strategic bombing was not a British invention. Third,
        Snow's advice to dispense with the services of a
        Lindemann is not very helpful. How can a government
        distinguish between the right and wrong kind of
        scientist? a Lindemann or Tizard? 1450w

B568   WEEKS, EDWARD. "Decision Makers." <u>Atlantic</u>, 207,
        no. 4 (April 1961) 108.
             "This small book, so bold, so lucid, and so full
        of character, goes straight to the heart of government
        in an atomic age, whether the government be totalitarian
        or democratic." 600w

<u>The Affair</u> (Play). 1961.

B569   CHAPMAN, JOHN. "Drama of Passionless Intellect."
        New York <u>Daily News</u>, 21 September 1962, p. 51.
             Mostly plot summary. Observes that it is a drama
        of intellect, devoid of passion and concludes, in
        cryptic fashion, that there is an impenetrable fog
        between the two halves of the world." [Reprinted:
        B146a]

B570   DENNIS, NIGEL. "Under the Combination Room." <u>Encounter</u>,
        17, no. 6 (December 1961) 51-52.
             [Joint review. His remarks on <u>The Affair</u> form a
        lead-in to his second and longer review of <u>Beyond the
        Fringe</u>.] Professes to be appalled at the depiction of
        professors in the play, and his tone is one of amused
        and amusing dismay. He found the dons dead, selfish,
        bitter, senile, imbecile, "hide-bound skeletons in their
        leather chairs." [The following quotation is a good
        example of the tone and drift of his remarks]. "When
        [professors] first start teaching at Cambridge, they
        still have childish traits of inborn decency and
        humanity, but as the years pass they purge themselves
        of these and dedicate their lives exclusively to the
        pursuit of status, prestige, wine, and other forms of
        absolute selfishness."

B571   KEOWN, ERIC. "At the Play." <u>Punch</u>, 242 (10 January
        1962) 113.
             Keown delighted in catching up with a play that
        was already a hit in London. He found the new cast
        excellent, the plot fresh, but caught some errors in
        the portrayal of the Establishment. He mentions no
        eternal truths, despises Donald Howard, but thought
        <u>The Affair</u> one of the best plays in London.

B572   KERR, WALTER. "First Night Report: <u>The Affair</u>."
        New York <u>Herald Tribune</u> (21 September 1962) p. 10.
             Underlines the ironies of the play. The conflicting
        motives which animate the players in the drama leave
        Kerr impatient. "The wonder is not that half-justice is
        ever done but that the race itself, presumably at its

most intelligent, is able to stir from the frogpond."
The characters, in their various contrived postures,
do not convince him that they are people with histories
and backgrounds. "There is intelligence, there is
complexity; but we are analyzing a pattern rather than
visiting sustained and incontrovertible life."
[Reprinted: B146a.]

B573   MCCLAIN, JOHN. "Theme Dulls Superb Effort." New York
Journal American, 21 September 1962.
       "It is superbly performed and all the trappings
are immaculate; it starts off with a roar and winds
up with an asthmatic wheeze." McClain believes the
central theme is improbable. The firing of a surly
"liberal" by an imbecilic Court of Seniors is an
unlikely event. It simply would not occur in England
or America. [Reprinted: B146a.]

B574   NADEL, NORMAN. "'The Affair' at the Miller." New York
World-Telegram and Sun, 21 September 1962, p. 20.
       Highly favorable review of this "morally invigor-
ating entertainment from England." Finds the play
stands well above ordinary theater because "Snow has
refused to settle for the storybook concept of right and
wrong as white and black." Praises Snow's enduring
moral values, the playwright and cast. [Reprinted:
B146a.]

B575   TAUBMAN, HOWARD. "Theater: Issue of Justice. 'The
Affair,' Adaptation of Snow Novel, Opens." New York
Times (Daily), 21 September 1962), p. 34, c. 2.
       It is a play for adults. It is on the side of
the angels. It has a viewpoint which is wise and mature.
Unfortunately, it is mainly thesis, and the blood runs
thin and cool. "The play does not dig deeply enough
into the hearts and motivations of important characters.
One does not learn enough about the young wife to
understand why she will not stop fighting even after her
husband's name is cleared, and one must take on faith
the bursar's rigidity. These two [Howard and Nightingale]
in short, are symbols of the extreme left and right
rather than fully realized persons." Brewster Mason as
Lewis Eliot pursues justice. The cast is accomplished.

B576   _____. "Sparkle of Ideas." New York Times (Daily),
Section II, 7 October 1962, p. 1, c. 1.
       The play makes two points: justice must be even-
handed, and the bloody contentions between the extremists
of the left and right must end. These issues are pursued
with a "sense of decency and, in the last act, a touch

of passion. Yet it cannot be acclaimed without reser-
vations. One respects its devotion to reason and its
magnanimity of spirit, but one is not sufficiently
seized and stirred by the conflict. Its characters
are consciously manipulated, and its dramaturgy, though
neat and business-like, tends to be mechanical." Shaw,
the great dramatist of the conflict of ideas, has set a
standard unattainable by lesser men.

B577   WATTS, RICHARD. "Striking Drama of Academic Life."
        New York Post, 21 September 1962.
            "The fear that a novel by C.P. Snow might make
        heavy going on the stage proves entirely unfounded."
        This opening sentence of Watts's review is matched by
        his last, "'The Affair' is a stimulating drama." In
        between, he praises the plot, the craftsmanship of the
        playwright, and the cast--particularly Brenda Vaccaro
        as the wife. [Reprinted: B146a.]

B578   WEST, ANTHONY. "From the Top Drawer and the Bottom."
        Show, 2, no. 12 (December 1962) 34-35.
            [West makes allegations about Snow and Leavis,
        and Snow and Lindemann not found elsewhere in the
        literature.] First, The Affair was doubtless inspired
        by Sea and Sardinia, in which Lawrence states, in an
        aside, that he wants judges with warm hearts, not
        abstract intellects. Second, the figure of Lester
        Ince in the play of the book, was deliberately intended
        as a portrait of Dr. F.R. Leavis and hence, by extension,
        of a Lawrentian rascal. Third, Snow and Lindemann took
        part in a conflict of wills that led to a diminution of
        Snow's influence in the Civil Service: Lindemann
        successfully argued the case for an independent Atomic
        Energy Authority. "Had the. . . Authority remained
        under civil service control [Snow] would have shaped
        it and in effect determined its policies by exercising
        his function of selecting its directors and its research
        workers." This defeat in British closed politics in
        the immediate post-war years led Snow to deliver the
        Godkin lectures. "They contain as vicious an attack
        on the reputation and achievement of a public figure
        as has been written in England for American consumption."
        Considers the play pure hokum, similar in its effects
        to the melodramatic mystery dramas of the 30s. 2500w
        [Reprinted: B10.]

The New Men (Play). 1962.

B579 ANON. "Audience in London Sees the Premier of The New
Men." New York Times (Daily), 7 September 1962, p. 35.
[A news report rather than a review. Announces
the opening of the play, and includes excerpts from
the favorable reviews of London critics. Bernard
Levin dissents. For Levin's review, see B581.]

B580 ANON. "The Bomb Kept Under Control. Strand Theatre:
The New Men." The Times (London), 8 September 1962,
p. 15.
  It has a strong narrative line, the ethics of the
bomb, an appealing glimpse of high political and
academic life and, in the person of Walter Luke, an
angry young man whose picturesque vocabulary delights
the straight-laced stalls. "The dialogue is all solid
and literary, and those involved meet every crisis,
external or internal, in the best stiff upper lip
traditions of the British stage at its stuffiest."
The characters unfortunately remain merely stereotypes.
Paul Daneman as the sensitive, scrupulous and basically
weak Martin Eliot is well cast. Ernest Clark as Lewis
Eliot makes him appear oily and priggish. Some of the
bit players are stagy to a fault.

B581 LEVIN, BERNARD. "My Concern Is not the Play But What
Is Behind It." Daily Mail, 7 September 1962, p. 3.
  [Snow sued Levin and his publishers on the appearance of this review. It was argued that Levin represented Snow as a fellow-traveller. The court sided
with Snow, and he gave the resulting money damages to
the British Migraine Association. See The Times
(London), 1 August 1963, p. 8.] Leavis' criticism
neglects Snow's dubious politics. Snow chooses to
remain blind to Soviet expansionism, and he minimizes
this threat by his emphasis on accidental nuclear war.
The play condemns the dropping of nuclear bombs on
Hiroshima and Nagasaki. It also argues that reliance
on the H-bomb is wrong and a form of corruption. This
argument is "nothing less than a shockingly unscru-
pulous piece of political sleight-of-hand, and its
denunciation must take precedence over the more
traditional aspects of dramatic criticism."

Postscript to Science and Government. 1962.

B582   ANON. "Two World Communication." Times Literary
Supplement, 27 July 1962, p. 535.
      Observes that Snow glosses his remark that "Tizard's
was the best scientific mind that in England had applied
itself to war" and records Snow's response to the appearance of Birkenhead's The Prof. The Strategic Air
Offensive Against Germany, 1939-1945 appears "to have
consolidated Snow's main contention." The arguments
between Tizard and Lindemann were about priorities--
with Lindemann consistently arguing for a lower priority
for radar. 675w

B583   HENGIST, PHILIP. "Accommodation Through Mutual Terror."
Punch, 243, no. 6379 (12 December 1962) 875.
      Omnibus review. "Sir Charles himself returns to the
anti-Lindemann attack. . . .By skilfully collating the
biographies of Sir Roy Harrod and Lord Birkenhead he
more than makes his point that "the Prof," besides being
a particularly unpleasing human being, was a disastrous
scientific overlord in time of war." 100w

B584   JONES, R.V. "Lord Cherwell's Judgment in World War II."
The Oxford Magazine, 3, no. 18 (9 May 1963) 279-86.
      [A long and detailed defence of Lindemann's
scientific judgment based on the written records of the
Committee for the Scientific Study of Air Defence and on
an examination of Lindemann's minority report dated
11 July 1936.] On radar: Lindemann's argument in favor
of aerial mines took into account the difficulties of
destroying German bombers at night and, while he pressed
this case, he nevertheless continued to give the highest
priority to the development of radar. On strategic
bombing: it is reasonable to accept the verdict of the
anonymous Times reviewer [see B548] that the bombing
policy attacked and defended was not Lindemann's policy.
In any case, Tizard's position on strategic bombing was
not enormously at variance with that of Lindemann. Also
provides comment on Lindemann's position vis-a-vis
operation 'Window,' the V2 rocket and on Tizard's
responsibility for atomic energy in the post war period.
"It is therefore quite reasonable--or at least it was
quite reasonable within the frame of reference of
military decision in World War II--for a Chief of Staff
to call for some one scientist to give the final
assessment of the scientific evidence. . . . Provided

that the scientist concerned does not isolate himself from the experience and opinions of his fellow scientists, but instead takes care to consult them, he may provide the best possible link between a non-scientific administration and the scientists on which it so heavily depends."

B585   TOULMIN, STEPHEN. "Scientist-Overlord." Spectator, 209 (27 July 1962) 104-05.
        Birkenhead's The Prof and The Strategic Air Offensive Against Germany, 1939-1945 confirm that Lindemann's scientific judgment was poor. Snow, in this restatement of the problem, observes that it is dangerous to have a scientist in a position of isolated power. This observation, while intrinsically sound, is not practical. A Prime Minister cannot constitutionally be debarred from appointing his own scientific adviser, and the appointment of a Scientific General Staff, a step Snow implies, does not solve the difficulty. The true solution is to educate politicians.

Stories from Modern Russia. 1962.

B586   ALLEN, GAY WILSON. "Reality in a Monolithic State." Saturday Review, 45, no. 14 (7 April 1962) 28.
        These stories may be more important than Dr. Zhivago in illustrating the activity and status of Russian writers. However, it is difficult not to read the stories as documents in the Cold War. The stories reveal "living conditions which the West would regard as intolerable. . . ." Considers that these stories are marked by more "vigor, passion and compassion" than contemporary English fiction. Followed by brief comments on Paustovsky's "The Telegram," Tendrayakov, Sholokhov's "One Man's Life" and "Bob" by S. Zalygin. 750w

B587   ANON. "New Fiction." The Times (London), 7 December 1961, p. 18.
        The introduction tactfully avoids the Cold War banalities, and properly concentrates on literary criticism instead, but the stories themselves are a disappointment. "Potholes" is the only undisputed success. "The Stovemakers" is amusing but light-weight, and "Bob" suffers from a failure of characterization. "The contributions of Mikhail Sholokhov, Nikolay Yevdokimov and Konstantin Paustovsky are negligible, but this one tale and the introduction make the book well worth while."

B588   ANON. "Without Pretensions." <u>Times Literary Supplement</u>,
        8 December 1961, p. 877.
            What has happened to the former Russian genius in
        writing novels? These stories possess a blessedly easy
        unpretentiousness compared to the contortions that
        accompany the Western writer's search for a personal
        idiom. "Altogether this is a most satisfying and
        interesting collection. Chekhov, after all, was not
        a full stop. The editors have established a promising
        bridgehead across which, let us hope, the [Russian]
        literary shock troops will soon be pouring." 350w

B589   ANON. Review of <u>Stories from Modern Russia</u>. <u>Kirkus</u>,
        30 (15 February 1962) 194.
            The perennial problem is that of translation.
        "Potholes," exciting but somewhat commonplace, suffers
        little from translation. But Sholokov's "One Man's
        Life" is less than well translated: the translation
        loses the pithy phrase, brutal image and lyric
        introspection typical of the author. "The Stovemakers"
        is gently boring, but the translation of "Light from
        Other People's Windows" is regrettable. "These stories
        are more 'of interest' than interesting."

B590   ANON. "Without Fireworks." <u>Newsweek</u>, 59, no. 14
        (2 April 1962) 89.
            The stories are tame, tepid, unalarming. "Bob"
        is the best of the lot. "The half dozen stories in
        this wholly unexciting assemblage are elemental,
        sentimental, and just about as unrevolutionary as
        most of the artistic production in the Land of the
        Great Revolution." 270w

B591   ANON. Review of <u>Stories from Modern Russia</u>. <u>New
        Yorker</u>, 38, no. 8 (14 April 1962) 184.
            "Since [the stories] are one and all pious and
        sentimental Victorian tracts, and since we know that,
        from Isaac Babel to Boris Pasternak, another sort of
        Soviet fiction has been written, the whole venture
        seems inexplicable." 60w

B592   ANON. Review of <u>Stories from Modern Russia</u>. <u>Springfield
        Republican</u>, 15 April 1962, p. 4D.
            "Although written in the Soviet aura and reflecting
        the patriotic pride that Russians naturally have in their
        own people and native land, these are not essentially
        propaganda pieces, but are analytical views of everyday
        human life, as seen by the observant writer's eye and
        interpreted by the sensitive literary mind." [Review
        signed: H.B.H.]

B593 ANON. "Winter's Tales 7: Stories from Modern Russia."
      Booklist, 58, no. 17 (1 May 1962) 609.
      "This collection, perceptively introduced by the
      British scientist-novelist and his wife, offers the
      Western reader a revealing glimpse into everyday life
      behind the Iron Curtain." 50w

B594 ANON. "From Many Places." Prairie Schooner, 36, no.
      2 (Summer 1962) 192.
      Omnibus review. The stories have little technical
      interest and tend to be mood pieces; but the characters
      --as in "The Stovemakers" have a dignity and significance
      absent from the perverts and sick adolescents in
      Western "literary" fiction. 150w

B595 BELKNAP, ROBERT L. Review of Stories from Modern Russia.
      Russian Review, 21, no. 4 (October 1962) 393-94.
      "Except for the patronizing little introduction by
      the editors, the collection might be the work of one
      of the younger Soviet critics. . . .In short, this is
      a competent but unexciting sampling from a rather
      unexciting moment in the history of a great literature."
      200w

B596 BLUM, JULIUS M. "Stories." Slavic and East European
      Journal, 8, no. 2 (Summer 1964) 204-05.
      Tvardovsky's "The Stovemakers" is the best of the
      stories; it conveys, without any political overtones,
      the sympathetic and noble peasants of Turgenev's
      Zapiski oxotnika. The absence of bibliographical data
      is regrettable, and the translation has a distinctly
      British flavor. 500w

B597 BRYLDEN, RONALD. "With a Difference." Spectator,
      165, no. 6964 (15 December 1961) 908.
      "Communism can produce literature as fine and as
      humane as any in this century." Witness Aragon, Brecht,
      Dreiser, the young Malraux and Silone. But this work
      induces stodgily dutiful boredom, and it is clear that
      the "main effect of the volume is a cramping, painful
      sense of mature and talented minds forced to talk down,
      being bent to ends smaller than their capacities, and
      to pretend otherwise seems. . . a ludicrous misjudgment
      of Russian art and Russian living." 450w

B598 CONQUEST, ROBERT. "Snow on Their Boots." London
      Magazine, 1, no. 2 (January 1962) 82-84.
      [Attacks the introduction and the selection by the
      two editors.] To claim that Soviet literature must be
      read without political considerations is fantastic

253

impudence. Both Snow and his wife accept the stories
as a hearty endorsement of the Soviet Establishment and
bureaucracy, and so violate their call for an apolitical
reading of the contents. They stress the support of
Soviet writers for the social system and the Party. They
neglect to observe that the humanist Soviet writers are
opposed to bureaucracy, against the restrictions placed
on intellectual freedom, and they gloss over the labour
camps, firing squads and suicides which marked the lives
of literary men. Names some of his favorite Soviet
writers--not represented here--and observes that the
purges, to judge by official census figures, cost as
many lives as World War II. The Snows make no mention
of the purges, or of Nekrassov's "The Second Night," a
truly pitiful story on the theme of World War II. "This
sort of thing is simply a gross and insensitive insult
not just to common humanity, but to Soviet literature--
an attitude it would be charitable to call obtuse. . . .
On any barricade I can think of, there is many a
Communist I should prefer to have on my side than Sir
Charles." 2500w [Reprinted: B599.]

B599   _____. "The Snows and Burintern Solidarity." New
Leader, 45, no. 12 (11 June 1962) 24-25.
          [Reprint, with minor stylistic revisions, of B598.]

B600   FITZGIBBON, CONSTANTINE. "Where the Curtain Falls."
Time and Tide, 42, no. 52 (14 December 1961) 2119.
          "Potholes" is the best of the lot, but Sholokhov's
sentimental "One Man's Life" could have been better told
by Hemingway in half the space. The rest of the yarns
are poor. The introduction deserves a Disingenuity
award. It suggests that the stories are recent, but
not how recent. It comments on qualities lost in
translation, but the Snows probably do not know Russian
well enough to judge this quality. Finally, it gives
no intimation of the censorship prevalent in Russia,
fails to point out that Russian writers, while members
of the Communist Party, may well be ambiguous members
of the Party; and the statement that Russian writers
consider Communism as the "only imaginable and desirable
one" is untrue. The harshest anti-Stalinist stories are
not published here and the result is a tepid, non-
controversial volume. Caveat emptor.

B601   FRIEDBERG, MAURICE. "Stories from Modern Russia."
Slavic Review, 22, no. 1 (March 1963) 179-80.
          The translation is good, but includes several rough
spots. The introduction is permeated by pro-Soviet bias.
The thick Russian literary journals flourished in the

time of the Tsars. "Naturalism" is a stick to abuse
writers guilty of sexual frankness; the term is not,
as Snow claims, otherwise sharply distinguished from
"realism." It is not true to write that Soviet writers
are respected by their colleagues in the middle of
disagreements and disputes: consider Pasternak,
Soshchenko, Akhmatova.

B602   FUTRELL, MICHAEL. "Winter's Tales 7: Stories from
Modern Russia." Listener, 67, no. 1713 (25 January
1962) 185.
        Praises the selection of Tendryakov's "Potholes"
but finds most of the other authors light-weight or
amateurish by comparison. Also gives some reasons
why Snow's introduction is regrettable.

B603   GROSS, JOHN. "From Russia, With Love." New Statesman,
62, no. 1605 (December 1961) 931.
        "They make a rewarding, substantial collection,
and it would be a pity if anyone was put off by the
introduction, which stands like a dragon at the mouth
of the cave. A pity, but understandable, since C.P.
Snow and Pamela Hansford Johnson discuss the Russian
scene with a complacency which would be merely fatuous
if one had never heard of Babel, Pasternak, and people
like that, not to mention Zhdanov, Surkov and people
like that. To argue blandly that God's in his Kremlin,
all's right with the world, is in fact the surest way
of raising political issues which are mercifully
irrelevant to the stories themselves." 435w

B604   HAYWARD, MAX. "Facts of Soviet Life and Literature."
Manchester Guardian, 8 December 1961, p. 7.
        Tendryakov's "Potholes" reveals a preoccupation
with moral problems of a universal nature, and this
story (like the better "Three, Seven, Ace" and "The
Trial") do not suggest the inevitable triumph of the
new Soviet man over the past. The other stories are
comparatively undistinguished. The introduction
suggests that the literary situation in the Soviet
Union is normal. It is not normal. It would be
interesting to have the comments of Sir Charles on a
speech delivered by N.M. Gribachev at the Twenty-
second Party Congress in which the notion that writers
are entitled to their own ravings was scornfully
dismissed. It must be remembered that Nikita Khrushchev
gathered Soviet writers together and suggested that
"'his hand would not tremble' if it came to shooting a
few of those [Russian writers] who had strayed too far."

B605   LASK, THOMAS. "Books of the <u>Times</u>: <u>Stories from</u> <u>Modern Russia</u>." <u>New York Times</u> (Daily), 9 April 1962, p. 27.

        Provides a synopsis of each of the stories, and considers the introduction overly solemn. "A collection more bland, or one with less bite would be hard to compile. Still we do get a glimpse. . . of Russian life behind the subject matter: the poor roads, inadequate lighting and uncertain communications, the weight of the government [and these glimpses] seem to indicate that though much has changed, a good deal remains the same." 800w

B606   NEISWENDER, ROSEMARY. "<u>Stories from Modern Russia</u>." <u>Library Journal</u>, 87, no. 6 (15 March 1962) 1152-53.

        The introduction by Snow and his wife, Pamela Hansford Johnson, is illuminating and sympathetic. The stories "have an almost Chekhovian warmth and wry humor, and are refreshingly free of partisan bias or hortatory political content." The translations, particularly those by Peter Henry, are praised. 150w

B607   PISKO, ERNEST S. "Fiction: Soviet and Swedish: Fair and Warmer?" <u>Christian Science Monitor</u>, 19 April 1962, p. 7.

        Praises "Potholes" and considers the yarn a strong protest against the Soviet system. Tvardovsky's story on the building of a stove is charming while "The Telegram" is moving. Sholokhov's story is grim, but "Bob" and "Light from Other People's Windows" are pale and unduly stretched out. "Yet even in these. . . pieces one can hear a faint echo of the now sad and now exuberant melody that gives the best of Russian short stories the quality of a haunting folk song." 250w

B608   PRICE, R.G.G. "New Fiction." <u>Punch</u>, 252, no. 6330 (3 January 1962) 80.

        Omnibus review. The stories are stuffy and hamfistedly banal. Surely the Russians have a better quality of fiction on tap? And believes the fault lies in the selection. 200w

B609   RUGOFF, MILTON. "The 'Individual' Vs. the 'System.'" <u>New York Herald Tribune Book Review</u>, 22 April 1962, p. 10.

        The stories deal in obvious and simple narrative forms involving peasants and workers in themes of social conscience. "Potholes" pits the individual against an iron bureaucracy. "The Telegram" involves a somewhat simple juxtaposition. "The Stovemaker" has some universality. The bitter "One Man's Life" demonstrates why the Russians have not forgotten or forgiven the Germans. "Light from Other People's Windows" gives an intimate glimpse of life in the city. The translations are marred by incongruous British colloquialisms.

B610   SLONIM, MARC. "In Russia, at Long Last, It's Spring." <u>New York Times Book Review</u>, 15 April 1962, pp. 1, 30.
        An excellent collection which is representative of the liberating trend in the Soviet Union. To call the Russian authors pillars of Communist society, as Snow does, is not quite correct: they are, with the solitary exception of Sholokhov, considered ideological rebels by the guardians of Marxism-Leninism. These writers "battle not against the government but for the human-ization and renovation of life and art." 900w

B611   SWETLAND, ANITA. "Russians are People." <u>Humanist</u>, 22 (December 1962) 203-04.
        The short story is a particularly palatable form of promoting cultural understanding. These stories, while essentially Slavic in content, are happily free from the "rather sick searching of the sub and semi-conscious for motive." They will serve to refute the notion that all Soviet art has a propagandistic aim, and to demonstrate that Russian writers work within the framework of Communism as western writers do within the confines of democracy.

B612   WAIN, JOHN. "Fiction from Moscow." London <u>Observer</u>, 10 December 1961, p. 27.
        Writers who disregard the directives of the Communist Central Committee are commonly rejected from the Writers' Union--or they cease to function as writers. These stories are readable and sometimes admirable; they convey a typical Slavic melancholy along with the prescribed Communist optimism. The introduction evades the issue of the lot of the writer in the Soviet state.

<u>The Masters</u> (Play). 1963.

B613   ANON. "<u>The Masters</u> Wins Acclaim in London." <u>New York Times</u> (Daily), 1 June 1963, p. 16.

[A news report, not a review. Announces the opening of the play at the Savoy theatre in London and quotes brief critical opinions from The Times (London) and Daily Express.]

B614   DENT, ALAN. "At the Play." Punch, 244, no. 6405 (12 June 1963) 862.
After a slow and somewhat confusing beginning, the play takes on human interest and Valerie Taylor as Alice Jago is exquisite and unforgettable, Gerald Cross as Winslow is incisive, and Richard Hurndall as the dying Master, Royce, is condignly ashen-gray, wise and resigned. The last two acts have action as well as talk and it is, all in all, a lion of a play compared to Miss Janet Allen's The Hot Tiara.

The Two Cultures: and A Second Look. 1963.

B615   ANON. "Snow's Second Look." New Statesman, 67, no. 1721 (6 March 1964) 370-71.
Snow's remarks about the politics of Yeats, Pound and Wyndham Lewis pinpointed a "severe limitation [i.e. in these authors] which at this hour in the day most of us would equally deplore." If Snow dismisses modern writers, Leavis' lecture proves that he loves literature very little. Huxley's neglected Literature and Science, by contrast, provides abundant proof of that devotion. In this expansion of the 'Two Cultures' theme, the argument against the literary intellectuals, the natural Luddites, is carried somewhat further, but it is not very convincing. Snow should have answered the criticism of Lionel Trilling, and argued less against Leavis and Leavisites. Modern literature, as Snow himself reveals at one point, does not bulk large enough in the minds of those who favor industrialization. "The truth is that the forces against which men have to contend in their efforts to build a decent society are enormous and complex, and have very little to do with the fairly specialised area of modern literature on which Sir Charles has trained his guns." 1000w

B616   ANON. Review of The Two Cultures: and A Second Look. Times Literary Supplement, 3 July 1969, p. 738.
Review of paperback ed. The essays "have lost none of their relevance over the years." 45w

B617   ANON. "Short Reviews." <u>Scientific American</u>, 210,
        no. 6 (June 1964) 134.
        The Rede lecture did not deserve the resulting
        cheers and abuse; Snow's basic ideas were old, and they
        were not expressed with unusual clarity or cogency.
        Notes that Snow reaffirms his central position, and
        dilates on the characteristics of Snow's third culture
        which flourishes in the United States. Snow's opinions
        in this second essay ramble from demography to
        Dostoevsky, act as only loose support of his main thesis
        and demonstrate the catholicity of his interests.
        "Whatever else might be said, one cannot fail to take
        Snow seriously or to recognize his commitment to the
        cause of peace, intelligent action and human betterment."
        690w

B618   BARTLEY, ROBERT. "C.P. Snow's New-Found Optimism."
        <u>Wall Street Journal</u>, 22 May 1964, p. 10.
        Quotes two reasons for Snow's renewed optimism:
        the rise of a third culture of social scientists,
        doctors and architects, and the success of the test
        ban treaty. Snow's literary critics, who charged that
        Snow was a partisan of science, are answered by a
        pointed attack on modern literature which portrays
        highly individual experience at the expense of the
        broad concerns of society. "One wonders if [Snow]
        didn't much underestimate the hurdle of overpopulation,
        the immaturity of leadership in the emerging nations,
        and the difficulties inherent in the cold war. Mr.
        Snow is widely known for his studied indifference to
        any threat from Russian communism. But can even he
        remain complacent about underdeveloped nations when,
        say, the Chinese fan the fires of anti-white racism?"
        600w

B619   FAIRLIE, HENRY. "Cults, Not Cultures." <u>Spectator</u>, 211,
        no. 7062 (1 November 1963) 554.
        Applauds Snow's humanitarian impulses, but argues
        that there is only one culture, much less three.
        Snow asserts that there are "two contrary ways of
        thinking about the same experiences, whereas, as Mr.
        Aldous Huxley says [in <u>Literature and Science</u>] there
        are just different types of experience." Snow lacks
        a sense of history and the sense of an intellectual
        tradition. In the absence of both, he has produced
        ideology. Snow's "thesis does not make sense in terms
        of cultures, for they do not exist. But it does make
        sense in terms of opposed ideologies."

B620　FOSTER, KENELM. "Snow Against the Poets."
Blackfriars; A Monthly Review Edited by the English
Dominicans, 45, no. 527 (May 1964) 220-26.
　　　[A serious examination of Snow's indictment of the
poets, or literary intellectuals.] In the original
lecture, Snow accused the literary intellectuals of
blindness to the cultural value of science, of reactionary politics and an idealized view of the pre-
industrial world. His charge against them later shifts
in its emphasis and Snow accuses them of a radical
social and moral indifference to society which marks
the romantic conception of the artist. (Snow does
not explicitly define an alternative, or more central
and true conception of the artist.) He evidently feels
that the roots of the alienation experienced by the
modernist writers (Samuel Beckett is a prime example)
lie in the 'ahistoricity' and a 'static view' of the
human condition. The question is whether Snow objects
to the content of a certain literature, or to an
underlying motive or spirit which shapes and forces
that content? It is plausible to argue that Snow is
putting the case for a literature entirely subordinate
to the collectivity and precluded by fiat from resting
its independence on a title deed of freedom. ('Science
has examined the nature of man and it finds no such
power or faculty [as freedom]. If there be such a
thing, show us where it is. You are warned!') Such
an argument is easy to derive from Marxist materialism
but not from Snow's apparent liberal agnosticism. 2500w

B621　KEMENY, JOHN G. "The Tower of Babel Revisited."
Washington Post [S.F. Examiner etc.] Book Week,
1 November 1964, p. 14.
　　　There is a demonstrable cultural gap, not only
between physicists and biologists, but even between
algebraic topologists and point-set topologists. This
second look induces bewilderment. Snow is on the
defensive. "He seems to belabor the obvious. He
discusses apparently irrelevant issues. He brings in
endless literary references. And the tone throughout
is one of a man who has been deeply hurt." It is
possible that, after the venomous invective of F.R.
Leavis, Snow is "subconsciously motivated by a desire
to re-establish himself as a full-fledged member of
the literary culture." The cultural gap is less
pronounced in the U.S. than in Britain, but the communication takes the form of baby-talk.

B622   WALSH, JOHN. "C.P. Snow: Second Thoughts on the 'Two
        Cultures' Likely to Keep the Pot Boiling." Science,
        142, no. 3493 (8 November 1963) 653-54.
            [Not a review of the printed book, but a recapit-
        ulation, with discussion, of Snow's article in the
        Times Literary Supplement (see A293)] Includes some
        long excerpts from the TLS article, observes that
        Snow's distinction between the individual and social
        condition is central to his argument, and discusses
        the nature of Snow's quarrel with the literary culture.
        Notes that Snow's novels have not made him a favorite
        of the literary intellectuals and raises the question
        whether this fact has affected Snow's general theory.
        Points out that Snow's public pronouncements in
        Science and Government have also provoked a certain
        amount of stiff controversy.

Corridors of Power. 1964.

B623   ADAMS, ROBERT. "Pomp and Circumstance: C.P. Snow."
        Atlantic Monthly, 214, no. 5 (November 1964) 95-98.
            A bilious look at the politics of Corridors of
        Power ("It is not hard to portray liberals as wise
        and prudent men when one systematically ignores the
        problems which liberalism cannot solve") is followed
        by a judgment of Snow's fictional aim of resonance
        (not effective), and irreverent but appreciative notes
        on the courtship of Margaret and Lewis in Homecomings,
        the sole novel of the series in which Lewis Eliot's
        "nagging, corrupting sense of moral responsibility" is
        for once not allowed to prevail against the "voice
        of instinct, the voice of tragic need."

B624   ANON. "Of Men and Decisions." Time, 84, no. 12
        (18 September 1964) 118.
            The novel is the capstone of the series. Its
        originality is diminished only by Snow's success in
        transforming his ideas into commonplaces. The brilliant
        Roger Quaife is the most enigmatic, and most attractive,
        of Snow's characters. The plot summary which follows
        carefully describes the moral ambiguity of Quaife's
        idealistic campaign, and meticulously ticks off the
        reasons for Quaife's failure to make his gambit party
        policy. ". . . Author Snow has gambled and won. . .
        his characters still seem sometimes to move with the
        other-worldly pace of tropical fish seen through a glass
        bottomed boat [but] by the sweeping scope of the issue

and the struggle, the strength of Roger Quaife, the accuracy of observation and dialogue and the disturbing pertinence of the questions, Snow has brought off a compelling novel of high politics."

B625   ANON. "Living Newspaper." Newsweek, 64, no. 11 (September 1964) 94.
"The conception is heroic, but Snow is no Balzac, no Proust--not even Trollope. His native gift isn't equal to the epic task he has set himself; and his theory of fiction, of the nature and function of narrative art, is limiting to an almost disabling degree." Snow's talents are those of the scientist and administrator; his fictional analysis of motive and act is too simple. "Everything is seen-and seen vividly--in its externality, but beyond the brilliantly perceived facade, there is no interior, no densely experienced sense of internal life." The novel is a "triumph of the intelligence, a failure of imagination."

B626   ANON. "Books." Playboy, 11, no. 10 (October 1964) 42.
Short plot summary which favors the policy of British unilateral nuclear disarmament. "The pace is, as always, leisurely; the characters, as always, slightly fuzzy. Sir Charles has given us another of his civilized Snow jobs." 200w

B627   ANON. "New Fiction." The Times (London), 5 November 1964, p. 15.
The blurb is in error. This is not a great political novel. It is told with a knowing air but, although the wheels undoubtedly do go round as described, we are in the corridors, not the power house of politics. "There is a sub-plot of Quaife's marital infidelity, and human touches are given to various figures. But Lord Snow's writing is becoming more mannered--or is it beginning to pall?--and Corridors of Power is not the best of the Lewis Eliot novels."

B628   ANON. "The Realism of the Worldly." Times Literary Supplement, 5 November 1964, p. 993.
The reviewer, who evidently knows something of the inner workings of Whitehall, praises Snow for the accuracy of his realistic details. ". . . his picture of the operation of a ruling class and a senior bureaucracy is at any rate near enough to the mark to satisfy the generality of readers." In one paragraph, the reviewer doubts the accuracy of certain minor details.

The style is judged to be good, plain--and solemn.
Suggests that Snow's political novels in university
settings are preferable to Corridors of Power.

B629   ANON. "Briefly Noted." New Yorker, 40, no. 213
(7 November 1964) 243-44.
"That old know-it-all Lewis Eliot is back again,
grinding away like the mills of God but sounding in
this instance disarmingly like an educated Bertie
Wooster." [This alarming comparison is followed by
a long quotation from the novel. Includes nothing
of substance about Snow or his work.] 200w

B630   ANON. Review of Corridors of Power. Economist, 213
(14 November 1964) 710.
The central question of the book is whether the
fictional events resemble the political process.
Concludes that, to most outsiders and insiders, Snow's
account has a romantic air ". . . like butterflies
ritualistically dancing up and down, with horrid
interruptions when the people's parliament has to have
its way." 300w

B631   BOYLE, SIR EDWARD. "Sir Edward Boyle, a former
Cabinet Minister, Gives an Insider's Opinion of
Corridors of Power." London Observer, 1 November
1964, p. 27.
The behaviour of Snow's fictional Prime Minister,
Lenton, is pretty incredible. Any White Paper which
recommended the elimination of a British nuclear
deterrent would have caused a political and party
convulsion; and any real-life PM would have had a
great deal to say to a Minister like Quaife who
recommended the policy. Similarly, on an important
issue of this kind, the Chief Whip and the chairman of
the Party Defence Committee would have been deeply
concerned. The Cabinet committee with an oversight of
Quaife's problems is a curious body: it evidently
excludes the Service chiefs and interested parties
from the Treasury. Quaife's peroration in the House
of Commons is too personal and general. These
criticisms do "not mean that the book, considered
as a whole, leaves a false impression." Quaife himself
personifies "the attitude of those who carry responsibility, of those who believe in politics rather than
ideology, and the scene in which Quaife reveals his
determination not to compromise carries complete
conviction." 500w. See also: B206.

B632   BROCK, CLIFTON. "<u>Corridors of Power</u>." <u>Library Journal</u>,
        89, no. 15 (1 September 1964) 3187.
           The central concern seems to be the interplay of
        power and purpose through the individual; it will become
        <u>the</u> modern British political novel. The motives behind
        Quaife's unconventional policy and adultery are left in
        the dark. 250w

B633   BROWN, JOHN MASON. Review of <u>Corridors of Power</u>.
        <u>Book-of-the-Month Club News</u>, August 1964, pp. 2-3.
           It is an English version of Allan Drury's <u>Advise</u>
        <u>and Consent</u>, but superior in the mastery of its style
        and its greater subtlety about people and events. It
        evokes the England of the great aristocratic families,
        members of Parliament, warriors, scientists and
        political hostesses as well as the feel of the English
        countryside and clubs. The style is witty, vivid and
        deceptively simple, and its observations of men and
        values are shrewd, snobbish and drily realistic. "Its
        plea in terms of the intrigues of ambitious men and
        women is that England admit to herself that she is no
        longer a major power and by withdrawing from the
        missile race accept her new lot and set the world a
        sensible and needed example."

B634   BUCKMASTER, HENRIETTA. "How to 'Push on Open Doors.'"
        <u>Christian Science Monitor</u>, 17 September 1964, p. 11.
           [Mostly plot summary.] "C.P. Snow has no literary
        style and makes no special pretence of forming characters.
        This is to ensure a certain forcefulness, as though he
        is saying that neither individualized men or events are
        large enough to represent the total impact of society;
        that power is an extraordinary complex of defensiveness,
        a non-aggression holding tight." [It is a lovely
        example of pellucid English.]

B635   BURGESS, ANTHONY. "Powers That Be." <u>Encounter</u>, 24, no.
        1 (January 1965) 71-76.
           [An interesting but intricate review.] Confronts
        Snow's critical premises. Lord Snow would agree with
        Dr. Johnson's Imlac that the imaginative writer's
        business is "to examine, not the individual, but the
        species; to remark general properties and large
        appearances; he does not number the strokes of the
        tulip. . . ." Burgess, the reader of <u>Babbitt</u>, and the
        creator of Enderby the poet, denies the validity of
        this neo-classical approach. "The minutiae that make
        real novels are the taste of eggs and bacon, the bad
        tooth, and the pang of heartburn." The same point is

made in a number of different ways. The abstractions,
the moves towards generalized experience in Snow's
novels, are all lamented. He recalls that, in earlier
Snow novels, the characters were more recognisably
human. "Despite all these strictures, Corridors of
Power remains an impressive work, strong, highly idio-
syncratic, in some ways mythopoeic." Still, he cannot
rid himself of nagging doubts, and promptly begins to
sound like Dr. Johnson himself. "More novels like
Corridors of Power, and the novelist must be admired
more and loved less," and he worries that the Snovian
novel can, when it has the "weight and majesty of a
Snow behind it," shut more doors than it can open.

B636   CREWS, FREDERICK C. "Private Lives, Public Lives."
New York Review of Books, 3, no. 6 (5 November 1964)
14-15.
        Omnibus review. Snow's narrative method raises
emotional shallowness to a moral ideal. We learn
little or nothing about the emotions of Snow's
characters. The book is pervaded by a contagious
admiration for power and its thematic question "Who
has the power?" is almost wholly evaded. However, the
fact that Quaife's decline, and the failure of disarmament, cannot be explained by cabinet ministers,
scientists or munition directors gives an impression
of historical realism. We have witnessed, but not
understood, British history in the making.

B637   CURLEY, DANIEL. "Satan is Missing." New Leader,
47, no. 25 (7 December 1964) 24.
        The novel is inert. The political idealism that
prompts Snow to write in terms of morality, commitment
and responsibility makes it seem "to exist on the level
of pure idea and its fictional weakness lends support
to the theory of fiction as a charade: If responsibility,
say, is the subject, responsibility is the one word that
cannot be used in the charade." Further, the book lacks
a villain, a Satan who embraces an independent British
nuclear deterrent; the paranoid, Brodzinski, is a poor
candidate. Hence the opposition to unilateralism is
somewhat weakly described as a mere climate of opinion.
The characters are "professionally inscrutable and
[their] very existence depends on a surface that defies
dramatization." As a tract for the times, not as a
novel, Curley finds it is instructive, inspiring and
even frightening.

B638   DOLBIER, MAURICE. "C.P. Snow's 9th Volume: Old Friends,
        New Enemies." New York Herald Tribune Book Review,
        14 September 1964, p. 19.
            Roger Quaife's aim, the removal of England from
        the nuclear arms race, recalls Snow's speech before the
        American Association for the Advancement of Science
        [see A273]. Although Snow's fiction has been compared
        to Trollope, Galsworthy and Anthony Powell, his theme
        is the immensely more important one of the vital and
        often misused relationship between science and govern-
        ment in the atomic age. "Faces are dim, but voices are
        clear, even when what they are saying is purposefully
        ambiguous; the environment is quickly, but firmly,
        drawn. People have complained about a 'lack of poetry'
        in Snow's fiction, but power has a peculiar kind of
        poetry of its own, and Snow captures it, I think,
        impressively."

B639   DOLLEN, CHARLES. Review of Corridors of Power. Best
        Sellers, 24 (15 September 1964) 221-22.
            The book does not have the skill or fascination
        of Advise and Consent, or Seven Days in May. Quaife's
        failure to win support for his policy, intended to
        withdraw Great Britain from the race for nuclear arms
        supremecy, is somewhat ironic. That policy later
        became official British policy. It is also unfortunate
        that Snow should use the phrase "post-Christian morality"
        since the essence of the anti-nuclear case is based
        on Christian morality. The accounts of the brutal
        security investigations and right-wing machinations
        provide the best chapter in the book. 600w

B640   ENRIGHT, D.J. "Easy Lies the Head." New Statesman,
        68 (6 November 1964) 698-99.
            A long discussion of Snow's style. Debates whether
        it connotes smug self-satisfaction or a form of spiritual
        modesty which Snow enjoins upon his creations. He takes
        up the stock defence of Snow's style: that it represents
        a scrupulous, honest concern for accuracy. He finds it
        improbable that the spoken or written word is necessarily
        an accurate representation of people's thoughts and
        feelings. "When there is so much craft in human nature,
        we might as well permit our art to indulge in a little
        art." Snow's unrelenting temperateness, his judicial
        calm, can sometimes be mistaken for "orthodox Soviet
        writing: solemn, shrewdly simple, bucolically genial,
        heavily tolerant of minor sins, so ponderous in its
        humour as to be humourless--and apt to excite acute

suspicion and alarm in the not utterly credulous." In
this novel the rich are tedious and nerveless; Lewis
Eliot is uxorious. The novel gives an overall impression
of complacent smugness, and Enright comes away with the
belief that it "seems distinctly more wooden than the
majority of its predecessors." 1900w Reprinted: B245.

B641   FULLER, EDMUND. "C.P. Snow Deals with Nuclear Age
         Dilemma." Wall Street Journal, 15 September 1964, p. 18.
             Mostly plot summary followed by Fuller's praise and
         mild adverse criticism. The praise: Snow does not offer
         the "conventional kicks through sex and violence." The
         criticism: "Within the series, we would rank its effec-
         tiveness a little behind The Masters and The Affair,
         partly because he has attempted a picture of so much
         greater magnitude that the focus cannot be as sharp."
         Snow is thoughtful, humane, responsible.

B642   HART, JEFFREY. "To Wield the Scepter." America, 111,
         no. 13 (26 September 1964) 354.
             The novel is marred by melodrama. The advocates
         of the British nuclear deterrent are characterized
         as "moral and intellectual cripples . . . loutish
         chauvinists, selfish politicians;" its opponents are
         "idealistic, civilized and compassionate." The char-
         acters are sketchy. "Snow cannot present convincing
         action; the dialogue is wooden and the narrative prose
         strangely lifeless. We get almost no sense of sound,
         color or touch. Dr. Leavis' judgment of Snow's prior
         "performances is accurate for this one: 'There is no
         more significance in the completed book than there is
         drama--or life.'" 350w

B643   HICKS, GRANVILLE. "Politician in a Nuclear Quandary."
         Saturday Review, 47, no. 37 (12 September 1964) 33-34.
             Snow is intentionally an old-fashioned novelist--
         unlike his rival, Anthony Powell--and though his
         subject matter has, by design, a greater moral component,
         he may well end up behind Powell as a novelist of current
         British history and ideas. 800w

B644   HOGG, QUINTIN. "The Political Novelist's Dilemma."
         New Scientist, 24, no. 417 (12 November 1964) 459-60.
             The book includes little of scientific content
         and the reason for Quaife's loss of faith in the nuclear
         deterrent is not stated, but the real flaw is Snow's
         combination of a real setting and a fictitious cast of
         characters. "The reason is simple. The real contem-
         porary setting is created by the real people and

imaginary top people simply cannot be made to fit it at all." The details (despatch boxes, etc.) are right, but the real flavour of the inner rooms is missed. "The book is enjoyable but not heavy-weight. I prefer Sir Lewis Eliot in his Cambridge combination room, perhaps because I am less at home there. As I closed the covers I could not help sighing with shocking banality: 'Ou sont les neiges d'antan?'"

B645   HUSTON, MCCREADY. "Snow's Society--in British Corridors." San Francisco Chronicle This World Magazine, 13 September 1964, p. 26.
        There is a sub-art of the novel, and Snow is its most successful practitioner. These sub-novelists (Theodore H. White, Knebel & Bailey, and Burdick and Wheeler) deal with public themes while the literary novelists deal with purely private emotions. Snow describes an adultery, a love affair, and the downfall of a politician, but it is merely description; he does not substantiate. It will be bought by those who read for the story, not those with an interest in literary method or merit.

B646   JOHNSON, LUCY. "Arms and Men." Progressive, 29 (December 1964) 46-47.
        In this work, as in The Masters and The Affair Snow provides a study in group decision-making. The Masters is the best of the lot. The Affair is one of the least successful of the series, and Corridors of Power is not much better. The problem is that Snow's technique, despite the perfected realism, the firm control and the measured doses of sharp understanding, is becoming obvious. The situations are contrived; the characters lack conviction; and Snow is more concerned with his message than his art. He now needs to relate the public lives to the private interior life of his characters as he once did in The Light and the Dark.

B647   LUDLOW, GEORGE. "The Power of C.P. Snow." Time and Tide, 5 (11 November 1964) 20.
        It is a good work, but not the best novel Snow has written. Its publication coincides with Snow's appointment as No. 2 man to Frank Cousins in the Ministry of Technology. That fact guarantees massive publicity. Observes that Snow presented an outline of the plot to Harold Macmillan and explains the origin of the title.

B648   MACDONALD, ALASTAIR. Review of Corridors of Power. Queen's Quarterly, 72, no. 1 (Spring 1965) 205.

"Here is good insight into . . . the ways of
Whitehall and parliamentary procedure; and the amount
of political maneuvering, human drama, and heartbreak
behind even a single speech or vote in the Commons. It
is convincingly realistic; and he has generated a sense
of the bigness and violent portentousness of the issue."
Unfortunately, the work is neither moving nor frightening.
Compares it unfavorably to The Masters. He finds it
reminiscent of scientific or government papers, arid
stuff, dry-as-dust documentation. Plainly filled with
more sorrow than anger, he senses "less warmth than we
have known, less of the lyricism and reflective wisdom"
than in Snow's previous works.

B649   MACDONALD, ALASTAIR. "The Failure of Success."
        Dalhousie Review, 44, no. 4 (Winter 1964-65) 494-500.
            Snow's imagery can be linked to notions of struggles
        towards worldly success and away from failure. In this
        novel, Roger Quaife, another study of worldly failure,
        is not "as powerful and compelling a character as some
        of his earlier counterparts." The frequent reports of
        dinners, committee meetings, political weekends, or
        rising and falling reputations--the sheer density of
        incident in the novel--puts Snow's first person narrative
        technique to severe test. Lewis Eliot's reports and
        analyses of all these events convey a "summary, gossippy,
        dismissive" tone which leads to a sense of remoteness.
        "Though characters may be given more dialogue, the talk
        of one, in its rhythms and idioms and imagery, is not
        significantly different from that of another . . . ."
        This remoteness, this absence of individuality, "tends
        to make the novel reminiscent of the scientific paper
        and government document." The work produces an effect
        of barrenness unintended by the author. 2500w

B650   MACLEOD, IAIN. "The Incredible Snowman." Sunday
        Telegraph, 1 November 1964.
            It is an admirable political novel, but fails as
        an accurate description of high Tory politics. The
        relation between politicians and civil servants, and
        the orchestration of the various cells of power, are not
        accurately reported. High Tory politics, as described
        in Snow's novel, is conducted in startlingly tortuous
        ways. This apparently Tory preference for the roundabout
        and the oblique is prompted by Snow's use of the first
        person narrative: Eliot must be present at each crucial
        scene even when his presence is, in fact, unlikely.
        Confesses that he is an admirer of The Masters but states
        on the basis of his own inside experience, that ministers
        do not behave to their permanent or Private Secretaries

in the terms used by Snow. Lord Snow delights in the
little unimportant things of the political life. "If
only he had set his book in Ruritania it would have
been possible to give it full praise. But as a
portrait of Tory politics half a dozen years ago it
is charmingly square." Snow is describing, not the
Conservative political world of 1955-58, but the world
of his youth. 700w [Macleod, a Tory M.P., was Leader
of the House of Commons, 1961-63.]

B651   MCGUINNESS, FRANK. Review of Corridors of Power.
London Magazine, 4, no. 10 (January 1965) 102-03.
       [Plot summary combined with abusive wit.]
". . . it marks the ninth stage in C.P. Snow's laboured
assault on the rising scale of power that began in the
regions of donnish deviousness and threatens to go on
until the techniques of real omnipotence have been
thoroughly probed and examined." Lewis Eliot is
described as a master of sententious duplicity. Snow
moves with assurance through Whitehall. But alas:
"More relevantly perhaps to its merit as a novel, I
find it hard to believe that even the most vehement
left-winger would expect the Tory mandarins to be
quite so massively dull and emotionally constipated
as Snow depicts them. Indeed, by the side of this lot,
those footling academics suddenly seem vital and
amusing."

B652   MUGGERIDGE, MALCOLM. "Oh No, Lord Snow." New Republic,
151, no. 2610 (28 November 1964) 27-29.
       Muggeridge recalls meeting Snow when both were in
their twenties. He was left with an impression of
left-wing politics and romantic worldliness, and
". . . worldliness like his is a great promoter of
success in the field of action, though completely
inimical to any other than the most mediocre achievement
in the field of imagination." The novel itself is not
to his taste. "Considered as an exercise in political
strategy, the whole thing is quite exceptionally silly
and difficult to follow." Snow's vision of power is
imbecile. Remembers a line from the novel ("the gossip
began to swirl out from the clubs and the Whitehall
corridors") and lets loose a terrific 300 word philippic
against drab London clubs, and he denies, with vigour, in
200 words, that he has ever received a scrap of gossip
from any grey-faced inhabitant of Whitehall. The last
paragraph broods over Snow's appointment to the Ministry
of Labor. He is grateful for the divertissement. It
is "rather as though [D.H.] Lawrence had taken a job as

a game-keeper. . . . I give up. Sir Lewis Eliot, Lord Eliot, away! I want no more of you. Those last four volumes of yours, as far as I'm concerned, shall remain unread." 2000w

B653   _____. Review of Corridors of Power. Esquire, 43 (January 1965) 26.
          "Ponderous, pontifical, solemn and sententious; and yet, you know, in some odd way readable, and even touching." Quotes Leavis: Snow's work has no relation to literature or life. "Snow writes about power as D.H. Lawrence writes about sex; with the same fathomless fatuity." Snow believes in politics ". . .as Lawrence believed in those interminable orgasms in the woods when Lady Chatterley surrendered herself to Mellors the game-keeper." The work is a functionnaire's fairy tale.

B654   PICKREL, PAUL. "Novelist Laureate." Harper's, 229 (October 1964) 126-28.
          Terms Snow a major mystagogue. The theme is superb; the treatment is tedious. No major revelations about power emerge. The industrialist, Lufkin, merely fires an irrelevant blackmailer. The argument between Brodzinski and Luke contains not one line of intelligent opinion. The British decision to abandon an independent deterrent was based on economic grounds; the novel gives no hint of the fact. "What interests Snow . . . is not technology and society but that old preoccupation of novelists as different (and as great) as Thackeray and Proust: social snobbery." 440w

B655   PRESCOTT, ORVILLE. "A Novel About England's 'Closed' Politics." New York Times (Daily), 14 September 1964, p. 31.
          Considers Snow the successor to Joyce Cary as Britain's most interesting novelist. Corridors of Power is the least successful novel of the series. "Sir Charles has allowed Lewis Eliot to obscure [the theme] in a haze of hints, ambiguities, elliptical understatements and evasions which, he suggests, are the tribal customs of English politicians and civil servants." The characters only have mannerisms; they lack flesh and blood. The work conveys an impressive air of authority, but it lacks vitality, narrative drive and intellectual excitement. Snow is more sophisticated than Trollope by far, but Corridors of Power makes dull reading compared to Phineas Finn.

B656   PRICE, R.G.G. "New Novels." Punch, 247, no. 6480 (18 November 1964) 784.
          This cautiously vague story about the abandonment

of a British Bomb has a narrative that grips hard, but
it is odd that a scientist should see history "as the
product of whispers in clubs and over dinner-tables."
The bad press of the series is partly due to its
commercial success, Snow's left-wing views, his
partisanship of science, and the fact that the novels
seem false and stagy when he strays outside his limited
field.

B657   PRYCE-JONES, ALAN. "A Structure Built for Business,
        not for Living." Washington Post [S.F. Examiner, etc.]
        Book Week, 13 September 1964, p. 5.
            Snow has tackled an insoluble problem: a novel
        which excludes the actual political events as well as
        the real-life participants of those events. His
        intentions deserve high praise, but Snow's Lewis Eliot
        is devoid of irony and, as the political novels of
        Disraeli, Anatole France, Harold Nicolson (Public Faces)
        and Trollope all tend to prove, irony is essential to
        the genre. It is possible that Eliot is not interested
        in people except as vehicles. It is easy to be unkind
        to this novel, but Snow's series is a massive under-
        taking essential for understanding a certain type of
        British life over the last 50 years.

B658   SALE, ROGER. "Provincial Champions and Grandmasters."
        Hudson Review, 17, no. 4 (Winter 1964/65) 613.
            Omnibus review. Snow is at the bottom of his
        form. The Strangers and Brothers sequence is comparable
        to Upton Sinclair's Lanny Budd series. "The major
        result of both, certainly, is to convince an ordinary
        private citizen that he is much more intelligent,
        sensible, and aware than the men in power." 150w

B659   SCHLESINGER, ARTHUR. "When the Movers Meet the Shakers,
        Lewis Eliot Listens In." New York Times Book Review,
        13 September 1964, pp. 4, 28.
            Snow's work traces the rise of the new technocrats
        and the decline of the traditional ruling class.
        Prefers Anthony Powell's more oblique treatment of the
        same theme. This novel is also not to his taste.
        "The public problem posed . . . is important. But the
        book is curiously uninteresting and unconvincing. An
        important reason for this is the author's faltering
        grasp of the politics involved. One is never told
        exactly what Quaife's White Paper recommends; but
        surely, if it proposes revolutionary changes in the
        strategy of British security, it becomes, not the idle
        thoughts of an individual minister, but the responsibility
        of the Cabinet and the Prime Minister. Yet the Government
        in Snow's account appears to dissociate itself from

Quaife with extraordinary ease." Lewis Eliot is a
bore, a political voyeur and a social snob. Worse,
he is becoming something of a blank cartridge. "But,
beyond his voyeurism, his ritualistic leftism and his
extreme portentousness of comment, he is a blank."
The characterization is impoverished. "Sir Charles,
in a burlesque of Dickens, seems to suppose that he
can define a man by heightening a single trait."
The role of the women is to blush and flush, color and
bloom from one end of the book to the other. As an
essayist, Snow is perceptive. However, Corridors of
Power is "obtuse, overexplained and under-observed,
[and it] throws very little light on Sir Charles's
admirable and fundamental preoccupation—who has
power in a democratic society?" 2000w

B660   SHILS, EDWARD. "The Charismatic Centre." Spectator,
         213, no. 7115 (6 November 1964) 608-09.
              [A long, slow-moving plot summary which makes
         repeated references to Snow's Science and Government.
         It is punctuated, at intervals, less by adverse
         criticism than lugubrious reproach.] "Only Brodzinski
         goes in for 'open politics,' and Sir Charles certainly
         does not regard his accomplishment as an argument for
         the position he set forth in Science and Government."
         The long corridors lead to a humdrum center.

B661   STEINER, GEORGE. "'Never the Whole Truth'." Reporter,
         31 (8 October 1964) 50-52.
              Praises Snow's style: it makes "available to fiction
         and the literate imagination the wealth and scruple
         of the language of science." Snow's treatment of Lord
         Gilbey and Dr. Brodzinski, a man who recalls Edward
         Teller, indicates an "essential impartiality and gener-
         osity of imagination. Brodzinski is no contemptible
         figure." The technical success of the novel is attrib-
         utable to the fact that it is all dialogue and scenario.
         The absence of inwardness, the failure to explore
         feelings, is deliberate; it is part and parcel of Snow's
         purpose to say that "the life of politics takes its
         special toll. It is life at the surface." Finds that
         the views of Lewis Eliot closely resemble the opinions
         of Snow. Eliot's hope that eventually the inheritors
         of the Russian revolution will create a wonderful
         society is quoted. Disagrees with the mere materialism
         of Snow's convictions but states that it has the
         "strength and largesse of hope." Like Fuller, Steiner
         believes that the absence of the physical details of

sexual activity is a sign of an adult attitude. He praises the pleas for tolerance, for generosity of judgment found in Snow's work, and finds the main theme, "the mystery of how the political process is to absorb and handle the immense powers of the new scientific arsenal" an urgent one. 1800w

B662   TAYLOR, A.J.P. "Dark Corridors." New Statesman, 68 (6 November 1964) 698.
        Refers to the political novels, or the political element in, the works of Dickens, Trollope, Bennett's Lord Raingo and Hilaire Belloc. He prefers Belloc. Complains of the obscurity of the plot, and the unreality of the novel's events. ". . . this is a closed world . . . . The topic is not aired in the press. Nor does it seem that the question arouses any interest except among a few scientists and civil servants . . . . Could any of this have happened?" Taylor clearly doubts it. The characters are forbiddingly intense. He is puzzled and dismayed by the absence of laughter. Brodzinski, a compound of Lindemann and Teller, is a mere ranter who spins the novel out. ". . . it is not a political novel at all. It is a Victorian melodrama, told in stodgy twentieth century prose. The experienced novel-reader, who is trained to follow clues, may perhaps make some sense of it. For my part, back to Belloc."

B663   WALL, STEPHEN. "New Novels." Listener, 72, no. 1858 (5 November 1964) 732.
        Snow's corridors are wearisome. The people who walk there are making history, but Wall finds them undeveloped and flat. The fact is regrettable for Snow's own background should give them qualities of life and reality. 300w

B664   WALSH, JOHN. "C.P. Snow: Corridors of Power Is Novel About Nuclear Policy and Politics, Closed and Open." Science, 146, no. 3641 (9 October 1964) 234-36.
        Walsh calls it a good political novel. He considers it a textbook which conveys sociological and historical information about the inside operations of the British government. Puts the novel in its historical perspective and points out that the Labor Party embraced nuclear disarmament in the 1959 election campaign; the Conservative Party favored retention of the independent nuclear deterrent. Agrees with Snow that any campaign for nuclear disarmament must satisfy

the political Center and Right. Quotes, without comment,
a section of the novel which suggests that the current
generation of scientists is more politically inactive
than their predecessors--perhaps partly on the ground
that events have become too big for men.

B665   WAUGH, AUBERON. "Over-Privileged Intellectuals."
        National Review, 16, no. 40 (6 October 1964) 870-71.
            Lewis Eliot is complacent, self-important, univer-
        sally disliked, conceited, dreary and leftish. Disputes,
        on the basis of his own experience, that there is an
        inner circle of right-wing activists, or that important
        decisions are made in the clubs of St. James's. He
        observes that all the scientists are pacifist left-
        wingers and all the civil servants pacifists. He states
        that the theme of the book is British unilateral dis-
        armament and that it is not logical to argue that
        Britain's bomb is a) irrelevant to the East-West dialogue
        and b) of great import as a moral example to other powers.
        Further, "The idea that our disarmament will bring moral
        pressure to bear on such notoriously immoral countries
        as France, Egypt and China is puerile." In any case,
        the Bomb is useful as a memento mori. A brave man does
        not deliver speeches like Quaife's address to the
        Fishmongers. Retent. r . of British nuclear weapons is
        the best means to peace. The moral of the novel is that
        the Civil Service and Scientific Establishment should
        be purged of all Lewis Eliots. 1500w

B666   WEIGHTMAN, JOHN. "It's Tough at the Top." London
        Observer, 1 November 1964, p. 27.
            This work is not a great novel, but it demonstrates
        once again that Snow's themes are the "tactics of human
        intercourse in public affairs, the battle of wills in
        committee meetings, life seen as a series of manoeuvres,
        alliances and rivalries." The book is readable; the
        Establishment color is deftly supplied; but it is marred
        by snippets of physical description which induce an
        atmosphere of distinguished melancholy. Quaife does
        not come to life. Eliot is a curiously ambiguous
        character: is he intelligent, or an "obnubilated social
        voyeur" undone by his obsession with power? All the
        characters are fundamentally naive; they are redeemed,
        if that is the word, by a sense of tactical shrewdness;
        but this sense is not enough to let them perceive the
        vacuity of life at the top. "Sir Charles is very good
        at suggesting that power--the mere presence of power
        in the air--is somewhat like an electric charge which

gives a tingling excitement to the most banal situations."
Quaife's policy is not refuted or opposed by a coherent
political force. It has "merely foundered against the
dead weight of misunderstanding, stupidity and personal
enmity" which suggests that even Top People are not to
be envied. 1050w

B667   WEINTRAUB, STANLEY. Review of Corridors of Power.
        Books Abroad, 39, no. 2 (Spring 1965) 219.
            The work is marred by Whitehall jargon and the
        ponderous sensibility of Lewis Eliot. It includes
        echoes of the shabby Teller-Oppenheimer episode, faint
        suggestions of the Profumo affair, and adds nothing to
        Snow's stature as a novelist. ". . . this novel provides
        us with no well-drawn new characters, nor any substantial
        extension of the characterization of earlier person-
        alities in the cycle." 200w

B668   WILKIE, BRIAN. "C.P. Snow's Latest." Commonweal, 81,
        no. 2 (2 October 1964) 48-49.
            Finds the work an uneasy blend of documentary,
        novel and philosophical essay. It is absorbingly
        interesting as documentary material; as novel, it is
        marred by the limp chattiness of the style, which
        trivialises the issues. Snow's epic purpose, to explore
        the extent to which one man can influence national
        policy, is vaguely reminiscent of the last half of War
        and Peace. Snow unfortunately tends to find glamor and
        romantic trappings in Camorras of dull politicians.
        "There is a positive naivete in the assumption that the
        exchange of veiled innuendoes with the shooting set at
        country houses, full-regalia dinners and cocktail parties
        with crusty industrialists . . . are in themselves
        exciting. . . . he ought, one feels, to sense and convey
        better the wry irony that inheres in a situation where
        tempests are almost literally made in teapots and
        cocktail mixers, a situation which in the hands of a
        less reverent author might easily explode into bitter
        social comedy . . . . the book's virtues are those of
        a good documentary anatomy of the political and
        bureaucratic processes."

B668a   WILLIAMS, RAYMOND. "Public and Private Lives."
        Manchester Guardian Weekly, 12 November 1964, p. 10.
            It would be false to interpret this novel in the
        light of Snow's public actions and political career.
        Snow's intention is clearly to include social history
        and the working relationships of men in contemporary
        fiction. The function of Lewis Eliot is to move from

one group to another and get the widest possible range.
It is possible to sympathize with these aims, but
unfortunately Snow's novel is not public enough. It
must be compared, not to Pasternak, or Sartre, but to
Virginia Woolf. It remains the same fiction of
abstracted social relationships, and Snow's public
figures are emotionally blind and cold.

B669   WOOD, FREDERICK T. "Current Literature, 1964: Prose,
Poetry and Drama." English Studies; Journal of English
Letters and Philology, 45, no. 4 (August 1965) 361.
        The atmosphere of unreality conveyed by the book
may inhere in the subject. Snow is doing for the
contemporary Establishment what Trollope did for the
Victorian elite. "Trollope found that there was a
limit beyond which one could not go with a series of
novels of this sort. C.P. Snow may almost have reached
that limit."

Variety of Men. 1967.

B670   ADAMS, J. DONALD. "Characterized by Singularity."
Saturday Review, 50 (27 May 1967) 34.
        Man is fascinated by the peculiarities of his
fellow-men, and this book has its due share of human
oddity. "Primarily a tribute to a great scientist,
the picture of Lord Rutherford is discerning; Hardy's
and Hammarskjold's are lit by compassion for the
tragedy of their closing years." Snow's devotion to the
welfare state led to some overstatements in the sketch
of Stalin, but the portrait of Churchill is a skilfully
balanced piece of work. 1000w

B671   AGIUS, AMBROSE. Review of Variety of Men. Best
Sellers, 27 (1 May 1967) 60.
        The portraits read like well-bred conversation,
and the "deceptively simple style is vitalized by
keen observation." [Followed by sketches, permeated
by a Catholic point of view, of Snow's nine characters.]

B672   ANGOFF, ALLAN. "Variety of Men." Library Journal,
92, no. 6 (15 May 1967) 1151.
        Snow's varied background in the arts and sciences
enables him to bring an incisive insight into these
sketches. "The layman and the student as well as the
historian and researcher will find these sketches, with
their simple, spare prose, quite impressive." 190w

B673   ANON. Review of <u>Variety of Men</u>. <u>Publishers' Weekly</u>,
191, no. 7 (13 February 1967) 70.
"In most of the biographical essays, Snow is
asking, and answering, the questions: how does talent
show itself? Where does genius come from? What did
these men want out of life that they did not get? . . .
This is going very deeply into questions of character,
but Snow does so very readably with lightness and ease
. . . ." 100w

B674   ANON. Review of <u>Variety of Men</u>. <u>Kirkus</u>, 35 (March 1967)
327.
"Snow's profiles are more properly portraits, with
an occasional personal aside or marginal anecdote; all
of them have an integral interest to which Snow has
added not warmth, but dispassionate insights and
tempered judgments." 300w

B675   ANON. "Nine Characters Find an Author." <u>Times
Literary Supplement</u>, 18 May 1967, p. 411.
Snow the novelist pervades these biographical
sketches and the overall impression, despite some
touches of comic relief, is one of a dark world.

B676   ANON. "Voyeurs of Power." <u>Economist</u>, 223 (27 May
1967) 919.
[Joint review of Toynbee's <u>Acquaintances</u> and
Snow's book.] After Rutherford and the Cavendish
Laboratory are left behind, Snow's writing becomes
discreet in the style of the reticent Lewis Eliot.
The portrait of Churchill owes something to the
influence of Lord Hankey and Lord Moran. The essay
on Stalin is marked by the flatly neutral and
politically fair accents of the don in Whitehall.

B677   ANON. Review of <u>Variety of Men</u>. <u>New Yorker</u>, 43, no.
14 (27 May 1967) 152.
The men are described with an impressive objectivity,
insight and political sophistication. 180w

B678   ANON. "From <u>Variety of Men</u>: Two Towering Figures."
<u>National Observer</u>, 5 June 1967, p. 21.
[Not a review, but two 100 word excerpts from
Snow's book. Albert Einstein and H.G. Wells are the
two towering figures.]

B679   ANON. "Portrait Galleries." <u>Tablet</u>, 221, no. 6631
(24 June 1967) 695-96.
"Lord Snow is at his happiest writing about

Rutherford, and the heroic age of physics at Cambridge, when the apparatus was simple and improvised, but the discoveries far reaching and momentous, and Rutherford simple and boyish enough to exult in his own astounding success."

B680   ANON. Review of Variety of Men. Booklist and Subscription Books Bulletin, 63, no. 21 (1 July 1967) 1130.
        "Four of the profiles were previously published in American periodicals and all exhibit appreciation of unusual personality and a sense of style." 50w

B681   ANON. Review of Variety of Men. Best Sellers, 31 (1 August 1971) 216.
        The characters are interesting and interestingly presented. 250w

B682   BATES, LEWIS. "The Future-Makers." Punch, 252, no. 6611 (24 May 1967) 773.
        The tone is occasionally too fruity and knowing, but Snow's humane curiosity burns through. "His higher journalism shouldn't be underrated." 150w

B683   BEDIENT, CALVIN. "The Gaze Behind the Lens." Nation, 205, no. 2 (17 July 1967) 59-60.
        "Snow moves among this gathering cooly, not as a cat that looks at kings but as a great cat among great cats. . . . The book presents personal power as spectacle; it is an aesthetic record of genius and will." It is an engrossing book which communicates energy and it is a delight to read. 435w

B684   COCKBURN, CLAUD. "Mates." New Statesman, 73, no. 1889 (26 May 1967) 722.
        The chapters on Rutherford, G.H. Hardy and Einstein do not communicate a "fresh understanding of just how those particular brains worked." The chapter on Stalin is the best thing in the book, mainly because it conveys the reverent attitude of all Russian authorities (including Stalin in his role of supreme censor) to literature. "Snow shows that the grim supervision of the written word, the excesses of Russian censorship, are the complement of a respect for the written word which the 'free world' notably lacks." 350w

B685   FULLER, EDMUND. "C.P. Snow Discusses Nine Men of History." Wall Street Journal, 18 May 1967, p. 16.
        Most of the review is devoted to Snow's sketch of Stalin and Fuller observes that "Snow has ties of

respect and affection with many Russians, as he has with
enormous numbers of Americans. He perceives the
qualities of greatness in both these principal nations
in the world power struggle." The essay on Stalin is
remarkable for its balance and justice. 800w

B686   HOOK, SIDNEY. "Fluff on the Sleeve of History."
New Leader, 50, no. 17 (28 August 1967) 16-18.
        The sketches concentrate only on men of power and
fame; they suggest the interest of the arriviste. The
portraits of the scientists are devoid of specific
scientific content. These facts are regrettable.
Worse, Snow's sketch of Stalin is marred by a foolish
argument on censorship, historical errors, unwillingness
to introduce relevant evidence against Stalin (Lenin's
will), and failure to see that Stalin's great purges
impeded industrialization. The sketch suggests a
"sneaking and ill repressed admiration" of the dictator.
"Snow is not a Communist like his friend, John Bernal
. . . .But he is an impatient anti-anti-Communist
whose rancor against those who oppose Communist terror
is much more marked than his criticism of those who
practice it."

B687   IGOE, W.J. "Reflecting the Contemporary Mind."
Chicago Sunday Tribune Books Today, 28 May 1967, p. 3.
        This book unwittingly reveals the truth of Snow's
'Two Cultures' dichotomy. The treatment of the scientists
is good; the depiction of statesman is bad, naive, and
reveals an extraordinary incapacity of moral judgments.
The account of Stalin neglects to point out that his
interest in reading literature was that of Big Brother,
and Snow's analogy of Stalin's liquidation of many
Russians with the war-time decisions of Churchill and
Truman is inept and unfeeling. The sketch of Frost
shows a crude appetite for unsubtle denigration, and
Frost's return to nature is unjustly mocked. The style
is clumsy, but the book is readable in an uncompulsive
way.

B688   MADDOCKS, MELVIN. "Behind the Scenes at Snow's
Powerama." Life, 62, no. 18 (5 May 1967) 10.
        .Snow, a little like a clean-shaven Colonel Blimp,
and often found in an intellectual no-man's land, will
draw new fire from biographers and historians; he has
blithely depicted nine of the most complex figures of
the century. The reverential portraits of Hardy and
Rutherford suggest that Cambridge of the 1930s is
Snow's spiritual home. The true reason for the appeal of
these sketches, as for Snow's fiction is that, inside

the official Snow, a wildly subversive Snow is struggling
to get out. The subversive Snow wants to know: "What
initiates an extraordinary man's creativity? What stops
it? Why is extreme loneliness so often part of the
package?" It is these questions, rather than the solemn
prattle about power, that makes the book well worth
reading. 600w

B688a   MALOFF, SAUL. "Living with Spin." Newsweek, 69, no. 17
         (24 April 1967) 102.
             Repeats some of Snow's anecdotes about Hardy,
         Rutherford, Churchill, Lloyd George, Hammarskjold,
         Einstein and Frost. Finds Snow's recollections
         "completely enthralling."

B689   MANTHORNE, JANE. Review of Variety of Men. Horn Book,
         43 (December 1967) 769.
             These sketches of great men accomplish more than
         the customary glacial portraits of the great; they
         show them in their intimate moments--"calling a remark
         from behind a tailor's screen, moodily worrying about
         a love affair, boasting, or building myths about
         themselves."

B690   MUGGERIDGE, MALCOLM. "Mr. Worldly Wiseman." London
         Observer Review, 21 May 1967, p. 26.
             Snow, the political novelist of action, reveals
         his true self, a compound of Frank Harris and James
         Boswell, in these reminiscences. The exchange between
         Snow and Wells in the University Arms is very
         Harrisian, and Snow, a technological Boswell, is quite
         prepared to reveal the earthy truth--that Lloyd George,
         an amateur phrenologist, took an interest in the
         bumps on his head. Snow's portraits of the scientists
         are the best in the book. Albert Einstein is the only
         great man. Snow's judgments on characters other than
         Einstein are worldly and banal. "I always think of
         Snow as Mr. Worldly Wiseman; not one of Bunyan's major
         villains, but blind and foolish because, try as he will,
         he cannot disengage himself from the marks that are
         awarded, the prizes that are won."

B691   RYAN, A.P. "Mad Dons and Clergymen." The Times (London),
         18 May 1967, p. 15.
             Perceptive portraits of all seven men, but the
         sketch of G.H. Hardy, with his militant disbelief in
         Christianity and passion for cricket, is a delicious
         masterpiece.

B691a   TAYLOR, A.J.P. "Old Men Remember." <u>New York Review of</u>
         <u>Books</u>, 9, no. 2 (3 August 1967) 14-17.
              [Also reviews Arnold Toynbee's <u>Acquaintances.</u>]
         Both Toynbee and Snow have one thing in common. They
         are thought of more highly by the general public than
         by historians and literary critics. "Literary critics
         seem to be agreed that Snow is an imitation novelist,
         rather like the near-beer peddled during Prohibition,
         another Charles Morgan or John Galsworthy." Snow's
         subject sound like Snow's fictional characters. The
         best portraits are those of the scientists, Rutherford,
         Hardy and Einstein. Snow "seeks to convey that they
         were great men. But he does this by hammering away at
         their greatness rather than by describing it." The
         great men Snow writes about seem to be alike "perhaps
         because Snow can only write in one way or . . . he
         chose people of similar type. It will do no harm if
         he produces further biographical sketches, though it
         will also not do much good."

B691b   TURNER, A.C. "Ten from Three Worlds." <u>New York Times</u>
         <u>Book Review</u>, 23 April 1967, p. 3.
              Gives a brief sketch of Snow's life, praises the
         <u>Strangers and Brothers</u> series, and provides a synopsis
         of each one of Snow's character sketches along with
         some very brief comments. 1000w

B691c   WAIN, JOHN. "E Pluribus Unum." <u>New Republic</u>, 156,
         no. 21 (27 May 1967) 25-28.
              The book is written from the point of view of a
         fairminded administrator, and the subjects are all
         seen in one perspective--as men of action. Snow's
         administrator's impartiality, his willingness to
         suspend judgment, is best observed in the essay on
         Stalin. Most of the biographees took part in tempes-
         tuous events, and when Snow comes to these crises,
         the temperature is kept deliberately low. This general
         policy "is wise enough, but there are times when one
         longs for more involvement, more passion. The tone
         is so level, the prose so jog-trot, that life seems
         often to be leaking out of the subject." More detail,
         scientific and critical, would have given the work
         more intellectual bite. The treatment of Wells's
         disillusionment is far too casual, and the account of
         Stalin's relationship with Russian writers and
         censorship ignores the towering figure of Pasternak.

B692   WAUGH, AUBERON. "Men of Power." <u>Spectator</u>, 218, no.
         7251 (16 June 1967) 709-710.
              "I have seen cultured and sober men, inspired by

an almost simple-minded benevolence to the human race, roll their eyes and scream at the mention of Lord Snow's name. How does this amiable man excite such passions?" The answer is not that his novels are bad, or even stupendously bad, but the reaction is a revolt against Snow's present fame, which is due to defective critical standards. This work, unlike his novels, is one of endearing charm; it shows that Snow is a master of gossip writing, of the potted biography, and the best sketches are those of men he has known personally. Lewis Eliot is surely one of the greatest comic inventions of all time. He "enshrines every wrong idea . . . a pathetic optimism about Russia, an ill-thought-out pacifism in world affairs, an ineffectual solicitude for the plight of underdeveloped nations."

The Sleep of Reason. 1968.

B693   ANON. "Monsters at Bay." Times Literary Supplement, 31 October 1968, p. 1217.
        Quotes a passage from the book which suggests that the sleep of reason will only be temporary. Considers the message cheering but not plausible; it is not indicative of an attitude willing to understand the motives and actions of the murderers who are, in any case, dismissed as merely "titillating" and "trivial." Suggests that society bears guilt and responsibility for the killings. It also seems to suggest that Lewis Eliot should alleviate the misery of the world instead of trotting around in the corridors of power with his self-indulgent concerns.

B694   ANON. Review of The Sleep of Reason. Kirkus, 36 (1 November 1968) 1246.
        "This latest Snow is more of a dying fall than a storm." It is somewhat reminiscent of J.P. Marquand, and essentially a novel of fathers and sons, parents and children rather than the Moors murders. "Snow's approach is as massively ceremonious as ever. Each character is introduced by an organ chord of commentary; thoughts are as long as life; characters from other books are prodded into being. But there is a certain dogged majesty as Snow lumbers down the halls of power. Book-of-the-Month for January." 320w

B695   ANON. Review of The Sleep of Reason. Publishers' Weekly, 194, no. 20 (11 November 1969) 42.
        "C.P. Snow can always be counted on to come up with good reading. He never fails to be intelligent,

provocative, a superb chronicler of our times. . . .He draws our world, our lives, our days, in such a way that most readers could step into the novel and find their own proper place there."

B696   ANON. "Generation on Trial." Time, 93, no. 2 (10 January 1969) 72.
"In The Sleep of Reason [Lewis Eliot's] cool eye is cast on more amorphous matters as the author struggles with formulations about such things as free will, responsibility and human nature. . . .If [the novel] is any indication of Snow's ability to deal with speculative issues in fiction, the next novel will prove a rather tedious and drawn-out farewell to Lewis Eliot." Passant is made to stand for an innocent addiction to humanist hopefulness about man as well as a belief in unfettered personal freedom. The development of these themes has "produced a book that is bound to provoke a great deal of reflection--but that is also a very bad novel." Snow describes; he does not substantiate.

B697   ANON. Review of The Sleep of Reason. Booklist, 65, no. 12 (15 February 1969) 639.
That section of the novel "covering the trial of two young women for the torture murder of a boy may have general appeal, although Snow, through his narrator Lewis Eliot, is concerned with questions of sanity and responsibility. . . ." 50w

B698   ANON. Review of The Sleep of Reason. Publishers' Weekly, 200, no. 14 (4 October 1971) 61.
Announces publication of the Bantam, paperback ed. of this novel and Last Things. In Last Things "Snow takes on such subjects as death, crime, guilt, freedom, choice, etc., and the average reader will wish he stuck more to people and events. Critics are on both sides of the Snow fence." 50w

B699   BEAM, ALVIN. "Snow Mixes Up Good with Evil." Cleveland Plain Dealer, 5 January 1969) p. 7-H.
Lewis Eliot is reticent about sexual matters, the theme of murder is slow to develop, and Snow's ramblings on Eliot's second marriage, relationship with his father, and son are unfailingly interesting. The philosophical questions are not answered but they are raised with skill. "Snow, as usual, touches on a lot of goodness, quite realistically, in a novel dealing, quite realistically, with a great lot of evil and potential evil. He is an aware and civilized man. And more than a little an artist."

B700   BOROWITZ, ALBERT. "The Revolving Bookstand. . . The
        Snows on the Moors." American Scholar, 40, no. 4
        (Autumn 1971) 708-32.
            [A fascinating study, by a specialist in corporation
        and business law, of literary attitudes towards murder.
        The emphasis falls on P.H. Johnson's On Iniquity and
        two of Snow's novels (Death Under Sail, The Sleep of
        Reason) but it also includes references to Colin Wilson,
        Henry James, Emlyn Williams, Thackeray and others.]
        Both Snow and his wife stress the differences between
        the murderer and the "normal" citizen, and they do not
        excuse failures of individual morality by arguing that
        the crimes of Auschwitz and Hiroshima have tarred mankind
        with the same guilt; they do not endorse the shibboleth
        that "we are all guilty." Johnson finds the Moors
        murderers iniquitous, considers pornography at least
        partly to blame for the crimes, and Borowitz argues
        the case against this diffuse casual relationship.
        Snow, unlike his wife, discounts the effect of ideology,
        or the influence of literature, and he specifically
        refuses to attribute a baleful influence to literature
        along the lines suggested in The Two Cultures and the
        Scientific Revolution. Examines Snow's interest in the
        psychiatric case histories of the two murderers, the
        response of "normal" people to the murder, and concludes
        with a discourse on Miss Johnson's, Snow's and
        Thackeray's abolitionist attitudes towards capital
        punishment.

B701   BROWN, JOHN MASON. Review of The Sleep of Reason.
        Book-of-the-Month Club News, December 1968, pp. 2-5,
        13.
            Snow's series is comparable to Trollope's Barset-
        shire novels or Galsworthy's The Forsyte Saga in sweep
        and scope. The questions which arise out of the new
        sexual freedom are discussed with wit and wisdom.
        Although the novel includes a confusing number of minor
        characters, the work displays Snow's modesty, humor,
        humane tolerance, political courage and strong sense
        of the drama of ordinary life. Snow's plots are built
        with the care of a craftsman, and the autobiographical
        element adds to the fascination of the work. "Devotees
        of the Strangers and Brothers series and newcomers
        alike will not want to miss this new work by an author
        who has been described by the New York Times--and quite
        accurately to my mind--as 'the most eminent living
        English novelist.'"

B702   COLE, BARRY. "New Novels 1: Heavy Duty." Spectator,
        221, no. 7325 (15 November 1968) 700.

"I read The Sleep of Reason with an almost mental nausea. . . . It might have been Eliot's pomposity, his noseyness and self-satisfaction. The book is easy to read and things happen, but through it all runs something unpleasant, hard to define. It is possible that this was C.P. Snow's intention. If so, he has succeeded, and should be praised." 150w

B703   CORBETT, EDWARD P.J.   Review of The Sleep of Reason. America, 120 (8 February 1969) 173-74.
Calls the Strangers and Brothers series the most notable of the twentieth century novel sequences, but finds the theme of murder in this work untypical of Snow. The theme was probably suggested by the interest of Snow's wife in the Manchester Moors murders. It is unforgivable of a novelist of Snow's stature not to intimate what makes his characters tick. Lewis Eliot, once perceptive, is now virtually blind to the subtleties and mysteries of human relationships. "When one charts the steady decline of Lord Snow's powers since The Masters, one wonders whether there will be enough voltage left to produce the final novel in the series, or whether it will be worth our attention when it is produced." 420w

B704   DERRICK, CHRISTOPHER.   "You Get Carried Away."   Tablet, 222, no. 6708 (14 December 1968) 1246-48.
"In practise, most of us would find small difficulty in distinguishing the two cases. Casual bedwork is one thing, sadistic murder is another: society is not being inconsistent if it decides to "tolerate" the one but not the other. A workable point of balance needs to be dis-covered. But this will involve an assessment of par-ticular cases, and the task is made much harder by the prevailing romanticism of sweeping partisan commitment. Do we really have to choose between total permissiveness and total authority? That old Vice-Chancellor, judging the sullen fornicatory young too harshly, was firmly put down by his more liberal staff: in so acting, were they really voting against all restraint, and in principle for this other indulgence of swinging private fun, the slow, messy killing of a small boy by two Lesbians?" This book swings between these two extremes in erratic fashion.

B704a   FIELD, J.C.   Review of The Sleep of Reason.   Revue des Langues Vivantes, 37, no. 1 (1971) 93-97.
Compared to Powell's The Military Philosophers, Snow's novel is the work of a practised master. The

style has a relaxed simplicity of diction and syntax,
the three events are unified by references to the
consciousness of Lewis Eliot (which works by association),
and by locating the action in Eliot's home town. Snow's
novels are also more human than those of Powell; he is
less interested in events than in the interaction of
characters which produces those events.

B705   FULLER, EDMUND. "C.P. Snow's Efforts to Keep Reason
Awake." Wall Street Journal, 13 January 1969, p. 12.
        "Respect for reason is the quintessence of C.P.
Snow's personal values and of his art as a novelist."
Followed by a long and leisurely plot summary complete
with generous quotations from the novel which amplify
this theme. Concludes that Snow is one of the "most
mature, deep-questioning, informed and concerned
novelists working today." 1000w

B706   FULLER, ROY. "Restricted Vision." Listener, 80, no.
2066 (31 October 1968) 588-89.
        Despite themes which call for extended treatment--
the relationship of parents and children, the decay of
an accepted morality--the novel seems long and static.
The fault lies in the depiction of characters, failure
to develop these characters, and inadequate detail in
the presentation of social life. Eliot's faulty values
and Augustus Carp-like complacency also play their role.
Snow's work "remains in the category of the merely if
honourably entertaining and perhaps he has only himself
to blame if captious critics occupy themselves in
searching in it largely in vain for something higher."
960w

B707   GARIS, ROBERT. "Fiction Chronicle." Hudson Review,
22, no. 1 (Spring 1969) 157-58.
        Omnibus review. "C.P. Snow's Strangers and Brothers
used to offer, along with sluggish action, sawdust
characterization and uninterrupted self-importance, some
moderately interesting documentary and journalistic
information about proceedings in the various corridors
of power through which the author has passed. Almost
nothing of the sort appears in the latest installment
. . . ." The four main dark events of the novel are
"clumsily interwoven and insensitively equated. . .
Snow's entire inadequacy to his theme and the consequent
nullity of his achievement make extended criticism
impossible; criticism needs an object." 350w

B708   HALIO, J.L. "Fantasy and Fiction." <u>Southern Review</u>,
7, no. 2 (Spring 1971) 644-45.
        Omnibus review. Calls it a journalistic novel and
praises those parts of the book that describe the
relationship of fathers to sons. 200w

B709   HICKS, GRANVILLE. "Literary Horizons." <u>Saturday
Review</u>, 52, no. 2 (11 January 1969) 78-79.
        Leisurely review. Gives an account of Snow's
lecture entitled "The State of Siege" and includes
biographical facts about Snow's official career.
Praises all Snow's themes, but finds the courtroom
drama especially irresistible. ". . . Snow follows
the [legal] proceedings with as much assurance as if
he had had the legal training Lewis Eliot received.
At the same time he makes each of the participants
an individual, and the resulting drama is magnificent."
Briefly describes Lady Snow's response to the Moors
murders and remarks that Snow's reflections are more
subtle and more sad. "Whatever [Snow's] shortcomings,
his gifts are many, and never have they been displayed
more effectively than in this novel. . . .<u>The Sleep
of Reason</u> is both an exciting and a thoughtful novel."
2450w

B710   HOPE, FRANCIS. "Just How Good Is Snow?" London
<u>Observer</u>, 3 November 1968, p. 30.
        [A review written in the form of a parody.] As
a novelist, Snow has the conventional virtues: careful
plotting, economy of means, a sense of what to leave
out. In this fictional account of the Moors murders,
Snow is somewhat out of his depth, and he expresses
a somewhat stagy moral outrage. As a judge of character,
Eliot is apt to quantify the unquantifiable in order to
give an impression of authority. Snow writes to instruct,
but the book gives a modicum of pleasure. The figure of
the elder Pateman is a genuine comic creation.

B711   HILL, WILLIAM B. Review of <u>The Sleep of Reason</u>. <u>Best
Sellers</u>, 28, no. 20 (15 January 1969) 425-26.
        The grand project is being grandly fulfilled. This
work is diffuse, but still interesting, and Snow's
divagations lend a richness to the whole. It chronicles
the impoverishment of George Passant, and his ultimate
responsibility for the moral bankruptcy of many young
people. The novel is an "excellent probing of our time
through the experience of one man whose success and fame
have not placed him above common human crises but have
made him an acute observer and a sufferer who is perhaps
more bewildered than the rest of us." It is a real and
fascinating study of our times. 750w

B712   JACKSON, KATHERINE GAUSS. "Books in Brief: Fiction."
       Harper's, 238, no. 1425 (February 1969) 102.
       This critic, previously unfamiliar with Snow,
       concludes that his novels are peopled by nice characters
       who are nice to each other. ". . . one comes away with
       a sense, or hallucination, that somehow the best things
       of life will survive." 250w

B713   JELLINEK, ROGER. "Ombudsman to the World." New York
       Times (Daily), 11 January 1969, p. 31.
       Gives a brief biographical sketch of Lewis Eliot,
       Lord Snow's alter ego, and observes he has no literary
       friends. Objects to the length of Snow's windup: the
       first intimation of the murder occurs on p. 207. The
       characters are not discovered and their situations not
       explored. The murderers, interviewed by Lewis Eliot,
       are not brought to life on the printed page. "It is
       this bureaucratic style of thought (the style that
       imposes the idea of "Two Cultures") that drives people
       to sympathize with the unreasonable." 600w

B714   JOHNSON, ROBERT D. Review of The Sleep of Reason.
       Library Journal, 94, no. 4 (15 February 1969) 781-82.
       "Witty, learned even, although at times pedantic,
       Snow's alter ego Sir Lewis Eliot finds life, even for
       one at the very top, full of conflict, struggle, and
       unreason." 180w

B715   LOBDELL, J.C. Review of The Sleep of Reason. National
       Review, 21, no. 7 (25 February 1969) 191.
       The book makes for pleasant reading but conveys
       the impression that, for the narrator, all issues were
       resolved in the 30s. Reading it also led to the notion
       that he was "overhearing an interesting but allusive
       conversation not intended for me." 240w

B716   LOWE, NORMAN. "Here's Lord Snow Again--in Disjunct
       'Sleep of Reason.'" National Observer, 13 January
       1969, p. 23.
       The first half reads like a fictionalized diary;
       and, given its subject matter, it argues an obsession
       with committees. The characters are bloodless and
       intellectualized. It is difficult to see how they can
       be much affected, much less shattered, by the murder
       committed by the two Lesbians. The elder Pateman is
       well drawn, and the courtroom scenes are good but not
       outstanding. ". . . Sir Lewis' reserved approach to
       the case is hard to comprehend. Though the [murder]
       case is plainly meant to put the Snovian cast of charac-
       ters in fresh perspective, the reader will not be easily
       convinced that it does so."

B717   MCDOWELL, FREDERICK P.W. Review of The Sleep of Reason.
        Contemporary Literature, 11 (Summer 1970) 410-12.
            A disappointment. The murderess is not established
        in depth. There is little Dostoevskian insight or
        resonance. Eliot's analysis of the crime is perfunctory
        and undramatic. George Passant has become a shifty and
        garrulous old man. The strength of the book lies in
        its account of the day-to-day relationships of the
        middle classes living in some kind of community. "As
        a novel and work of art, it is not entirely satisfying,
        though there are many fine things in it. In sum, Snow
        as a metaphysician is naive; as an observer of human
        beings, he is often acute and illuminating."

B718   MCGUINNESS, FRANK. Review of The Sleep of Reason.
        London Magazine, 8, no. 10 (January 1969) 111-13.
            This work, the tenth novel in "C.P. Snow's monster
        chronicle of the last forty years as seen through the
        relentlessly boring but singularly unpentrative eyes of
        Lewis Eliot" shows us Eliot is more interested in
        passing the port than in radical causes. True enough,
        Eliot commands a curious respect, perhaps even
        affection, but these responses are due to the fact
        that he is a creation so monumentally cliché-ridden
        and plastic as to excite a certain morbid fascination.
        Followed by a somewhat sardonic plot summary ("a
        roman fleuve . . . of meandering sluggishness.")
        Believes the sanity of the principals is the main
        issue; but Snow's book will probably lead to the
        impression that permissiveness and pornography are
        the source of all British ills. The depiction of the
        defendants, and the trial scenes are competently done.
        "All the same, even as a piece of reportage, it would
        scarcely seem to merit the more extravagant praise of
        those critics who seem so frightened of the nasty and
        vulgar that they automatically assume anything written
        with some measure of restraint is authoritative and
        sound. I find this hard to stomach of a work that
        appears to endorse the younger Eliot's weighty pronounce-
        ment: 'Freedom rots.'" 750w

B719   MADDOCKS, MELVIN. "'Take It Off!' Cry the C.P. Snow
        Fans." Life, 66, no. 2 (17 January 1969) 8.
            [A biting attack on the remoteness, emotional and
        sexual, of Snow's fictional world.] In the language
        of the striptease, Lewis Eliot "just about has one coy
        arm out of his frock coat." The novel is a moral tract
        on freedom and responsibility, and Lewis Eliot is a
        tedious and predictable moralist, whose friends are
        ultra-respectable men of honor, professionals with high

principles or, at their most degraded, decent and
responsible men of affairs. It is virtually impossible,
from this distant perspective of high-principled probity,
to do justice to the civil war in the souls of Cora and
Kitty, the two murderers of the novel. "Why do we put
up with Snow's long-distance treatment of the human
heart--his stubborn refusal to come to intimate terms
with either good or evil? The answer is that while he
may be remote, he is never cold. There is a generosity
and, within limits, a curiosity to Snow. Keeping his
balance once again, he wins--or loses, depending on how
you look at it."

B720   MARSH, PAMELA. "Lewis Eliot Lectures His Times: Freedom
        and Responsibility." Christian Science Monitor,
        16 January 1969, p. 11.
            Argues, like Wain, that the separate events of
        the novel, form parts of one theme. The trial of
        Arnold Shaw prepares us for the murder trial. Quotes
        George Passant's speech on freedom and the following
        speculation which suggests that his remarks might have
        led directly to the murder. The work is ". . . .
        thoroughly readable . . . its emphasis typically on the
        discussion of events rather than on the events them-
        selves."

B721   MONOD, SYLVERE. Review of The Sleep of Reason.
        Etudes Anglaises, 23, no. 3 (July-September 1970)
        350-52.
            [In French.] The title somewhat inappropriately
        suggests that Lewis Eliot, man of reason, will find
        his own reason asleep. The novel is much concerned
        with family relationships, lacks unity, but it features
        the typical Snovian diction, and marks the appearance
        of many characters from the other books in the series.
        The trial scene, reminiscent of Dreiser's An American
        Tragedy, is excellently done, the character of Mr.
        Pateman is excellently drawn, and one looks forward
        to Last Things.

B722   MORRIS, ROBERT K. "The English Way of Life." Nation,
        208, no. 17 (28 April 1969) 546-47.
            Omnibus review. Snow's characters are intended to
        be literally true to life. They are also conformist
        to a fault. When they are not so, they "careen
        nakedly toward madness, anarchy, or the grave." The
        character of Lewis Eliot has diminished in importance.
        By contrast, that of Powell's Nicholas Jenkins has

increased his dramatic appeal. The peripheral themes,
the generation gap, student freedom and power politics,
reflect uneasiness. The theme of murder leads Snow
to reflect on man's responsibilities if the world is
to survive.

B723   MUGGERIDGE, MALCOLM. Review of The Sleep of Reason.
        Esquire, 72, no. 3 (March 1969) 54-55.
            The account of the murder case is extremely well
        done. In this novel Snow debates the issue of respon-
        sibility. Are the defendants to be considered not
        responsible for their actions simply because the crimes
        are so heinous? "In other words, have we decided
        that as there is no God and no Devel, there is no such
        thing as good and evil, and so no moral responsibility?"
        The question is not answered, but Snow, an able writer,
        demonstrates the dilemma with skill and telling effect.

B724   PARK, CLARA CLAIBORNE. "The Snows of Yesteryear,
        Updated." Chicago Tribune [Washington Post] Book
        World, 5 January 1969, p. 3.
            A disappointment. The series was once notable for
        clarity, subtle assessment of motives, and the occa-
        sional memorable phrase. Lewis Eliot has now become
        flat and dull, and his attempt to pin the blame for
        the crime on George Passant will be resisted by the
        reader. Leavis' gibe that Snow's books are composed
        by a computer named Charlie, which is fed instructions
        in the form of chapter headings, begins to look
        plausible.

B725   PRICE, MARTIN. "Reason and its Alternatives: Some
        Recent Fiction." Yale Review, 58, no. 3 (Spring 1969)
        464-66.
            Omnibus review. Offers some interpretations of
        Goya's "The Sleep of Reason Brings Forth Monsters,"
        detects some ironies in the "slow and sometimes point-
        less detail" of the novel, and argues that the murderers
        are "meant to evoke the sheer blind power of instinct
        or will that reason must try to understand." That
        instinct in turn is rooted in the will to survive.
        Snow's novels "move toward generalization, and this one
        more than most. Many episodes have little coherence
        with each other outside of theme, and the themes lie
        near the surface. . . .It is easy to be supercilious
        about Snow's achievements, especially since F.R. Leavis'
        attack. It is somewhat harder to be just to the moral
        earnestness, the cumulative weight of social detail,

the fascination with the prosaic forms of public administration. It is probably too much to say that Snow's novels read like a committee report, but the private voice becomes more and more lost in the public man who narrates them." 730w

B726   PRICE, R.G.G. "New Fiction." Punch, 255, no. 6686, (30 October 1968) 632.
        Omnibus review. "As always, in its grave way it is intensely readable and there are fascinated and fascinating glimpses of the lives of lawyers, academics and doctors. Eliot's toughness reflects his creator's toughness, his refusal to be laughed into writing more flashily. . . .This decent, worried book interested and impressed me. . . ."

B727   RICHARDSON, JACK. Review of The Sleep of Reason. New York Times Book Review, 19 January 1969, p. 5.
        Accuses Snow of reticence, and charges that Snow sees the world as a civil service examination. "Lord Snow obviously wants to present us with a mature, balanced sensibility taking on an ugly caprice of nature, but he manages only to make his detached character seem shallow, if not at times outright silly . . . . one of the book's main annoyances is its heavy moral promptings and thin excuses for human behavior to be debated in a manner and depth not unlike that of a television symposium." The trial is undigested. Snow's characters seem grafted together by the author's whim. Nothing important is said about a man when you say that he has won the Nobel Prize. "So many men and women drift through Lord Snow's novels without any more substance to them than the bureaucratic awards they have achieved. . . . Stripped of their honors, they vanish altogether as, indeed, The Sleep of Reason does in the very act of reading it."

B728   STEINER, GEORGE. "Last Stop for Mrs. Brown." New Yorker, 45, no. 21 (12 July 1969) 83-86, 89.
        Steiner asks why Snow's recent works have received insulting or ferocious dismissals by the critics. His answer suggests that Snow's fiction is not in fashion. First, Snow's fictional gifts are those of the "builder of scientific hypotheses and social models." Works of this kind are not appreciated by the current crop of jaundiced critics. Worse, recent fiction has been more than half in love with easeful death (Mann, Proust, Faulkner) and Snow, for all his darkness of vision and occasional rank pessimism, has a maddening robustness

of temper. Further, Snow's work is marked by an attempt
to reclaim for fiction the life of the mind; this
attempt flies in the teeth of American preferences.
In their fiction, Americans prefer an amused contempt
for abstractions. Observes that the account of the
trial in this novel, with its attendant subtleties and
intricacies of legal procedure, represents one way to
domesticate and contain the sordid facts of the case.
Snow "finds much of modern art and literature irre-
sponsible because it wilfully solicits chaos. He is
suspicious of brilliance and the cult of expressive
intensity; fireworks bring little light to the murk
of history." Praises that section of The Sleep of
Reason in which Charles Eliot has a talk with his
father in the hospital.

B729   TOMALIN, CLAIRE. "Decencies." New Statesman, 76,
        no. 1964 (1 November 1968) 587.
            Argues that decency is the prevailing charac-
        teristic of the series. The virtue perhaps flattened
        the prose of the books but they were, for all that,
        interesting studies in political motivation and those
        aberrant impulses that lead to the sacrifice of power.
        Quotes from Trilling's essay [see B435] on Snow's
        novels. In this work, the gap between the intention
        and achievement is too big. "The narrative is without
        tension or shape; nothing in the book could not have
        been better expressed or discussed in essay or auto-
        biography." The characters, despite their material
        success, are lifeless. The account of the eye operation
        is the best part of the book. "With the best of
        motives, the foul acts and giving of evidence are
        presented in a manner so muted, so deliberately
        calculated not to titillate the reader, that one is
        left at the end with, indeed, little to ponder but
        the decency of Lord Snow's intentions; horror and
        pity are dried out. In such a context it is difficult
        not to weigh the failure of the novel against its
        author's scrupulous approach to his subject, and allow
        him at least a certain triumph of character." 700w

B730   TREVOR, WILLIAM. "Lewis Eliot and the Avenging Age of
        Freedom." The Times (London), 2 November 1968, p. 22.
            Passant's remarks about freedom "come home to
        roost with a thud of vengence" when the two lesbian
        killers torture a child. The novel can be read in
        isolation from the series only at the expense of
        turning George Passant into a silly, pretentious man,
        and Lewis Eliot into a dullard. "One is in a world

that is side by side with the world of Anthony Powell, and how different those two very English estates are: the old Establishment of the one decrying in glorious comedy, the new Establishment of the other, sombre and ernest and intellectual, its air foggy with polemics, its voices jaded already."

B731   WAIN, JOHN. "Ruminating About Freedom." New Republic, 160, no. 5 (1 February 1969) 30-36.
        Wain, who approves of the Strangers and Brothers series when Lewis Eliot ("pursy, conventional") is not the main character, also approves of this book. The novel asks an old question: given the absence of God, why not let human nature rip and damn the consequences? This theme is worked out on a number of different levels--the Vicky Shaw-Pat Martin love affair, the cold sexual coupling of some students--and reaches its culmination when the two lesbians are accused, tried and convicted of murder. Considers that the male lesbian, Kitty Pateman, has been corrupted by the doctrines of that somewhat Lawrentian, facile old life-enhancer, George Passant, who taught self-fulfillment through gratification. Are freedom, the absence of sexual restraints, good or bad for society? "Nobody in the book has any convincing answers to these questions, which does not matter, because the putting of relevant questions is more important, at a time like this, than any cocksure answers." The fundamental theme of the book is the cultural and sociological gap between the old and new Left and Wain is "glad to have read [the book] in the last days of cold, gritty 1968."

B732   WEEKS, EDWARD. "The Peripatetic Reviewer." Atlantic, 223, no. 2 (February 1969) 127-28.
        Omnibus review. "C.P. Snow is at his best when writing about people under pressure: he makes the struggle of power of engrossing interest, and although he works in a now familiar background, each book in its different way has enriched our understanding." 600w

The State of Siege. 1969.

B733   ANON. Review of The State of Siege. Publishers' Weekly, 195, no. 11 (17 March 1969) 53.
        "In quiet terms he contrasts the extraordinary scientific advances of our day with a noticeable

withdrawal--of individuals into themselves, of nations into "enclaves"--that can be disastrous if continued into the world of the near future when a population explosion may have embittered human society. . . ."
75w

B734   ANON. Review of The State of Siege. Christian Century, 86 (21 May 1969) 713.
"Population growth and food shortages have reached such a critical point that Snow can only utter a cry from the depths and write a hymn of despair. He argues that the world can--but probably will not--face this dual problem." [This one sentence is the complete text of the review.]

B735   ANON. Review of The State of Siege. Science Books, 5, no. 3 (December 1969) 203.
"The lectures of this book are a passing note to a lasting problem--survival in a world of plenty. Until nations solve this problem above all others, there is no hope for the young or the yet unborn. It is hardly likely that even the eminence of C.P. Snow will make these lectures required reading."

B736   ANON. "Review of The State of Siege. Choice, 7, no. 2 (April 1970) 264.
This statement on the dangers of overpopulation includes little new information or analysis; its importance rests primarily on Snow's eminence. It has "already made a considerable impact as quotations from it have appeared in countless newspaper editorials and columns, but it will be of little value to students of either economics or contemporary social and political problems." 200w

B737   GARRETT, T.M. Review of The State of Siege. Best Sellers, 29 (15 June 1969) 125.
"The author claims we are in a state of siege because the world is closing in as the curve of rising population rushes to collide with the curve of lagging food production. He sees neither the rich countries nor the poor reacting in time, but feels that we must ask people to make great sacrifices. There is nothing new in the lectures and they have only the author's style to recommend them." 70w

B738   HESELTINE, ROBERT W. Review of The State of Siege. Library Journal, 94, no. 10 (15 May 1969) 1975-76.
Snow's discussion of the population explosion and

the sacrifices required of the West to industrialize
the poor nations, is not a pleasant prospect, but it
is an honest appraisal.

B739   MUDRICK, MARVIN. "The End of the World or Else."
       Hudson Review, 22, no. 3 (Fall 1969) 555-56.
         Describes Snow as a "deep thinker" and gives an
excerpt from the lecture which states that Snow
neglected detailed discussion of the population crises
in his "Two Cultures" to avoid hurting other people's
religious sensibilities. "The man is all heart
(exactly how often did he love those religious
friends of his?), and it's an awful jolt when he
comes right out in public with his most private
feelings about the end of the world if not worse:
'I have to say that I have been nearer to despair
this year, 1968, than ever in my life.'" 300w

Last Things. 1970.

B740   ANON. Review of Last Things. Kirkus, 38 (15 June
       1970) 656.
         Lewis Eliot confronts death and the troubles of
his son Charles with all his optimism unimpaired,
propelled by a process of renewal, hope or will not
really his own. "Mr. Snow is so eminently sane and
reasonable that he cannot but persuade the reader
even where he fails to engage him on more personal
terms and the audience for these russet-toned
reflections is not only certain but further assured
by its Book-of-the-Month Club selection, for August."
330w

B741   ANON. "The World of Power and Groups." Times
       Literary Supplement, 23 October 1970, pp. 1223-25.
         The Strangers and Brothers series creates a
composite portrait of twentieth-century man. Lewis
Eliot, who must not be completely identified with Snow,
unfortunately never achieves an identity of his own;
but he is vulnerable on a number of grounds, and so
perfectly suited to convey the nature of that composite
portrait. This aim, not resonance, is Snow's real
fictional purpose. "The world shown by him through
the eyes of this almost invariably judicious observer
is one where matters are decided by groups and
committees which form and reform, change shape and
character but remain entities more important than the
individuals whose lives they order." Six of Snow's

novels are briefly examined to prove this point.
Numbers, the counting of votes in committees and the
House of Commons, are important in solving the problems
of Snow's fictional world, and these problems are solved
or resolved with a notable narrative skill that reso-
lutely excludes the irrelevant. The series is an
impressive and personal statement about the power
relations of men in organized society. Snow depicts
the losers--those unable to accept the structure of
power and the limits it places on behavior (Passant,
Calvert), but Snow's finest portraits are those of
the winners: Hector Rose, Walter Luke, Bevill. "The
whole sequence is finer and deeper than any single
work within it, and it offers a view of professional
British life in the twentieth century magnificent in
its scope and remarkable for the faithfulness with
which it is maintained. . . . Few other novelists
in our time have attempted as much, few have spoken
with such generosity and lack of malice, none has
shown insights into his chosen material that are
more delicate and true." 3000w

B742   ANON. "Islands in the River." Economist, 237 (21
November 1970) xvii.
        The backcloth of the novel is student rebellion
and the generation gap and, on another plane, the
relations between father and son. The grand theme of
the sequence as a whole is, quite simply, that each
man is an island unto himself. "There are partings
and there are homecomings. The life cycle gives them
an organic unity. The individual human being cannot
hope for more. Lewis Eliot is serene."

B743   ANON. Review of Last Things. Booklist, 67, no. 2
(15 September 1970) 83-84.
        ". . . the novel is balanced by vitality, the
delicate understanding of personality interaction,
and a gentleness toward life." 50w

B744   ANON. Review of Last Things. British Book News,
January 1971, p. 84.
        The work concentrates on Lewis Eliot's inner
circle and Lewis Eliot himself, and the strongest
new relationship is that between Lewis Eliot and his
son Charles. "The volume does not possess a dramatic
shape nor an easily identifiable theme, as one of its
predecessors, but it provides an admirable coda to a
monumental chronicle and commentary upon the professional
and personal life of our times." 250w

B745   no entry

B746   ANON. Review of Last Things. Publishers' Weekly,
        200, no. 14 (4 October 1971) 61.
        [Brief review of the Bantam paperback ed.] "Snow
        takes on such subjects as death, crime, guilt, freedom,
        choice, etc., and the average reader will wish he
        stuck more to people and events. Critics are on both
        sides of the Snow fence." 100w

B747   BONNET, JACKY. "Last Things: Snow's Refusal of Man's
        Tragic Individual Condition." Langues Modernes, 66,
        no. 3 (1972) 302-04.
        The resonance technique within this novel takes
        an unpredictable turn. Both Austin Davidson and
        Sammikins, confronted by death, lose interest in their
        previous affairs. But Lewis Eliot, confronted by his
        cardiac arrest, has a different and more optimistic
        response. He sees visitors, takes a sympathetic
        interest in the doings of his son and, open to external
        influences, even changes some of his attitudes towards
        Muriel. "Lewis's psychological maturation has reached
        its climax, he is no longer pining for unattainable
        cosiness and safety; he has reached the state of peace,
        of undisturbed calm he so longed for. . . ."

B748   BRADBURY, MALCOLM. "Snow's Bleak Landscape."
        New Statesman, 80 (30 October 1970) 566.
        Snow "has made his peculiar mixture of the reason-
        able, neo-scientific, positivistic literary imagination
        into a kind of test case, a radical opposite to literary
        despair." It is true that the public lives of Snow's
        characters move towards optimism and give credence to
        notions of progress. Witness, for example, Snow's
        treatment of the meritocratic class, the New Men, a
        treatment which makes him seem like the exact heir of
        Wells. Witness also Snow's concern with the life of the
        family, that social repository of the forces of reason
        and growth. Still, the overall movement of the cycle is
        from public optimism to private despair. Lewis Eliot,
        once a man of affairs, full of attention and moral
        energy, now finds the big world shrivelling, and Last
        Things is "an epic of ungracious survival." This
        movement, this reduction of Eliot from public man to
        private emperor of angst, is prefigured in the early
        novels of observed experience: the emotions depicted
        there are "typically those that lie outside order and
        pull in the direction of desperation. . . . The circle
        is rounded off with the fading of the hope that let

that dense, substantiated fictional world of the early
novels take on such compelling power, the power of
being a culture co-existent in time and fiction. For
a writer who, it is often said, has no gift to move
us, it is a terrible story." [Reprinted, with additions,
in B310.]

B749   CORBETT, E.P.J. Review of Last Things. America, 123,
no. 4 (22 August 1970) 100.
Considers it an impressive end of an impressive
series. Snow's sentence structure is varied, and his
prose is sesquipedelian. "In his autumnal years, Lord
Snow seems to be indulging his sheer delight in the
lexical and syntactical resources of his native language."

B750   CRUTTWELL, PATRICK. "Fictional Chronicle." Hudson
Review, 24, no. 1 (Spring 1971) 178-80.
Comments on the absence of formal religious beliefs
in Snow's works, decides that Eliot's brooding about
last things is evidence of naive and plodding truthfulness and finds the account of the younger generation
fantastically unconvincing. "As long as things and
people behave decently, rationally, and expectedly,
Snow can understand them, and deal with them intell-
igently and convincingly." Unfortunately, the twentieth
century has not been rational; this fact explains the
interest in the novels of Dostoevsky, Golding, Camus,
Kafka, Hesse. "C.P. Snow will not go down as one of the
great English novelists; but there is no need to go from
this conclusion to the. . . frenzied denigration
exhibited by Leavis, which seems to be based on a
personal hatred and envy. . . ." The series will be
read by sociologists and those with an interest in the
history of ideas. "It will be read: with interest, and
perhaps with an emotion and a kind of pity which its
author had never imagined or intended it could generate."
900w

B751   DAWSON, HELEN. "Briefing: Paperbacks." London
Observer, 5 November 1972, p. 35.
[50 word mention of the paperback ed.]

B752   EDELMAN, MAURICE. "The Cycle Closes in Snow-Land."
Life, 69, no. 8 (21 August 1970) 8.
Snow's claim to be a major novelist rests firmly
on his creation of a Snovian world of men in groups
who struggle for success and power. Snow's description
of Eliot's eye operation and cardiac arrest is without
precedent in literature; it also exemplifies the line--

'Each man dies alone'--of the Rede lecture. The
motives Snow imputes to the young Charles Eliot and
to the Jews in the cycle are perhaps too generous.
Still, "In the great deluge of contemporary fiction,
it's hard to find three writers whose oeuvre has a
comparable coherence. Snow stands out not only as a
novelist who has recognized the problems of his age
and offered solutions, but also as one to whom in a
hundred years' time readers will turn and say, 'That's
how it was!' and add, 'It's just like that now!'"
570w

B753   FULLER, EDMUND. "C.P. Snow Concludes his Awesome
        Project." Wall Street Journal, 24 August 1970, p. 6.
            Briefly praises the sheer substance and solidity
        of Snow's accomplishment, and devotes most of the
        review to capsule summaries of the ten other novels
        in the series. Followed by plot summary of Last Things.
        "C.P. Snow's large achievement commands respect, and,
        we think, thanks from those who care about thoughtful,
        ripened writing." 1000w

B754   GRIFFIN, LLOYD W. Review of Last Things. Library
        Journal, 95, no. 13 (July 1970) 2521.
            "Working in the great tradition of novel writing,
        he reveals again that prose can be controlled yet
        effective, and that in the hands of a good novelist
        almost all the social actions of man will repay
        scrutiny." 200w

B755   HALIO, JAY L. "First and Last Things." Southern
        Review, 9, no. 2 (April 1973) 461-62.
            Omnibus review. This is the best novel of the
        sequence. It shows "a direct grasp of the subject--
        a direct, lived experience of the soul confronting
        the death of one's last friends, relatives, even
        oneself. . . ." Of the four last things, death,
        judgment, heaven and hell, "Lewis Eliot's frankly
        secular outlook. . . renders the last three terms
        figurative--the heaven and hell one makes in his own
        life, the judgments delivered upon others or oneself."
        Eliot discovers that life manifests itself in a form
        of continuous creation, a process which leads him to
        take a renewed interest in the doings of his son
        Charles. 350w

B756   HAWKES, PETER. "The Day Thou Gavest." Spectator,
        225, no. 7428 (7 November 1970) 563-64.
            [Preceded by short, amusing parody in which God

summons <u>Saint</u> Lewis for advice.] Dickens and Balzac
were successful in novels which showed young men from
the provinces assaulting the capitals. Snow fails in
the same high enterprise because 1) the style is
offensively explanatory, 2) his similes are bizarre,
3) the book has no plot or tension, and 4) the raw
sex of <u>Homecomings</u> and <u>Time of Hope</u> [surely one of
Hawkes's little jokes] is transmuted to pious sexual
apothegms. Only a few dull things occur in this
novel. 600w

B757   HILL, WILLIAM B. "Fiction." <u>America</u>, 123, no. 17
        (28 November 1970) 464.
            Short notice. 50w

B758   _____. Review of <u>Last Things</u>. <u>Best Sellers</u>, 30
        (15 September 1970) 83–84.
            As the older generation dies off, and the younger
        generation takes part in revolutionary activities,
        Snow makes it clear that the young are now the center
        of the stage. During three quarters of its length
        the movement is glacial, but the canvas is large, and
        nothing can be cut. "It is not a novel to be read
        at a sitting, or in isolation from the rest of this
        series; taken at full length, and with some background,
        it is a very fitting end to a remarkably fine series."

B759   JONES, D.A.N. "Inconclusive." <u>Listener</u>, 84, no.
        2170 (29 October 1970) 598–99.
            The work is inconclusive. The story line is thin,
        and Lewis Eliot conveys an air of stoicism or grim
        satisfaction when he talks of death. The novel, at
        times, seems to consist of notes for future novels.
        The talk of enclaves suggests only that the various
        enclaves will exist much as before. "Perhaps that
        statement, 'We die alone,' signifies Lewis's regret
        at leaving his enclaves." The priest advises Lewis
        Eliot not to be too hard on himself "though we might
        not have guessed that he was likely to be so." [For
        correspondance, see November 12, 1970, p. 663 (C.P.
        Snow); November 26, 1970, p. 738 (Morris Shapira);
        December 10, 1970, p. 817 (Colin Ross). Snow protests
        the use of the 'babu expression' "We die alone."
        Shapira backs Leavis. Ross protests that Shapira is
        no Leavis.]

B760   JONES, RICHARD. "The End of the C.P. Snow Affair."
        <u>Atlantic</u>, 226 (September 1970) 112–17.
            The sequence is plainly autobiographical, and it
        celebrates the theme of getting-on. Occasionally, the

inadequate transposition of Snow's life to fiction is
clearly evident: we get the outer, but not the inner
development. Further, Snow's aesthetic misjudgment
hangs over the books like a primal disaster. Eliot
prepares himself for death but this tremendous theme,
as treated by Snow, is vexatiously commonplace. Eliot's
eschatological meditations are almost touching, but
Snow's sub-Trollopian style and Eliot's unlovely
personality give these musings a mere uncomfortable
eloquence. The antics of the young in this book leave
Lewis Eliot baffled. Presumably he is dismayed by
their "absence of competitive bitchiness, their apparent
inability to recognize the main chance when they see it."
Lewis Eliot, a Khan of the Civil Service, is a mere
philistine, and the sequence is marked by the narrowness
of Snow's intention, the poverty of his style, and the
philistinism of Lewis Eliot's life and interests. 2400w

B761   LE CARRÉ, JOHN. "Vocation in a World of Pain."
London Sunday Times, 25 October 1970, p. 27.
        The series conveys a hatred of violence which
accounts for Lewis Eliot's obsessive preoccupation
with death and the potential of man's self-destruction.
The theme of ambition has dispelled the potential
morbidity always present in Snow's work. The same
theme, more closely observed, results in Snow's interest
in those men who contrive to repell the agents of chaos:
sex, ambition and love when these passions are "no
longer harnessed to the humanitarian cart. . . .What
Snow has finally given us. . . is a vision of men
mystified by the undertow of life's brutality. . . .
As one might expect of a dynastically minded socialist
obsessed with the creation of an elite, it is a vision
rich in paradoxes. . . .Sometimes, by preaching a
doctrine of such desperate inhibition, Snow leaves us
wondering whether he is actually contributing to the
collision he so anxiously seeks to avoid." Snow
inspires a new definition of a writer: he who can
make a philosophy out of his bewilderment.

B762   MCDOWELL, F.P.W. "Time of Plenty; Recent British
Fiction." Contemporary Literature, 13, no. 3
(Summer 1972) 363.
        Omnibus review. The novel includes a poor grasp
of last things: attainment of power and satisfaction
of personal ambition, two of Snow's insistent themes,
perhaps lessen his philosophical perceptiveness. But
the perceptiveness is there when Snow examines domestic

and social relationships, and the most moving pages of the book concern Eliot's relationship with his son Charles. The book is inferior to Snow's early fiction, but superior to The Sleep of Reason and Corridors of Power, its immediate predecessors. 900w

B763 MADDOCKS, MELVIN. "Lord of Limbo." Time, 96, no. 8 (24 August 1970) 62.

Snow's false self-advertisements—the claim that he serves as a link between the two cultures, the comparisons to Proust, the sorry pretence of profundity in this novel—have obscured his real merits. It is true that introspection, tragedy, disasters have little place in the largely optimistic series, and it is true that he has been clearing his throat for a revelation that never comes, but Snow's real and substantial gift is that he has described how, but not why, men act. "The guises and disguises of ambition, the glint of fever in the eye. . . the way a New Man on the make can use the old steppingstones (Cambridge common room, St. James club)—all this Snow knows with first-hand certainty." Snow is not apocalyptic; he is the Lord of Limbo; he has written the record of middling men and middling ways in an often middling time. Like Galsworthy, he has "made honest drama out of the undramatic stuff of compromise."

B764 MALLET, GINA. "Boiler Room in the Ship of State." Chicago Tribune [Washington Post] Book World, 23 August 1970, p. 5.

"The final volume. . . is farewell then, and frankly, it was time." The series has become increasingly the monograph of a self-made, self-satisfied, elitist mandarin and raging egomaniac, Lewis Eliot. It provides a limited view of life, and it does so by curtailing the growth of characters like Roy Calvert, the Rev. Mr. Knight, Mrs. Jago and Arthur Brown. This castration of character is counterbalanced by Snow's subject, contemporary England, and by his skill at handling plot. Lewis Eliot, once uptight, is now sealed away forever. He has told us about his mind, spirit, health; he has lectured us on ethics; he has never shown us his soul.

B765 MORRIS, ROBERT K. "Thematic Skeletons Fleshed Out with Plot and Character." Saturday Review, 53, no. 34 (22 August 1970) 43-45, 55.

Snow, author of a "formidable, energetic and readable chronicle of our age" has literary faults

that probably stem from his scientific training. His
characters are the exponents of moral positions. His
style--accurate, direct, simple, controlled--is
incapable of conveying resonances. In the hands of
that non-stylist, Lewis Eliot, "resonance fades into
something like a numbing hum." Lewis Eliot, for all
his public virtues, is incapable of complex feelings.
Eliot's rationalism remains intact and indomitable
throughout the cycle, and the quality is passed on to
Charles Eliot the younger. "One would like to feel,
though it daily grows more difficult, that Snow is not
too optimistic with too little cause. Should time
prove his optimism justified, however, one may uncover
between the lines of his dutiful, marching prose more
truths than in all the crackling rhetoric of handbooks
by Che or Mao, and as many provocative insights as in
the anti-utopian novels of Aldous Huxley, George Orwell,
Anthony Burgess, or Yevgeny Zamyatin. In any event,
Snow will be remembered, I think, for giving us in
the Lewis Eliots of our century possible models of
privileged intellect worthy of emulation." 2400w

B766   OSTERMANN, ROBERT. "C.P. Snow Winds up His Series with
a Banal and Tiresome Novel." National Observer, 31
August 1970, p. 17.
        "C.P. Snow may be one of the novelists whom critics
have in mind when they insist the novel is dead." The
series as a whole is in many ways a breath-taking
performance, but this tedious and mechanical book
highlights faults that should not be overlooked in
the final scholarly assessment: the supernatural
omniscience of the narrator and the prevailing stilted
dialogue.

B767   PARKER, DOROTHY. "A Monument Completed." Christian
Science Monitor, 27 August 1970, p. 11.
        Snow is the novelist of the middle ranges of
experience. The vitality of this last novel, despite
its share of appropriate eschatological content, is
due to the concerned attention paid to the younger
generation's "ardors and agitations." As for the
series: "If it is never elegant or penetrating, neither
is it ever merely clumsy or meretricious." It is
marked by intelligence, uncompromising decency, a
deep sense of what finally matters in human intercourse.

B768   RAYMOND, JOHN. "Eliot Comes Through." London Financial
Times, 22 October 1970, p. 27.
        A fine and absorbing novel. The account of the
student protest operation is shrewdly imaginative and

exciting. Eliot's "death" in the operating room
inevitably engrosses too much of the reader's attention.
Includes brief comments on the other novels in the
series and concludes "If you are one of those who are
generally uninterested in the power game--then the
world of Lewis Eliot, or a large part of its content,
is not for you."

B769   SAAL, ROLLENE W. "Pick of the Paperbacks." Saturday
Review, 54, no. 52 (25 December 1971) 33.
        Prompted by the Bantam paperback editions of
The Sleep of Reason and The Light and the Dark. "In
its own stately, cool, and very English fashion [Snow's
series] remains one of the major literary works of our
time." 100w

B770   SCOTT, PAUL. "No News from the Other World." The
Times (London) 22 October 1970, p. 8.
        This valedictory volume is less independant than
other works in the sequence, and its themes--politics,
sexual and parental love, solitary existence--are
stated not illustrated. Snow's weakness as a novelist
is that he has a first-class mind. Fiction seems to
require an obsessive and enclosed ability to deal in
lies and approximations; and Snow lacks this obsession.
As a novelist, he can entertain, but he fails to
convince the reader of the existence of a special
reality. The best writing in the series is found in
the first part of Homecomings and the best novels are
The Masters, The New Men and The Affair.

B771   SHAPIRO, CHARLES. "Political Fates." Novel; A Forum
on Fiction, 5, no. 1 (Fall 1971) 88-89.
        Lewis Eliot has progressively become more tedious
and dull, and the human knowledge conveyed by the
series is that of public men wearing public faces.
"What Snow has given us, through eleven novels, is
little more than a collection of mildly humorous
eccentrics whose serious problems are made cozy for
us by Eliot's everlastingly kind observations." Snow's
work is more comparable to R.F. Delderfield than to
Anthony Powell. The dullness of this book extends to
politics. Eliot broods a great deal about the specious
idea of enclaves. "There is almost as much of this
moralizing [about enclaves and other things] in Last
Things as there is awkward prose to bear it." 500w

B772   SHRAPNEL, NORMAN. "Great Intimations." Manchester
Guardian Weekly, 31 October 1970, p. 19.
        Snow is the first major novelist of the cybernetic

age. [The remark recalls a gibe by F.R. Leavis; it is
not a compliment.] He has contributed, although in a
chilling sense, to an understanding of contemporary
British life. For Lewis Eliot has revealed the
"deadness, the emptiness at the heart of these socio-
professional performers. We seem to have landed
ourselves in a spiritual boneyard, and Snow emerges
as a kind of literary undertaker." Snow's literary
technique does not convey the illusion of life. Both
The Sleep of Reason and Last Things flounder on the
brink of great intimations, but the promise is not
fulfilled. "Are we near revelation at last?. . .
The hope is useless. Snow is too sensible and
scientific to have any metaphysical pretensions. . . .
What his hero achieves is over-tidy, a kind of life
after death on this earth. In his end is his son's
beginning."

B773   SOKOLOV, RAYMOND A.   Review of Strangers and Brothers.
       Newsweek, 76, no. 7 (17 August 1970) 88-90.
            Half review, half interview. Snow's various and
       deeply studied characters have helped him to cover the
       English scene with the thoroughness of an enlightened
       census taker. The genealogy at the end of the book is
       a cut and dried coda. The interview, by Seth
       Goldschlager, describes Snow's office and Belgravia
       house; Snow's writing habits and future writing plans
       (The Malcontents); the possible teleserialization of
       of his works [not televised as of December 1978]; and
       Snow's editorial revisions of the series [which resulted,
       in 1972, in the publication of the Omnibus Edition by
       Macmillan and Scribner.]

B774   WEIGHTMAN, JOHN. "End of the Corridor." London
       Observer, 25 October 1970, p. 34.
            Snow's series covers more ground than Galsworthy's
       Forsyte Saga, less than Jules Romains' Men of Good Will.
       The vicious attack by Leavis changed the minds of some
       of Snow's admirers, but in fact the strengths and
       weaknesses of Snow's series have remained constant for
       30 years. Snow is comparable to John Buchan. One
       believes in the British Gentleman; the other in the
       Top Man in a given line. When Charles Eliot opts to
       become a pundit by way of a stint as a foreign corre-
       spondent, the decision demonstrates Snow's theme of a
       Top Man in a given line.

B775   WEINTRAUB, STANLEY. "An Elegiac Ending to C.P. Snow's
       11-Novel Cycle." New York Times Book Review, 23 August
       1970, p. 4.

Examines all the novels in the series in the
attempt to assess Snow's work as a whole. Includes
references to Galsworthy, Trollope and the much debated
issue of resonance. The style--flat, precise, un-
emotional--fits Lewis Eliot; and, in any case, Snow's
narrative gifts will get him the attention of thoughtful
readers. "The long and memorable cycle has ended, and
through it as in no other work in our time we have
explored in depth the inner life of the new classless
class that is the twentieth century Establishment."
3400w [Reprinted; B776.]

B776 _____. "Last Things: C.P. Snow Eleven Novels After."
Mosaic (University of Manitoba) 4, no. 3 (Spring 1971)
135-41.
[Reprint of B775.]

B777 WADE, ROSALIND. Quarterly Fiction Review, 218, no.
1260 (January 1971) 45.
Omnibus review. Calls it an impressive new novel.
Eliot's development is brilliantly precise and orderly.
He remains interesting. His mind is packed with
relevant detail and an understanding of every con-
ceivable human predicament. "Last Things provides
unerring comment not only on how things are at this
moment, but how they have become so." 200w

B778 WOOD, MICHAEL. "End of the Line." New York Review
of Books, 16 (11 March 1971) 41.
[A series of decisively stated judgments of the
"Strangers and Brothers" series followed by a short,
adverse judgment of Last Things.] The generalizations
in the novel are apt to be silly. Wood does not
endorse Eliot's opinion that closed politics in
Cambridge, the Vatican or the Politburo are "much the
same." But the major problem of the whole series is
the sensibility of Lewis Eliot, which is marked by
endless self-congratulation, an ostensibly healthy
selfishness, and the repetitive structure of his
insights. "There is what people usually think. There
is what Eliot knows. What Eliot knows is the opposite
of what people think, and he is right." In spite of
these deficiencies, in spite of the dull characters
and dead prose, Snow's work is often intelligent,
efficiently plotted and full of the right kind of
trivial detail. "There is a sense of life being
lived in Snow's work, however stiff and stupid that
life appears." The novels convey, in an appealing way,

the illusion that Snow is about to disclose secrets. "Last Things, however, is a falling away from this small, but not negligible achievement. It is a wistful, tired, uncertain book." 1000w

Public Affairs. 1971.

B779   ANON. Review of Public Affairs. Kirkus, 39 (1 September 1971) 1008.
     A welcome collection of Snow's public statements. 60w

B780   ANON. Review of Public Affairs. Publishers' Weekly, 200, no. 12 (20 September 1971) 46.
     [A somewhat vague and inaccurate summary of the contents and the polemical point of Snow's book.] The bitter feud between Tizard and Lindemann is described as an "incredible and spell-binding story [which] beautifully illustrates Snow's theory of the dangers of entrusting governmental powers to scientific men . . . .An important work and a major statement of faith which may surprise with its sales power." 180w

B781   ANON. "It's That Culture Gap Again." Times Literary Supplement, 19 November 1971, p. 1448.
     Snow's Rede lecture has become a classic in the history of science, and his Science and Government, included in this book, demonstrates the danger of permitting one scientist, Lindemann, to assume a position of predominant power among non-scientists. 800w

B782   ANON. Review of Public Affairs. Choice, 9 (March 1972) 133.
     "Lord Snow is an excellent writer, and experience in both science and government have given him opportunities to observe some of the relationships between science and public policy which he discusses in these highly readable essays. . . .Interesting prologue and short epilogue are new. . . .Good for undergraduates and graduates, science and non-science majors." 160w

B783   ANON. Review of Public Affairs. Booklist, 68, no. 10 (15 January 1972) 405.
     "Seven of Snow's statements made from 1959 to 1970 develop his concern with contemporary problems. . . ." 75w

B784   ANON. Review of <u>Public Affairs</u>. <u>British Book News</u>,
        March 1972, pp. 186-87.
        The 'Two Cultures' essays stand the test of time;
        they have been maligned, but not successfully challenged.
        Snow's preoccupation with poor nations has been less
        widely accepted, while <u>Science and Government</u> is
        partisan. "Unlike his public utterances, his novels
        are in vogue, but there is a fair chance that the
        ideas expressed in the former will live the longer of
        the two."

B785   ANON. Review of <u>Public Affairs</u>. <u>Science Books</u>, 8,
        no. 1 (May 1972) 13.
        This reprint of Snow's seven essays indicate that
        his views may change but not moderate and if warnings
        such as these are not heeded, the result of technological
        advances may be a tragic outcome. "Scientists and
        intelligent laymen should read this anthology."

B786   BOYTINCK, PAUL. Review of <u>Public Affairs</u>. <u>Library
        Journal</u>, 96, no. 21 (1 December 1971) 4018.
        This collection of Snow's published lectures
        "shows him to be a moralist of profound dignity who
        recognizes that the problems which tug at him and
        terrorize him are perhaps insoluble." 190w

B787   BURNS, ALAN. "Snow of Yesteryear." <u>Books and Bookmen</u>,
        17 (December 1971) 47.
        The issues Snow resurrects are now dead. "One
        would have thought that Dr. Leavis's splendid polemic
        . . . had finally disposed of this non-issue and
        decent silence would ensue." For Snow to state that
        he has turned his back on the art of Yeats, Pound
        and Wyndham Lewis is pompous neo-Johnsonian nonsense.
        "There is hardly a trace of creative imagination in
        the whole dank series of 12 long novels. . . ." Snow
        became a bureaucrat because he knew that his novels were
        no good. Snow's political analysis is merely utopian;
        it does not convey the means to his ends. His notions
        of education are simplistic and pathetic. The Epilogue
        is "predictable and dreary. How well placed is Charlie
        Snow in the House of Lords. Such good manners. So
        much false modesty. So much gentlemanly yap about the
        poverty of nations and the education of our youth
        . . . . There he goes, tottering after his grandchildren
        . . . even anxious to ingratiate himself, to show how
        liberal he is, to lecture us, to bore the pants off us,
        to drone on. . . ."

B788   CASEY, JOHN. "Snowballs." <u>Spectator</u>, 227, no. 7483
        (27 November 1971) 770.
        [A series of arguments against selected statements
        in <u>The Two Cultures and Scientific Revolution</u> and <u>The
        Two Cultures: and A Second Look.</u>] Snow's weightiness of
        tone is at variance with the vagueness of his actual
        remarks on the subject of the religious and political
        beliefs of scientists. The third culture, "slouching
        towards Akademgorodok to be born," which consists of
        social history, sociology, etc., is not likely to be
        more truthful than, say, moral philosophy, history, or
        literature. The comparison between the Second Law of
        Thermodynamics and the works of Shakespeare is misguided.
        One can appreciate the Second Law only after a degree in
        natural science. By contrast, one can get some sort of
        emotional and moral education from the literary culture,
        and there is no precise analogy for this process in the
        sciences. His dismissals of Ruskin, Morris and Lawrence
        "deserve to be re-read as a <u>locus classicus</u> of bland
        ignorance." Serious attempts were made in the
        nineteenth century to make distinctions between the
        "aesthetic" and "scientific" consciousness. "Snow has
        not advanced the debate significantly. He is only the
        solemn second fiddle of the intellectual orchestra."

B789   CLAIBORNE, ROBERT. Review of <u>Public Affairs</u>. <u>New
        York Times Book Review</u>, 26 December 1971, pp. 2, 13.
        The book is stimulating but superficial. Concentrates
        on the issue of mass bombing or terror bombing and
        Lindemann's role in the strategy. The decision to bomb was
        due to political reasons; it was not, as Snow alleges, the
        result of scientific ignorance at the top (the relevant
        calculations involved simple arithmetic). The British
        were intent on finding a cheap way to win the war that
        would conserve British manpower; and the Air Force generals
        wanted to believe that their arm was decisive. The way to
        prevent such blunders is to subject "secret" decisions to
        public scrutiny and debate. "The need for policy decisions
        that are both rational and moral will not be met by altering
        the mix of scientists and non-scientists in the murky and
        tortuous corridors of power, but by letting in the light
        of public scrutiny." 1500w

B790   CRICK, BERNARD. "The More It Snows." <u>New Statesman</u>,
        82, no. 2119 (29 October 1971) 591-92.
        [Includes comments on the Snow-Leavis confrontation
        <u>Corridors of Power</u>, <u>The Masters</u> and <u>dicta</u> on Snow's whole
        novel sequence.] Snow's ideas are somewhat sketchy; it
        would be useful if he gave details on a nuclear and

population policy. Expresses disatisfaction with
Snow's use of the word culture. Crick is not
convinced that "in any valid sense of culture
scientists have a sub-culture any more distinct
than that of the university-educated as a whole
compared to the rest, or of North and South, still
less of classes." Suggests that Snow's concerns
over the bomb, population, food and technical
education do not call for scientific, literary or
political solutions. Action on these issues is a
"matter of widely shared doctrines and beliefs"
and socialism, an ideology which values both
science and freedom, is the best means to Snow's
intended ends.

B791   DUNN, JOHN. "Science and C.P. Snow." Listener, 86,
       no. 2224 (11 November 1971) 656-57.
            Snow casts himself as a serious political prophet,
       but his contention that the culture of natural science
       is conducive to virtue and social responsibility is
       open to question. "The pursuit of scientific inquiry
       is by a priori necessity an activity in which men cannot
       know the consequences of their actions. . . .Nothing
       can guarantee moral security in the scientific career,
       and it is quite clear that knowledge of the social
       and political world is just as essential as scientific
       insight to being socially responsible as a scientist."
       The moral undependability of science is part of
       historical tradition and popular culture (Dr. Faustus,
       Prometheus). Still, the beast of modern science and
       modern industry is loose now, and it can be tamed only
       by mind and energy but Snow, in attempting to deal
       with the issue, merely dispenses abstract moral
       injunctions. 1800w

B792   FISHLOCK, DAVID. "Moguls at Work." London Financial
       Times, 28 October 1971, p. 34.
            Snow has never engaged in debate with that
       Cantabrigian mogul, F.R. Leavis, on the ground that
       Leavis is given to misquotation and other faults
       that disqualify him from serious debate. Snow's
       portrayal of that other mogul, Lindemann, is less
       than objective. He gives the impression that all
       Lindemann's decisions were erroneous, and does not
       provide or investigate Tizard's record in giving
       advice during the post-war years. In discrediting
       Lindemann's record, Snow may have provided the literary
       culture with a stick with which to beat the scientists.

B793   FULLER, EDMUND. "Lord Snow's Humane Advices."
        Wall Street Journal, 3 January 1972, p. 6.
            Includes summaries of the principal essays in this
        volume and a quotation from Snow's address entitled
        "On Magnanimity." "C.P. Snow is a ripened, humane
        counsellor, a man worldly-knowledgeable but imbued with
        that magnanimity to which he gently calls us, for our
        bodies' and our souls' sakes." 1100w

B794   HAMPSHIRE, STUART. "Suspect Sages." New York Review
        of Books, 19, no. 4 (21 September 1972) 12-13.
            Omnibus review. Challenges Snow's assertion that
        technology must be used to oppose the bad effects of
        technology, and defends the literary response to the
        unbearable ugliness and deformities produced by un-
        controlled technological progress. It is both
        reasonable and necessary to defend an existing pre-
        technological Eden, the dream of the pastoral life;
        the strength of that impulse is proved by houses and
        gardens everywhere in Britain. Observes that different
        technologies compete with each other and, in a free
        market, high technology in the form of advanced hospital
        treatment, may drive out the technology necessary "to
        support efficient public health services, the spread
        of literacy, and a better diet at the bottom of the
        scale." 1150w

B795   MCALEER, JOHN J. Review of Public Affairs. Best
        Sellers, 31 (15 January 1972) 465.
            Snow concedes that the threats of nuclear war,
        rampant population growth and the gap between the
        rich and poor nations were all the result of technology.
        His exhortation to use more technology to combat the
        bad effects of technology invites an abrogation of
        the traditional disciplines of society which runs the
        danger of creating anarchy. The polemics of Snow the
        moralist are marred by the literary self-indulgence
        of Snow the novelist, and technology "simply cannot
        give everyone America's high standard of living by the
        year 2000, even if birth control advocates are given
        every aid short of nuclear weaponry."

B796   MARCH, ROBERT H. "The Future of Science." Science
        and Public Affairs (formerly Bulletin of the Atomic
        Scientists) 18, no. 3 (March 1972) 45-48.
            In America, the effect of the 'Two Cultures'
        lecture "led to a renewed effort on the part of
        scientists to communicate with the general public."
        Snow's political point in "The Case of Leavis and
        the Serious Case" is that generalists must have

greater scientific literacy. However, the Rostows
and McNamaras who took part in the direction of the
Vietnam war certainly fit Snow's general prescription,
which does not make for a self-evident endorsement of
Snow's case. Young scientists may dispute Snow's
view that only technology can be used to oppose the
bad effects of technology. The failure to concentrate
effort on a few vital problems, in a process analogous
to the military effort in World War II, is the main
political failure which may lead to disaster. The
Western Left is politically inactive. China may offer
the model for developing countries, but the facts are
not yet in. Cites some reasons why Snow, a moderate
man, has acquired his quota of enemies. Scientists
must formulate their research in terms intelligible
to and approved by the intelligent public. "We need
scientists who understand their own work as part of a
truly humane culture. If this can come to pass, the
gulf between the two cultures can be closed. If it
does not, the future of science may be in grave
jeopardy." 3400w

B797   WEINTRAUB, STANLEY. "Sage's Summa." New Republic,
165, no. 22 (27 November 1971) 23.
      Gives the publication history of Snow's long-
standing concern with education, the 'Two Cultures'
dispute and his humanitarian interest in the issues
of population control and food supply. Provides
summaries of Snow's major arguments found in the
different essays that make up this book. "The world's
store of contemporary wisdom is small, and as his
public statements incorporated in Public Affairs
have proven, Lord Snow can move men's minds." 2300w

The Malcontents. 1972.

B798   AMIS, MARTIN. "Generation Gap." London Observer, 2
July 1972, p. 31.
      Snow is clueless about the younger generation.
His observations on the language of the young are
dated, his account of the drug-scene is incredible,
and the characters are stereotyped and unreal. But,
"despite the howlers, one can only continue to admire
Snow's tolerance and honesty, and his eloquence when
writing about the possibilities of doing good and the
difficulties of behaving well."

B799   ANON. Review of <u>The Malcontents</u>. <u>Kirkus</u>, 40 (1 March
        1972) 280.
            The collected, ruminative tone is reminiscent of
        the <u>Strangers and Brothers</u> series. Snow does not seem
        to know these malcontents, more moneyed and hygienic
        than their American counterparts, all that well. The
        novel is a set piece discussion of moral choice. "As
        one of the older members of what the younger members
        refer to as the 'machine' or 'the bourgeoisie' comments
        'Minimum force. It's usually a good maxim.' For a
        conservator."

B800   ANON. Review of <u>The Malcontents</u>. <u>Publishers' Weekly</u>,
        201 (6 March 1972) 56.
            ". . . remains essentially an elderly man's view
        of the drives behind rebellious youth, not uninteresting
        but never very convincing." 150w

B801   ANON. Review of <u>The Malcontents</u>. <u>New Yorker</u>, 48, no.
        12 (13 May 1972) 145-46.
            ". . . a well-meaning but not very convincing
        drama of suspicion, recrimination, and self-knowledge."
        100w

B802   ANON. "Reasonable Revolutionaries." <u>Times Literary
        Supplement</u>, 30 June 1972, p. 737.
            The young people virtuously accept the power of
        reason as those in <u>The Sleep of Reason</u> viciously
        rejected it. The work has a powerful storyteller's
        grip. Still, there is a certain amount of deliberate
        vagueness about the Rachmanism, and the characterization
        of the young people lacks suppleness and subtlety.
        The relationships of the young and their parents,
        between Stephen Freer and his mother, and the solicitor
        Hotchkinson, are some of the finest things in the
        book. 1300w

B803   ANON. Review of <u>The Malcontents</u>. <u>Choice</u>, 9, nos. 5-6
        (July-August 1972) 648.
            Although Snow solves the intricate mysteries of
        the plot, the reader loses patience with the whole
        artificial business. ". . . Snow simply does not
        understand his subject. His characters are convincing
        neither as young people nor as radicals. . . he lapses
        into a parody of his own style. . . .Snow's theme, the
        uses and abuses of idealism, is a worthy one; and,
        as always, he brings into play a fine ethical
        intelligence." 230w

B804   ANON. Review of <u>The Malcontents</u>. <u>British Book News</u>,
        September 1972, pp. 816-17.
            The subject of young students, organized for
        social protest and action, permits Snow to show the
        separate reactions of individuals under stress. The
        suspense is real enough, but the individuals taking
        part in the action are not made credible. The
        dialogue put in the mouths of the protestors emphasizes
        Snow's remoteness from the younger generation.

B805   BELL, PEARL K. "Falling Snow." <u>New Leader</u>, 55
        (29 May 1972) 16-17.
            The work lacks, to use a Hegelian term, mediation:
        the breaking down of the abstract and the generalizing
        of the particular, and "Snow has fallen into the trap
        of schematizing his political generalities through his
        characters, making the book too manipulative to be
        convincing." The young student conspirators are
        "Fitted into their slots on his fictional blueprint,"
        and "they are stiff and bloodless, pompously donnish
        in their talk and awkward in their aggressiveness, like
        adolescents unaccustomed to independence." The source
        of the Core's energy and action is never adequately
        explored. 1300w

B806   BLUMBERG, MYRA. "Moral Passports." <u>New Statesman</u>,
        84, no. 2155 (7 July 1972) 26-27.
            Courage and magnanimity are indispensable moral
        virtues in Snow's scheme of things, but this work
        reveals an extraordinary moral passion. The central
        question is whether it is possible to be good or do
        good without committing harm or criminal actions. It
        is notable that, at the end of the book, two of the
        main characters retain their commitment. 650w

B807   BROYARD, ANATOLE. "New Tricks for an Old Don."
        <u>New York Times</u> (Daily), 26 April 1972, p. 43.
            Snow has no natural aptitude for fiction; he
        ignores all the twentieth century advances of the
        art; and he has none of the comfortable and cozy
        qualities of the nineteenth century writers. His
        characters are forever musing on elementary feelings.
        "As if this were not enough. . . Lord Snow adds the
        reflections and surmises of other characters on the
        first character, so that we see him or her in a three-
        way mirror, standing stock-still, foursquare and flat-
        footed." Snow's style seems modeled on that of Helen
        MacInnes. The plot is incredible and possibly anti-
        semitic. The fictional moral is unclear. "It is not

like Lord Snow to toy with ambiguity, but who knows?
This fictive contact with the young may have infected
him. If you lie down with dogs, you may get up with
tics."

B808   CRAIN, JANE LARKIN. Review of The Malcontents.
         Saturday Review: World, 2, no. 8 (11 January 1975) 26.
             Although the novel includes brooding over Britain's
         decline, Snow's pronouncements do not have a doomsday
         quality. It is "a satisfying novel that seeks to
         illuminate, not merely to disparage, the era with
         which it is pre-occupied." 200w

B809   FRAKES, J.R. "Sketches in Poster Paints." Chicago
         Tribune [Washington Post] Book World, 7 May 1972, p. 13.
             "Every gesture, every dialogue, every switch of
         loyalty is accompanied by murky, determinedly styleless,
         plodding musings about motivation, ambition, humanity,
         opportunism, innocence, maturity, conscience and
         monopoly capitalism. And over all, like a stuffed-owl
         voice of experience, broods the omniscient author,
         interpreting, patronizing, clucking away. . . ."

B810   HILL, W.B. Review of The Malcontents. Best Sellers,
         32 (15 May 1972) 95.
             "Lord Snow has a diagnostic eye and a meticulous
         care about exposing every nerve of his characters. . . .
         What may surprise a reader new to [his] novels is the
         remarkably leisurely pace of a novel about what is, after
         all, a social conspiracy. . . .The very quest for the
         traitor observes strictly the social amenities. There
         is the possibility that for some readers an air of
         unreality may emerge. . . .Yet this is an intriguing
         book. . . .Lord Snow's plots always move slowly because
         he never wants to leave a character until it is fully
         articulated. And for all its slowness, the story is
         fascinating; a reader is not apt to leave it unfinished,
         will always be glad to get back to it. There is merit
         in style, and C.P. Snow has an especially distinguished
         one." 450w

B811   HOBSON, HAROLD. "Snow's Summer Cloud." Christian
         Science Monitor, 17 May 1972, p. 13.
             The book is a very agreeable diversion, part
         mystery story, and part scrutiny into the ambitions and
         impulses of youth today. The analysis of the motives
         that lead the young to social revolt is conducted with
         sympathy "But perhaps with a certain complacency. He
         concludes that with time all troubles will pass away,
         leaving no more impression that a summer cloud."

B812   JONES, D.A.N. "Fils a Papa." Listener, 87, no.
2257 (29 June 1972) 873-74.
    The novel is told in the third person, but the
pervasive class-consciousness of Lewis Eliot strengthens
the novel, as does Snow's pervading tone of gravity.
Speculates if the title is reminiscent of Marston's
play The Malcontents (1604).

B813   MORRIS, ROBERT K. "C.P. Snow: Nevertheless." Nation,
214 (29 May 1972) 696-97.
    This relevant and moral novel proves again that
Snow writes thesis novels at the expense of character
and technique. But the thesis is so honed and precise
that it redeems his flat prose, wooden dialogue and the
caricatures he calls characters. Snow is an important
novelist. He is honest and straightforward, the epitome
of hope, reason, probity, decency and good will. The
characters of this novel are bloodless abstractions,
and Snow implicitly flogs them with knotty questions
of ethics. "And since the reader soon loses empathy
for the characters, he is in danger of losing interest
in the ethics." Unlike that best of Snow's novels,
The Masters, the characters do not change or develop.

B814   PARKER, ROBERT ANTHONY. Review of The Malcontents.
America, 126, no. 23 (10 June 1972) 618-19.
    The work is controlled, relevant, passionless,
ironic. The young malcontents think, talk and act
alike. "The problem is that we enter the book after
the action, the plotting of the scandal, has stopped.
Then we leave it before the seven [conspirators] can
confront the next episode in their lives. Meanwhile
moral responsibility vies with self-preservation in
an endless series of conversations that indicate
Snow sees drama in talk rather than action." The
book is devoid of restlessness, indignation, passion,
action, or confrontation. Questions Snow's position
as an artist. 600w

B815   PORTERFIELD, CHRISTOPHER. "Notable." Time, 99
(12 June 1972) 89-90.
    Snow merely provides a distant echo of the youth
culture, and his claim that these revolutionaries will
determine the future is mistaken. "On closer examination, however, they turn out to be merely incipient
Snow men, i.e., earnest, solemn, long-winded committee
members." The style is prosaic and clumsy. 230w

B816   SCHLUETER, PAUL. "Unconvincing Radicals." Christian
Century, 89, nos. 39-40 (1 November 1972) 1105-07.

The motivation is unclear and unconvincing; the
plot is anti-climatic. The ". . . characters are wooden
and stereotyped (the radicals, for instance, include a
sexually emancipated girl, an impractical idealist,
a decadent pothead, a Jewish intellectual and a visionary
girl suitably named Emma)." The style is clumsy and
graceless. The moral, that people are venal and grasping,
is a truth suitable for kindergarten.

B817   SPACKS, PATRICIA MEYER. "Fiction Chronicle." Hudson
Review, 25, no. 3 (Autumn 1972) 508.
Omnibus review. Both dons and revolutionaries
struggle for power and hope to achieve love. In the
process, they shape nations and individuals. The thesis
may be true, but the novel seems mechanical and therefore
false. 200w

B818   THWAITE, ANTHONY. "In the Comfortably Ruminative Snow
Manner." New York Times Book Review, 7 May 1972, p. 5.
"The tone is flat and explicatory, laying down
sentences like railroad ties, without graces but also
without many foibles. . . . The characterization is
matchingly stolid. . . ." Snow's obsessions are power
and its motives. The novel is too willed. The student
meetings are reminiscent of cadres and cells of the
30s rather than the 70s. "Snow is always serious,
humane and concerned. What is missing, here as elsewhere in his novels, is an essential grip on so much
that makes people various, complex and mysterious, and
any real imaginative apprehension of anything beyond
the decencies and conventions." 650w

B819   WAUGH, AUBERON. "C.P. Snow: Shows Promise." Spectator,
229, no. 7515 (8 July 1972) 54.
Snow's social observations are inept and his
moral judgments venal, but he reveals the talents of
a detective thriller writer in this book. The dialogue
of the young conspirators is bad; it misses the
essential solemnity of their drug-taking rituals. The
book has a technical fault: too many characters are
introduced at the beginning, a fact which leads to
confusion, and forces the reader to develop his critical
faculties "at the expense of his willingness to suspend
disbelief."

B820   WEBER, BROM. Review of The Malcontents. Saturday
Review, 55, no. 25 (17 June 1972) 76-77.
The novel provides fascinating evidence that
science can enrich literature. Witness Stephen Freer's
references to entropy in an early part of the book,

319

and the reference to Werner Heisenberg's principle
of indeterminacy in one of the last chapters. "The
Malcontents is an exciting novel, displaying not only
the continued ripening of Snow's literary art, but also
a model for those still doubtful that science and art
can be harmoniously combined." 550w

B821   WEEKS, EDWARD. Review of The Malcontents. Atlantic,
        229, no. 6 (June 1972) 110-11.
        ". . . Lord Snow is expert in the scenes which
tell us why Stephen has turned against his parents
and through them against society, and how in all like-
lihood he will be reconciled by his love for his camp
follower, Tess. Readers who persevere through the arid
beginning will be rewarded." 450w

B822   WILLIAMS, DAVID. "Good Intentions on Strange Ground."
        The Times (London), 29 June 1972, p. 12.
        You must be surefooted to write about the younger
generation, and Snow fails in the attempt. His
vernally green desperadoes surely could have given
themselves away without help from an inside traitor.
For them to meet together in order to spot the Judas
is a very odd thing to do. The novel is easy to read;
it conveys some idea of certain terrible notions of
duty; and it refuses to leap from the unknown to certitude
with the help of image or phrase. "But somehow these
youngsters never talk right. You feel their dialogue
has been listened to intently through an ear trumpet,
and become, with the best of intentions, garbled in the
writing down." 400w

In Their Wisdom. 1974.

B823   ANON. Review of In Their Wisdom. Kirkus, 42 (1
        September 1974) 963.
        Snow, like Galsworthy, examines the manners and
morals of the British Establishment. The style is
not comparable to that of Anthony Powell, but the
sequence has become a "literary document of our time."
The "transcendent moments" of this book are the death
of a proud man, the healing of a sick one, and Jenny
Rastall's rationale for her love. "All in all a
thoughtful and rewarding book."

B824   ANON. Review of In Their Wisdom. Publishers' Weekly,
        206 (30 September 1974) 52-53.
        He is an old-fashioned but solidly satisfying story

teller whose "Powers of observation are first-rate as
he looks at his people, muses on many aspects of
heritage and inheritance in this rewarding novel."

B825   ANON. "A Matter of Money." Times Literary Supplement,
11 October 1974, p. 1109.
        Snow, often criticized for his failure to show
the whole of life, has here written a novel that, in
its breadth and compassion, compares well with the best
of the Strangers and Brothers sequence. Praises Snow's
probing of the nerve ends of his characters: ". . . the
terror and isolation of facing a painful and messy death,
the humiliations of disease, the subterfuges and self-
deception of obsessive sexual love." The book is
pervaded by pessimism; but it is an invigorating
pessimism which sharpens perception.

B826   ANON. Review of In Their Wisdom. Booklist, 71, no. 5
(1 November 1974) 269.
        "The story line is comfortable but the style
unremarkable." 50w

B827   ANON. Review of In Their Wisdom. Economist, 253, no.
6849 (30 November 1974) 8.
        [See the separately paged "Survey" section of
this work.] The work is inferior to any volume in
the Strangers and Brothers sequence. England's decline
into barbarity and the pervasiveness of death are
natural themes for a man of 70. The Snow of the sequence
is better than Galsworthy, but in its depiction of the
relations between men and women, this book ranks below
Galsworthy.

B828   ANON. "Briefly Noted." New Yorker, 50, no. 47
(13 January 1975) 90.
        "His characters are entangled in a web of financial
maneuvers and lethal medical facts. Dignity, manners,
intelligence, accomplishment, and honor are the main
distinctions in this cold world. Love and happiness
exist, but almost in the form of clinical specimens.
Lord Snow's style, which is marked by a personal
mixture of off-handedness and solemnity, seems
appropriate for expressing his bleak views." 200w

B829   ANON. Review of In Their Wisdom. Choice, 12, no. 1
(March 1975) 78.
        The novel "is often turgid in style, some of the
characters are unmemorable (and hard to distinguish
from each other), and the several plots—political,

legal, romantic, and even medical--are held together
only tenuously. Nevertheless, the author is very
wise in a worldly way and his concerns are worth
attending to. He is also frequently entertaining."
100w

B830   CUNNINGHAM, VALENTINE. "Money Talks." New Statesman,
        88 (18 October 1974) 848.
             Suggests that, for all Snow's professed concern
        with money, he neglects the genuinely poor; therefore
        the novel is low on reality and high on social myopia.
        The two redeeming events of the book, the marriage of
        the poor peer to the litigant's daughter, and the
        successful operation for Parkinson's disease, do not
        redeem the work.

B831   FULLER, EDMUND. "Absorbing Battle Over a Man's Will."
        Wall Street Journal, 28 January 1975, p. 16.
             The Malcontents was disappointing, but this
        account of a struggle over a will almost ranks with
        the best of the Strangers and Brothers sequence.
        It is aimed at the mind, not the guts and genitals
        and, for all its restrained pessimism, Snow's symbol
        of hope is the successful cryogenic brain surgery for
        Parkinson's disease. It is "timely, compellingly
        interesting, and worldly-wise in a non-Bunyanesque,
        non-cynical sense."

B832   GRAY, LARRY. Review of In Their Wisdom. Library
        Journal, 99, no. 19 (1 November 1974) 2873.
             The novel left him apprehensive and bored. "The
        central problem is that the reader never really gets
        down to caring who wins the law suit and the auxiliary
        characters and the subplots simply don't provide enough
        interest." The most significant and engaging parts of
        the book are inner musings of the characters about
        their destiny in an England grown gray and second-rate.
        180w

B832a   HILL, WILLIAM B. Review of In Their Wisdom. Best
        Sellers, 34 (1 March 1975) 528-29.
             "All these people are vital and enlist sympathy
        or antipathy. The adoration of Mrs. Underwood and
        Liz for the unspeakable Julian awakens just the
        reaction it should. . . But the mantle of Trollope
        has fallen all too heavily on Lord Snow's shoulders.
        He is as precise as the surgeon who operates on Lord
        Sedgwick. Precision in words, however, can often be

achieved only at the price of verbosity, and as an
admirer of Lord Snow's work I must finally admit that
he is tedious. Yet there is no prose more accurate
than his." 350w

B833   JONES, D.A.N. "In Their Enclaves." New Review, 1
        (November 1974) 76.
            The book explores the ways in which natural human
        feeling is affected by the transfer of money from one
        generation to another. The older characters indulge in
        much wounding self-introspection; they accuse themselves
        of selfishness and then, in ritualistic formulas, excuse
        themselves on the ground that they are no more selfish
        than the run of the human race. These casuistic exer-
        cises prepare the way for chapter 36, "a beautiful
        account of pure, unselfish feelings working in harmony.
        This is the climax." It is excellently constructed
        and therapeutic in the sense that one passage suggests
        that rich men have no right to be rich. "Among
        several noteworthy elements in Lord Snow's attitudes is
        an extreme left-wing tendency kept under careful control."

B834   MADDOCKS, MELVIN. "Cash and Curry." Time, 104, no. 22
        (25 November 1974) 120-E7.
            "C.P. Snow continues to operate as the self-
        assigned recording secretary of the last gentleman's
        club on earth [i.e. The House of Lords]." Reminds
        Maddocks of Trollope--and reading Trollope is like
        walking down corridors of carpet. The novel merely
        confirms that power and justice are two different
        things, a point Snow readers were told a dozen novels
        ago. At the time of the Angry Young Men, he would
        have been called a banal old fogy.

B835   O'HARA, J.D. "C.P. Snow; Like Chinese Water Torture,
        the Persistent Drip of Platitudes." New York Times
        Book Review, 27 October 1974, p. 7.
            The novel is marred by platitudes, commonplace
        insights and farfetched plotting. The assertions
        about the law, the House of Lords, the current state
        of England, are all vague. The writing is bad. "A
        coronary is described as not heartening, a character
        is able physically to retract her tears. Another is
        invincibly acquiescent." Snow was manful in the face
        of Leavis' silly attack, but this work is pedestrian,
        an example of "Late Victorian Humdrum, that style in
        which an all-knowing but coy narrator. . . sluggishly
        unfolds a story patched together from conventional
        plot elements. . . ." 750w

B836   OKA, TAKASHI. "C.P. Snow's Lovingly Crafted New Novel."
<u>Christian Science Monitor</u>, 30 January 1975, p. 10.
     Considers it "pleasant but minor Snow, lacking
the bite and vigor of the <u>Strangers and Brothers</u> series
and its march through the corridors of power. Most
of the novel's characters have their lives behind them;
'wisdom' lies not in challenging fate but in coming to
terms, gracefully or reluctantly as the case may be,
with gathering twilight." 270w

B837   PARKER, DEREK. "Fiction." <u>The Times</u> (London), 10
October 1974, p. 13a.
     Snow displays a slight impatience with plot and
his true interest in the development of human
character has enabled him to present two brilliantly
effective set pieces: a meeting of two elderly, dying
peers and an account of a brain operation.

B838   PARKHILL-RATHBONE, JAMES. "The Public and Private Faces
of C.P. Snow." <u>Books and Bookmen</u>, 20 (March 1975) 55-56.
     The upper class characters are surrounded by an
invisible bubble of well being, and the reader's
sympathy cannot penetrate this bubble even when the
characters are on their deathbeds. The book is somber,
and Snow has the ability to describe the rich and
powerful members of the <u>ancien regime</u>. "Stripped for
the surgeon like Hillmorton; naked to an unrewarding
passion like Liz, the powerful rich are here touched
where the nerves are laid bare, where suffering is at
its most universal." 800w

B839   SHRAPNEL, NORMAN. "Life and Love Above the Snow-Line."
<u>Manchester Guardian Weekly</u>, 19 October 1974, p. 20.
     [Omnibus review.] "The distinguished characters
. . . . so mix their medical and financial operations
that you can never be sure which slipped portfolio or
which falling equities are going to prove fatal. But
even the most devoted lawyers and accountants, the
priesthood of those socio-professional orders, can't
save us from the great Tax Collector in the end."
The novel has a feeble heartbeat. The best scene in
it concerns two oldish, dying peers who discuss their
lack of achievement with bleak realism. 200w

B840   SYMONS, JULIAN. Review of <u>In Their Wisdom</u>. <u>Critic</u>, 33
no. 3 (March-April 1975) 73.
     Snow creditably avoids smugness, bad temper or mere
repetitiveness—those dangers of a novelist in his
late sixties. "The characterization varies between

assurance in dealing with the peers and lawyers to distinct uncertainty in handling Julian Underwood and his mistress. Sexual activities are something Snow cannot bring himself to deal with except by indirection, and here his evasions make the account of a relationship inadequate. . . .Yet it is still a fine novel in a tradition of total naturalism, very evidently the work of a generous and humane mind." 850w

B841   STORY, JACK TREVOR. "Lid Off the Lords." Listener, 92, no. 2376 (10 October 1974) 482.
       "All the conniving, and the conspiracies, all the ambition and force you found in the Lewis Eliot books have come down to the depressions and confusions you get at the end of an epoch--this is Snow's message." Recalls a meeting with Snow when Story was employed by Marconi and William Cooper on Snow: 'I call him Snowball, he calls me Snowflake and Pamela Fairy Snow.'

B842   THWAITE, ANTHONY. "A Matter of Money." London Observer, 13 October 1974, p. 29.
       Snow is clearly interested in the workings of small groups racked by abstract power struggles and the quirk of individual temperment. In this novel he deals with the law and the House of Lords. "Here, as before, I'm impressed by Snow's massive, bleak but humane urge to display the collective drives and impulses of a varied cast, much less impressed by the magisterial yet indelicate way in which he actually gets the job done." The style is rough and ready; the characterization is glutinously ponderous; and Snow's generalizations are stated with a neutralising blandness.

B843   WEEKS, EDWARD. Review of In Their Wisdom. Atlantic, 234, no. 6 (December 1974) 124-25.
       Mostly plot summary with asides on Julian Underwood ("an ill drawn charlatan") and praise for the thoughtful characterization of Lords Hillmorton, Ryle and Lorimer. "The trial with its savor of scandal, the loquacity of the judge, and the fraternity of the rival barristers are admirably described." 440w

B848   no entry

Trollope: His Life and Art. 1975.

B845   ANON. Review of Trollope: His Life and Art. Kirkus, 43 (15 September 1975) 1110.

". . . undoubtedly the season's lushest bit of
Trollopia, but it will be of more interest to people
who don't want to know an awful lot about Trollope
than people who do." Snow does his best with Trollope's
prosaic later life, but the material is slender, and
the biographical speculations based on Trollope's novels
seem somewhat arbitrary. The notion of percipience is
awkward but pleasing. Analysis of Trollope's novels
is replaced by a system of mathematical ratings. "In
sum, an affectionate, highly personal, meandering
tribute marred by a high-handed tone and occasional
critical naivete."

B846   ANON. Review of Trollope: His Life and Art. Publishers'
Weekly, 208, no. 16 (20 October 1975) 68.
        Trollope's claim that he wrote only for money
damaged his reputation for years. Snow's belief that
Trollope was more than a social historian is evident.
"Snow's wisdom, wit and insight make this an attractive
and worthy tribute from one public servant and novelist
to another."

B847   ANON. "Dogged As Does It." Economist, 257 (1 November
1975) 103-04.
        There are no real affinities between Trollope and
Snow, and the biography sheds no dazzling new light.
The Post Office records are skilfully deployed; the
dissertations on the survival of Victorian U-speech
patterns and on the problem of presenting the working
of an individual mind in a convincing literary way are
brief but valuable. The style is reminiscent of
Daily Express but the book is still "the best all-round
account we have of the enigmatic ironist in whom the
Victorian character found its most faithful and honest
recorder. . . ."

B848   ANON. "Trollope: His Life and Art." Booklist, 72
(15 December 1975) 541.
        A brilliant psychological and literary delineation
of Trollope's life and art.

B849   ANON. Review of Trollope: His Life and Art. New
Yorker, 51, no. 47 (12 January 1976) 91.
        "A short but fulfilling and even probing study of
perhaps the most durable of the great Victorians." The
review quotes Snow's definition of percipience, said
to be a combination of insight, empathy, and a
diachronic vision that enabled Trollope to see a person,
not only in the present, but in the past and future.
210w

B850   ANON. Review of <u>Trollope: His Life and Art</u>. <u>British Book News</u>, January 1976, pp. 61–62.
        The illustrations are of high quality, and the treatment of Trollope is sympathetic; but it should be noted that Snow is at times "pleasantly speculative" when the facts are unknown and unknowable. The claim to scholarship is unsound and unwarranted. "Snow's scholarship is the weakest feature of a book which contains many small and some large errors. This should not deter the general reader from this very handsome and enjoyable work." 200w

B851   ANON. Review of <u>Trollope: His Life and Art</u>. <u>Choice</u>, 12, no. 12 (February 1976) 1576.
        Snow's reassessment, which counters the somber image of Trollope by Victorian critics, will place Trollope "alongside those of Dickens and Thackeray as major contributions to Victorian fiction. This work will bring about a renewed interest in Trollope's work and a reevaluation that will raise him in the estimate of modern critics." 170w

B852   ANON. Review of <u>Trollope: His Life and Art</u>. <u>Horn Book</u>, 52, no. 3 (June 1976) 321–22.
        Considers it a warm, personal appraisal of Trollope.

B853   BROOKES, GERRY H. "Trollope Illustrated." <u>Prairie Schooner</u>, 50, no. 2 (Summer 1976) 182–83.
        It is a pleasant introduction which supplements the <u>Autobiography</u> and Sadleir's biography. Snow himself, a knowledgeable guide, bulks somewhat large as the book begins, but the writing becomes more unobtrusive as he deals with Trollope as author and civil servant. Snow's emphasis on Trollope's unfortunate childhood and relationship with Kate Field is noted. The comments about Trollope's art are "just enough to make a specialist reader wish he'd say more. Altogether this book is spirited, a bit of an adventure. Trollope readers will enjoy it, and it may set others to reading his novels. . . ." 400w

B854   CAPOUYA, EMILE. Review of <u>Trollope: His Life and Art</u>. <u>Nation</u>, 221, no. 18 (29 November 1975) 573.
        The biography is informative, and Snow's "pleasant tone and andante pace" conceal the fact that a great deal of ground is covered. Snow's common sense and decent restraints are also useful for a would-be biographer of Trollope. 400w

B855   CARY, CECILE WILLIAMSON. Review of <u>Trollope: His Life</u>
        <u>and Art</u>. <u>Antioch Review</u>, 34, no. 3 (Spring 1976)
        374-75.
            Finds the book a delight. Snow's defense of
        Trollope's machine-like writing habits is sound, and
        his insistence on Trollope's stature is justified.
        200w

B856   DENNIS, NIGEL. "Keeping the Secret." <u>New York</u>
        <u>Review of Books</u>, 22, no. 20 (11 December 1975) 34-35.
            The book is "badly written in a self-assured manner,
        and very scatterbrained." It reveals the jumpy tempo
        and intermittent vagaries more appropriate to a lecture,
        or work of dictation. Snow fails to explain the
        excellences of Trollope which endeared themselves to
        Tolstoy. To state, as Snow does, that Trollope's
        excellence is due to his percipience, is to substitute
        a word for an explanation. If Trollope's excellence
        is to be found in the dialogue of his novels, Snow
        does not penetrate the secret of that hidden special
        quality; he merely gives a "long talk on British speech
        habits instead, a subject of comparatively little
        interest and quite beside the point." 1350w

B857   FULLER, EDMUND. "Fresh Recognition for an Enduring
        Author." <u>Wall Street Journal</u>, 15 December 1975,
        p. 12.
            Snow and Trollope were both interested in the
        inner workings of the British Civil Service and
        fascinated by worldly and political affairs in
        ecclesiastical societies (Trollope) and university
        groups (Snow). Both novelists show "great detachment
        in observing a range of types and political styles
        within these arenas." Fuller also states that Snow
        demonstrates the quality of percipience for which
        Trollope is praised. The rest of the review is a
        biographical sketch of Trollope culled from Snow's
        book. 1000w

B858   GERSH, GABRIEL. Review of <u>Trollope: His Life and Art</u>.
        <u>Western Humanities Review</u>, 30, no. 2 (Spring 1976)
        175-77.
            This extended biographical essay on Trollope is
        appropriate because Snow and Trollope "share an interest
        in the surface and details of life, a style capable of
        deeper resonances than is apparent, an unobtrusive but
        remarkable sense of reality, a psychological percep-
        tiveness that can easily be missed, and a deep concern

for political institutions and the moral pressures
exerted on politicians and civil servants." Snow's
assumption that John Eames is a Trollopian self-
portrait of the Post Office period is unwarranted, and
his discussions of Trollopian dialogue and characters'
states of mind are embarrassingly sketchy.

B859   GREEN, BENNY. "Snow Bound." Spectator, 235, no. 7686
        (18 October 1978) 511.
            Trollope wrote that an author's first duty is to
        make himself pleasant. This work is marred by
        hackneyed phrases, baffling constructions (which
        can be understood only "with the aid of a block and
        tackle and a few sticks of gelignite"), bad proof-
        reading, wretched jargon, and misleading advice about
        the desirable order in which to read the Barchester and
        Palliser novel sequence. If, for all these reasons,
        Snow's book cannot be understood, it is clearly not
        pleasant.

B860   HALL, N. JOHN. Review of Trollope: His Life and Art.
        Nineteenth Century Fiction, 31, no. 2 (September 1976)
        212-16.
            The work makes a modest contribution to Trollope
        studies, and Snow "writes with obvious delight and
        enthusiasm for his subject." New material and original
        insights are present in Snow's account of Trollope's
        Post Office career. The two chapters on Trollope's
        fiction fall "sadly short of uncovering the secret of
        Trollope's art." Snow's shortcomings included un-
        warranted inference, undue emphasis on Henry Taylor
        and an "informal, somewhat slangy" style. Tolstoy's
        remark "Trollope kills me. . . with his excellence"
        refers to The Bertrams (1865) not to The Prime Minister
        (1877) and Snow's propensity to link Tolstoy and
        Trollope partly on the strength of that remark leads
        Hall to quote references to Trollope culled from the
        90 volume Jubilee edition of Tolstoy's works. 1500w

B861   MARVIN, JOHN R. Review of Trollope: His Life and Art.
        Library Journal, 100, no. 20 (15 November 1975) 2139-40.
            Trollope's chief admirers were his fellow novelists
        Tolstoy and James, and "Snow's own social perceptions
        seem ideally suited to this truly full-dimensional
        portrait. . . .The whole of it is a work of art as
        well as of notable scholarship." 110w

B862   MILLER, J. HOLLIS. "The Truth about Trollope." Yale
        Review, 65, no. 3 (Spring 1976) 450-55.
            The illustrations are splendid, but often tangential.

[Many of the other reviewers made the same comment.]
Snow rightfully awards Trollope a high place among the
world's great novelists, and compares him to Proust,
Stendhal, Galdos--even to Dostoevsky! Notes Snow's
high regard for Trollope's American critics, the
enduring nature of Trollope's dialogue, and Trollope's
intimate knowledge of the Church and Civil Service.
However, Snow's reaffirmation of the paradigm of
realism, and his use of words like percipience are
somewhat inadequate critical terms which oversimplify
the problem of theorizing about the novel form.

B863   MORRIS, JOHN ROBERT. Review of <u>Trollope: His Life and
        Art</u>. <u>Best Sellers</u>, 35 (January 1976) 328.
             The biographical profile of Trollope comes
        perilously close to psychological guesswork. Snow
        seems compelled to treat the writer and his family as
        fictional characters rather than people. The critical
        section Trollope's art is perceptive and convincing.
        "Of course Snow is a brilliant prose-writer. One is
        delighted to encounter a great writer through the eyes
        of another. . . .Snow's English is a complete joy to
        read."

B864   NYE, ROBERT. "Trollope Revival Bid." <u>Christian
        Science Monitor</u>, 17 December 1975, p. 19.
             This well-written and capably researched book
        makes the critical case for a Trollope reappraisal
        with penetrating intelligence. "All in all, this
        is an attractive and absorbing study of a fine novelist,
        and I hope it succeeds in its declared aim of winning
        new readers for the best of Trollope's books." 330w

B865   RABAN, JONATHAN. "The Secrets of Survival." <u>New
        Statesman</u>, 90, no. 2327 (24 October 1975) 505-06.
             Trollope, a secretive man, pathological ironist
        and consummate actor, has eluded his biographers.
        His fiction, equally elusive and "morally icy," has
        eluded his critics. "He is an engrossing, dangerous,
        maddening character; and people who write books about
        him usually end up wrecked on that huge, self-protective
        reef of Trollope's irony. C.P. Snow succeeds in
        avoiding being wrecked by employing the cautious but
        useful tactic of not trying very hard to land. . . .
        Nevertheless, it is to be welcomed for the way in which
        it clears a few patches and corners of the dreadfully
        oxidized portrait of one of the most misunderstood
        writers in the language." Snow's notion of percipience
        does not go far enough, and to praise the plain
        Trollopian prose is to neglect the complex Trollopian

narrator. [Brilliant essay--but much more about
Trollope than Snow's Trollope.]

B866   RICHARDSON, JOANNA. "Pallisers and Barchester."
       History Today, 25, no. 12 (December 1975) 859-60.
             Notes that Snow consulted unpublished Trollope
       letters at Princeton as well as the Post Office
       records and observes that these researches confirm
       some known facts. "It is perhaps best described as
       an affectionate impression of Trollope and his times.
       Lord Snow writes in a relaxed, not to say colloquial
       manner about a fellow novelist." Quotes Hawthorne's
       judgment of Trollope's novels, and considers the book
       a useful introduction to Trollope and his world.

B867   SHRAPNEL, NORMAN. "Troubled Trollope." Manchester
       Guardian Weekly, 26 October 1975, p. 27.
             Trollope is one of the literary plain dealers
       who, for various reasons, has baffled posterity. His
       biography is equally baffling. Snow's supposition
       that Trollope's novel, The Three Clerks, describes
       Trollope's early adult life, may be tenable. Snow
       describes Trollope's remark that his early adult life
       was an uncommonly happy one as shouting against the
       dark. The remark is shrewd and sympathetic. It is
       a welcome critical picture book above all for its
       contrast between the sun-lit scenes of Harrow and the
       actual psychological hell endured there by the day-
       boy, Anthony Trollope.

B868   SISSON, C.H. "Romance and Red Tape." Times Literary
       Supplement, 5 December 1975, p. 1464.
             In this goggle-box of a book Snow has interpreted
       new material on the Post Office career of Trollope and
       "we should have been more interested in the originals"
       than the interpretation. The tone of the text is
       jaunty and helpful--but Snow does not present the
       proof that the Americans have done penetrating work
       on Trollope. Snow defends Trollope with "superfluous
       stoutness"--and Trollope can well defend himself.
       "Lord Snow, one sometimes feels, is tempted to identify
       his own case with that of his subject." Snow is more
       interesting on Trollope the civil servant than the
       novelist. 1400w

B869   TOWERS, ROBERT. Review of Trollope: His Life and Art.
       New York Times Book Review, 16 November 1975, pp. 5, 16.
             Considers the similarities between the novels and
       careers of Trollope and Snow. Praises Snow's zeal in

establishing the facts of Trollope's later Post Office career. "He gives us a vivid and coherent image of the gregarious, noisy, fox-hunting clubman who regularly wrote two thousand words before breakfast—a proud, diffident, wounded man who deliberately tried to thicken his own skin." 1300w

B870   WADE, ROSALIND. "A Fresh Assessment of Trollope." Contemporary Review, 228, no. 1321 (February 1976) 108-09.
"With the sympathy for the man and his personal problems, C.P. Snow is entirely successful in bringing Trollope to life. One has the impression of Lord Snow walking alongside his subject, noting and interpreting his virtues and shortcomings, like a trusted confidante." 300w

B871   WALL, STEPHEN. "Snow's Trollope." London Observer, 19 October 1975, p. 27.
Snow's book adds very little to existing scholarship and is marked by speculation about Trollope's early life and the real-life sources of his heroines. He does not give a detailed technical or psychological analysis of Trollope's supposed percipience. His discussions of Trollope's dialogue and his characters' states of mind are embarrassingly sketchy. The book is marred by small errors of various kinds.

B872   WEINTRAUB, STANLEY. Review of Trollope: His Life and Art. New Republic, 173, no. 17 (25 October 1975) 30-31.
Snow "has written a critical biography of the nineteenth century novelist whose fiction is often thought of as an earlier counterpart to his own. The result is striking. . . .Snow furnishes the reader, in spare, matter-of-fact prose, the fabric of the milieu in which Trollope lived and worked, provides insights into Victorian bureaucracy, publishing and society, and offers lessons—from a professional—in the making of the psychologically realistic novel of moral choice." 1150w

B873   WILDMAN, JOHN HAZARD. "Trollope: Re-emphasis of a Reputation." Southern Review, 12 (April 1976) 419-21.
It is a magnificent and warm introduction to the work of a master, and Snow's account of Trollope's percipience puts the case for Trollope's ability to depict a character in the round with satisfying precision.

The Realists. 1978.

B874   ANON. Review of The Realists. New Yorker, 54, no.
        40 (20 November 1978) 234.
            "These essays are wholly engaging. Lord Snow
        is a shrewd critic, alive to the imperfections of the
        masterpieces he discusses, as well as to the infirmities
        of character of their creators, and he never lets us
        forget that he is dealing with extraordinary human
        beings, all of whom, in one way or another, prevailed
        over circumstantial adversities."

B875   ANON. "Eight of the Best." Economist, 269, no. 7058
        (9 December 1978) 123-24.
            Snow provides recherché, sometimes speculative
        details, about his subjects. Dostoevsky receives
        the best treatment. The sketch of Henry James is
        patronizing, and the portrait of Dickens is not very
        convincing. "Although he attempts no very scholarly
        analysis of their work, in his own hyperbolic and
        eccentric manner Lord Snow presents them with an
        immediacy as vivid as their fiction, to which the
        book is a lively introduction."

B876   BYATT, A.S. "Worldly Wise." New Statesman, 96, no.
        2485 (3 November 1978) 586-87.
            "There is room," as in Snow's work, "for a study
        of bureaucracy, or jobs, or heritage that is not
        presented only as a grotesque phantasmagoria." So it
        would have been valuable if Snow's study of eight
        realists had concentrated on those factors that led
        to their choice of subject matter. In fact, Snow's
        book consists of mannerly biographical essays which
        sum up the plots and values of certain great realistic
        novels. The biographies read like Snow's novels,
        worldly-wise, judicious with curious excursions into
        the sexual energies and proclivities of his novelists.
        Summarizes Snow's conclusion that literary realists
        tend, as a group, to be short, fat, and bad at
        mathematics; and they flourish in energetic societies
        characterized by individual and social hope. "I found
        the essays interesting in proportion as I knew less
        about the writer concerned. . . .I only really enjoyed
        the chapter on Galdos, of whose work I was ignorant,
        and whom I now want to read."

B877   CORY, JAMES M. "Lord Snow as Critic and Critical
        Object." Philadelphia Inquirer, 14 January 1979,
        p. 12K.

"Snow's portraits are loaded with information and affection. They are drawn so skillfully and with such discrimination that they succeed in giving the reader a flesh-and-blood sense of the novelists and their work." Observes that Balzac the immoralist made many people happy; Tolstoy the aspiring saint "treated his wife like a fleshpot" and ignored his illegitimate son. The chapter on Proust is a biography in miniature. "Included among his "Realists" are the greatest novelists who ever have lived. Whether Snow may join their ranks cannot yet be decided."

B878   CRAIN, JANE LARKIN. Review of The Realists. Saturday Review, 6, no. 1 (6 January 1979) 56.
        Snow's congenial premise is that we turn to great literature for magnification, clarification and insight into the stuff of actual experience, is exhilarating and consoling. This work animates the lives of the great realists. Some of Snow's judgments will continue to be debated as long as there are readers. "A love of literature itself, and a passionate curiosity about the human enterprise, animate every page of The Realists. The book does what the best criticism ought to do-- sends us back to the texts themselves, to be overcome once again with their power to move and enlighten us."

B879   GRUMBACH, DORIS. "Without Benefit of Critics: C.P. Snow as Dr. Seuss." The Chronicle of Higher Education, 17, no. 13 (27 November 1978) R12.
        As a serious work of criticism the work is a failure: the biographical material, extracted from standard sources, is repeated on different pages; the syntax is repetitive and deadening; and Snow's bio-graphical interest is focussed on the height, sex lives and earnings of his authors. As a "primer for fiction, a good-humored guide for the beginning student of literature," this ungrammatical work, filled with casual slang and unending, enthusiastic superlatives, may be considered a success.

B880   KIRBY, DAVID. Review of The Realists. America, 139, no. 22 (30 December 1978) 501-02.
        This book raises the suspicion that the realists are the great egoists of literature rather than the romantics. Snow does an excellent job of whetting the appetite of his readers. Unfortunately, Trollope, Flaubert, George Eliot, Howells, Twain, Turgenev and Hardy are omitted. Stendhal seems out of place in this company. Snow refers to James' The Traveller,

when he plainly means The American. Still, despite
these critical cavils, the book is written with charm
and lucidity. The main strength of the book "lies in
its attention to detail and [which] tells us, among
other things, that both Balzac and Tolstoy lost their
teeth early ('but nineteenth century women must have
been accustomed to dental inadequacies.')"

B881   WEBSTER, HARVEY CURTIS. Review of The Realists. New
Republic, 179, no. 25 (16 December 1978) 30.
        Of these bio-bibliographical essays, or psychographs,
as they were called by Gamaliel Bradford, the one on
Balzac is perceptive and empathetic, while those on
Proust and Tolstoy are disappointing. "Dostoevsky seems
to Snow to be a spiritual brother despite the entire
lack of superficial resemblances between them. . . ."
Notes that the dialectic between the free and dissident
soul and the decencies of social behavior, one of
Dostoevsky's preoccupations, is also "to understate,
a major concern in Snow's Strangers and Brothers."
600w

Appendix I

<u>Snow in the London Times; A Chronological Account</u>

Appointment, September 21, 1945, p. 2c.

Directorship, March 13, 1947, p. 9g.

<u>View Over the Park</u> reviewed, August 31, 1950, p. 6e.

<u>The New Men</u> reviewed, May 1, 1954, p. 8f. Plays in Authors v.
    Book League Cricket match; photo, June 10, 1954, p. 16.

<u>The New Men</u>: award, March 2, 1955, p. 10d.

Novel [<u>Homecomings</u>] September 13, 1956, p. 13b.

K.B. [Knighthood] January 1, 1957, p. 4a. On Hungarian authors
    (letters with others), October 29, 1957, p. 11f.

<u>The Conscience of the Rich</u>, March 27, 1958, p. 13d. University
    appointment, October 27, 1958, p. 10e.

Plans for Rede lecture, January 22, 1959, p. 12d. Rede lecture,
    May 8, 1959, p. 7a. Honorary degree plans, July 30, 1959,
    p. 8b. Honorary degree, November 9, 1959, p. 12d.

Honorary degree, January 13, 1960, p. 14e. On Russian book
    exhibition [letter] February 10, 1960, p. 11g. On Spanish
    prisoners (1. with others) March 1, 1960, p. 11d. Novel
    [<u>The Affair</u>] April 14, 1960, p. 15b. Honorary degree, May 2,
    1960, p. 7c. University appointment, July 14, 1960, p. 7e.
    In United States--delivers Godkin lectures, December 2, 1960,
    p. 13c. On nuclear warfare [speech] December 28, 1960, p. 8a.

Comment on Lord Atlee's statement on Hiroshima atom bomb, March 28,
    1961, p. 6a. On dispute between late Prof. Lindemann and

337

Henry Tizard [letter] April 8, 1961, p. 9e. Rectorial candidate, June 24, 1961, p. 10b. The Affair: dramatization plans, July 17, 1961, p. 14c. On nuclear disarmament [speech] September 5, 1961, p. 6e. Correspondence, September 12, 1961, p. 11e; [letter] September 14, 1961, p. 13e. On libraries [speech] September 20, 1961, p. 5g. St. Andrews University rectorship: candidature, October 31, 1961, p. 12c. The Affair, September 22, 1961, p. 16a. Elected rector of St. Andrews University, November 13, 1961, p. 14e. Editor, Winter's Tales 7, December 7, 1961, p. 18b.

To have eye operation, April 9, 1962, p. 10b. Welcomed by St. Andrews University students before inauguration as Rector, April 13, 1962, p. 14d. Installed: photo, April 14, 1962, p. 5a. Criticism by Dr. F.R. Leavis, March 1, 1962, p. 12d. Eye operation unsuccessful, May 1, 1962, p. 6f (and 12a in 5*). The New Men: stage adaptation, September 7, 1962, p. 15a. The Affair: stage performance in New York, September 25, 1962, p. 14d. To have eye operation, October 30, 1962, p. 12c. Eye operation: condition, November 3, 1962, p. 8b; November 5, 1962, p. 10b; November 6, 1962, p. 12f. Sight saved, November 10, 1962, p. 8a; November 13, 1962, p. 12f. Leaving hospital: photo, November 14, 1962, p. 6e. Gift to St. Andrews University Students Representative Council, November 15, 1962, p. 15b; luncheon in honour--on art [speech] December 8, 1962, p. 5f. The Affair: United States tour closing early, December 22, 1962, p. 6d.

Russian university honorary degree--invited to Rostov to receive degree, March 26, 1963, p. 14c. On House of Lords reform [letter] March 28, 1963, p. 13c. On Oxbridge snobbery [speech] May 2, 1963, p. 7a. The Masters; adapted for stage, May 6, 1963, p. 6b. On business school proposal; underdeveloped countries [speech] May 7, 1963, p. 7c. Signatory to declaration against performance of plays in South African theatres with colour bar, June 26, 1963, p. 12d. On typhoid outbreak [speech in Parliament] July 2, 1963, p. 14b. Libel action by, August 1, 1963, p. 8d. Russian honorary degree, October 4, 1963, p. 12c. "The Two Cultures: A Second Look," October 25, 1963, p. 12c. Leading article reference, October 25, 1963, p. 13d. Correspondence, October 31, 1963, p. 13e.

"The Two Cultures: And a Second Look," February 20, 1964, p. 16e. Two Cultures: Civil Service experiment, May 6, 1964, p. 9a. The Fool in the Family, May 19, 1964, p. 16a. On underdeveloped countries [speech] July 14, 1964, p. 6f. In Russia, August 15, 1964, p. 5d. Calls on Mr. Wilson, October 19, 1964, p. 12b. Parliamentary Secretary, Ministry of Technology, October 20, 1964, p. 12c. Photo, biographical note, October 20, 1964, p. 8e.

Appendix I

Resigns directorship, October 24, 1964, p. 6g. Baronetcy:
style and title, October 31, 1964, p. 8g. Corridors of Power,
November 5, 1964, p. 15b. Maiden speech—management education
[speech in Parliament] November 19, 1964, pp. 6a, 12d. Science
education [speech in Parliament] December 3, 1964, p. 16a.
Extract published in Pravda [i.e. of Corridors of Power]
December 7, 1964, p. 8d. Engineers [speech] December 15, 1964,
p. 5e. Resigns from British Council, December 31, 1964, p. 7b.

On B.B.C. educational channel, broadcasting licenses [speech in
Parliament] January 21, 1965, p. 12e. Business lunches [speech]
January 29, 1965, p. 7f. Science and technology, growth rate
[speech in Parliament] February 5, 1965, p. 6g. Secondary
education [speech in Parliament]: son's education discussed
in House of Lords, February 11, 1965, p. 14b. At Harwell,
February 16, 1965, p. 8g. Speech by R. Pedley, February 18,
1965, p. 17c. Water desalination [speech in Parliament]
March 12, 1965, p. 16c. Women engineers [speech] March 23,
1965, p. 16e. Addresses Conference of Institute of Public
Relations: science and technology, two cultures [speech]
March 27, 1965, p. 10e. Opens autonomics laboratory: on
computers [speech] April 6, 1965, p. 14c. (7*). The Light
and the Dark: South African ban, April 12, 1965, p. 10f. On
fishing industry [speech] June 1, 1965, p. 16g. On arts
patronage [speech] June 24, 1965, p. 16b. Opens London
International Youth Science Fortnight: photo, July 30, 1965,
p. 7d (5*). On universities [speech in Parliament] November
3, 1965, p. 18a. On science and technology [speech in
Parliament] November 4, 1965, p. 16b. On higher education
[speech in Parliament] December 2, 1965, p. 8c. Comments on
Mr. Frank Cousins, December 4, 1965, p. 64. Leading article,
December 10, 1965, p. 13d.

To visit United States, January 19, 1966, p. 8c. In United States
—awards, January 24, 1966, p. 9e (5*). Honorary fellow,
Christ's College, February 8, 1966, p. 12c. Post Office
Savings Bank [speech in Parliament] March 1, 1966, p. 16a (5*).
On computers [speech in Parliament] March 3, 1966, p. 16a.
Health, March 5, 1966, p. 8g. Engineers, March 25, 1966,
p. 7g. To retire, March 31, 1966, p. 12b. Letter from Prime
Minister, April 7, 1966, p. 8d. Speech, April 9, 1966, p. 5e.
Cybernetic revolution [speech] April 14, 1966, p. 6e. On
Atlantic Treaty [speech in Parliament] July 3, 1966, p. 7c.
On economic situation [speech in Parliament] August 2, 1966,
p. 6a. Unveils H.G. Wells plaque: photo, September 22, 1966,
p. 12. Corridors of Power—T.V. production rehearsals: photo,
September 22, 1966, p. 20. H.G. Wells centenary lecture,
December 6, 1966, p. 12f. On brain drain [speech in Parliament]
December 22, 1966, p. 5a. On Italian flood victims [speech in
Parliament] December 22, 1966, p. 5a.

National Youth Theatre Council member, January 16, 1967, p. 12d.
On nuclear weapons [speech in Parliament] March 9, 1967, p. 22g.
Variety of Men, May 18, 1967, p. 15b. Letter, with others,
opposing war in Vietnam, May 23, 1967, p. 9. Photo, September
14, 1967, p. 14. In United States--speech on gifted children,
October 7, 1967, p. 4c. On National Library [speech in
Parliament] December 14, 1967, p. 8b.

On science [speech in Parliament] February 29, 1968, p. 5a. At
Beckshire assizes, March 29, 1968, p. 8g. On Rhodesian sanctions
[speech in Parliament] June 19, 1968, p. 6b. On Civil Service
[speech in Parliament] July 28, 1968, p. 13b. Opens Harrogate
Festival, August 9, 1968, p. 2f (6*). Diary note, September
27, 1968, p. 10h. The Sleep of Reason; cartoon, November 2, 1968,
p. 22a.

Clayesmore lecture, March 8, 1969, p. 8a. On genetic and racial
differences, April 2, 1969, p. 4g. Lord Snow compared to Dr.
Goebbels, April 9, 1969, p. 1e. Correspondance: April 11,
1969, p. 11e; April 16, 1969, p. 11c. On gifted children
[speech in Parliament] May 15, 1969, p. 6b. Invited to join
group to advise Post Office, December 3, 1969, p. 1b; article
on, December 5, 1969, p. 4f (6*).

Strangers and Brothers: plans for television series. Diary note,
August 12, 1970, p. 6d. Radio serialization, August 13, 1970,
p. 6e. Last Things, October 22, 1970, p. 8e. Views on food
population collision made in 1968 published by Oxfam; photo,
December 17, 1970, p. 3d.

Strangers and Brothers to be television series, January 14, 1971,
p. 16f. On censorship [speech in Parliament] February 4,
1971, p. 6f. To be member of Arts Council of Great Britain,
February 9, 1971, p. 14b. On population [speech in Parliament]
February 11, 1971, p. 8a. On Strangers and Brothers [complete
novel sequence] March 13, 1971, p. 17. Strangers and Brothers
to be adapted for television, March 29, 1971, p. 12e. On
joining the Common Market, May 17, 1971, p. 12c. Gives
interview on status of writer in Britain and Soviet Union;
diary note, August 11, 1971, p. 10c. Article on translation
of literature in minority languages, September 25, 1971, p. 10.
Correspondance: September 28, 1971, p. 13d; September 29,
1971, p. 15g; October 1, 1971, p. 17d; October 4, 1971, p. 13e;
October 6, 1971, p. 15d. On new novel, December 14, 1971,
p. 12f.

On regional arts grants [speech in Parliament] March 23, 1972,
p. 14b. The Malcontents, June 29, 1972, p. 12f.

George Passant, formerly Strangers and Brothers, March 8, 1973,
p. 12d. The Light and the Dark, March 8, 1973, p. 12d. On

the future of the arts, [speech in Parliament] March 22, 1973,
p. 14b. Polytechnics [speech] Times Higher Education Supplement,
May 11, 1973, p. 1b. College of Arms Bill [speech in Parliament]
May 11, 1973, p. 14d. Suggests Duke of Norfolk stage musicals,
Sunday Times, May 13, 1973, p. 2d.

Retires, February 5, 1974, p. 14b. Teacher militancy [speech in
Parliament] July 11, 1974, p. 10e. Teacher militancy [speech]
Times Educational Supplement, July 19, 1974, p. 8e. To speak
at Lord Longford's conference, September 4, 1974, p. 4f.
In Their Wisdom, October 10, 1974, p. 13a. In Their Wisdom;
photo, Sunday Times, October 13, 1974, p. 36e. Finalist for
Booker prize, October 24, 1974, p. 20d.

Performance rating in Lords; photo, May 30, 1976, p. 17.

Appendix II

Snow in The New York Times: A Chronological Account

C.P. Snow on effects of science in the novel. "Storytellers for
the Atomic Age. Novelists, says C.P. Snow, Must Face Today's
World and Link Mankind to It." January 30, 1955, Section VII,
p. 1.

J.D. Adams on C.P. Snow January 30 article on effect of science
on the novel. February 13, 1955, Section VII, p. 2, c. 2.

Snow to give Godkin lectures, Harvard University, March 27, 1960,
p. 20, c. 5.

Dartmouth College gives honorary degrees to Ambassador Chagla,
Snow, others. September 11, 1960, p. 48, c. 1.

C.P. Snow calls for more scientists in high government posts in
Western world, Godkin lecture, Harvard. December 4, 1960,
Section IV, p. 7, c. 4.

Sir Charles Snow in speech on Moral Un-Neutrality of Science at
AAAS convention urges scientists spread fruits of research
to underprivileged areas.--Sir Charles P. Snow warns that
12 or more nations have capacity to manufacture nuclear
weapons within 6 years and that it is "statistical certainty"
that in 10 years some bombs will be exploded through "accident,
folly or madness" in speech New York City. Urges scientists
take direct responsibility to seek curbs. Urges United States
to take risks inherent in tests ban. Reverend T.M. Hesburgh
and Dr. W.O. Baker query Snow views. December 28, 1960, p.
1, c. 7. Excerpts: December 28, 1960, p. 14, c. 7-8.

B. Atkinson comments on Sir Charles Snow view that humanists are
scientific illiterates. Sees need for literate scientists to
communicate with humanists. January 3, 1961, p. 26, c. 3.

Appendix II

Letter lauds Sir Charles P. Snow December 27, 1960 speech to AAAS warning of nuclear race and urging scientists take direct part in curbing it. January 7, 1961, p. 18, c. 5.

Ten British and American leaders on what they consider to be the world's greatest need. April 2, 1961, Section VI, p. 7.

Sir Charles P. Snow accepts fellowship at Advanced Studies Center, Wesleyan University. Wife Pamela Hansford Johnson gets fellowship. April 21, 1961, p. 31, c. 6.

Snow writes letter on Lewis L. Strauss review of Science and Government. Strauss replies on same page. April 23, 1961, Section VII, p. 44.

Foreign writers and artists (including Snow) elected honorary members of the National Institute of Arts and Letters. May 2, 1961, p. 42, c. 1.

B. Atkinson on Kenyon College symposium on problem of communication between humanities and science, theme propounded by Sir Charles Snow. Professor Blanshard, Dr. Teller views noted. November 3, 1961, p. 32, c. 5.

F.R. Leavis attacks author C.P. Snow as "ignorant" and his novels as "intellectual nullities." Scores Snow's famed "two cultures" concept of Western world. Snow comments. March 10, 1962, p. 23, c. 6.

British writers and scientists score Leavis' attack on Snow. March 16, 1962, p. 33, c. 8.

Letter on Professor H.R. Trevor-Roper refers to book Science and Government; editorial notes forthcoming appendix to book. March 25, 1962, Section VII, p. 38.

Snow comments on coming inauguration as Lord Rector of St. Andrews University. April 1, 1962, Section IV, p. 10, c. 3.

W. Allen article on Leavis' attack on Snow, excerpts from Leavis' lecture. April 1, 1962, Section VII, p. 10.

Snow defers eye operation to give inaugural speech as St. Andrews University rector. April 11, 1962, p. 39, c. 6.

Snow gets honorary degree. Sir C.P. Snow bids rich nations aid poor in speech at St. Andrews University. Says poverty can be ended. April 14, 1962, p. 3, c. 2.

Edmund Fuller letter on Leavis-Snow dispute. April 22, 1962, Section VII, p. 24.

Appendix II

Operation to replace detached retina fails. May 1, 1962, p. 5, c. 2.

Snow arrives United States with wife and daughter. Gives interview in article headed "Snow, on Visit, Talks of Faculty Raiding." June 13, 1962, p. 37, c. 7.

Gets honorary degree, Polytechnic Institute of Brooklyn, gives speech in which he favors more vigorous education. Deplores view that pure science is superior to applied science as "snobbish." June 14, 1962, p. 30, c. 1.

C.P. Snow, in pamphlet published as appendix to his book Science and Government, renews criticism of strategy decisions made by late F.A. Lindemann (Lord Cherwell) during World War II. Lauds role of late Sir Henry Tizard. July 12, 1962, p. 6, c. 3.

H.C. Schonberg, using music as example, disputes Snow thesis on lack of communication between arts and sciences; sees common goals. September 16, 1962, Section II, p. 15, c. 1.

Snow in New York City. Time of Hope, by V. Ketels, based on C.P. Snow novel. Article on adaptation by Mrs. Ketels, New York City teacher. She and her husband illustrated. Snow comments. September 29, 1962, p. 14, c. 5.

Snow recovering after new eye operation. November 4, 1962, p. 22, c. 1.

Remaining sight in left eye saved. November 10, 1962, p. 3, c. 4.

Snow gets honorary degree from Syracuse University. June 3, 1963, p. 59, c. 2.

Snow on importance of bridging "dangerous gulfs", gives speech in Washington. June 12, 1963, p. 40, c. 5.

Snow gets honorary degree from Temple University. June 14, 1963, p. 27, c. 5.

With Lady Snow visits U.N. Secretary General U. Thant. June 20, 1963, p. 20, c. 4.

Warns of need to limit atomic arms manufacture and tests in interview held in New York City. Criticizes United States haste to send man to moon; sees most dramatic developments on next decade in research on life processes. Snow lauds graduate education, reply to Minister Hailsham charges of inadequacy. June 21, 1963, p. 11, c. 3.

Snow reviews dispute stemming from his '59 assertion of split
between literary and scientific cultures in article published
in Times Literary Supplement [no. 3217 (October 25, 1963) 839–44].
Says "3d culture" of intellectuals from various fields rises
to bridge gap. Sees education as chief hope. Replies to
detractors, including F.R. Leavis. October 25, 1963, p. 33,
c. 8.

Dr. Hornig, soon to become Presidential science adviser, says
Snow's thesis on lack of communication between science and
humanities must be proved wrong in United States. Holds
nation can understand science if more explanations offered.
Says research pace in pure science will ultimately require
system of national priorities for basic research. Sees need
to widen geographical distribution of research centers.
November 16, 1963, p. 12, c. 3.

Sir Charles Snow urges those continuing to work after retirement
age to "step down slightly" and not block advancement of younger
persons in a speech delivered at the Governors' Conference on
Aging, New York City. Stresses he is not against employment
of elderly. May 2, 1964, p. 29, c. 2.

Named Parliamentary Secretary to Technology Minister. October 20,
1964, p. 12, c. 2.

Named peer: to be known as Lord Snow of Leicester. October 31,
1964, p. 3, c. 4.

Lord Snow comments on appointment to Technology Ministry. Glad
to return to government. November 1, 1964, p. 21, c. 1.

Lord Snow campaign against system of British education detailed.
January 13, 1965, p. 80, c. 3, 5.

Lord Snow chided for sending son to Eton and acquiring coat of
arms (design illustrated). February 27, 1965, p. 5, c. 1.

Lord Snow to get honorary degree and Centennial Engineering Medal
at Pennsylvania Military College. December 27, 1965, p. 2,
c. 5.

To get honorary degree, Bridgeport University. January 16, 1966,
p. 69, c. 3.

Lord Snow holds industrial nations are at start of a "cybernetic
revolution" in statement made before House Committee on
Science and Astronautics. Holds world poverty is chief
challenge of science. January 26, 1966, p. 19, c. 2.

Appendix II

Resigns as Parliamentary Secretary to Technology Minister. Seeks
more time for writing and travel. February 26, 1966, p. 6,
c. 4.

Lord Snow holds railway service between London and Stratford upon
Avon is inadequate and hurts tourist trade. Statement in House
of Lords. Lord Champion defends service. Daily Mail columnist
Bernard Levin backs Snow. December 4, 1966, p. 168, c. 1.

Lord Snow and wife Pamela Hansford Johnson attend USSR Writers'
Congress. May 23, 1967, p. 12, c. 3.

Snow discusses his "nonhope" for the world in interview conducted
by Robert Reinhold in Fulton, Missouri. Says signs are not
pointing to global cooperation. November 12, 1968, p. 37, c. 3.

Snow holds poorer nations must revolutionize food production to
help avert "sea of famine" by year 2000. Lectures on world
problems, Westminster College, Fulton, Missouri. November 13,
1968, p. 1, c. 4. For excerpts of speech, the John Findley
Green Foundation lecture of 1968, see: November 13, 1968,
p. 29, c. 1.

Snow sees sadistic violence accompanying growth of affluence,
gives interview in New York City on forthcoming novel, The
Sleep of Reason. November 17, 1968, p. 123, c. 3.

Critical Quarterly Society publishes booklet critical of liberal
ideas of progressive mass education. Lord Snow warns nation
faces danger of neglecting her most gifted children because of
obsession with egalitarianism and lessened regard for academic
excellence, speech. Other reaction to publication noted.
March 31, 1969, p. 10, c. 1.

Lord Snow, British physicist and author, says he is prepared
to believe that Jews are genetically superior to other people
in speech, Hebrew Union College--Jewish Institute of Religion,
New York School, New York City. Holds Jewish performance
has been astonishing in all kinds of human excellence.
Declines comment on Jensen theory which holds that intelligence
is determined largely by heredity and cannot be altered
significantly by improving environment. April 1, 1969, p. 37,
c. 3, 4. W.R. Van Meter letter scores Snow for applying
stereotypes to whole group of people: April 6, 1969, Section IV,
p. 11, c. 7. M.H. Bell letter warns of dangers of Snow's
"benign racism:" April 8, 1969, p. 46, c. 5. R.L. Sisson
letter calls Snow's comment irrelevant: April 11, 1969, p. 44,
c. 6.

Snow named to head panel of "think tank" advisers to study improve-
ments in British postal service. December 7, 1969, p. 120, c. 2.

Lord Snow comment on <u>New York Times</u> disclosure of secret Pentagon papers on Vietnam war holds such disclosures could not have happened in Great Britain, and that British legal processes would have strangled them before birth. Says British method of extracting information from the executive and keeping it in check is to make executive directly responsible to Parliament. July 12, 1971, p. 27, c. 3.

Snow comments on interest in Great Britain in United States Presidential election. Notes there is far less than the usual partiality. October 28, 1972, p. 31, c. 6.

Scholars (in <u>New York Times</u> survey) assess Apollo program on the eve of launching Apollo 17, which will mark nation's final mission to moon in decade. Snow comment noted. December 3, 1972, p. 1, c. 3.

James Reston article comments on Great Britain's economic and political outlook in the wake of February 28 general election. Compares present British attitudes to those in '39-40. Cites assessments of situation by Reginald Maudling, Rebecca West, Arnold Toynbee, Lord Snow and Lord Franks. March 1, 1974, p. 29, c. 1.

British writer and scientist C.P. Snow presents to U.N. Secretary General Waldheim declaration stressing urgency of world food and population problems. Document speaks of "responsibility of governments to provide their people with birth control information and equipment." Snow makes presentation on behalf of 1,000 persons from 94 countries who signed or supported document called Declaration on Food and Population. Declaration notes U.N. is providing leadership on solving both food and population problems. Waldheim, in accepting declaration, does not specifically endorse its recommendation concerning birth control, but says that "unprecedented growth of world's population is compounding man's difficulties in feeding himself." Declarations's supporters include United States delegate John A. Scali, Senator Jacob K. Javits, Representatives Jonathan B. Bingham and Bella S. Abzug, former Attorney General Elliot L. Richardson, anthropologist Margaret Mead, writer Bernard Malamud, Italian industrialist Giovanni Agnelli, Swedish economist Gunnar Myrdal and Cambodian President Lon Nol. April 26, 1974, p. 4, c. 7.

New York University awards novelist-scientist C.P. Snow honorary Doctor of Letters degree. Snow portrait. March 14, 1976, p. 32, c. 1.

Appendix II

Comment on controversy over '77 National Book Awards; criticism
centered on judges, their nomination and omissions, even
more than their final choices, and fact that Englishman,
C.P. Snow, is main speaker at ceremony for American authors.
April 13, 1977, Section III, p. 25, c. 1.

Index

This index is primarily an author-title index, but it also includes personal names used as subjects and selected subject entries. It excludes the book reviews by C.P. Snow and Appendices I and II.